THE MARYLAND SEMMES

AND

KINDRED FAMILIES

RAPHAEL SEMMES

Commander C. S. S. *Alabama,* Rear-Admiral Confederate States Navy.

THE MARYLAND SEMMES AND KINDRED FAMILIES

A Genalogical History of Marmaduke Semme(s), Gent., and His Descendants, Including the Allied Families of Greene, Simpson, Boarman, Matthews, Thompson, Middleton, and Neale

Harry Wright Newman

HERITAGE BOOKS
2007

HERITAGE BOOKS
AN IMPRINT OF HERITAGE BOOKS, INC.

Books, CDs, and more—Worldwide

For our listing of thousands of titles see our website
at
www.HeritageBooks.com

Published 2007 by
HERITAGE BOOKS, INC.
Publishing Division
65 East Main Street
Westminster, Maryland 21157-5026

International Standard Book Number: 978-0-7884-2308-6

CONTENTS

ILLUSTRATIONS

FOREWORD

More than a third of a century ago, Raphael Thomas Semmes of Savannah, Georgia, bequeathed to the Maryland Historical Society his voluminous collection of genealogical data concerning the Semmes and related families, the compilation of which had consumed many years of careful and zealous personal research. A book based on his work, entitled *The Semmes and Allied Families,* was published after his death in a very limited edition, and has long been out of print.

Upon examining these papers it seemed to me that although they have always been made available, in Baltimore, to genealogists and others interested, they contain much of rather widespread interest since they relate to some of the earliest and most prominent of Maryland's settlers. I was gratified in interesting the Maryland Historical Society in publishing some of these data and have helped defray the cost by a grant to the Society.

We were fortunate in securing the services of Mr. Harry Wright Newman, of Washington, D. C., one of the foremost American genealogists and the author of many Maryland genealogical publications, to compile for publication the genealogical history of the Maryland Semmes and kindred families.

Mr. Newman has completed his painstaking research, in which he has, of course, had the benefit of his own extensive Maryland genealogical data, and this work is presented as an authentic and interesting history of several of Maryland's early and distinguished families.

Detroit, Michigan.
1956

PREWITT SEMMES

INTRODUCTION

The Semmes family of Southern Maryland is considered to be of Norman origin with the name appearing in England after the Conquest in various forms such as Sim, Sims, Simms, Syms, Simme, and the like. The progenitor wrote his name as Semme and likewise his widow when she signed her last will and testament. By the third generation distinct differences in orthography occurred with the descendants of Anthony Semmes, though not always, adopting the shorter form of Simms and using it today, while the descendants of James, the second son, consistently used Semmes.

An English writer stated that the family appears to be of Scottish or border origin and the blazonry of the family coat-armour indicates some connection with Norway. In 1221 one Riccard de Syme was granted land at Handboville, Normandy, by Philippe Augustus, and as Normandy was conquered by the Norsemen or tribes from the region which is now Norway, the Norman tradition fits into the historic pattern. In the sixteenth century, however, the name was found among the county families of Northamptonshire and Gloucestershire.

The progenitor to Maryland was schooled in letters, for his signature appeared upon numerous public documents, and his wife was likewise learned. Although her family name is unknown, the fact of her being literate definitely indicated county-gentry background, for many maidens of even the nobility in the seventeenth century were unable to write their names.

The family name of Milburn given as a Christian name by a son of the emigrant leads to positive belief that it is a name connected with the distaff side—possibly the family name of Fortuna, his mother. Then the family name of Cleburne appeared as a Christian name in the second generation which also lends credence to another relationship on the maternal side.

The four sons married well, one contracting an alliance with a great-grand-daughter of Jane, Lady Baltimore, consort to Charles, 3d Baron of Baltimore, and thus cementing his position among the aristocracy of Southern Maryland.

In religion the family were members of the Roman Catholic Church which was further proved in 1714 at court when John Semmes, a younger son of the emigrant, was declared to "profess ye Romish Religion."

In the matter of public service during the colonial period, on account of their faith, they were prevented from participation by laws following the revolution of 1689 which abolished the franchise for all Roman Catholics and prohibited them from holding office. In public life after the American Revolution the family assumed its place in the political life of the Republic and many held high offices of State and commissions in the Army and Navy. The most famous member has been Admiral Raphael Semmes, C. S. N., who commanded the *Alabama* during the War between the States and who is regarded as one of the most colorful, daring, and courageous sea-fighters of any time.

The spelling of Christian and family names is ever a perplexing question for the family historian. The Semmes family was, as noted in the foregoing, certainly no exception, and the kindred families also presented a problem. Governor Thomas Greene spelled his own name with a final *e* which the Kentish family used, but the later generations did not adopt it to any great extent. The orthography of Mathews also was difficult. Thomas Mathews wrote his name with a single *t*, while the later generations for the most part used the double consonant. A consistent policy therefore is difficult to follow, for often an individual was never himself consistent. John Maccubin, the Emigrant, is the outstanding example, for he spelled his name five different ways in his own will. In this book the usual genealogical practice of spelling names as written in the instrument under consideration has been followed.

HARRY WRIGHT NEWMAN

Washington, D. C.
1956

THE MARYLAND SEMMES

AND

KINDRED FAMILIES

MARMADUKE SEMME, GENT.

16– –1693

MARMADUKE SEMME, the progenitor of the Semmes family of Southern Maryland, was in the Province as early as April 2, 1662, when he was sworn in as door keeper to the Council or Upper House of the General Assembly. It was not until April 7, 1666, however, that he proved his rights to 50 acres of land for his emigration into the Province, thus proving that he financed his own passage.

He was single upon his arrival, so it can be assumed that he was yet in his twenties. By July 7, 1668, however, he was courting Madam Fortuna Mitford,* the widow of Bulmer Mitford who had emigrated to Maryland about 1664 and who died within the next few years. On the former date Marmaduke Semme gave bond to the widow for a deed of trust, stating in the instrument that a marriage between them was about to be consummated. Accordingly, Fortuna Mitford, widow, negotiated a deed of gift to her two sons, Thomas and Joseph Mitford, for 100 acres of land on the west side of St. George's River, but the land was to be held in trust by Henry Hide, George Macall, and Marmaduke Simms (*sic*), reserving to herself the use of the plantation during her natural life.

Her husband, Bulmer Mitford, of St. Mary's County, had drawn up his will on July 23, 1665, and bequeathed his entire estate real and personal to his wife, Fortuna. No date of probate was noted. He was deceased by March 20, 1665/6, for on that date his widow bought for 7,000 lbs. tobacco the plantation of 100 acres which she subsequently deeded in trust for her two sons.

After his death the widow applied for his rights to land as follows:

> Fortune Metford administratrix of Bulmer Mettford demands land due to Bulmer Metford her deceased Husband for his the said Bulmer's transporting himself into this Province as also for the transporting her the said Fortune his then wife, Thomas his son,

* Her name appears at times as Fortune, but it is believed that it was pronounced in three syllables, for in several instances the final letter is definitely an *a*.

John Brothers, James Young, and Elizabeth Waddy their servants and further for transporting William Champ all in the year 1664. Fortune Metford above named made oath to this rights in usuall this 11 feb. 1666/7.

By his marriage to the Widow Mitford, Marmaduke Semme acquired in 1669 the patent for 250 acres of land, above applied for, which had been due Bulmer Mitford before his death. William Champ who had been transported by Bulmer Mitford died testate and without issue in 1667 and had made Madam Mitford the residuary heir. After his marriage with Madam Mitford, Marmaduke Semme completed the administration of the estate of Champ and thus acquired the greater portion of his estate.

Children of Marmaduke and Fortuna Semme

1. Anthony Semmes married twice. *q.v.*
2. James Semmes married Mary Goodrick. *q.v.*
3. John Semmes married Elizabeth Clarkson. *q.v.*
4. Marmaduke Semmes married Mary Higdon. *q.v.*

He settled first in St. George's Hundred on the west side of St. George's [now St. Mary's] River and then moved later to the settlements north of the Wicomico River then in St. Mary's County, but which by a readjustment of the boundaries fell into present Charles County. His seat was known as " St. George's " which he purchased from his neighbor Thomas Simpson.

On February 23, 1674/5, as Marmaduke Semme, of St. Mary's County, Innholder, he bought from Andrew Woodberry, of Salem in New England, Mariner, for 5,000 lbs. tobacco the tract " Middle Plantation " of 300 acres lying on the Sassafras River in Cecil County. On November 14, 1685, he was granted by Lord Baltimore 400 acres of land lying on the Elk River in Cecil County which he named " Symmes Forrest."

His will, dated August 17, 1690, was admitted to probate in St. Mary's County on March 20, 1692/3, by John Cornish, Thomas Simpson, Sarah Graves, Richard Edelen, and Thomas Cullum. It gave

To son Anthony 200 acres of land out of a tract bought of Mr. Thomas [Sympson] in St. Mary's Co., adjoining Westwood Manor and land of Major Boarman; 400 acres of land in Cecil Co. called " Simms Forrest."

To wife Fortuna the dwelling-plantation during life with all the remaining land except that given son Anthony.
To son James 300 acres of land in Cecil Co. called "Middle Plantation."
To sons John and Marmaduke the dwelling-plantation after the death of their mother to be divided equally between them upon their coming of age, John to have the first choice.
Personal estate to be divided equally among wife and sons Anthony, James, John, and Marmaduke.
Executrix—wife Fortuna Simms.

By a codicil added August 17, 1690, he revoked Anthony's participation in the personal estate.

His widow completed the administration of his estate and lived until 1701. Her will, dated May 1, 1699, was proved in Charles County on December 8, 1701, by her sons, John and Marmaduke Semme. She signed the instrument as Fortuna Semme.

To son John 319 acres being part of tract of 838 acres called "St. George's" which deceased husband bought of Mr. Thomas Sympson.
To son Marmaduke 319 acres being another portion of "St. George's" containing the houses, etc . . . , son Anthony already in possession of 200 acres of same tract.
To son Thomas Medford 20 shillings to buy a ring.
To grandson Thomas Medford, son of Thomas, a heifer.
To son Anthony 10 shillings for a mourning ring.
To son James 10 shillings for a mourning ring.
To grandson Marmaduke Semme of Anthony a colt.
Residue to be divided between sons John and Marmaduke.
Executors—sons John and Marmaduke.

An account filed in 1702 showed 428 lbs. tob. paid to Mr. Jonathan White for "ye Furneral Sermon."

ANTHONY SEMMES[2]

AND

HIS DESCENDANTS

ANTHONY SEMMES, son and heir of Marmaduke Semmes and his wife Fortuna, was born about 1670 in that part of St. Mary's County north of the Wicomico which later fell into Charles County. In 1703 he and Robert Hagan were appointed overseers of the highways for Newport Hundred.

He married Ann Sissons who may not have been his first wife. On December 11, 1706, her mother Alice Sissons who declared herself to be the relict of Edward Sissons of St. Mary's County negotiated her will and bequeathed her daughter Anne Simes (*sic*) one hive of bees. Alice Sissons, Sr., had also been the widow of William Tenahill who died in 1667. At the September Court for 1707 Anthony Simms and Ann his wife filed their account as the administrators of the estate of Nicholas Brown. Sometime after September, 1707, and before August, 1708, he had married Dussabella [Barker] who survived him. If there were any issue by his last wife, it had to be the youngest child, Jane, as an instrument of 1738 states that Mary was the sister of the whole blood to Marmaduke, Alexius, Fidelmus, and Bathia.

Children of Anthony Semmes

1. Marmaduke Semmes, born 1694, married Mary ———. *q.v.*
2. Anthony Semmes married Sarah Maddox. *q.v.*
3. Electius Semmes married Virlinda ———. *q.v.*
4. Fidelmus Semmes married Elizabeth ———. *q.v.*
5. Bathia Semmes married John Higton.
6. Mary Semmes, died spinster.
7. Jane Semmes.

The will of Anthony Semmes, dated August 15, 1708, was probated in Charles County, on January 12, 1708/9, by John Higton, John Semmes, and Susannah Buckley.

> To sons Anthony and Marmaduke 200 acres of "Sems Settlement," but Marmaduke to have the dwelling-plantation.

To children Electious, Fidellmus, Mary, and Bathia 400 acres "Semms Forest" in Cecil Co.
To daughter Jane personalty.
To wife Dussabella, extx., residue of personal estate for maintainance of 4 children first named; in event of death of wife or remarriage, her share of estate to pass to brother James Semmes, he to provide for children and to have charge of Anthony, Electious, Fidellmus, and Bathia; friend Barnaby Anctill to have charge of Marmaduke, Mary, and Jane during minority.

At a court held in Charles County during April, 1710, Marmaduke Semmes, aged 16 years, came into court and made choice of "his mother-in-law" Dosebella Semmes as his guardian until his 21st birthday.

On July 1, 1738, Marmaduke Sims, Alexious Sims, Fidelmus Sims, and Bathia Higton conveyed to their brother Anthony Sims, "Semmes' Forest" of 400 acres in Cecil County, which had been willed them by their father, stating that their sister "Mary Sims of the whole blood" had died unmarried and without issue. Mary Sims wife to Marmaduke, Virlinda Sims wife to Alexious, and Elizabeth Sims wife to Fidelmus, waived their dower interests.

In 1755 some question arose over the right of descent and ownership of certain land, whereas Richard Edelen, Sr., aged 83, deposed that he was well acquainted with Marmaduke Sims about 70 years ago and that the latter had been dead about 60 years, that his eldest son was Anthony Sims with whom he was intimately acquainted, and that the said Anthony's eldest son was Marmaduke Sims with whom he was also very well acquainted, and that the said Marmaduke's eldest son was named Anthony Simms who was then alive.

Christian Lemaster, aged 75, and Elizabeth Machone, aged 76, both recalled the death of Marmaduke Sims, Sr., and made practically the same deposition as Richard Edelen. Thomas Sympson, Sr., aged 60, deposed that Anthony Simms was reputed by all the neighbors to have been the eldest son of Marmaduke Simms ever since he could remember, whereas the same statement was made by William Sympson, aged 57.

MARMADUKE SIMMS [3]

1694–1738

MARMADUKE SIMMS, son and heir of Anthony Simms and his first wife, was born about 1694, having in 1710 at sixteen years of age made choice of his step-mother as his guardian. His wife was Mary ——.

Children of Marmaduke and Mary Simms

1. Anthony Simms married Elizabeth ——. *q.v.*
2. Marmaduke Simms married ——. *q.v.*
3. James Simms, extant in 1756.
4. Jane Simms.

His undated will was proved in Charles County on January 17, 1738/9.

> To son Anthony the plantation whereon Thomas Higdon now lives.
> To son Marmaduke "New Design" which I am settling.
> To son James the plantation whereon I now dwell.
> To three above named sons 50 acres in Zachia Swamp called "Semmes' Chance."
> To cousin Ann Cooksey 50 acres of "St. Georges" already laid out, she paying 6 shillings.
> To son Anthony and daughter Jane personalty.
> To wife Mary dwelling-plantation during life and half of the orchards and all buildings.

The widow was living as late as May, 1744, when she was cited by the court for the failure to file an account upon the estate of her deceased husband.

On September 5, 1756, his two sons Marmaduke Simms and James Simms, of Charles County, and the widow of his son Anthony Simms, of Prince George's County, sold to Charles Smoot, of Charles County, for 11,000 lbs. tob. "Sims' Chance" lying on the east side of Zachia Swamp. No wives waived dower.

ANTHONY SIMMS [3]

16– –1749

ANTHONY SIMMS, son of Anthony and his wife, was born at "St. George's" in Charles County, a portion of which he received by the will of his father in 1709. He married Sarah Maddox after the death of her father, Notley Maddox, of St. Mary's County in 1716, who named her in his will. As Sarah Simms, she shared in the will of her mother, Margreten Maddox, of St. Mary's County, in 1739 and that of her unmarried brother, Samuel Maddox, in the same year.

Children of Anthony and Sarah (Maddox) Simms

1. Jane Simms married George Baxter.
2. Anthony Simms married Sarah ———. *q.v.*

He established his seat in St. Mary's County, the native county of his wife, and there on December 9, 1736, he deeded to his brother, Marmaduke Simms, of Charles County, for 6,000 lbs. tob. 100 acres of " St. George's " which had been willed him by his father. On July 1, 1738, he bought of his brothers and sister Bathia Simms " Semms' Forrest " in Cecil County, which on August 7, following, he sold to George Forbes, of St. Mary's County, Merchant, for £50 plus 5,000 lbs. tob. Sarah Simms, his wife, waived all dower rights.

His last will and testament, written on October 14, 1749, was proved in St. Mary's County, on February 20, 1749/50.

To daughter Jane Baxter all land called " Batchelor's Comfort " during life, then to my grandchildren John and Ann Simmes Baxter, and negroes.
To son Anthony Simmes 5 shillings.
To Mary Horsey a suit of mourning and mourning ring.
All moveable estate to grandchildren—John Baxter, Ann Simms Baxter, Anthony Baxter, and Elenor Baxter at the age of 16 or 20.
Executor—Son-in-law George Baxter.

ELECTIUS SIMMES [3]
17– –1752

ELECTIUS SIMMES, son of Anthony Simmes and his wife, was born in Charles County. About February 1733/4, he married Virlinda, the widow of John Sanders who had died testate in Charles County in 1732.

Children of Electius and Virlinda Simmes

1. Joseph Simms, born Nov. 1733, married Catherine Culver. *q.v.*
2. Winifred Simms, born Nov. 1735, married ——— Thompson.
3. Edward Simms, born Apr. 1739, *d.s.p.* 1804.

4. Ignatius Simms, born June 1740, married Eleanor ———. *q.v.*
5. Anthony Simms, born Mar. 1742, married Sarah ———. *q.v.*
6. Sarah Simms, born Mar. 1744, married ——— Thompson.
7. Mary Simms, born Mar. 1747, married Thomas Dudley Green. *q.v.*
8. Virlinda Simms, born May 1752, married Harry Pierce.

Electius Simms died intestate in Charles County during 1752, when his widow, Virlinda Simms, was granted letters of administration, with William Coomes and Leonard Mitchell as her sureties. The personal estate was distributed on August 25, 1753, among the following heirs—Joseph aged 20, Winifred aged 17, Edward aged 14, Ignatius aged 13, Anthony aged 12, Sarah aged 10, Mary aged 7, and Virlinda aged 2.

At the same time the personal estate of Ignatius Sanders, the son of Virlinda Simms by her first husband John Sanders, was distributed by Alexius Simms and Virlinda his wife among the following heirs; his mother Virlinda Simms; Prudence Mitchell at age; Joseph Semmes aged 20; Winifred Simms at age; Edward Simms aged 14; Ignatius Simms aged 13; Sarah Simms aged 10; Anthony Simms aged 12; and Mary Semmes aged 7. The inventory of his estate had been taken on January 12, 1750.

The widow, Virlinda Sanders-Simms, died intestate in 1755, when her son-in-law Leonard Mitchell was made the administrator. Joseph Simms and Winifred Simms approved the appraisement of the inventory, and when all disbursements were made, the balance was distributed among the following heirs—Prudence Mitchell, Joseph Simms, Winifred Thompson, Edward Simms, Ignatius Simms, Anthony Simms, Sarah Simms, Mary Simms, and Virlinda Simms.

Their son, Edward Simms, married Anne, born 1744, daughter of Philip and Jane (Gardiner) Edelen, of Prince George's County, but if any issue resulted, they failed to mature. She predeceased her mother who died testate in 1793, but Edward Simms approved the appraisement of the estate in that year. He died in 1804, and by his will probated in the District of Columbia, a number of relationships are proved.

To Alexius Simms, son of Joseph, a negro.
To Edward Simms, son of Alexius, $25.00.
To Edward Simms, son of Marsham, $25.00.
To William Sims half of my pewter.

To Cecily Clark, daughter of William Clark, half of my pewter and $50.00.
To William Clark all wearing apparel.
To sister Winifred Thompson $100.00.
To sister Sarah Thompson a negro.
To Mary Clark, wife of William Clark, furniture.
To Rody Clark, daughter of William Clark, personalty.
To Eleanor Sanders, wife of Joseph Sanders, furniture.
To Catherine Clark, daughter of William Clark, negroes.
To Sarah Simms, daughter of Ignatius Simms, a negro.
To Sophia Sanders, daughter of Joseph Sanders, $100.00 in the hands of Thomas Simms, son of Joseph Simms, to be paid her at 16.
To Mary Ann Boarman, daughter of Charles Boarman, a negro, household goods, $100.00, spiritual books, china, crockery, and bottles.
To Thomas Simms, son of Joseph Simms, a negro on condition that he pay to testator's sister, Virlinda Pierce's daughters, $100.00.
To said Thomas Simms a negro during the life of Mrs. Ann Rhodes, and residue of estate after all bequests were made.
To following priests $25.00—Francis Neale, John David, William Matthews, and Notley Young, also like amount to Rt. Rev. Bishop Neale.
To poor of Trinity Church $50.00.
Executor—Thomas Simms of Joseph.

FIDELMUS SEMMES [3]

17– –1776

FIDELMUS SEMMES, son of Anthony Semmes and his wife, was born in Charles County. His share in the parental estate other than the personalty was a portion of "Semmes' Forest" in Cecil County. His wife was Elizabeth ——— who was undoubtedly connected with the Bryan (Byran) family. In 1736 he and his wife, Elizabeth, were joint grantors on a portion of "Eaton's Delight" to Edward Sanders which Charles Byran and his wife had likewise conveyed to Edward Sanders. In 1762 he and his wife were again joint grantors of a portion of "Friendship" which had been divided between Mary and John Smallwood and Charles Bryan and Mary his wife. How Fidelmus Semmes acquired these tracts it is not known, but with his wife joining with him in the deed, it indicated that she had vested rights in the land.

Children of Fidelmus and Elizabeth Semmes

1. John Semmes married Elizabeth ———. *q. v.*
2. Mark Semmes married several times. *q. v.*
3. Elizabeth Semmes married [Basil] Knott.
4. ——— Semmes married ——— Higdon.
5. ——— Semmes married James Simpson. *q. v.*

On May 23, 1745, he bought of John Baptist Boarman for 5,000 lbs. tob. a 59-acre portion of "St. George's." Elizabeth Boarman, wife of Thomas, waived all dower rights. In the same year he bought of his brother, Anthony Semmes, of Prince George's County, for £44 a 66-acre portion of "St. George's" which adjoined the former portion of John Baptist Boarman. On March 10, 1755, he deeded for natural love and affections which he held for his son, John, the two portions of "St. George's" which were contiguous. On February 1, 1758, he bought of Abel Carrico another portion of "St. George's," at which time Anne Carrico waived her dower interest.

His will, dated March 6, 1776, and admitted to probate in Charles County on June 14, same year, devised no realty, but slaves and personalty to his daughter Elizabeth Knot, and 10 shillings each to the following grandchildren—Francis Higdon, Elizabeth Higdon, Anne Higdon, Winifred Higdon, Thomas Simpson, Charity Simpson, and Mary Simpson. The residuary estate was willed equally to his two sons—John and Mark.

ANTHONY SIMMS [4]

17— -1756

ANTHONY SIMMS, son of Marmaduke and Mary Simms, was born in Charles County, but removed to Prince George's County, where he died intestate in 1756 leaving a widow Elizabeth and daughter Mary. Letters of administration were issued to his widow; the inventory of the personal estate was filed in Prince George's County on November 1, 1756, with Marmaduke Simms and Abraham Davenport approving as the kinsmen. At the distribution on September 11, 1758, the balance was paid to "Mary Simms, the only daughter of Anthony and Elizabeth Simms." The daughter died unmarried as proved by the deed of Marmaduke Simms, her uncle, when he declared himself as heir to his brother's landed estate. The widow married secondly Francis Green, a widower, of Prince George's County, and died testate in 1777, naming no heirs of her body.

MARMADUKE SEMMES[4]

17— -17—

MARMADUKE SEMMES, son of Marmaduke and Mary Semmes, was born in Charles County. By the will of his father he received "New Design," the dwelling plantation. On February 9, 1762, he conveyed to James Cole, son, and heir of Edward Cole, Jr., late of Charles County, land known as "Stone's Delight" which his brother, Anthony Semmes, had sold to Edward Cole, Jr., but before the legal delivery Anthony Semmes died, and it descended to him, Marmaduke, as the only brother and heir-at-law of Anthony Semmes. No wife waived dower. On August 9, 1774, he again made the title to "Stone's Delight" valid by deeding it to Ignatius Fenwick, Jr., of St. Mary's County, who held it in right of his wife Sarah. This property had descended to Ignatius Fenwick, Jr., from James Cole, late of Charles County, deceased, the son and heir of Edward Cole, Jr.

He removed to Prince George's County, where he subscribed to the Oath of Allegiance in 1778.

He became an heir of his sister-in-law, Elizabeth, the widow of his brother, Anthony Simms, who married secondly Francis Greene, and the three Simms legatees of her will undoubtedly belong to his family group. As Elizabeth Greene, widow of Prince George's County, by her will of 1777, she devised to her brother-in-law, Marmaduke Simms, all land "I hold or have any claim to" and all negroes "I now have . . . Susannah, James, Henrietta, and David." Among her other legatees were Darkey Simms,* widow, to whom she bequeathed 5 bushels of wheat, Margaret Nailer Simms, who received "feather bed and furniture she now uses," and Mary Ann Simms, the cow with the broken horn. As late as March 6, 1790, the estate was unsettled, for on that date Marmaduke Simms filed an account on the estate of Elizabeth Greene, who was the administratrix of Francis Greene, late of Prince George's County.

* In 1790 Darkey Simms was head of family in Prince Georges Co., with 2 males under 16, and 4 females.

He was not the head of a family in Prince George's County at the first census, but he could be the Marmaduke Sims who was the head of a family in Montgomery County with himself and another male over 16, one male under 16, four females, and two slaves.

ANTHONY SIMMS[4]

1722–1770

ANTHONY SIMMS, son of Anthony Simms and Sarah his wife, was born perhaps in St. Mary's County where his father was domiciled at the time of his death. During the colonial period he remitted quit rents on "Wickehandick," being the only member of the Semmes family owning land in St. Mary's County prior to the Revolution. His wife was Sarah ——.

Children of Anthony and Sarah Simms

1. Anthony Simms. *q.v.*
2. Bennett Simms, *d.s.p.* St. Mary's Co., 1770.
3. James Simms married Sarah Eleanor Anne Lee. *q.v.*
4. Ignatius Simms, *d.s.p.* 1786.
5. Jane Simms married Charles Green. *q.v.*
6. Anne Simms married Thomas Fowler.
7. Sarah Simms.
8. Patty Simms married Edward Mattingly.

His will, dated April 11, 1769, was probated in St. Mary's County on March 7, 1770, by James Mills and Benjamin Smith. He willed his wife Sarah during widowhood the use of the dwelling-plantation, also four Negroes, furniture, and livestock. After the marriage or death of his widow, the dwelling-plantation was to revert to his son Bennett. Negroes were bequeathed to the following children—James Simms, Ignatius Simms, Ann Simms, Sarah Simms, Patty Simms, and Jane Green. Five shillings each were willed to his son-in-law, Charles Green, and to his sons Anthony Simms and Bennett Simms.

The son, Bennett, died unmarried and by his will which was probated in St. Mary's County in 1770 he devised his entire landed estate to his mother, Sarah Simms, but the 150 acres of land near Taney Town, bought of Edward Digges, were to revert to his brother, Ignatius, at the death of his mother. Other bequests were made to his brother, James, and his three youngest sisters–Anne, Sarah, and Patty.

The unmarried son, Ignatius Simms, predeceased his mother, his will being proved in Botetourt County, Virginia, as well as Charles County, Maryland, on November 14, 1786, showing that he was a partner of the firm Simms & Dyson. His legatees were his mother Sarah M. Simms, sister Mattingly, sister Sarah Simms, sister Ann Fowler, and niece Sarah Maddox.

A petition was made to the High Court of Chancery by Philip Key, of St. Mary's County, by which it was shown that the " Widow's Purchase " of 217½ acres lying in Chaptico Manor, British confiscated property, was acquired by Sarah Simms in her lifetime on December 3, 1783; that James Simms, Anthony Simms, Ann Fowler, and Edward Mattingly and Patty his wife were the legal representatives of the said Sarah Simms who had assigned the land to him, Philip Key; that the said Sarah Simms died intestate and that the land descended to her children as named above.

JOSEPH SIMMS [4]
1731–1791

JOSEPH SIMMS, son of Electius and Virlinda his wife, was born February 22, 1731, according to the statement of his great-granddaughter. On May 28, 1753, he married Catherine Culver, born April 20, 1736. From 1766 to the Revolution he remitted quit rents on " Second Addition to Culver's Chance," according to the Debt Books of Frederick County.

Children of Joseph and Catherine (Culver) Simms

1. Joseph Milburn Simms married Elizabeth Mudd. *q.v.*
2. Anne Simms married ——— Clarke and ——— Rhodes [Roads].
3. ——— Sims married [Elisha] Fowler.
4. William Simms.
5. Henrietta Simms, born May 10, 1761, died Feb. 17, 1835, married Jan. 24, 1784, Robert Clarke of Robert, born Apr. 7, 1758, died Feb. 20, 1834.
6. Alexius Simms married Mary Mudd. *q.v.*
7. Virlinda Simms married John Jarboe.
8. Walter Simms.
9. Thomas Simms married Elizabeth ———. *q.v.*
10. Ignatius Simms married Sarah Ann Spalding. *q.v.*

11. Mary Simms, born June 6, 1760, died Jan. 18, 1828, married Feb. 20, 1776, William Clarke of Robert, born Mar. 16, 1750, died Mar. 10, 1809.

In 1778 as Joseph Simms he subscribed to the Oath of Allegiance and Fidelity in Montgomery County before Judge Edward Burgess. In 1790 he was the head of a family in Montgomery County with 4 males under 16 years of age, 3 females, and 7 slaves. He died intestate on December 28, 1791. The administration was granted to his widow, with Jesse Baily and Robert Clarke as her bondsmen.

On November 6, 1793, the various heirs gave their receipts to "Mrs. Catherine Simms executrix of Joseph Simms, late of Montgomery County." The heirs were: Joseph Milburn Simms; Ann Clarke; Ann Fowler, and Elisha Fowler, Jr.; William Simms; Robert Clarke; Alexius Simms; Virlinda Simms; Walter Simms; Thomas Simms; and Ignatius Simms.

His widow died on April 30, 1805. Her will was dated December 31, 1804, and proved in Montgomery County on January 24, 1805.

To son Ignatius Simms £42 due him by me as his part of his father's estate for which Robert Clark became my security and as my said son Ignatius is not yet of age and consequently not paid I desire that so much of my property not hereafter willed and bequeathed may be sold as will pay my said son and to be paid him by my executors when he reaches 21 years of age.

To son Elexious Simms $12.00.

To daughter Mary Clarke all the money due on William Clark's bond to me but without recourse to me or my heirs.

To daughters Henrietta Clarke, and Ann Roads, personalty.

To sons William Simms, Thomas Simms, Walter Simms, and Ignatius Simms personalty including Negro slaves.

To grandchildren Francis Simms, Joseph Simms, and Anne Simms personalty.

To the Rev. Mr. Plunkett and Verlinda Jarboe personalty.

Residue to sons Walter Simms and Ignatius Simms.

Executors—son Walter Simms and son-in-law Robert Clark.

IGNATIUS SIMMS[4]

1740–1794

IGNATIUS SIMMS, son of Electius and Virlinda Simms, was born June 1740 in Charles County. His wife was Eleanor ——.

Children of Ignatius and Eleanor Simms

1. Sarah Simms married ——— Rhoades.
2. Mary Anne Simms married ——— Speake.
3. Elizabeth Simms married ——— Clarke.
4. Jean Simms married Thomas James Mudd.
5. Eleanor Simms, died spinster in D.C. 1814.
6. Ignatius Robert Simms married twice. *q.v.*
7. Jesse Simms.
8. Marsham [Massey] Simms married Margarey Ann ———. *q.v.*
9. Bennet Barton Simms. *q.v.*

In 1778 he took the Oath of Allegiance before Judge Samuel Hanson. He served during the war as a private in the militia company of Captain William McPherson.* In 1790 he was the head of a family in Charles County with two males besides himself over 16, one male under 16, six females and 13 slaves.

His will, dated April 12, 1793, was proved in Charles County on October 20, 1794, by J. A. Russell, Thomas Sanders, and Catherine Sanders.

To his wife Eleanor and five daughters—Sarah, Mary, Elizabeth, Jean, and Eleanor—during their unmarried lives the lease of the dwelling plantation.

To wife Eleanor the use of the entire estate during her single life, with the proviso that the children not already educated may have such education out of estate as is necessary equal to their brothers and sisters.

Son Ignatius to be maintained out of the estate until his majority.

At age or marriage each child to have £50, including sons Jesse and Massey Simms.

To son Bennett B. Simms £19/8/9 over and above what he already had.

What remains upon the death or marriage of wife to be divided equally among nine children above mentioned.

To Eleanor Cusick £10 annually as far as there are assets.

The will of his widow, Eleanor Simms, was probated in Alexandria, District of Columbia, on November 23, 1805, having been dated October 19, previous. She bequeathed Negroes and other personalty to her daughters Sarah Simms, Elizabeth Simms, Jane Simms, Mary Ann Speake, and Eleanor Simms. To her sons Jesse Simms, Bennett B. Simms, and Massey Simms she willed a limited amount of currency and to her son Ignatius Simms "one case of

* Militia List, p. 53, Maryland Historical Society, Baltimore.

white glass bottles." She named her daughter, Sarah, as the executrix.

Ellender Simms, the unmarried daughter, died testate in the District of Columbia in 1814, and by her will she placed her estate in trust with William Rhoades and James Hoben for the use and benefit of her sister, Mary Speake, during her life and at her death it was to be divided equally among the testatrix's brothers and sister—Ben Simms, Massey Simms, Ignatius Robert Simms, and Jane Mudd.

ANTHONY SIMMS [4]
1742–1775

ANTHONY SIMMS, son of Electius Simms and Virlinda his wife, was born in March, 1742, in Charles County. His wife was Sarah ———.

Children of Anthony and Sarah Simms

1. Susannah Simms, born Nov. 4, 1766, [married ——— Stewart].
2. Eleanor Simms, born Sept. 24, 1769.
3. Catherine Simms, born Sept. 24, 1772.
4. Anthony Simms, born Jan. 6, 1775.

He died testate in Charles County leaving a widow and four young children. Letters of administration were issued to the widow, when John Baptist Wills and Edward Semmes went her bond. The inventory of the personal estate was approved by Edward Semmes and Ignatius Semmes as the kinsmen. It was distributed on December 13, 1777, to the widow and the following children—Susannah aged 11 on November 4 last, Eleanor aged 8 on September 24 last, Catherine aged 5 on September last, and Anthony aged 3 on January 6 next. By the time of a second distribution on August 14, 1786, the widow had married William Stewart by whom there was at least one issue.

By the will of Allen Stewart, of Charles County, proved in 1796, he bequeathed his estate to his mother, Sarah Stewart, during life then to his "own sister" Mary Stewart, and his half-sisters—Susannah Stewart, Eleanor Simms, and Catherine Simms.

The widow died testate in 1797, leaving her estate to her daughters—Susannah Stewart, Eleanor Simms, Catherine Simms, and Mary Stewart. Her daughter Mary Stewart and Charles Semmes were named as executors.

JOHN SIMMS [4]

17– –1811

JOHN SIMMS, son of Fidelmus and Elizabeth Simms, was born at "St. George's," Charles County, Maryland. He was married as early as 1766, when Elizabeth his wife waived dower on "Simms' Grief," a portion of "St. George's," at his conveyance to his father and brother. In 1778 he took the Patriot's Oath of Allegiance before Judge John Parnham. At the first census he was the only John Simms in Maryland, with himself and three other males over 16, two males under 16, four females,, and one slave.

After the first census and before April 4, 1796, he and his family removed to Washington County, Kentucky. He apparently had received a land grant on Hardin Creek, for in 1796 he and his wife Elizabeth conveyed four distinct parcels of land on that creek totaling 600 acres. On June 6, 1798, he purchased from Thomas Turnham and Eve his wife, 100 acres of land on Pleasant Run for £100. The 1799 tax list for Washington County shows him a proprietor of 100 acres on Beach Fork which is probably the Pleasant Run tract. Also were listed Thomas and Mark Simms on the same fork but without land.

Children of John and Elizabeth Simms

1. Francis Simms married Alethea Spalding. License Nov. 7, 1810, Washington Co., Ky. *q.v.*
2. Johns Simms married Sarah Luckett and Mary ———. *q.v.*
3. Mark Simms.
4. Mary Simms married James Hayden.
   Bond Nov. 23, 1798, with father John Simms as surety, Washington Co., Ky.
5. Sarah Simms married John Hayden.
   Bond Apr. 15, 1799, with father John Simms surety, Washington Co., Ky.
6. Eleanor Simms married Joseph Tucker.
   Bond Apr. 18, 1797, with father John Simms as surety, Washington Co., Ky.
7. Susannah Simms married ——— Buckman.
8. Ann Simms married ——— Simpson.
9. Thomas Simms married Eleanor Spalding of Bennett.
   Bond Aug. 23, 1800, Washington Co., Ky.
10. Bernard Simms.

11. Elizabeth Simms married Benjamin Luckett.*
Married Jan. 20, 1790, Charles Co., Md., by Father Henry Pile.

The will of John Simms, Sr., was dated August 29, 1811, and probated in Washington County, Kentucky, by Benedict Spalding, Sr., Nicholas Smith, and James F. Smith on December 11, 1811. He signed the instrument.

To wife Elizabeth all estate real and personal during her life, but reserving the management of the estate to son Francis Simms. At death of wife all estate to son Francis, but he to pay $1.00 each to the following my daughters (Mary Hayden, Sarah Hayden, and Eleanor Tucker) and to the children of the following deceased daughters—Elizabeth Luckett, Susanna Buckman, and Ann Simpson—and to my sons John and Mark Simms.
To son Thomas Simms the mare I formerly lent him.
To son Bernard Simms the gun which he has.

MARK SIMMS [4]
17– –1821

MARK SIMMS, son of Fidelmus and Elizabeth Simms, was born in Charles County. In 1776/7, he bought land from his brother John and the latter's wife. After 1774 he married Susanna Burtles, daughter of William Burtles, but at that time the widow of his kinsman, Marmaduke Simms, with three children–Aloysius, Sarah, and Marmaduke.

His wife Susanna was deceased by 1789, for in that year Mark Simms was appointed the guardian of his step-children–Aloysius, Sarah, and Marmaduke. At a court held in Charles County during August, 1791, Mark Simms was cited to show cause why he had not filed an annual account upon the estate of his wards, according to law.

In that month or on August 9, 1791, he married Mrs. Catherine Simpson, then the widow of James Simpson, late of Charles County. He, his wife, and Thomas M. Simpson settled the estate of James Simpson on August 12, 1793; the balance was distributed to the widow and seven children, namely, Thomas M., Charity, Mary, Catherine, James, Benedict, and Gustavus Simpson.

* For the Luckett family, see, Newman's *The Lucketts of Portobacco.*

At the June session of the court for Charles County Mark Simms was again issued citations by the Sheriff to show cause why he had not made a final account or settlement of estates of Alexius [Aloysius] and Marmaduke Simms.

In 1790 he was the head of a family in Charles County with himself and three other males over 16 years of age, 3 males under 16, 5 females, and 10 slaves.

He established his seat upon his marriage with the Widow Simpson on her deceased husband's land, for on November 5, 1801, Thomas M. Simpson sold his share of "St. Thomas," the parental plantation, as the son and heir, to Joseph Green except "one-third part thereof which Catherine Simpson widow of the said James Simpson had her life of dower in and which Mark Simms who intermarried with the said widow now dwells on containing in the whole 150 acres."

Mark Simms died intestate in Charles County, when letters of administration were issued to his widow, Catherine Simms, on March 13, 1821, with Benedict Simpson and John Mudd as her bondsmen.

Children of Mark Simms

1. Chloe Simms.
2. Charles Simms. *q.v.*
3. Rebecca Simms married John B. Wathen, June 1, 1791.
4. Francis Simms married Eleanor Mudd. *q.v.*
5. Cibilla Simms married ——— Wathen.
6. Ann Simms married ——— Wathen.
7. Elizabeth Simms.

The final distribution of the estate was made in Charles County on October 1, 1822, by the widow when the balance was divided among the widow and the following seven children—Chloe Simms, Charles Simms, Rebecca Wathen, Francis Simms, Cibilla Wathen, Ann Wathen, and Elizabeth Simms.

His widow died in 1833, when the administration of her estate was granted by the court to her son Benedict Simpson. Distribution was made on October 16, 1833, when the heirs were Gustavus Simpson, Benedict Simpson, and Elizabeth Simms.

Elizabeth Simms, reputed to be the only issue of Mark Simms by his last wife, on September 27, 1838, sold to Benedict Simpson and his daughters, Elizabeth E. Simpson and Mary Rose Simpson, for $200 portions of "Semms' Grief" and "Boarman's Folly" in Charles County containing 130 acres.

ANTHONY SIMMS [5]

17— -1824

ANTHONY SIMMS, son of Anthony and Sarah Simms, was born in St. Mary's County. The name of his first wife is not known, but it is said that he married secondly Elizabeth Fenwick, to whom license was issued in St. Mary's County on January 16, 1795.

Children of Anthony Simms

1. Francis Simms. *q. v.*
2. Anthony Simms married Sarah Brooke. *q. v.*
3. John Simms married thrice. *q. v.*
4. Mary Simms married Benedict Drury. License St. Mary's Co., Mar. 5, 1810.
5. Martha Simms married Edmund Rice. License Dec. 13, 1818, St. Mary's Co.

During the Revolutionary War he was enrolled in the militia of St. Mary's County.*

The will of Anthony Simms was proved in St. Mary's County on April 6, 1824, having been written on December 31, 1823. He devised his son, Francis Simms, the plantation in "Beaver Dam Manor" of 129½ acres, and also the tract which had been bought of Ignatius Dorsey adjoining; to his grandson, Anthony Brooke Simms, the plantation whereon he (testator) was then living which had been purchased of Colonel Uriah Forrest. Other bequests or devisees were made to his son John Simms, his daughters Mary Drury and Martha Rice, his granddaughter Dorothy Simms, and to three Catholic priests. His sons, John and Francis, were named executors.

The balance of his estate amounting to $8,600 was distributed in St. Mary's County on April 21, 1830, by John Simms and Francis Simms to the following heirs—son John Simms, son Francis Simms, grandson Anthony Brooke Simms, daughters Mary Drury and Martha Rice, and granddaughter Dorothy Simms.

* Militia List, p. 166, Maryland Historical Society, Baltimore.

LIEUT. JAMES SIMMS[5]

17– –1807

JAMES SIMMS, son of Anthony Simms and Sarah his wife, was born in St. Mary's County, but removed to Charles County where on June 9, 1781, he married Sarah Eleanor Ann Lee, the daughter of Arthur and Charity (Hanson) Lee, of Charles County, but then the young widow of James Key.

On December 10, 1776, he was commissioned an Ensign in the First Maryland Regiment and promoted to 2d Lieutenant on April 17, 1777. On May 27, 1778, he was advanced to 1st Lieutenant, but was taken a prisoner by the British on September 16, 1778, and was not released until January, 1780. For his distinguished service in the war one descendant under the Rule of 1854 is entitled to membership in the Society of the Cincinnati.

In 1792 he was High Sheriff of Charles County. Soon after his tenure of office, he and his wife liquidated their estates in Charles County and removed to Columbia County, State of Georgia. Before going, however, he and Sarah Eleanor Ann his wife conveyed to Robert Ferguson and John Campbell in trust " Betty's Delight," " St. Nicholas," " Round Hills " and " Chandler's Hills " which had been devised to a certain James Key, late of Charles County, and former husband of the aforesaid Eleanor Ann Simms. The land was to be sold and the proceeds to be applied for the payment of the debts of James Key, deceased; if any surplus remained, it was to be paid to Thomas Key, son of the said James Key, deceased.

He died intestate in Columbia County, Georgia. Letters of administration were issued to his widow, Sarah E. A. Simms, and Arthur L. Simms on May 4, 1807. The inventory of his estate consisted among other personalty of 24 slaves, one-half of which was claimed by Arthur L. Simms.

JOSEPH MILBOURN SIMMS [5]

17– -181–

JOSEPH MILBOURN SIMMS, son and heir of Joseph and Catherine (Culver) Simms, was born perhaps in Frederick County. During the Revolutionary War he served in the Middle Battalion of Militia for Montgomery County in the same outfit with his brother Alexius.* In 1778 he subscribed to the Oath of Allegiance in Montgomery County before Judge Edward Burgess.

On February 2, 1790, he secured license in Prince George's County to marry Elizabeth Mudd. In the same year he was the head of a family in Montgomery County with himself and another male over 16 years of age, one male under 16, his wife, and five slaves.

Children of Joseph and Elizabeth (Mudd) Simms

1. Francis X. Simms married Verlinda Hagan. License Prince George's Co., July 11, 1814.
2. Joseph Simms married Tabitha ———, removed to Scott Co., Ky.
3. Anne Simms.

In 1793 he received his legacy from his father's estate, and being the eldest son, he inherited the entire landed estate. He died before 1804, but his three children shared in the will of their grandmother Catherine Simms. His widow married secondly ——— Thompson.

On December 31, 1814, Francis X. Simms, of Prince George's County, and Joseph Simms, of Montgomery County, conveyed to John Baker and Edward Davis, of Georgetown, D. C., for $1,050 "Culver's Chance," formerly the property of Milburn Simms in Montgomery County of 100 acres, subject to the dower estate of Elizabeth Thompson. Verlinda Simms, wife of Francis X, and Tabitha Simms, wife of Joseph, waived dower. On January 1814, Elizabeth Thompson, of Georgetown, for $1.00 quit all claims to her dower interest in the tract.

The son, also styled as Joseph M. Simms, settled in Scott County, Kentucky, and on September 9, 1818, the court of Montgomery County, Maryland, recorded the receipt of $200 which Joseph M. Simms "of the County of Scot in the State of Kentucky" had paid James Beall of James, of Montgomery County, for a "negro woman Slave Hannah aged about 40 years of Black complection."

* Militia List, p. 135, Maryland Historical Society, Baltimore.

ALEXIUS SIMMS [5]

1756–1823

ALEXIUS SIMMS, son of Joseph and Catherine (Culver) Simms, was born in 1756, presumably in the Lower District of Frederick County which later became Montgomery. At the beginning of the Revolutionary War he enlisted in the company of Captain Edward Burgess of the militia of the Lower District of Frederick.* In 1778 he took the Oath of Allegiance to the State of Maryland in Montgomery County before Judge Joshua Sanders. In 1779 and 1780 his name is found on the extant militia rosters for Montgomery County showing him at one time to be of the Middle Battalion and another of the 29th Battalion.**

He married a maiden of Charles County, Mary Mudd, the daughter of Henry and Blanche (Spalding) Mudd. Her father by his will of 1810, but not probated in Charles County until 1818, bequeathed "to the three youngest sons of my daughter Mary Simms, viz., Aloysius, Joseph, and Alexius, two Negroes to be divided among them when the youngest son arrives at the age of 21 years and then they are to pay £5 annually each to Mary Simm during her natural life." To his granddaughter Cecily Spalding he willed a Negro boy.

Children of Alexius and Mary (Mudd) Simms

1. Cecily Simms married John Spalding.
2. Catherine Simms married Capt. William Easbey.
3. Alexius Simms married Euridice Franzoni. *q.v.*
4. Joseph Simms.
5. Aloysius Simms married ——— Huffman.
6. Henry Simms married 1824 Margaret Brengle at Catholic Church, Frederick, with Alexius Simms as witness.†
7. Edward Simms. *q.v.*
8. Thomas Simms, died in young manhood.

In 1790 he was the head of a family in Montgomery County with one male under 16 years of age, three females, and five slaves.

* Archives of Maryland, vol. 18, p. 42.

** Militia List, pp. 135, 146, Maryland Historical Society, Baltimore.

† "Married 5 Nov. 1824, by Rev. Mr. McCloy, Henry Simms to Miss Margaret Brengle, daughter of Nicholas Brengle, all of this county." *Frederick Herald, 6 Nov.*

After the Revolutionary War he removed to Frederick County where he died intestate. The following obituary appeared in the *Frederick Herald* of March 1, 1823: " Fallen another of the patriots of '76. Died Saturday 22 February 1823, at his residence on Linganore, Alexius Simms, aged 67 years. He left a widow and seven children."

Letters of administration upon his estate were issued in Frederick County on April 8, 1823, to Joseph Simms and Henry Simms. The distribution was made on April 4, 1826, to the following heirs—Mary Simms, widow; Alexius Simms; Joseph Simms; Aloysius Simms; John Spalding in right of his wife Cecily; William Easbey in right of his wife Catherine; Henry Simms; and Edward Simms.

THOMAS SIMMS [5]
1773–1829

THOMAS SIMMS, son of Joseph and Catherine (Culver) Simms, was born in what is now Montgomery County in or about 1773. He was made the executor of his uncle's will who died without issue in 1804. He married Elizabeth, born 1774, daughter of Richard and Sarah (Harrison) Edelen, of Charles County.* They established their seat in Prince George's County. The names of their children were furnished by a granddaughter, Sister Mary Aloysia.

Children of Thomas and Elizabeth (Edelen) Simms

1. Philip Simms, *d.s.p.*, New Orleans, 1888.
2. N——— H——— Simms married Juliana T. ———.
3. John M. Simms, later of Harris Co., Texas.
4. Theresa Simms married ——— Bowling.
5. Joseph E. Simms, born 1808, married Mary Jane Dyer. *q.v.*
6. Elizabeth Simms married Francis Burch.
7. Benedict Simms, bachelor.
8. Milburne Simms.
9. Ann Sophia Simms married George Henry Gardiner.
10. Thomas Simms, married and lived in New Orleans; died in Jersey City; he and wife buried in New Orleans.
11. Robert Simms.

On April 23, 1813, styling himself as Thomas Simms of Joseph, of Prince George's County, he conveyed to Joseph Boone, of Charles

* For the Edelen family, see, *Charles County Gentry*, by Newman.

County, for \$1.00 all his rights and interest in "Hagan's Folly" 46½ acres which had descended to him by the will of Edward Simms. On the same day, Joseph Boone reconveyed to him the same plantation for a consideration of \$200.00.

On December 1, 1815, he bought of Mary Spalding and her two sons, John Spalding and Thomas P. E. Spalding, of Prince George's County, for \$3,600 "Edenton" and "Edelen's Addition Resurveyed." Cecilia Spalding, wife of John, and Ann Spalding, wife of Thomas P. E., waived all dower rights.

On November 11, 1818, he conveyed to Benjamin Gibbons, of Charles County, for \$2,000 "Hagan's Folly" adjoining "Hagan's Addition" and "St. James" which lay on the road leading from Newport to Bryantown. Elizabeth his wife waived dower.

Before his death he settled in Charles County, where he died intestate on September 29, 1829. His gravestone in the burying grounds at St. Mary's Catholic Church at Bryantown reads "Thomas Semms died September 29, 1829 in his 56th year."

Letters of administration were issued to his widow, Elizabeth Semmes, on February 13, 1830, with William F. Bowling and George H. Gardiner as her sureties. The personal estate was inventoried on July 13, 1830, and appraised at \$5,338, including 19 Negroes.

The first account filed by the widow on June 14, 1831, showed a balance of \$6,132.49. Numerous accounts were rendered, one on June 16, 1835, showed disbursements to John F. Dent for the tuition of the minor children, and also to De Arcy A. French for tuition, and to Miss Eliza Doyle for board and tuition of Elizabeth Semms, minor daughter of the deceased. The final acount was passed on September 3, 1844, showing a balance of \$4,685.97, but no distribution to the heirs.

On August 1, 1836, his son, Joseph E. Simms, of Charles County, conveyed to Philip I. Ford, of the same county, "Edelenton" and "Edelen's Adition Resurveyed," lying in Prince George's County, in accordance with a decree of the Court of Chancery of Prince George's County to sell the realty of which Thomas Simms died seized in order to pay his debts. The tracts consisted of 143½ acres and were sold at \$10.25 per acre.

In 1850 his widow, Elizabeth Simms, aged 76, was living with her son, Joseph E. Simms, aged 42, of Bryantown, and his wife, Mary J. Simms, aged 29. Her gravestone at St. Mary's Catholic Church beside her husband reads "Elizabeth Semms died July 18, 1852, in her 78th year."

The son, Joseph E. Simms, died on July 19, 1855, in his 48th year according to his gravestone at St. Mary's Church, Bryantown. His will, dated 1852, was probated in Charles County on July 31, 1855. He devised to his wife, Mary J. Simms, a life interest in his landed estate, including the dwelling-plantation "Lanturnum" and at her death it was to revert to his sister, Elizabeth Burch. The personal estate was likewise willed to his wife except the Negress Julianna who was to be held by her during life, then the slave and her increase were to be divided between his brothers, John M. Simms and Benedict Simms.

Philip Simms, son of Thomas Simms and his wife, settled in New Orleans, amassed a fortune, and died without issue. His will, dated August 6, 1885, was proved on January 31, 1888, naming a number of his nieces and nephews.

> To Mrs. Julian T. Simms, of New Orleans, widow of my deceased brother N. H. Simms, $5,000; to her 8 children—Virginia Simms Hardin, Philip S. Simms, H. B. Simms, Dixie L. Simms, Bell B. Simms, Robert H. Simms, Walter B. Simms, Florence B. Simms, $6,000 each.
>
> To brother John M. Simms, of Harris Co., Tex., $3,500.
>
> To niece Mary E. Boarman the farm she lives on in Charles Co., Md., and $7,000.
>
> To niece Miss M. Agnes Gardiner, of Baltimore, $12,000.
>
> To niece Ann Gardiner, known in religious orders as Sister Mary Aloysius, of Washington, D. C., $5,000.
>
> To nephew Emanuel S. Gardiner, of Louisiana, $14,000.
>
> To nephew William Mason Burch of Charles Co., Md., the farm he lives on being one-half of "Lantuman" and $8,000.
>
> To nephew Marcellus Burch, of Charles Co., Md., the farm he lives on being one-half of "Lantuman" and $8,000.
>
> To nephew A. M. Bowling, of Charles Co., Md., his debt due me of $12,500 and to his wife $5,000.
>
> To nephew Thomas Bowling of New Orleans, $14,000.
>
> To nephew B. F. Bowling of Charles Co., Md., $12,000.
>
> To nephew John Bowling, of New York, $14,000.
>
> To niece Miss Ann Bowling, of Charles Co., Md., $12,000.
>
> To niece Miss E. S. Bowling, of Charles Co., Md., $12,000.
>
> To nephew William F. Bowling, of Charles Co., Md., the farm he lives on known as part of "Boarman's Manor" and commonly known as "Poplar Hill" and $8,000.
>
> To sister Mrs. Theresa Bowling, of Charles Co., Md., $10,000.

To sister-in-law Mrs. Mary Jane Simms, of Charles Co., Md., widow of my deceased brother, Joseph E. Simms, the mortgage for $1,185 I hold on her farm and $5,000.

To Mr. J. Borland of the house of Tale & Bowling $5,000 in token of esteem and friendship.

To my godchild Philip Simms Wanen, of Washington, D. C., son of William J. Wanen, $2,000.

To Miss Nina Falwell, of Magazine St., New Orleans, $2,000.

To godchild B. Winchester Bowling, son of Joseph Bowling, of New Orleans, gold watch and chain, and $2,000.

To the Jesuit fathers of the Church of the Immaculate Conception on Baronne St., New Orleans, $500.

To the Redemptorist Fathers of New Orleans $200.

To Horace Hester my faithful servant providing he remains with me to my death $2,000.

To the Little Sisters of the Poor, of New Orleans, $2,000.

To the Convent of the Good Shepherd of New Orleans, $2,000.

To the Asylum of St. Vincent de Paul on Magazine St., New Orleans $2,000.

To St. Theresa Asylum of New Orleans $2,000.

To the Convent of Perpetual Adoration $1,000.

To the Convent of Mercy, New Orleans, $1,000.

To Georgetown College, Washington, D. C., $5,000.

To nephew Nicholas Bowling, of New Orleans, $16,000 which amount is to be taken out of the obligation I hold of his for $25,000.

To godson Nicholas Bowling, son of Nicholas, $2,000 to be taken out of the obligation of his father mentioned above.

To nephew Joseph Bowling, of New Orleans, all the remainder of my estate after paying said legacies, funeral expenses, and settling estate.

IGNATIUS SIMMS [5]

17– –18–

IGNATIUS SIMMS, son of Joseph and Catherine (Culver) Simms, was under age in 1804. On January 2, 1810, he obtained license in Prince George's County to marry Sarah Ann Spalding who was the daughter of James and Mary Spalding.

On November 3, 1815, Ignatius Simms and Anne his wife, of Prince George's County, conveyed to Thomas Simms, of the same county, for $349.50 all their right and interest to "Edenton" and "Edelen's Addition Resurveyed" of 149 acres; inasmuch as James Spalding, the father of the said Anne Simms, was entitled to one-fourth of the above-named tracts, and whereas Anne Simms together with her mother Mary Spalding and her two brothers, John and Thomas P. E. Spalding, and Susan Spalding did on August 26, 1810, sell the said land to Thomas Simms for $1,862.50, then Ignatius Simms and Ann his wife conveyed their undivided share to Thomas Simms.

IGNATIUS ROBERT SIMMS [5]

1783–1852

IGNATIUS ROBERT SIMMS, son of Ignatius Simms and Eleanor his wife, was born November 5, 1783, in Charles County. On September 24, 1805, he married Sally Hanson Fowke, born June 20, 1784, the daughter of Roger Fowke and Sarah his wife.*

Issue of Ignatius and Sally (Fowke) Simms

1. Sarah Eleanor Simms, born Jan. 24, 1807, married William B. Logan.

His wife died on April 8, 1808. At Locust Hill, the home of the bride's parents, on August 15, 1809, he married Harriet Middleton, the daughter of Samuel Ward Middleton and Catherine Taliaferro Hooe his wife. The bride was born in Charles County on May 9, 1793.

Issue of Ignatius and Harriet (Middleton) Simms

1. Louisa Middleton Simms, born Sept. 24, 1810, Charles Co., married Dr. Samuel M. Prosser.
2. Samuel Robert Simms, born Dec. 20, 1812, Madison Co., Ky., married Sarah Ann Freeman. *q. v.*
3. Chatham Hooe Simms, born Oct. 1, 1814, Madison Co., Ky., married Anna Margaret Prosser. *q. v.*
4. Jane P. Simms, born Mar. 9, 1818, in Madison Co., Ky, married James Berdam.
5. Mary E. Simms, born Sept. 27, 1820, Madison Co., Ky., became the second wife of Dr. Samuel M. Prosser upon the death of her sister.
6. William W. Simms, born 1822, died unmarried 1849.
7. Harriet A. Simms, born July 15, 1826, in Madison Co., Ky, died a spinster 1849.
8. Middleton Ward Simms, born Mar. 17, 1828, Madison Co., Ky., married Elizabeth M. Jones; settled in California.

---

* For the Hanson lineage of Sally Fowke, see, Newman's *Charles County Gentry*.

About 1811 he left Charles County and settled in Madison County Kentucky. Before his death he removed to Jacksonville, Illinois, where he died on October 28, 1852, aged 69 years. His wife predeceased him, dying on September 8, 1851, aged 58 years.

MASSEY SIMMS [5]
17– –1818

MASSEY SIMMS, son of Ignatius and Eleanor Simms, was born in Charles County. There are indications of two marriages, for on July 26, 1806, he negotiated a bond in the District of Columbia for his son, Edward Simms, with John Mitchell and Charles Adams as his sureties. His widow was Margarey Ann Simms who was the mother of the three youngest children.

Children of Massey Simms

1. Edward Simms, born 1798.
2. Alexius Simms, born July 11, 1809.
3. Jane Simms, born Mar. 20, 1812.
4. Catherine Simms, born May 8, 1813.

On March 6, 1810, he and his wife Margarey Ann Simms conveyed to Joseph Wright four tracts of land in Durham Parish, namely "Smith's Garden," "Skinner's Grub," "St. Barbara's Manor" and "Pennyworth Wit," being the surviving partner of Simms & Adams. In 1800 and 1810 he was the head of a family in Durham Parish. In February, 1815, he negotiated a bond as the guardian of Edward Simms, aged 17.

He died intestate. Letters of administration were issued to his widow Margarey Ann Simms. His personal estate was inventoried on August 11, 1818, being appraised at $3,898.95. The widow was made the guardian of the three orphans at the December court in 1818.

The widow died intestate shortly afterwards, for Edward Simms was granted letters of administration, and her estate was inventoried on December 2, 1819. At the December court of 1826 held in Charles County Alexius Simms, a minor of 17 years, was placed under the guardianship of his uncle Charles Adams.

BENNET BARTON SEMMES[5]
1766–1832

BENNET BARTON SEMMES, son of Ignatius Semmes and Eleanor his wife, was born 1766 in Charles County. He married first —— Tyer [Tiar], of his native county. He resided in Port Tobacco Parish, where he was a large slave owner.

Children of Bennet Semmes

1. Bennet Barton Semmes.
2. Ann Harriet Semmes married William A. Tiar.
3. Eleanor Ann Semmes married John Douglas Freeman.
4. Jesse M. Semmes, born 1791, married Etheldra McPherson and Mary A. E. McGlue. Only child died young.
5. George W. Semmes, *d.s.p.*

After the death of his wife he married secondly a distant cousin, Eleanor, daughter of Robert Doyne Semmes. Their only child, George W. Semmes died at the age of 18 years.

The marriage of his daughter was carried in the *National Intelligencer* on September 2, 1823: " 19 August 1823, married John D. Freeman, of Washington, to Eleanor Ann, daughter of Bennett B. Semmes, Esq., of Charles County."

The notice of his death was also carried in the *National Intelligencer* of September 29, 1832: " Died 25 September 1832, aged 66, in Charles County, Bennett B. Simms."

The death of his son, Jesse Mitchell Semmes, was carried in the *National Intelligencer* of November 17, 1823: " Died 15 Nov. 1823, at his residence in Washington, D. C. in his 32d year, Jesse M. Semmes, son of Bennett M. (*sic*) Semmes, Esq., of Charles Co."

The will of Bennett B. Semmes, dated March 29, 1832, was proved in Charles County on October 17, 1832, by Charles A. Pye, Mary Clare Neale, and Elizabeth Sanders.

To son Bennett B. Semmes personalty.
To son George W. Semmes personalty including gold watch, chain and seal, and bed and furniture which belonged to his deceased mother; he to continue at Georgetown College until Aug. 1833.
Residue to be divided equally among 4 children—Ann Harriet Tiar, Eleanor Ann Freeman, Bennett B. Semmes, and George W. Semmes.
Executor—son-in-law John Douglas Freeman.

The distribution or division of his slaves was made in four lots on November 10, 1832, as follows: William A. Tiar in right of his wife; George Semmes a minor, John D. Freeman in right of his wife, and Bennet B. Semmes.

FRANCIS SIMMS [5]

17– -1844

FRANCIS SIMMS, son of John and Elizabeth Simms, was born in Charles County, Maryland. He accompanied his parents to Kentucky before 1796, but was apparently under age in 1799, for he was not listed as a tithable in Washington County in that year. By bond negotiated in Washington County on November 7, 1810, he contracted to marry Alethea Spalding, of a Maryland Catholic family which had settled in Washington County. She was probably the mother of all his children, for his youngest daughter bore the name of Mary Alethea. He, however, married secondly Elizabeth ———, who survived him.

Children of Francis Simms

1. Joseph G. Simms.
2. John Simms.
3. Ann Simms married William Berry Mudd on May 20, 1808, by Father Jarboe.
4. Martha Ann Simms married ——— Buckman.
5. Francis X. Simms.
6. Benedict Joseph Simms, born Nov. 18, 1825, died Oct. 20, 1891, married Harriet ———, born July 22, 1828, died Mar. 10, 1888; both buried at St. Rose.
7. Catherine Lucetta Simms.
8. Thomas W. Simms.
9. Mary Alethea Simms.

Francis Simms drew up his will on January 16, 1844, it being probated in Washington County, Kentucky, on January 22, following, by Green Forrest and John P. McAllister.

> To wife Elizabeth one-third of estate during life and at her death to revert to all my heirs except such property as may be otherwise disposed of.
>
> To son Joseph G. Simms $650 and 17½ acres of land purchased of John Sandusky adjoining my home farm.
>
> To following children—John Simms, Ann Caroline Mudd, Catherine

Lucretta Simms and Martha Ann Buckman, personalty and slaves.

To son Francis X. Simms the farm purchased of J. F. Smith to include the schoolhouse and spring.

To son Thomas W. Simms the south half of the farm, if he should remain on the place with his step-mother and be raised and educated.

To youngest daughter Mary Alethea Simms Negroes.

Executors—sons Joseph G. and John Simms.

JOHN SIMMS [5]

17– –1847

JOHN SIMMS, son of John and Elizabeth Simms, was born at "St. George's," Charles County, Maryland. He settled in Port Tobacco Parish, where in 1778 he subscribed to the Oath of Allegiance before Magistrate Daniel Jenifer. During the conflict he served as a private in the militia company of Captain Benjamin Lusby.*

He married Sarah Luckett, the daughter of Thomas and Mary (Griffin) Luckett, of Port Tobacco Parish.** It can be assumed that he removed to Kentucky with his father and other Catholic families, for on April 10, 1797, he and Sarah his wife of Nelson County, Kentucky, with the other heirs of Thomas Luckett, late of Charles County, deceased, liquidated their land in Charles County. Another heir was Benjamin Luckett who on January 10, 1790, had been married to Elizabeth Simms, sister to the said John Simms.

His second wife was Mary ——, who survived him, by whom there were issue.

Proved children of John Simms

1. James Luckett Simms, born Oct. 27, 1792, died Mar. 22, 1866, according to tomb at St. Rose, Washington Co., Ky.; married Ann Matilda Mudd by bond Jan. 1820, with Richard Mudd, surety, Washington Co.; "Ann M. Simms, wife of J. L. Simms born Oct. 4, 1798, died June 14, 1876."
2. Elizabeth Pamela Simms.

His will, dated September 24, 1842, was probated in Washington County, Kentucky, on October 24, 1847. He bequeathed his wife,

* Militia List, p. 56, Maryland Historical Society, Baltimore.

** For the ancestry of Sarah Luckett, see, Newman's *Lucketts of Portobacco.*

Mary, and his daughter Pamela Simms, all household and kitchen furniture and one-third of the cash money and the personal effects. To the children of his first wife, two-thirds of the cash money and the residue of the personalty, but his son, James Luckett Simms, was to have $50.00 over and above the others. The latter he appointed executor.

CHARLES SIMMS [5]

17– -1822

CHARLES SIMMS, son of Mark Simms and his wife, was born in Charles County. He died intestate about 1822. On August 2, 1824, Chloe Simms was made the guardian of his two minor children—John Thomas Simms, aged 16, and Charles Williams Simms (*q. v.*), aged 15—with Joseph Simms and David Simmons as her sureties.

His son, John Thomas Simms, married Margaret C. ——— and through his wife he became possessed of a portion of "Pennsylvania" of 300 acres lying in Cobb Neck. They sold their interest in this tract for $360.00 to William J. Mollyhorn, stating that the late James Bailey died seized thereof and that his wife, Margaret, inherited one-fifth of the undivided tract from her mother.

FRANCIS SIMMS [5]

17– -1840

FRANCIS SIMMS, son of Mark Simms and his wife, was born about 1780 in Charles County. His wife was Eleanor, the daughter of Bennett and Ann Mudd of the same county.

Children of Francis and Eleanor (Mudd) Simms

1. Lucy Ann Simms, died young.
2. Mark Levi Simms, born 1805, married Mary Emeline Nally and Elizabeth Louise Lewis. *q.v.*
3. Lucretia Ann Simms married John Stone.
4. Lucinda Ann Simms married Charles Sewall; removed to Memphis.
5. Francis Anthony Simms, died a bachelor after 1870 in District of Columbia.
6. Rosetta Ann Simms, born Mar. 31, 1818, died Nov. 22, 1897, in D.C.; married Thomas Jefferson Davis.

Lucy Mudd, the unmarried sister of Mrs. Simms, made her will on December 12, 1822, and bequeathed property to her nieces,

Lucretia Ann and Lucinda Ann Simms, daughters of Francis Simms and " my sister Eleanor Simms' children," also appointing them the executrixes of her estate. Lucretia Simms made the final account with the court in Charles County in 1832.

His undated will was proved on April 29, 1840, in Charles County. He devised his landed estate equally to his children—Francis, Levi, and Rose. Personalty were bequeathed to his daughters Louisa Stone and Lucinda Sewell, with the remainder of his estate equally to his three children—Francis, Levi, and Rose.

FRANCIS SIMMS [6]

17— -18—

FRANCIS SIMMS, son of Anthony Simms and his wife, was born in St. Mary's County. Upon the death of his father he received the dwelling-plantation on " Beaver Dam Manor," and in 1830 he and his brother settled the parental estate.

On July 10, 1806, he secured license in St. Mary's County to marry Teresa Brooke. On March 3, 1824, he bought of Samuel Maddox, of St. Mary's County, the plantation whereon Robert Herbert then lived in Charles County on the Wicomico River. On December 17, 1830, he re-conveyed the same plantation to Samuel Maddox, but no wife waived dower.

ANTHONY SIMMS [6]

17— -1811

ANTHONY SIMMS, son of Anthony Simms and his wife, was born in St. Mary's County. By license obtained in that county on November 25, 1804, he married Sarah Brooke. By this union was born one son—Anthony Brooke Simms. (*q. v.*) He died intestate. Letters of administration were issued on October 15, 1811, to his brother Francis Simms. The distribution was made in St. Mary's County on June 8, 1830, when Francis Simms settled one-third of the personal estate or $504.35 on the widow, with the remainder, or $1,088.71, to the son Anthony Brooke Simms.

JOHN SIMMS[6]

17– –1837

JOHN SIMMS, son of Anthony Simms and his wife, was born in St. Mary's County. Sometime before May 13, 1795, he married Dorothy ——, who as his wife waived dower when he conveyed "Brother's Agreement" in Frederick County to Daniel Delozier.

Issue of John and Dorothy Simms

1. Joseph Simms, born 1797, married Sarah Mattingly. *q.v.*

As a widower he secured license in St. Mary's County on July 17, 1803, to marry Elizabeth Brooke.

Issue of John and Elizabeth (Brooke) Simms

1. John Francis Simms married Mary Ann Greenwell. *q.v.*

On February 22, 1823, he and William Floyd, of St. Mary's County, negotiated an administration bond for Teresia Fenwick, the widow of Joseph Lewis Fenwick. As Teresia Fenwick she had married her cousin by license of February 14, 1815. On January 24, 1825, he, John Simms, secured license to marry the widow.

Children of John and Teresia (Fenwick) Simms

1. John Abden Simms married Lucy McFadden. Indian agent at Colville Reservation, Washington State.
2. Sarah A. Simms married William F. Combs. License May 3, 1853, St. Mary's Co.
3. Eliza Ann Simms married William H. Drury. License St. Mary's Co., Nov. 25, 1851.

He died intestate in St. Mary's County. The bond of his administrator was dated March 15, 1837. The final accounts were made on July 27, 1843, and November 13, 1844, when the personal estate was distributed among the widow, Teresia Simms, and the following children—Joseph Simms, John Francis Simms, John Abden Simms, Sarah Simms, and Eliza Simms.

The estate of his widow, Teresia Simms, was settled in St. Mary's County on February 22, 1851, when the balance was divided among her children—Aloysius Fenwick, John F. Fenwick, Jane M. Greenwell, John A. Simms, Eliza A. Simms, and Sallie A. Simms.

At the 1850 census for St. Mary's County, the two daughters,

Sarah A. Simms aged 21, and Eliza Simms aged 20, were each possessed of realty appraised at $5,000. They were living in the home of their brother uterine, John F. Fenwick, aged 29.

ALEXIUS SIMMS[6]

18– -1854

ALEXIUS SIMMS, son of Alexius and Mary (Mudd) Simms, was born perhaps in Frederick County. He settled in the National Capital and there he married Euridice Franzoni, the daughter of Guiseppe Franzoni, a native of Carrara, Italy, and son of a former president of the Academy of Fine Arts in that city. He was engaged by Benjamin Latrobe to do the sculpture for the original Capitol, all of which was destroyed when the British burned the Capitol in 1814. He arrived in Baltimore from Italy in February, 1806, and died in Washington during 1824.

Children of Alexius and Euridice (Franzoni) Simms

1. Anna Clementina Simms.
2. Frances B. Simms married Crane McIntyre. License D. C., Dec. 27, 1867.
3. Maria Antoinette Simms married Robert Holtzman.
4. Sabina Matthew Simms married Frank W. Miller. License D. C., Oct. 9, 1872.
5. Rosa G. Simms.
6. Thomas F. Simms, died in young manhood.

He died in Washington, D. C. Letters of administration were issued to his widow, Euridice F. Semmes (*sic*) on March 7, 1854, with Nathaniel Carusi and E. A. Whipple as her sureties. On March 14, 1854, she gave bond as the guardian of her five minor children—Fannie Simms, Maria A. Simms, Sabina M. Simms, Rosa G. Simms, and Thomas F. Simms.

The widow, Euridice F. Simms, drew up her will on February 29, 1860, in the District of Columbia, and to her children—Anna Clementina, Frances B., Maria Antoinette, Sabina Matthew, Rosa G., and Thomas F.—all her estate real and personal absolutely in fee simple as tenants in common. The instrument was probated in the District of Columbia on November 25, 1881.

EDWARD SIMMS [6]

18– –18–

EDWARD SIMMS, son of Alexius and Mary (Mudd) Simms, was born perhaps in Montgomery County. He became a resident of Washington, D. C., and according to family records he married ——— Hardy, of Charles County. His children were: Dr. Constantine Simms who married ——— Onderdunk and practiced medicine in New York; Sienna Simms who married Judge Smith; Richard Simms who married and left issue; Virginia Simms, spinster; Georgiana Simms, spinster; and Edwina Simms who married William Warren and left issue; Mary G. Simms, spinster; William Simms; and Philip Simms.

The unmarried daughter, Mary G. Simms, died testate in Washington, D. C., in 1898, leaving a large and affluent estate. After numerous legacies to Catholic institutions, she named her brother-in-law, William J. Warren, the executor, willing him $500.00. To her sister, Catherine Virginia Simms, she bequeathed her diamond earrings and $1,000, and to her niece and goddaughter, Georgie Douglass, she bequeathed $25,000 to be invested for her benefit. Other heirs were her nephews William Edward Warren and Philip Simms Warren.

SAMUEL ROBERT SIMMS [6]

1812–18–

SAMUEL ROBERT SIMMS, son of Ignatius and Harriet (Middleton) Simms, was born December 20, 1812, in Madison County, Kentucky. His wife was Sarah Ann Freeman. Their children were: Nelly B. Simms who married Thomas B. Crouch, of St. Louis; and Ida Hooe Simms.

CHATHAM HOOE SIMMS [6]

1814–18–

CHATHAM HOOE SIMMS, son of Ignatius and Harriet (Middleton) Simms, was born October 1, 1814, in Madison County, Kentucky. His wife was Anna Margaret Prosser.

Children of Chatham and Anna (Prosser) Simms

1. Edward C. Simms married Emma McCatchen.
   Issue: Clarence L; Bissia L.; Eugene C.; and Gracia Simms.
2. John L. Simms married Angeline Letna Atkins.
   Issue: Julia W., and Annie Margaret Prosser Simms.
3. Julian R. Simms married Jessie M. Linney.
   Issue: Florence and Horace Linney Simms.

CHARLES WILLIAM SIMMS[6]
1809–1844

CHARLES WILLIAM SIMMS, son of Charles Simms and his wife, was born about 1809 in Charles County. He married Anne Eliza Stewart, daughter of Ignatius Stewart and Mary Boswell his wife. He was at one time High Sheriff for Charles County. He died in 1844 and was buried at Pomfret. His children were Josephine, John Oscar, and Christopher Columbus Simms.

MARK LEVI SIMMS[6]
1805–1780

MARK LEVI SIMMS, son of Francis and Eleanor (Mudd) Simms, was born about 1805 in Charles County. His first wife was Mary Emeline Nally. One son, Lewis Sanders Simms, was born about 1840 and died unmarried May 28, 1868.

He married secondly on January 8, 1849, in Washington City, Elizabeth Louise Lewis, of Charles County, born June 2, 1818, daughter of William Wheeler Lewis, of Nanjemoy, and his wife Elizabeth Tyer. The license was obtained in Washington on January 6th.

Children of Mark Levi and Elizabeth (Lewis) Simms

1. Elizabeth Rose Simms, born Oct. 28, 1849, married Jan. 7, 1880, William Mortimer Howard, born Sept. 30, 1852.
2. Jane Almedia Simms, born Dec. 10, 1854, married Feb. 22, 1811, Andrew Augustine Mullen, of Washington, D. C., born Jan. 6, 1848, at Baltimore.
3. Clara Emeline Simms, born Feb. 13, 1856.
4. Charles Eugene Simms, born and died 1857.
5. Mary Ellen Simms, born Aug. 31, 1851, entered Order of Holy Cross, St. Mary's Convent, Notre Dame, Ind.

On November 10, 1845, he received from Francis A. Simms, Rose A. Davis and her husband Thomas A. Davis, of Charles County, for $5.00 all their interest in 150 acres of "Partnership" then in the possession of the said Mark L. Simms, of which Francis Simms, late of Charles County, died seized.

He died May 21, 1870, in his 66th year. Letters of administration on his estate were issued on July 25, 1870, to Louisa E. Simms and James E. Higdon, with John W. Wills and F. Matthew Lancaster as the bondsmen.

ANTHONY BROOKE SIMMS[7]
1809–1864

ANTHONY BROOKE SIMMS, the only son of Anthony and Sarah (Brooke) Simms, was born about 1809 in St. Mary's County. He was a minor at the death of his father in 1811, but it was not until August 7, 1822, that the court officially appointed his mother, Sarah Simms, the guardian. Upon application of Francis Simms, the administrator of his father's estate, the court appointed Joseph Howard and Benedict Heard commissioners to divide the estate of Anthony Simms, deceased, between the widow and son. He settled in Charles County, where he married first ——— Jameson.

Children of Anthony Brooke and ——— (Jameson) Simms

1. Robert Simms, died 1881, John J. Jenkins, adm.
2. Thomas Simms, *d.s.p.* testate Charles Co., 1883, leaving most of his estate to an old sweetheart.

After the death of his first wife he married secondly Jane, daughter of George Neale, of Charles County.

Children of Anthony Brooke and Jane (Neale) Simms

1. Antoinette Simms, born Apr. 3, 1851, married John J. Jenkins.
2. George Neale Simms.
3. Mary Celestia Simms.
4. Mary Bertha Simms married Francis Plowden Jenkins.
5. Henry Simms married Clara Jenkins, sister to John J. Jenkins.
   Issue: Henry Plowden, John J. Jenkins, Estell Jenkins, and Malcolm Austin Simms.

He died intestate in Charles County. Thereupon letters of administration were issued on May 10, 1864 to Jane Simms and

Robert Simms, with Columbus L. Lancaster and Benjamin A. Jameson as the sureties. The widow was granted the guardianship of her minor children, namely, Antoinette, George, Mary, Bertha, and Henry, with Robert Simms and Thomas Simms as her bondsmen.

On July 17, 1877, his landed estate was divided among his heirs, at which time it was recorded that Robert Simms, one of the children and heir-at-law, had died intestate, leaving his brother, Thomas Simms, of the whole blood as his only heir-at-law.

His widow, Jane Simms, died 1884, in Charles County. Administration was granted to her son George N. Simms and her son-in-law John J. Jenkins. The sureties were Henry Simms and Mary C. Simms.

The will of Thomas Simms who died without issue was proved in Charles County on July 11, 1883.

> Personalty to the priest at St. Mary's Catholic Church at Cobb Neck.
>
> To half brothers and sisters, *i. e.*, George N. Simms, Henry Simms, Antoinette Jenkins, Mary Bertha Simms, and Mary C. Simms, all realty being part of "Charleston" allotted to me and my brother, Robert Simms, deceased, in the division of the real estate of my father and brother, provided the said half brothers and sisters pay to Robert Crain $1,000 in two years after my death.
>
> To Mrs. Eleanor Maria Crain all my personal property and also that she shall enter into immediate possession of my said land from the day of my death.
>
> Executrix—Mrs. Eleanor Maria Crain.

JOSEPH SIMMS [7]

1797–1867

JOSEPH SIMMS, son of John Simms by his first wife, was born about 1797 in St. Mary's County. On January 11, 1825, he secured license to marry Sarah Mattingly.

Children of Joseph and Sarah (Mattingly) Simms

1. James Simms died 1873; administration granted to John Edward Simms, of St. Mary's Co.
2. John E. Simms, born 1831.
3. Regina H. Simms married F. F. Spalding. License St. Mary's Co. Jan. 25, 1859.

4. Mary M. Simms married John F. Fenwick, son of Lewis and Teresia (Fenwick) Fenwick. License St. Mary's Co., Jan. 28, 1845.

At the 1850 census he was the head of his family in St. Mary's County, aged 53; his wife Sarah P., aged 58, and the following two children at home—Regina aged 21 and James aged 17.

The will of Joseph Simms, dated December 4, 1866, was probated in St. Mary's County, on March 12, 1867.

To son James Simms part of " Fenwick Manor," being the dwelling plantation of 270 acres, upon the condition that he pay to the children of my deceased daughter, Mary Fenwick, that is, Mary Jane Fenwick and J. Simms Fenwick, $250.
To Ella Fenwick $250 at 18 years.
To Nanie Fenwick $250 at 18 years.
To son James Simms all those tracts in St. Mary's Co. called " Moore Town " and " Blackman's Delight," being the lands which the testator's son, John E. Simms, cultivated at that time, and the said lands were to be held in trust for son John E. Simms.
To Daughter Regina H. Spalding, the wife of F. F. Spalding, $1,000.
To son James residue of estate.
Executors—sons John E. Simms and James Simms.

JOHN FRANCIS SIMMS [7]
18— -1845

JOHN FRANCIS SIMMS, son of Anthony Simms and his wife, was born in St. Mary's County. On February 14, 1832, he obtained license in St. Mary's County to marry Mary Ann Greenwell.

Children of John and Mary Ann (Greenwell) Simms

1. Mary Elizabeth Simms married Joseph Van Reswick. License St. Mary's Co., Apr. 16, 1849.
2. Caroline Simms.
3. Lydia Ann Simms married George F. Maddox. License St. Mary's Co., Apr. 20, 1852.
4. Francis X. Simms, born Dec. 8, 1841, served in Confederate Army, died of consumption Aug. 28, 1876.
5. William H. Simms, killed at Gettysburg in charge on Culp's Hill, C.S.A
6. George A. Simms married Mary Combs; resided in Baltimore.

He died intestate. Letters of administration were issued in St. Mary's County to his brother Joseph Simms on April 22, 1845.

At the 1850 census his widow, aged 36, was the head of her family in St. Mary's County, with realty appraised at $5,000. Other members of her household were Lydia A., aged 15, Caroline M., aged 11, George A., aged 13, Francis X., aged 7, and William H., aged 6.

The administration bond on her estate was dated April 14, 1858, and issued to George A. Simms, with G. F. Maddox and J. F. Fenwick as the sureties. The balance was distributed on September 27, 1864, when one-sixth each went to the following heirs: daughter Elizabeth Van Rishwick; daughter Caroline Simms; granddaughter Kate Maddox; son Francis X. Simms; son William H. Simms; and son George A. Simms.

JAMES SEMMES [2]

AND

HIS DESCENDANTS

JAMES SEMMES, second son of Marmaduke Semmes and Fortuna his wife, was born about 1670, being aged 50 in 1720. Before September 28, 1701, he married Mary Goodrick, born March 13, 1673/4, daughter of Robert Goodrick, but then the widow of John Anderson, with one or more children.

Children of James and Mary (Goodrick) Semmes

1. Marmaduke Semmes married Henrietta Jenkins. *q.v.*
2. Joseph Milburn Semmes married Rachel Prather. *q.v.*
3. Ignatius Semmes *d.s.p.* 1740 intestate.
4. Mary Semmes married William Cavanagh [Cavenough].
5. Anne Semmes married Augustine Ward.
6. Juliana Semmes, died spinster 1735.
7. James Semmes married twice. *q.v.*
8. Susannah Semmes married ——— Johnson.

Not receiving any portion of the parental lands around Newport Hundred, but only the tract in Cecil County which he quickly disposed of upon his majority, he moved westward and established his seat in or near Chandler's Town, later to be known as Charles Town and then Port Tobacco, at that time the center of commerce for Charles County as well as the county seat and social center. He purchased several plantations from the Chandlers who developed the port and gained much afluence in shipping as well as agricultural pursuits.

In 1712 his wife, Mary Semmes, received a legacy of 20 shillings from the will of her brother, Edmond Goodrick, to purchase a ring. In September 1721, his wife deposed in court that the mulatto called James, who belonged to Notley Rozer, was born sometime before her son, Edward Anderson, who was 31 years of age sometime in August next. In 1727 his wife, Mary Semmes, and her sister, Juliana Simpson, approved the appraisement of their brother's, George Goodrick, estate, at which time, William, Robert, and Benjamin Goodrick were the executors.

He died in the spring of 1727/8, aged about 58 years. His will dated August 5, 1727, was proved in Charles County on March 12, 1727/8, by the Rev. Peter Attwood, Juliana Simpson, Robert Hanson, and James Nicoll.

> To William Chandler title "Burnt Quarter" at Portobacco bought of the said Chandler.
> To son Marmaduke "Chandler's Invention."
> To wife Mary the dwelling-plantation during life and residue of "Chandler's Invention"; at her decease to revert to sons Joseph Milburn Semmes and Ignatius Semmes.
> To daughters Mary, Ann, Juliana and Susannah, personalty.
> To son James personalty.
> Residue of estate to aforesaid children.
> Executors—wife and son Marmaduke.

By a codicil of August 7, 1727, he bequeathed to his son, James, the money in Liverpool which Gerard Slye was empowered to recover, but the legacy to James was not to exceed £70—any surplus was to go to his wife who was bequeathed one-third of the stock and household stuff.

His widow married as his second wife, John Speake, of Port Tobacco, by whom there were no issue. He died testate in 1731, leaving his town house at Port Tobacco to his widow during life, then to his grandson John Speake of Thomas.

The nuncupative will of the unmarried daughter, Juliana Semmes, was proved at court on February 2, 1735/6, when Mary Speake swore that her daughter shortly before her death gave to her brother, Ignatius Semmes, a Negro boy which had been bequeathed Juliana by her deceased father.

In November 1745 at court as Mary Speake she deposed that she was more than 70 years of age and that her father was Robert Goodrick, late of Charles County, deceased. She died within the next year testate.

Her will, dated September 25, 1746, was proved on October 31 following in Charles County. She bequeathed Negroes and other personalty to her sons, Marmaduke Semmes, James Semmes, and Joseph Milburn Semmes, as well as her grandchildren Ignatius Semmes of James, and Monica Johnson. The items in the chest were to be divided by her Sister, Julianna Simpson, among the testatrix's daughters Mary Cavenough, Ann Ward, Susanna Johnson, and Elizabeth ——. To Augustine Ward, the father of her granddaughter Julianna Ward, she bequeathed 3,000 lbs. tob. to purchase a Negro for her granddaughter. A bequest was made to her cousin, William Goodrick, while the residuary estate was to be divided between her daughters, Anne Ward and Susanna Johnson.

MARMADUKE SEMMES[3]
1701–1772

Marmaduke Semmes, son of James and Mary (Goodrick) Semmes, was born about 1701 in Charles County, being aged 43 in 1744. He married Henrietta, daughter of George and Susannah (Cole) Jenkins, of the same county. She was born about 1712, deposing to be 32 in 1744. Susannah Jenkins, mother-in-law to Marmaduke Semmes, by her will of 1760 and proved 1763, bequeathed personalty to her daughter, Henrietta Semmes, whereas George Jenkins, his brother-in-law, who died a bachelor in 1775, left legacies to his sister Henrietta Semmes and her sons—Thomas, Edward, and Marmaduke, making Thomas the executor of his estate.

Children of Marmaduke and Henrietta (Jenkins) Semmes

1. Edward Semmes married Sarah Middleton. *q.v.*
2. Marmaduke Semmes married Martha Middleton. *q.v.*
3. Violetta (Letitia) Semmes.
4. Martha Semmes married Henry Hagan.
5. Mary Ann Semmes married William Rhody Luckett.*
6. Susannah Semmes married Thomas Boarman. *q.v.*
7. Thomas Semmes married Anne Queen. *q.v.*

On November 9, 1741, styling himself as the heir and elder brother of Ignatius Semmes, late of Charles County, deceased, he conveyed to his brother, Joseph Milburn Semmes, for £10 and other causes his right to the plantation containing 300 acres which, by the will of their deceased father had been devised to Joseph Milburn and Ignatius, and which was to be divided equally between the latter two after the decease of their mother.

The will of Marmaduke Semmes, dated March 31, 1772, was probated in Charles County on September 23, 1772.

* For their descendants, see Newman's *The Lucketts of Portobacco.*

To son Dr. Edward Semmes 27 acres of land in Charles Co., called " Semmes' Help " and also as much to be taken off " Hargisses Hope " and " Hungerford's Hope " as will make up the 27 acres to 200 acres to be run out so as to include dwelling house.

To son Marmaduke Semmes all the remainder of both tracts with the water grist mill.

To daughters Violetta Semmes and Martha Semmes 100 acres more or less in Charles Co. called " Turle " and 50 acres of manor land which was held by lease. If either died, the whole to go to the survivor; to have liberty to live in mansion house during their single lives.

To children Mary Ann Luckett, Thomas Semmes, and Susannah Boarman personalty, also personalty to grandchildren Eleanor Luckett, Henrietta Luckett, and Catherine Boarman.

To son Marmaduke if he marries before his mother's death and if his mother desires him to remove from the parental home, he to have the plantation and house bought of Charles Hungerford; after wife's death clock and desk over and above the distributive share, so that clock and desk may not be removed from the premises.

To wife Henrietta £30 for distribution to the poor and during her life the mansion house and dwelling-plantation.

By a codicil he bequeathed his wife the residuary estate and also debts due him. At the probation, Thomas Semmes, the son and heir, was present.

The will of his widow, Henrietta Semmes, dated October 10, 1774, was proved in Charles County on December 31, 1774. Personalty was bequeathed to her six children, Susannah, Thomas, Edward, Letitia, Martha, and Marmaduke, also her grandchildren—Eleanor Luckett, Henrietta Luckett, Joseph Luckett, and Thomas Luckett. Her daughter Letitia was made the guardian of Eleanor and Henrietta Luckett, and her son Edward was made the guardian of her grandson William Luckett. Her children Susannah, Thomas, Edward, Letitia, and Martha were willed equally £100 in hands of Robert Mundell, and her son Marmaduke was willed one hogshead of tobacco more than his share of the growing crop, and the residue was to be divided equally among the other children.

JOSEPH MILBURN SEMMES[3]

17– –1764

JOSEPH MILBURN SEMMES, son of James and Mary (Goodrick) Semmes, was born in Charles County. Between September 1, 1728, and July 21, 1732, he married Rachel Prather, daughter of Thomas Prather and Martha his wife, but then the widow of William Pottenger, of Prince George's County. Thomas Prather died testate 1712 in Prince George's County and bequeathed a legacy to his daughter, Rachel, and devised his wife, Martha, several plantations. The widow married secondly ——— Yoakley and died testate in Charles County during 1742, leaving five shillings to her daughter Rachel Semmes.

Of nine children born to Joseph Milburn Semmes and his wife, seven daughters and the only son entered Holy Orders. His daughters—Rachel, Elizabeth, Mary Anne, Catherine, Clare, Martha, and Teresa—all entered the Benedictine Convent at Pontoise, France. The son, Joseph, entered the Society of Jesus at Liege, Belgium, and died at Stonyhurst, England, on September 26, 1809.

His will dated August 25, 1763, was probated in Charles County on October 20, 1764, by Henry Hagan and Hezekiah Turner. He devised his daugter, Eleanor Adams, during life 100 acres of "Leitchfield Enlarged" which he had bought of Archibald Johnson, and at her decease it was to revert to his grandson Richard Adams. Various legacies were made to his daughters and son, and £30 were bequeathed to the Rev. George Hunter for the poor of the parish.

JAMES SEMMES[3]

17– –1787

JAMES SEMMES, son of James and Mary (Goodrick) Semmes, was born in Charles County. He was bequeathed personalty in the will of his father in 1728 and in that of his mother in 1746, which also provided for his son and heir, Ignatius. He married first Anne, the daughter of Henry Barnes, who died testate in Charles during 1739 and named his daughter Anne Semmes. Some years later, or in 1783, a lawsuit developed over the inheritance of the landed estate of Thomas Rookwood, late of Charles County. A number of depositions were taken from the oldest inhabitants among which was one from John Machatee, aged 83, who stated that Thomas Rookwood "married Henrietta Barnes the daughter of old Henry Barnes and sister to James Simmes' wife."

Issue of James and Anne (Barnes) Semmes

1. Ignatius Semmes married Mary Doyne. *q.v.*

He married secondly Mary Simpson after November 2, 1744. On the latter date her father, Andrew Simpson, drew up his will and bequeathed Negroes and other personalty to his daughter, Mary Simpson. Her mother was Mary Green, the granddaughter of Thomas Green, Esq., the second Governor of Maryland.

Children of James and Mary (Simpson) Semmes

1. Joseph Semmes married Henrietta Thompson. *q.v.*
2. Thomas Semmes married Mary Ann Ratcliff. *q.v.*
3. Andrew Green Semmes.
4. James Semmes, Officer of the Maryland Line.*

According to the quit-rent rolls for Charles County, his landed estate consisted of "Simms' Amendment" and "Amendment." In 1778 he subscribed to the Oath of Allegiance and Fidelity to the State of Maryland in Charles County before Magistrate Warren Dent.

The will of James Semmes, dated April 1, 1785, was probated on February 26, 1787, in Charles County by James Dunnington, Rhoda Maddox, and Ignatius Adams.

> To son Joseph the tract "Amendment" of 200 acres and "Semmes' Amendment" of 54 acres; negro Aaron, and one-half of his

* Commissioned Ensign, 1st Md. Regt. Dec. 10, 1776, advanced to 2d Lieut. Apr. 17, 1777, advanced to 1st Lieut. May 27, 1778, taken prisoner Sept. 16, 1778, discharged as a prisoner Jan., 1780. Ref: War Dept. On May 9, 1781, Treasurer of the Western Shore ordered to pay Lieut. James Simms, 1st Regt., £46/6/–, and also 2 gals. of rum and 128 lbs. of sugar. Ref: *Archives*, vol. 45, pp. 428-429. On July 3, 1781, Commissary delivered to Lieut. James Simmes, 1st Md. Regt., cloth and trimmings sufficient for a suit of clothes and linen for 4 shirts for the year 1780. Ref: *Archives*, vol. 45, p. 493. Nov. 1812 Maryland Legislature granted him a pension: "Lieut. James Semmes, of Charles Co., late lieut. in Rev. War" equaled to the half pay of a lieutenant. Ref: Brumbaugh's *Maryland Records*, vol. 2, p. 389. Under the Rule of 1854, a descendant is entitled to membership in the Society of the Cincinnati.

livestock and household furniture, and 1 set of blacksmith's tools.

To wife Mary negro Ruth during life and at her decease said Ruth and her increase to son Thomas Semmes; also negro Philip and one-half of the livestock and furniture.

To grandchildren—Joseph Semmes, Robert Doyne Semmes, Ann Simpson and Mary Semmes 1 shilling each.

To sons Joseph and Thomas, each one-half of the tract in Prince William Co., Va., called the "Walker's Tract," of 260 acres.

Executor—son Joseph Semmes.

DR. EDWARD SEMMES [4]

17– –1789

EDWARD SEMMES, son of Marmaduke and Henrietta (Jenkins) Semmes, was born in Port Tobacco Hundred, Charles County. By the will of his father in 1772, he received "Semmes' Hope," portions of "Hargus' Hope" and "Hungerford's Hope." He studied medicine and during his life was one of the leading doctors in Charles County. In 1778 he subscribed to the Oath of Allegiance in Charles County before Magistrate Joshua Sanders. His wife was Sarah, daughter of Smith and Mary (Hawkins) Middleton.

Children of Edward and Sarah (Middleton) Semmes

1. Elizabeth Semmes married Mar. 2, 1794, as his 2d wife Francis Tolson, per rites St. John's Episcopal Church, Broad Creek.
2. Mary Hawkins Semmes married Stanislaus Hoxton. License Prince George's Co. Jan. 17, 1799.
3. Thomas Semmes married Sophia Wilson Potts. *q.v.*
4. George Semmes, born 1782, *d.s.p.* Apr. 14, 1846, married Mary H. Tolson. High Sheriff for Prince George's Co., Member of Congress.

His will, dated October 5, 1789, was proved on November 2, same year, in Charles County, by Alexander McPherson, John B. Thompson, and Raphael Boarman, Jr.

To father-in-law Smith Middleton personalty.

Children placed under care of their grandfather Smith Middleton and to live with him until youngest child reaches 18 years.

Children—Elizabeth Semmes, Thomas Semmes, George Semmes, and Mary Hawkins Semmes to have that part of the testator's estate including stock, household furniture, and plantation not disposed of by the executor.

Daughters—Elizabeth Semmes and Mary Hawkins Semmes to have

2 slaves on their wedding day or when youngest son George reaches 18 years.

Sons—Thomas Semmes and George Semmes all lands with the proviso that the use thereof be given all children until his youngest child attains 18 years.

Residuary estate to all children—Elizabeth Semmes, Mary Hawkins Semmes, Thomas Semmes, and George Semmes.

Executor—Friend Theodore Middleton.

On June 7, 1804, his sons, Thomas and George Semmes, of Alexandria, sons and devisees of Dr. Edward Semmes, late of Charles County, deceased, deeded to Gabriel Moran, of Charles County, for £1,115 a 91-acre portion of "Boarman's Manor" and another portion of 55 acres of the same manor.

MARMADUKE SEMMES[4]

17— -1806

MARMADUKE SEMMES, son of Marmaduke and Henrietta (Jenkins) Semmes, was born in Charles County. He was unmarried at the writing of his father's will in 1772, but he received the grist mill and portions of "Semmes' Help," "Hargiss' Hope," and "Hungerford's Hope." His wife was Martha, the daughter of James and Sarah (Smith) Middleton.

Children of Marmaduke and Martha (Middleton) Semmes

1. Sarah Semmes married ——— Digges.
2. Teresia Henrietta Semmes.
3. Leticia Harriet Semmes married Francis Patrick Hamilton.

During 1778 he subscribed to the Oath of Allegiance and Fidelity to the State of Maryland in Charles County before Judge Robert Young. He was enrolled in the militia of Charles County and served as a private in the company of Captain John Hanson.*

On June 13, 1789, he and his brother, Dr. Edward Semmes, agreed to a division of their interests in "'Hargus' Hope" and "Hungerford's Hope" which had been devised "by our deceased father Marmaduke Semmes." In 1790 he was the head of a family in Charles County with four females and 19 slaves.

* Militia List, p. 33, Maryland Historical Society, Baltimore.

His will was admitted for probate in Charles County on September 14, 1806, having been written on June 5, 1802.

> To his daughter Sarah Digges slaves and other personalty.
> To daughters Teresia Henrietta and Leticia Harriet slaves and all lands in equaled division; if one marries, the single one to maintain the dwelling house.
> To granddaughter Martha Digges a slave.
> Residue to daughter Teresia Henrietta and Leticia Harriet, having given daughter Sarah £300 at time of marriage.
> Executrix—daughter Leticia Harriet Semmes.

When the administration bond was issued on August 18, 1808, his daughter and executrix, Leticia had married Francis Patrick Hamilton, to whom letters of administration were issued.

On January 3, 1816, Letitia H. Hamilton and Teresa H. Semmes, of Washington, D. C., sold to Samuel Chapman for $500 the land in Charles County which was devised them by the will of their father, Marmaduke Semmes, dated June 5, 1802, and appointed Ignatius and Alexander Mathews, of Charles County, their attorneys.

THOMAS SEMMES[4]

17– –1832

THOMAS SEMMES, son of Marmaduke and Henrietta (Jenkins) Semmes, was born in Charles County. He married Anne, the daughter of Marsham Queen. The latter by his will of 1771 probated in Charles County bequeathed a Negro to his daughter Ann Simms.

Children of Thomas and Anne (Queen) Semmes

1. James Semmes, born Feb. 19, 1755.
2. Henrietta Semmes, born Nov. 7, 1757, married Apr. 14, 1779, Aquilla Scott, of Harford Co.
3. Edward Semmes, born Sept. 14, 1759, married twice. *q.v.*
4. Anne Semmes, born Mar. 4, 1760.
5. Jean Semmes, born Sept. 25, 1762.
6. Mary Semmes, born Nov. 5, 1764, married Thomas Semmes. *q.v.*
7. Joseph Milburn Semmes, born Nov. 28, 1766, married Anne Semmes. *q.v.*
8. Ignatius Semmes, born Nov. 11, 1768, married twice. *q.v.*
9. Catherine Semmes, born June 12, 1770.
10. Elizabeth Semmes, born May 12, 1772, married Thomas H. Luckett, resided in Georgia.
11. Martha Semmes, born Mar. 20, 1774.

In 1778 he subscribed to the Oath of Allegiance in Charles County before Magistrate Walter Hanson. On April 11, 1778, he and Alex McPherson negotiated a bond in the favor of Zephaniah Turner, Esq., of Charles County, who had been appointed Auditor General for the Council.*

He drew up his last will and testament on September 14, 1785, at which time he was one of the most wealthy members of the Semmes family. While officiating as Tobacco Inspector at Port Tobacco a felon struck him on the head with a heavy club which caused a mental illness from which he never recovered.

In 1789 Joseph Milburn Semmes and Anne Semmes, two of his children, petitioned the High Court of Chancery setting forth that their father was no longer responsible for his acts and requested that they be made his guardians. Since his illness of about 4½ years past they had been managers of the estate and had been in charge of the family. They furthermore asked protection from their two brothers, James and Edward, the first and second sons, who had attempted to injure the property and were not worthy to act as guardians, and could not be trusted. They had conveyed two tracts of land, namely, " Hall's Lot " and " Hall's Place," but that there was still an estate of about 1,200 acres. The court declared him *non compos mentis* and the management of his estate was awarded to the two petitioners.

At the first census he was domiciled in Port Tobacco with two males over 16, three males under 16, nine females and 23 slaves—being the largest slave owner of the family.

Several of his children settled in the State of Georgia, taking their father with them. He died at the plantation of his son, Dr. Ignatius Semmes, in Wilkes County during 1832.

The will of Thomas Semmes, one time of Charles County, was probated in Wilkes County, Georgia, as well as Charles County, Maryland, the latter being on May 25, 1832, 47 years after the writing.

> To son James Semmes that part of the plantation I now dwell on, on the east side of Port Tobacco.
>
> To son Edward Semmes that tract on Wheeler's Branch and one-third of " The Heates."

---

* *Archives of Maryland*, vol. 21, p. 29.

To son Joseph Milbourn Semmes one-third of the remaining plantation whereon I dwell.
To son Ignatius all remaining part of the dwelling-plantation and one-third of "The Heates."
To daughters Henrietta Scott, Anne Semmes, Catherine Semmes, Elizabeth Semmes, and Martha Semmes Negroes and other personalty.
Executors—daughter Ann and friend Henry Hagan.

IGNATIUS SEMMES[4] √
1730–1764

IGNATIUS SEMMES, son and heir of James Semmes by his first wife, was born about 1730 in Port Tobacco Hundred, Charles County. About 1752 he married Mary Doyne, born 1731, the daughter of Robert Doyne, of Nanjemoy, Gent., and his wife Jane Green. His father-in-law died testate in Charles County during 1760, and directed his tract of 520 acres in Stafford County, Virginia, be sold for the benefit of his five daughters, one of whom was Mary Semmes. He furthermore bequeathed a Negro slave to his grandson, Robert Doyne Semmes.

By his last will and testament, he named only his wife and three daughters, but we are indebted to the preserved record book of his son, Robert Doyne Semmes, for a list of his children.

Children of Ignatius and Mary (Doyne) Semmes

1. Robert Doyne Semmes, born Nov. 11, 1753, married thrice. *q.v.*
2. Roger Semmes, born 1755, died 1778.
3. Dorothy Semmes, born 1758, died 1775.
4. Ethelbert Semmes, born 1762, died 1777.
5. Mary Semmes married Joseph Milburn Semmes. *q.v.*
6. Ann Semmes married Ignatius Simpson and Richard Mason. *q.v.*
7. Joseph Semmes had four wives, but *d.s.p.* 1832 in Georgetown.
8. Jesse Semmes. *q.v.*
9. Roger Semmes, died Nov. 16, 1778, aged 23 yrs.

Quoting from the record book of his son, "My dear father Ignatius Semmes departed this life the 25 March 1764." His will was dated March 21, and probated in Charles County on March 31, by the oaths of Sarah Doyne, Roger Smith, and John B. Wills. He devised the entire estate to his wife, Mary, with the exception of several Negroes whom he bequeathed to his daughters—Mary, Ann, and Dorothy Semmes.

The personal estate was valued at £396/8/3, with receipts or debts owing the estate amounting to £1086/6/3. The final account was passed at court on November 5, 1770, showing no distribution to the heirs.

On January 24, 1788, his widow, Mary Semmes, of Charles County, deeded to her daughter, Anne Simpson the wife of Ignatius Simpson, for natural love and affections two Negro slaves. In 1790 she maintained her own household in Charles County with three females besides herself in the immediate home and seven slaves. On May 2, 1798, she made a deed of gift to her granddaughter, Mary Ann Pye, the wife of Edward Pye, and to their daughter, Sarah Pye, and any other children that they may have, the Negroes she had purchased from Edward Pye their father, but her daughter, Ann Simpson, was to have a life interest in them. Quoting from the record book of her son, " My dear Mother departed this life in April 8, 1799 in her 68 year of her life."

Although the son Joseph Semmes had four wives, if there were any children, none reached maturity. His first wife is said to have been a Miss Brooke. By July 30, 1793, he had married Margaret Pye, the widow of Jesse Matthews, late of Charles County. On October 9, 1814, he secured license to marry Sarah Scott. The notice of her death appeared in the *National Intelligencer* on September 7, 1815: " Died on Sunday evening last in the 28th year of her age Mrs. Sarah D. Semmes, the consort of Mr. Joseph Semmes, of Georgetown, survived by her husband." On September 10, 1816, he obtained license in the District of Columbia to marry Ann Beatty who was the widow of Thomas Beatty.

He maintained his residence in Georgetown, where he died testate in 1832. He made his wife, Ann, the executrix, and bequeathed her certain articles of personal property. Other bequests were made to his niece Ann Pye; the daughters of Joseph M. Semmes by his (testator's) sister, Mary Semmes, of Georgia, namely Ann and Eliza Semmes; to Sarah Ann Scott, Eleanor Speake Scott, Mary Scott, Catherine Beatty Scott, all daughters of his relative John D. Scott. The latter and his kinsman, Raphael Semmes, were named executors with his wife.

On March 21, 1833, his widow was granted a pension by the

State of Maryland for the services of her husband, Lieut. Thomas Beatty, during the Revolutionary War. She died in Georgetown, when letters of administration were issued on August 26, 1834, to Bazil Brawner.

JOSEPH SEMMES [4]

1753–1824

JOSEPH SEMMES, son of James and Mary (Simpson) Semmes, was born about 1753 in Port Tobacco Hundred, Charles County. By the will of his father of 1787, he received the dwelling-plantation which consisted of "Amendment" and "Semmes' Amendment." He married Henrietta, the daughter of Richard and Henrietta (Boarman) Thompson, born January 18, 1755, in Charles County.

Children of Joseph and Henrietta (Thompson) Semmes

1. Henrietta Semmes married John Kennedy.
2. Alexander Semmes married Eleanor Beatty. *q.v.*
3. Samuel Milburn Semmes.
4. Richard Thompson Semmes, born 1784, married Catherine Middleton. *q.v.*
5. Raphael Semmes, born Aug. 21, 1786, married Matilda Jenkins. *q.v.*
6. Benedict Joseph Semmes, born Nov. 1, 1789, married Emily Elizabeth Edelen. *q.v.*
7. Mary Charlotte Semmes, born 1790, married Richard H. Winter.
8. Thomas Felix Semmes, born 1793, married Mary Olivia Edelen. *q.v.*

In 1778 he subscribed to the Oath of Allegiance in Charles County before Magistrate Warren Dent. During the war he served as a private in the militia company of Captain Sinnett of Charles County.*

At the first census, he, as Joseph Semmes of James, was domiciled in Charles County with four males under 16 years of age, three females, and 12 slaves.

On August 3, 1808, he purchased of George W. Grayson, of Fauquier County, Virginia, for £397 "Fagg's Advenutre" of 143 acres, "Adams' delight," "Enlargement," "Patterson's Chance," and "St. David's," including all buildings and other improvements. The conveyance was confirmed on November 7, 1809, by Robert Harrison Grayson, of Mason County, Kentucky.

On February 7, 1818, he made a deed of gift of the above-named

* Militia List, p. 59, Maryland Historical Society, Baltimore.

tracts to his son, Richard Thompson Semmes, for natural love and affections and the additional consideration of one dollar, the tracts all lying in Durham Parish. On February 2, 1819, his son, Richard T. Semmes, then of Georgetown, reconveyed the identical tracts to him for a consideration of $3,300. On January 7, 1822, he deeded the same tracts to his son, Raphael Semmes, of Georgetown, and to his son, Benedict Joseph Semmes, of Prince George's County. In all indentures he signed his name as "Jos Semmes," but no wife waived dower rights.

No court administration can be found in Charles County for the administration of his estate, but family records state that he died in 1824.

On April 20, 1833, Raphael Semmes, Sr., Thomas F. Semmes, Raphael Semmes, Jr., of Washington County, District of Columbia, and Benedict J. Semmes and Samuel M. Semmes, of Prince George's County, Maryland, conveyed to Benjamin Burgess, of Charles County, for a consideration of $1,250 all those several tracts of land in Charles County of which Joseph Semmes died seized and which constituted the dwelling-plantation of the late Joseph Semmes, they being entitled to four-sixths of the estate. Mary Matilda Semmes, wife of Raphael Semmes, and Emily Semmes, wife of Benedict J. Semmes, waived all dower rights.

His widow lived until 1833 and was buried in the old Catholic cemetery between Georgetown College and the Convent of the Visitation. Her headstone reads "Mrs. Henrietta Semmes relict of Joseph Semmes of Charles County, Maryland, died 27 May 1833 in the 73 year of her age." Nearby is the headstone of her daughter "Mrs. Mary C. Winter relict of Richard H. Winter, of Charles County, Maryland, died 28 Dec 1831, in the 42 year of her age."

Her last will and testament, dated May 31, 1833, was probated in the District of Columbia, on August 17, 1833. Negroes, silver plate, and household furniture were bequeathed to her children—Benedict Joseph Semmes, Thomas F. Semmes, and Raphael Semmes. Personalty including Negroes were left to her grandchildren—John H. Semmes, Alexander A. Semmes, and Mary V. Semmes. Mourning rings were willed to Catherine Winter, Emily Semmes, and Matilda Semmes. The residuary estate was bequeathed to Mrs. Servilla Carberry in trust for the poor. She appointed her son, Benedict Semmes the executor, but in the event that he could not serve, then her son Raphael Semmes.

LIEUT. THOMAS SEMMES[4]
1754–1824

THOMAS SEMMES, son of James and Mary (Simpson) Semmes, was born at "Semmes's Amendment" in Charles County during 1754. In February, 1779, he married Mary Ann Brawner, the widow of Bennett Brawner, who died in Charles County in 1776. The latter's estate was settled on January 18, 1779, when the balance was distributed to the widow, Mary Ann Brawner, and two sons—Henry Brawner aged 4 and Daniel Brawner aged 2. She had been born a Miss Ratcliff, a family which had settled early in Charles County.

Children of Thomas and Mary Ann (Ratcliff) Semmes

1. Roger Semmes married Jane Sanders. *q.v.*
2. Andrew Green Semmes, born Dec. 2, 1781, married twice. *q.v.*
3. James Ratcliff Semmes, born 1783, married Mary Powell. *q.v.*

At a meeting of the Committee of Observation for Charles County on Februray 26, 1776, he was recommended as 1st Lieutenant of the Militia of Captain Walter Hanson's Company. The recommendation was subsequently approved and he was commissioned by the Council of Safety on March 7, 1776 *

His wife died about 1790, and a few years later he married secondly Mrs. Ann Protheser (Wheeler) Tiar, the widow of Joseph Tiar who had died in 1792. In 1805 when the estate of her father, Clement Wheeler, was settled in Charles County, it was stated that his daughter, Ann Semmes, was living in the State of Georgia with her husband Thomas Semmes. After her death he married his kinswoman, Mary, the daughter of Thomas and Ann (Queen) Semmes. No issue resulted from either the second or third unions.

At the first census he was listed as the head of a family in Nanjemoy Hundred, Charles County, with five males under 16 years of age, one female, and seven slaves. In or about 1800 he was among that group of Catholic families which left Southern Maryland and settled in Wilkes County, Georgia. At the lottery of 1803 when the State of Georgia was making a distribution of some recently acquired Indian land, granting certain sections to those who had been domiciled in the State for at least a year, "Thomas Simmes

* *Archives of Maryland*, vol. 11, pp. 186, 205-6.

from Nanjemooy," as a planter with a family, was granted two draws.

The Bible of his son, Andrew Green Simpson Semmes, records his death as follows: "Thomas Semmes Senr. died in Wilkes County the 16th June 1824 in his 71st year."

The will of Thomas Semmes, dated May 3, 1821, was proved in Wilkes County, Georgia, on July 24, 1824.

> To infant daughter of my son James R. Semmes by his lawful wife in the Island of Cuba, $2,500 at 18 years.
>
> To Andrew and Albert Semmes eldest sons of my son Andrew G. Semmes $1,000 each.
>
> To Thomas Semmes, Jr., only child of Roger Semmes deceased $1,000.
>
> Residue of estate to son Andrew G. Semmes and his heirs and Thomas Semmes, Jr., the only child of Roger Semmes, deceased, equally,
>
> If infant daughter of James R. Semmes should die before 18 years of age, her legacy to be divided equally between Andrew G. Semmes and Thomas Semmes; if Thomas Semmes should die before lawful age leaving no lawful child then to my son Andrew G. Semmes.
>
> Executor—Andrew G. Semmes.

By a codicil of May 31, 1823, he bequeathed to his five grandchildren—Frances, Paul, John, Caroline, and Joseph, the children of Andrew G. Semmes and his wife Mary—the sum of $1,500, or $300 each.

DR. THOMAS SEMMES [5]

1778–1833

THOMAS SEMMES, son of Dr. Edward Semmes and Sarah Middleton his wife, was born August 13, 1778, in Prince George's County, according to family records. He first studied medicine under Dr. Dick, but later entered the medical college of the University of Pennsylvania from which he was graduated in 1801. He then studied in Paris and St. Petersburg, Russia, before returning to the States, but upon arrival in Maryland he discovered that practically all of his patrimony had been consumed through careless guardianships.

He settled in Alexandria, Virginia, where in 1808 he married

Sophia Wilson Potts, the daughter of John Potts and Eliza Ramsey his wife of that city.

Children of Thomas and Sophia (Potts) Semmes

1. Thomas Semmes, born Nov. 11, 1812, married, Eliza F. Bernard. *q.v.*
2. Anna Sophia Semmes, born Aug. 1, 1815, married June 10, 1834, at Alexandria, Rev. Philip Clayton Slaughter, of the Episcopal Church.
3. Mary Elizabeth Semmes, born Aug. 13, 1820.
4. Douglas Ramsey Semmes, born May 9, 1822, married Virginia Flynn. License District of Columbia, Nov. 30, 1857.
5. Sarah Wilhelmina Semmes, born May 4, 1830.
6. William Hawley Semmes, died bachelor.

He was a vestryman of Christ Episcopal Church in Alexandria and a member of the Masonic Order. He died in Alexandria during 1833.

His will, dated July 29, 1833, was probated in Alexandria on 12, following. He bequeathed Mrs. Eliza Potts $850, being the amount of her money which stood in his name on the books of the Bank of Alexandria. The residue of the estate was willed to his wife to bring up "our children." The executors so named were his wife, William G. Gardiner, Bernard Hooe, and Samuel I. Potts.

His widow, Sophia W. Semmes, died testate in Alexandria, Virginia, during 1839. She named her children—Sarah Wilhelmina, styling her the youngest daughter, William Hawley Semmes, Douglas Ramsey Semmes, Mary Elizabeth Semmes, Thomas Semmes, and Ann Sophia Slaughter. Her son, Thomas, and her brother, Samuel I. Potts, were named executors.

EDWARD SEMMES[5]

1759–18–

EDWARD SEMMES, son of Thomas and Anne (Queen) Semmes, was born September 14, 1759, at Port Tobacco, Charles County. As Edward Simms (*sic*) Jr. he took the Oath of Allegiance and Fidelity to the State of Maryland in Charles County before Magistrate Walter Hanson.

When his father was declared mentally ill by the court, he stated that before his illness he had promised him certain land and made his will accordingly about 1781, when he [Edward] married his present wife. The latter statement would lead one to believe that he had been married previously, and the parlance in a deed of trust would indicate that there was at times some conflict in his nuptial relations.

On December 17, 1787, as Edward Semmes, Jr., he negotiated a deed of trust with Daniel Jenifer, whereby for natural love and affections for his children Ann, Thomas, and Jane he conveyed to Jenifer all his rights in "Litchfield Enlarged," "Small Profit" and one-third of a tract on Pomonkey Road. His daughter Ann was to enjoy "Litchfield," his son Thomas "Small Profit," and his daughter Jane the other unnamed tract, but his wife was to receive the profits.

On September 8, 1788, as Edward Semmes, Jr., "for and in consideration that my wife Elizabeth Semmes on returning to live with us and performing the legal duties of a wife," he made over to her "Litchfield" of 150 acres and also his stock and household furniture during life or the life of the said Edward for the purpose of jointly maintaining them and after the decease of one or the other the property was to be divided equally among "any children that may be born under our re-union and in case of no future children the said land and other property was to be divided equally among my present children," that is, Ann, Thomas, and Jane.

Children of Edward Semmes

1. Anne Semmes.
2. Thomas Semmes.
3. Jane Semmes.

On September 11, 1779, he was commissioned an Ensign of the 1st Md. Regiment, and on October 19, following, the Maryland treasurer was ordered to pay him $2,000 in lieu of articles for the year allowed by the Assembly. He resigned his commission in the Maryland Line on February 7, 1780. On June 19, 1781, he was commissioned a 1st Lieutenant of the 12th Battalion of Militia in Charles County and served under Captain Henry Boarman and Captain Alexander McPherson.* He was the head of a family in Charles at the censuses of 1790 and 1800.

* *Archives*, vol. 18, p. 161; vol. 21, p. 521; vol. 45, p. 280; Md. Militia List, p. 40, Maryland Historical Society.

JOSEPH MILBURN SEMMES [5]

1766–1821

JOSEPH MILBURN SEMMES, son of Thomas and Anne (Queen) Semmes, was born November 28, 1766, in Port Tobacco Hundred, Charles County. In 1789 he and his sister, Mary Semmes, were made the guardian of their father. He married his cousin Mary, the daughter of Ignatius and Mary (Doyne) Semmes, in Charles County. Two of his daughters were named as heirs in the will of their uncle, Joseph Semmes, of Georgetown.

Children of Joseph and Mary (Semmes) Semmes

1. Anne Semmes.
2. Eliza Semmes.

During the Revolutionary War he served as a private in the militia company of Captain Francis Mastin.*

After 1800 he removed to Wilkes County, Georgia, where he died intestate. On June 4, 1821, his brother, Ignatius Semmes, gave bond as the administrator of his estate, with John Scott as one of the sureties.

Note: License was issued in Warren County, Ga., on January 1, 1812, for Joseph Milburn Semmes and Mary Torrence, widow, the ceremony being performed by the Roman Catholic Church.

DR. IGNATIUS SEMMES [5]

1768–1834

IGNATIUS SEMMES, son of Thomas and Ann (Queen) Semmes, was born November 11, 1768, at his father's seat near Port Tobacco, Charles County. He emigrated to the State of Georgia and settled in Warren County. There on June 9, 1799, he secured license to marry Henrietta Thompson, a scion of the Maryland family, and daughter of Joseph Thompson.

Children of Ignatius and Henrietta (Thompson) Semmes

1. Ann Semmes married Joseph W. Luckett and Hugh Ward.
2. Henrietta E. Semmes married Apr. 18, 1826, Cornelius O'Leary.

* Militia List, p. 57, Maryland Historical Society, Baltimore.

After the death of his first wife at a young age, he married secondly Mary Cooksey.

Children of Ignatius and Mary (Cooksey) Semmes

3. Jane Semmes born July, 1811, married Sept. 22, 1829, Thomas Turley, and secondly James Brooke, born Oct. 31, 1807.
4. Catherine C. Semmes married Aug. 16, 1832, Dr. W. T. Quillan, and secondly Dr. Pierce O'Leary.
5. Francis Semmes married Mary Elizabeth Hubert, License Mar. 19, 1842, Warren Co., Ga.; married by Patrick N. Maddux, Methodist preacher; removed to Meridian, Miss.
6. John Thomas Semmes married in Madison Co., Miss., Julia Luckett, daughter of Gustavus Luckett and Nancy Towns his wife.

He died on June 6, 1834, in his 66th year. His will was probated in Wilkes County, as well as Taliaferro County, on September 5, 1834, having been dated July 27, 1832. He appointed his wife, Mary, the executrix, and provided for the following children—Nancy Ward, Henrietta O'Leary, Jane Turley wife of Thomas Turley, Catherine Semmes, Francis Semmes, and John Semmes.

His widow married secondly Thomas Gibson by license obtained on February 2, 1839, the ceremony being performed in Warren County three days later by Father Whelan of the Catholic Church.

ENSIGN ROBERT DOYNE SEMMES[5]
1753–1814

ROBERT DOYNE SEMMES, son of Ignatius and Mary (Doyne) Semmes, was born in Charles County. It is his Record Book given him by his mother in 1775 from which much information is obtained not otherwise available. "Robert Doyne Semmes was born in the year of our Lord 1753 on November 11th and was married on October 22d 1774 to Mary Ryan in her 16 year of her age." Her father was Ignatius Ryan, a planter of Charles County.

Children of Robert and Mary (Ryan) Semmes

1. Susanna Semmes, born and died 1776.
2. Ignatius Semmes, born Aug. 22, 1778, married Mary Holmes. *q.v.*

His wife, Mary, died on November 11, 1783, ". . . three years wanting 27 days a widower. Robert Doyne Semmes was married on October 17th 1786 to Anne Pye in the 22d year of her age."

Children of Robert and Ann (Pye) Semmes

1. Walter Semmes, born 1787, died 1788.
2. Robert Semmes, born Apr. 3, 1789, died Oct. 26, 1789.
3. Walter Semmes, born Apr. 3, 1789, died May 29, 1816.

Ann, his second wife, died on April 4, 1789, the day after the birth of her twins. "Robert D. Semmes lived a widower two years five months and eight days and was married to Mary Neal on September 11th 1791. Mary Neal was about 25 years of age." She was the daughter of Raphael and Sarah (Howard) Neale, a family who in the early days of Maryland held manorial rights on Wollaston Manor.

Children of Robert and Mary (Neale) Semmes

1. Eleanor Semmes, born Sept. 4, 1792, married Bennett B. Semmes. *q.v.*
2. Sarah Semmes, born Dec. 26, 1796, married David Joseph Floyd.
3. Mary Doyne Semmes, born Apr. 27, 1798, took Holy Orders.
4. Robert Semmes, born Feb. 14, 1800, married Mary Worthington. *q.v.*

On May 9, 1778, he was commissioned an Ensign in Captain William Winter's Co., of the 26th Battalion of Militia in Charles County.* During the same year he subscribed to the Oath of Allegiance and Fidelity to the State of Maryland before Judge William Harrison of Charles County. In 1790 he had in his household besides himself two males over 16 years of age, two males under 16 years of age, and 10 slaves.

"Mary Semmes wife of Robert D. Semmes, departed this life 9 June 1802, aged 36 years. Robert Doyne Semmes departed this life 27 September 1814 aged 60."

The will of Robert Doyne Semmes, dated September 23, 1814, was probated on October 22, same year, in Charles County, by John B. Wills, John Matthews, and John C. Layman.

> To son Walter Semmes one-half of profits from plantation in Cornwallis Neck, my dwelling-plantation, and appointed son Ignatius Semmes trustee for son Walter, and son Ignatius to apply the profits for the use of Walter during his natural life, and at the death of Walter then to my daughters—Eleanor Semmes, Sarah Semmes, Mary Doyne Semmes, and son Robert Semmes.

---

* *Archives of Maryland*, vol. 21, p. 72; Militia List, p. 65, Maryland Historical Society, Baltimore.

To my four children—Eleanor, Sarah, Mary Doyne, and Robert the other half of the profits of the dwelling-plantation and residue of personal estate.

Executor—son Ignatius Semmes.

JESSE SEMMES [5]

17– –18–

JESSE SEMMES, son of Ignatius and Mary (Doyne) Semmes, was born in Charles County. He enlisted in the 3d Maryland Regiment, and on May 24, 1780, the commissary was ordered to issue him 1 shirt and 1 pr. of shoes.* By 1788 he had settled in Alexandria where he witnessed a deed for Charles Simms. On May 24, 1796, as a resident of Alexandria he conveyed to Francis Peyton a lease on a tract of land in Alexandria. On the same day he deeded to Jesse Green, of Sussex County, Delaware, for £150 a square in the town of Alexandria.

ALEXANDER SEMMES [5]

17– –1826

ALEXANDER SEMMES, son of Joseph and Henrietta (Thompson) Semmes, was born in Charles County. He settled in Georgetown, where on September 26, 1820, he married Eleanor Harrison Beatty. She was born October 22, 1802, the daughter of John Beatty, of Georgetown, and his wife Ann Harrison.

Children of Alexander and Eleanor (Beatty) Semmes

1. John Harrison Semmes, born Mar. 10, 1823, married Eliza Robinson. *q.v.*
2. Alexander Alderman Semmes, born Jan. 18, 1825, married Mary Dorsey. *q.v.*
3. John Beatty Semmes, born Dec. 14, 1826, married Edmonia Edelen. *q.v.*

Alexander Semmes became the owner and master of a large sailing fleet with Georgetown as the home port. One of his first ships was the "Elizabeth" built for him in 1808 with a burden of 77 tons. Other vessels were the "Farmer's Friend" of which his brother Richard Thompson Semmes held half interest, the "Leo-

* *Archives of Maryland*, vol. 43, p. 181.

nidas," "James Madison," and the "'Eleanor H. Semmes" built in 1820 with a burden of 122 tons.

He sailed from Georgetown on one of his vessels on December 21, 1826, and was lost at sea. His widow in 1830 married at Georgetown Basil Brawner, and died in Washington, D. C., on April 16, 1865.

RICHARD THOMPSON SEMMES[5]
1784–1823

RICHARD THOMPSON SEMMES, son of Joseph and Henrietta (Thompson) Semmes, was born 1784 in Nanjemoy Hundred, Charles County. In 1808 he married Catherine Middleton, daughter of Samuel Middleton and Catherine Taliaferro Hooe his wife, but then the widow of Captain William Winter, of Effton Hills, Charles County.

Children of Richard Thompson and Catherine (Middleton) Semmes

1. Raphael Semmes, born Sept. 27, 1809, married Anne Spencer. *q.v.*
2. Samuel Middleton Semmes, born Mar. 5, 1811, married Eleanor Guest. *q.v.*
3. Henrietta Thompson Semmes, died in childhood.

After the death of his wife, he married secondly Kitty Brawner, of Charles County. With his consent she placed her landed estate in trust with William Perry and Richard W. McPherson which included her interest in the land belonging to the estate of Major Samuel McPherson, deceased, and "Woodlanding" which she had purchased from Clement Kennedy, deceased, also her 11 slaves, carriages, horses, and numerous other articles of personal property.

He died intestate during 1823 leaving three minor children who were placed under the guardianship of their uncle Benedict Joseph Semmes. His personal estate was appraised on July 2, 1823, by John Perry and Heza Dunnington, with Henry Brawner as the administrator.

Within a few years after his death Elizabeth Perry and John T. R. Perry, executors of John Perry, deceased, and Benedict J. Semmes, guardian to Raphael and Samuel M. Semmes, minors and infant heirs of Richard T. Semmes and Catherine A. T. his wife formerly Catherine A. T. Middleton, late of Charles County, deceased, petitioned the court for a sale of the real estate of Richard Thompson Semmes and also the real estate they were entitled as the heirs of their mother Catherine A. T. Semmes.

RAPHAEL SEMMES [5]

1786–1846

RAPHAEL SEMMES, son of Joseph and Henrietta (Thompson) Semmes, was born August 21, 1786, in Charles County. He married on October 6, 1818, Mary Matilda Jenkins, of Charles County, born December 28, 1800, the daughter of Captain Thomas Jenkins and Mary Neale his wife. His father-in-law, Thomas Jenkins, by his will of 1822, provided for his daughter Mary Matilda Semmes. About 1819 he removed from Charles County to Georgetown, where he and his family became identified with the social life of that community.

Children of Raphael and Mary Matilda (Jenkins) Semmes

1. Ann Maria Semmes, born 1819, died 1820.
2. Mary Virginia Semmes, born Mar. 13, 1821, married Apr. 4, 1864, her widowed brother-in-law Rice Winfield Payne.
3. Benedict Joseph Semmes, born June 15, 1823, married Jorantha Jordan. *q.v.*
4. Thomas Jenkins Semmes, born Dec. 16, 1824, married Myra Eulalie Knox. *q.v.*
5. Ann America Semmes, born July 3, 1826, married Rice Winfield Payne. *q.v.*
6. Alexander Ignatius Semmes, born Dec. 17, 1828. *q.v.*
7. Clara Elizabeth Semmes, born Aug. 5, 1830, married Nov. 4, 1850 (license D.C. Nov. 2) William Bushby FitzGerald, C.S.N., son of Edward and Mary Hite (Bushby) FitzGerald, married Feb. 22, 1815, Clarksburg, Md.; said William FitzGerald, one-time officer in U.S.N., later Capt. in the Confederate Navy, died Aug. 9, 1862, Greenville, S.C.
8. Mary Sabina Semmes, born Dec. 6, 1832, married Sept. 20, 1856, at Washington, Dr. Alphonso Thomas Semmes. *q.v.*
9. Cora Matilda Semmes, born June 26, 1834, married Joseph Christmas Ives, U.S.A. *q.v.*
10. Raphael Semmes, born June, 1836; lost at sea 1853 from S.S. "Antelope" en route from San Francisco to New York City.
11. Ada Eliza Semmes, born June 4, 1838, died Oct. 20, 1893, married Oct. 6, 1858, Richard Henry Clarke.

12. Peregrine Warfield Semmes, born Mar. 12, 1841, died Feb. 15, 1906, Memphis, Tenn., unmarried.
13. William Gaston Semmes, born 1843, died 1844.

About 1818 Raphael Semmes instituted action in the court of Charles County against his sister Mary C. Winter, widow and Henry F. Winter, and Catherine T. H. Winter, heirs of Richard H. Winter, deceased, to show cause why they had not negotiated a deed of conveyance on portions of "Effton Hills," "Perry's Last Chance," "Brit's Adventure," "Verlinda," and "Hudson's Exchange," according to a bond made and executed by Richard H. Winter in his life time. The court appointed Samuel Hanson guardian to the two Winter orphans who on March 19, 1819, according to a decree of the Circuit Court, deeded the plantations in question to Raphael Semmes.

As resident of Georgetown on July 17, 1822, he conveyed to Alexander Gray, of Charles County, "Effton's Hills" which he had purchased from Richard H. Winter and also "Addition to Perry's Last Chance," being a portion of a tract likewise conveyed or purchased from Winter, and also "Hudson's Exchange" of 98 acres which he had purchased from Edward Brawner, inasmuch as he, Raphael Semmes, had agreed to convey to Henry Posey who on January 22, 1822, had assigned to Alexander Gray.

On July 7, 1824, he and his wife, Matilda Semmes, of Georgetown, conveyed to Lewis A. Jenkins, of Charles County, two-tenths of "Gill's Land" which had descended to Matilda Semmes by the will of her deceased father Thomas Jenkins.

The will of Raphael Semmes was dated January 4, 1945, and proved in the District of Columbia on October 30, 1846.

To wife Matilda during life the house and lot on 1st St. in Georgetown where he lived; the house and lot occupied by Mrs. Buck on Pennsylvania Avenue in Washington; two small brick houses and lots on Frederick St., Georgetown; and all household and kitchen furniture.

To his six daughters—Virginia, America, Clara, Sabina, Cora, and Ada—joint tenancy in the house and lot at 4½ St. and Pennsylvania Avenue, then occupied by John Suter; also the house and lot then occupied by him in Georgetown, at death of his wife.

To sons Raphael, Warfield, Alexander, Benedict Joseph, and Thomas personalty.

Executors—brother Benedict Joseph Semmes and son Benedict Joseph Semmes.

His widow was thrown from her carriage and injured fatally on June 16, 1881, near Warrenton, Virginia, where she died five days later. She was buried on June 23, 1881, in Trinity Church Cemetery, Georgetown.

BENEDICT JOSEPH SEMMES [5]
1789–1863

BENEDICT JOSEPH SEMMES, son of Joseph and Henrietta (Thompson) Semmes, was born November 1, 1789, near Port Tobacco, Charles County. On November 11, 1823, by license issued in Prince George's County, he married Emily Elizabeth Edelen, born March 22, 1800, the daughter of Joseph and Catherine (Edelen) Edelen.*

Children of Benedict Joseph and Emily (Edelen) Semmes

1. Henrietta Semmes, born 1824, died young.
2. Charlotte Semmes, born 1826, died 1829.
3. Benedict Joseph Semmes, born 1827, died young.
4. Matilda Semmes, born Mar. 13, 1830, married Oct. 15, 1857, Pembroke Augustine Brawner, born May 22, 1831, in Charles Co., died June 25, 1893, at Chattanooga.
5. Eugenia Semmes, born 1831, died 1843.
6. Benedict Joseph Semmes, born Aug. 15, 1833, married twice. *q.v.*
7. Alice Semmes, born 1835, died young.
8. Celestia Semmes, born Oct. 15, 1839, died Mar. 16, 1876, at Chattanooga.

After attending the rural schools in his native Charles County and being taught by private tutors, he was admitted to the medical college in Philadelphia, but soon left and entered the Baltimore Medical College from which he was graduated in 1811. He practiced medicine at Piscataway as well as engaged in farming, but ultimately became interested in politics. He served in the Maryland House of Delegates from 1825 to 1828, being one-time Speaker, then he served for a brief period in the State Senate. He was elected to the U. S. House of Representatives and served from March 4, 1829, to March 3, 1833, as a Democrat. After an interval from the activity of politics, he reentered in 1842 the Maryland House of Delegates and served one term.

* For the Edelen family, see, Newman's *Charles County Gentry*.

His wife died on December 5, 1853; he died on February 10, 1863, at his seat Oak Lawn in Prince George's County.

THOMAS FELIX SEMMES[5]

1793–1868

THOMAS FELIX SEMMES, son of Joseph and Henrietta (Thompson) Semmes, was born about 1793, near Port Tobacco, Charles County. On June 2, 1835, at Piscataway he married Mary Olivia Edelen, born June 8, 1808, at Mt. Air, the daughter of Joseph and Catherine Alice (Edelen) Edelen.*

Children of Thomas Felix and Mary (Edelen) Semmes

1. Thomas Felix Semmes, born 1836, died 1839.
2-3. Alfred and Celestia Semmes, twins, born and died Apr. 15, 1838.
4. Joseph Semmes, born and died May 17, 1839.
5. Mary Josephine Semmes, born 1842, died unmarried 1914.
6. James Hall Semmes, born Dec. 26, 1844, married Minnesota Dennison. *q.v.*
7. Emily Edelen Semmes, born Aug. 13, 1846.
8. Thomas Felix Semmes, born Dec. 3, 1847.

He resided in Washington City where his children were born. He died in Baltimore on February 26, 1868. Letters of administration upon his estate were issued on March 21, 1868, to John Harrison Semmes.

ROGER SEMMES[5]

1779–1804

ROGER SEMMES, son of Thomas and Mary Ann (Ratcliff) Semmes, was born about 1779 in Charles County. In Georgia he married Jane Sanders, born December 4, 1782, the daughter of John Francis Regis Sanders and his wife Ann Wheeler.

Issue of Roger and Jane (Sanders) Semmes

1. Thomas Semmes, born Jan. 19, 1802, married twice. *q.v.*

He died in Wilkes County, Georgia. On September 19, 1804, citations were issued to Thomas Semmes and Jane Semmes to obtain

* For the Edelen family, see, Newman's *Charles County Gentry.*

letters of administration upon the estate of Roger Semmes, deceased, late of Wilkes County, Georgia. Letters were ultimately issued with William Thompson and Benjamin Hill as her sureties.

On December 1, 1808, the widow married secondly William Luckett, the license being obtained in Warren County.

The estate of Roger Semmes, deceased, paid William R. Luckett $100.00 or the services of two Negroes for the board, clothing, and schooling of Thomas Semmes, the minor son of Roger Semmes, deceased, for the period of August, 1809, to March 4, 1811.

ANDREW GREEN SIMPSON SEMMES [5]
1781–1833

ANDREW GREEN SIMPSON SEMMES, son of Thomas and Mary Ann (Ratcliff) Semmes, was born at Nanjemoy Hundred, Charles County, "on the second day of December Seventeen hundred and eighty-one," according to his Bible record, which stated on the fly-leaf that it was bought for $7.00 in New York in July, 1807. He accompanied his father and his step-mother to Wilkes County, Georgia, about 1800, and there on September 22, 1807, according to his Bible, he married Frances Herbert.

Children of Andrew and Frances (Herbert) Semmes

1. Thomas James Andrew Semmes, born Aug. 7, 1808, married Antoinette Tait. *q.v.*
2. Albert Gallatin Semmes, born Aug. 28, 1810, married Isabella Semmes. *q.v.*
3. Mary Ann Frances Semmes, born 1811, died 1812.

His first wife died on December 16, 1811. He married secondly on December 12, 1812, Mary Robertson, born June 23, 1788, in Orange County, Virginia.

Children of Andrew and Mary (Robertson) Semmes

1. Frances Semmes, born at Montfords Plantation, Nov. 15, 1813, died May, 1863, in Mississippi, married May 13, 1830, William L. Harris, Chief Justice of Supreme Court of Mississippi, born July 6, 1807, in Oglethorpe Co., Ga., died Nov. 26, 1868.
2. Paul Jones Semmes, born June 4, 1815, married Emily Hemphill. *q.v.*
3. John Robertson Semmes, born Aug. 27, 1817, married Lucy Sophia Stone. *q.v.*

4. Caroline Maria Semmes, born Washington, Ga., Oct. 8, 1819, married Mar. 14, 1837, William Clayton; she died Apr. 4, 1893, Atlanta, Ga.
5. Joseph Green Semmes, born Washington, Ga., Feb. 12, 1822, *d.s.p.*
6. Sarah Hillhouse Semmes, born Washington, Ga., Mar. 26, 1824, married Benjamin Conley, one-time Governor of Georgia; she died in West End of Atlanta, Ga., Dec. 31, 1903, the last surviving child of her parents.
7. Alexander Webster Semmes, born Washington, Ga., June 9, 1826, died young.
8. Mary Antoinette Semmes, born Washington, Ga., Oct. 13, 182–, died Dec., 1852, in Mississippi, married Oct. 1845, William Moore, of Mississippi.
9. Alexander Webster Semmes, born Washington, Ga., June 22, 1828.
10. Abner Grigsby Semmes, born Apr. 22, 1833, Washington, Ga.

He died on August 8, 1833, in Washington, Wilkes County, Georgia, in the 52d year of his age. His will, dated December 1, 1832, was probated on December 20, 1833.

Executors to pay legacies left certain children by their grandfather at age or marriage; to pay $300 with lawful interest beginning Jan. 1, 1825, to children Sarah, Mary and Alexander, the youngest children, in order to place them on equal footing with my children Frances, Caroline, Paul, John and Joseph who received legacies from testator's father.

To oldest son Andrew $3,496 with interest, personalty, and confirmed gift to land already given.

To son Albert lot in town of Washington, 253 acres of land in Abbeville District, S. C., $3,900 with interest, and other personalty.

To son-in-law William L. Harris brick house and lot, Negro, and $6,000.

To wife Mary Semmes and 7 youngest children—Paul, John, Caroline, Joseph, Sarah, Mary, and Alexander Webster—residue of estate real and personal equally, to be distributed by executors when son Paul arrives at age of 21 years.

If "it please Providence to bless my wife with another birth and the child survives," child to share equally with other children.

Executor—wife Mary Semmes.

His widow died in Washington, Georgia, on December 24, 1838, in the 51st year of her age.

JAMES RATCLIFF SEMMES [5]

1783–1821

JAMES RATCLIFF SEMMES, son of Thomas and Mary Ann (Ratcliff) Semmes, was born about 1783 in Charles County, Maryland. He was taken to Georgia by his parents, he married Mary Powell. One daughter—Isabella who married Judge Albert Gallatin Semmes—was born. He died May, 1821.

THOMAS SEMMES [6]

1812–1843

THOMAS SEMMES, son of Dr. Thomas Semmes and Sophia Wilson Potts his wife, was born November 11, 1812, presumably in Alexandria. In 1839 he married Eliza F. Bernard, of Port Royal, Caroline County, Virginia. He died a few years later leaving an only son. Thomas Middleton Semmes, born September 4, 1840, *q. v.*

His will was dated September 3, 1841, and probated in Alexandria on September 4, 1843. He made several bequests to his brothers and sisters—Douglas R. Semmes, William H. Semmes, Sarah Wilhelmina Semmes, who received a diamond breast pin, and Ann Sophia Slaughter who was willed the silver plate which he expected to receive from the estate of his mother. To his son, Thomas Middleton, he bequeathed his law library and the silver watch which had been given him by his father. The residuary estate was willed to his wife, Eliza F. Semmes, whom he appointed executrix, but in event of her remarriage, then his friend, George FitzHugh, of Port Royal, was to act. At the probation the widow renounced the administration of the estate of her mother-in-law, Mrs. Sophia W. Semmes, which was then unsettled and requested that Thomas Semmes be appointed.

IGNATIUS SEMMES [6]

1778–1826

IGNATIUS SEMMES, son of Robert Doyne and Mary (Ryan) Semmes, was born August 22, 1778, in Charles County. On April 25, 1781, Ignatius Ryan, of Charles County, made a deed of gift to his grandson, son of Robert and Mary Simms, of four Negroes. On February 15, 1801, he married Mary Holmes, and of 13 children born to the union, only one, Ignatius, the youngest, born September 6, 1821, survived infancy. According to the Bible of his father and continued by him, " My dear wife departed this life on 9th June 1825 in her 48th year." She was buried at Mt. Carmel where her headstone speaks of her as the " Consort of Ignatius Semmes, Esq." His death was carried in the Baltimore *American* as of January 4. 1826, " Died 2 January 1826 aged 47, Ignatius Semmes, late of Rose Hill, Charles County."

He wrote his will but neglected to have it witnessed. However, the court of Charles accepted it in June, 1827, and it was probated accordingly. To his brother, Robert Semmes, he devised his storehouse and lot at Port Tobacco and to his sisters, unnamed, each $500. To his sister, Mary, he willed his carriage and horses. The residue of his estate was devised to his son, Ignatius, but in the event that he died without issue and under age, the dwelling-plantation " Rose Hill " was to revert to the testator's brother, Robert Semmes, and the personal estate equally to his two sisters. His brother, Robert, was named as guardian to the son Ignatius.

The will of the bachelor son, Ignatius Semmes, was dated April 27, 1843, and proved on June 13, same year, in Charles County. He bequeathed legacies to his Aunt Sarah Floyd, his Uncle William Holmes, his Aunt Mary D. Semmes " now in the Monastery in the City of Baltimore," and to the children of David I. Floyd, that is, Mary Floyd, Olevia Floyd, and Robert Semmes Floyd. All of his silver plate was bequeathed to the Catholic Church of St. Thomas. A number of his slaves were freed. He provided for the erection of a frame dwelling with brick chimney on his plantation " Rose Hill " for several of his manumitted servants. Legacies were also willed to his friend, Walter Mitchell, whom he appointed executor. The residuary estate was devised in trust with his Uncle Roger Semmes, for the use and benefit of the latter's children.

ROBERT DOYNE SEMMES [6]
1800–1845

ROBERT DOYNE SEMMES, son of Robert Doyne and Mary (Neale) Semmes, was born February 14, 1800, in Charles County. By license obtained in Baltimore County, on October 26, 1829, he married Mary Tolley Johns Worthington, born Jan. 8, 1804, daughter of Charles and Susan (Johns) Worthington, of Garrison Forest, Baltimore County.*

Children of Robert and Mary (Worthington) Semmes

1. Mary Elizabeth Semmes, born and died 1831.
2. Susan Johns Semmes, born Dec. 26, 1832, at Rose Hill, Charles Co., died Apr. 29, 1904, in the District of Columbia, married John Nelson Lloyd Milnor.
3. Charles Worthington Semmes, born Jan. 27, 1834, married Elizabeth Ann Johnson.
4. Robert Doyne Semmes, born Apr. 11, 1835, died Dec. 17, 1891, married Julia Eggerton. *q.v.*
5. Richard Johns Worthington Semmes, born 1838, died 1843.
6. Rosetta Worthington Semmes, born and died 1840.

On August 18, 1832, Robert Semmes and Mary J. T. Semmes, his wife, of Charles County, and Mary D. Semmes, of Baltimore County, conveyed to Joseph Watson, of Charles County, for $785.00 "Mt. Pleasant" of 392½ acres lying in Charles County.

He died about 1845. His widow was made the guardian of her children—Susan J., Charles W., and Robert D. Semmes. At the July court of 1848, she as their guardian, protected their rights in realty at Port Tobacco which had been devised her deceased husband, Robert Semmes, by Ignatius Semmes. She returned to Baltimore and died on October 19, 1885.

JOHN HARRISON SEMMES [6]

1832–1898

JOHN HARRISON SEMMES, son of Alexander and Eleanor Harrison (Beatty) Semmes, was born March 10, 1823, in Georgetown, D. C. On June 19, 1850, he married at Washington Eliza Wadsworth Robertson, daughter of Samuel Robertson, Paymaster, U. S. N., and his wife Ann Murdock. He died at Chevy Chase, Maryland, on June 7, 1898.

* For the genealogy of the Worthington family, see, Newman's *Anne Arundel Gentry*.

Children of John and Eliza (Robertson) Semmes

1. Eleanor Murdock Semmes, born June 10, 1852, at Washington, married Apr. 12, 1887, Bordley Calhoun, born Sept. 8, 1859.
2. Susan Robertson Semmes, born Apr. 1, 1854, died 1865.
3. Lillie Harrison Semmes, born July 17, 1856, spinster.
4. Bessie Wadsworth Semmes, born Oct. 21, 1857, at Washington, married Oct. 21, 1885, Leon Emil Dessez, born Apr. 12, 1858, at Washington, son of Leon J. B. Dessez and Wilhelmina Gebhart his wife.

COMMODORE ALEXANDER A. SEMMES, U. S. N.[6]
1825–1885

ALEXANDER SEMMES, son of Alexander and Eleanor Harrison (Beatty) Semmes, was born January 18, 1825, at Georgetown. On October 22, 1841, he was appointed a midshipman to the Naval Academy, from which he was graduated. He was one of the few members of the family who did not espouse the principles of State sovereignty during the War Between the States, but remained in the Federal Navy. At the time of his death on September 22, 1885, at Hamilton, Virginia, he held the rank of commodore and was the commandant of the Washington Navy Yard. On February 9, 1864, at Baltimore he married Mary Mortimer Dorsey, daughter of Edwin Mortimer Dorsey and his wife Grace Tyler. His only son died in infancy and his two daughters, Grace and Eleanor, never married and died in Washington at advanced ages.

JOHN BEATTY SEMMES[6]
1826–1865

JOHN BEATTY SEMMES, son of Alexander and Eleanor Harrison (Beatty) Semmes, was born December 14, 1826, in Georgetown. On February 1, 1860, at Mt. Air, near Piscataway, Prince George's County, he married Edmonia, born December 26, 1830, the daughter of Dr. Horace Edelin and his wife Eleanor Catherine.* A son and daughter both died in infancy, but their second son, Alexander Harrison, born December 7, 1861 (*q. v.*), married Mary Hodges and left issue. John Beatty Semmes died in Washington on November 19, 1865; his widow died in Washington on April 13, 1903.

* For the genealogy of the Edelen family, see, Newman's *Charles County Gentry.*

ADMIRAL RAPHAEL SEMMES, C. S. N.[6]
1809–1877

RAPHAEL SEMMES, son of Richard Thompson and Catherine (Middleton) Semmes, was born at "Effton Hills," Charles County, Maryland, on September 27, 1809. At the death of his father in 1823 he was placed under the guardianship of his uncle, Benedict Joseph Semmes, of Prince George's County, one-time Member of Congress. Another uncle, Alexander Semmes, maintained a merchant fleet of ships which sailed from the port of Georgetown, and no doubt in his youth he sailed with his uncle to foreign ports and gained not only his early training in seamanship, but his love for it as well.

On April 1, 1826, he was appointed a midshipman in the U. S. Navy, and on September 8, following, he was ordered to the U. S. S. "Lexington" for duty with the Mediterranean Squadron where he remained about two years. In September, 1828, on account of ill-health, he returned to the United States.

It was at this period that he received a leave of absence from the service during which time he studied law and practised in both Maryland and Ohio. During his legal career in Ohio he met and married Anne Elizabeth Spencer, of Cincinnati, who had been born in that city on June 2, 1819, the daughter of Oliver Marlborough Spencer and his wife, Electra Oliver, and the granddaughter of Colonel Oliver Spencer and his wife, Anna Ogden, of New Jersey. Colonel Oliver Spencer had distinguished himself in the Continental Army during the Revolutionary War and was one of the original members of the Society of the Cincinnati. The marriage of then Lieutenant Raphael Semmes and Anne Spencer occurred on May 5, 1837.

Children of Raphael and Anne (Spencer) Semmes

1. Samuel Spencer Semmes, born Mar. 4, 1838, married (1) Pauline Semmes and (2) Frances Morris. *q.v.*
2. Oliver John Semmes, born Aug. 29, 1839, married Amante Gaines. *q.v.*
3. Electra Louisa Semmes, born Jan. 29, 1843, married Pendleton Colston. *q.v.*
4. Catherine Middleton Semmes, born Apr. 9, 1845, married Luke Edward Wright. *q.v.*
5. Ann Elizabeth Semmes, born May 27, 1847, married May 5, 1875, Charles Bailey Bryan, born 1836, in Robertson Co., Tennessee,

HOME OF ADMIRAL RAPHAEL SEMMES, C.S.N.

In 1871 this house at 802 Government Street, Mobile, Alabama, was bought for Admiral Semmes by popular subscription.

son of John Hardy Bryan and Margaret Bailey his wife. Issue: Raphael Semmes Bryan, born Feb. 3, 1877, at Memphis, married Nov. 8, 1900, Georgia Scott; Charles M. Bryan, *d. s. p.*

6. Raphael Semmes, born Apr. 17, 1849, married Marion Adams. *q. v.*

On February 9, preceding his marriage, he had been recalled to duty, promoted to lieutenant, and had been assigned to duty at the Norfolk Navy Yard. From then until the outbreak of the Mexican War he was engaged in surveying the southern coast on the U. S. S. "Consort"; had a tour of duty at the Pensacola Navy Yard; served on the U. S. S. "Warren," and was in command of the U. S. S. "Poinsett" for the survey of the Gulf of Mexico from August 10, 1843 to April 8, 1845. Then assignments on the U. S. S. "Porpoise" and the U. S. S. "Cumberland" followed.

On October 23, 1846, he was transferred temporarily to the command of the U. S. S. "Somers" then engaged in the blockade of Vera Cruz. On December 8, the "Somers" with two of her officers and part of her crew was lost during a sudden squall. He requested a court of inquiry which acquitted him of all blame and commended him for his gallantry during the catastrophe. By March, 1847, he was on shore with the naval artillery at the bombardment of Vera Cruz.

In April, 1847, as a volunteer aide to Major General Worth he participated in the expedition against Tuxpan and accompanied General Winfield Scott on his triumphant entry into Mexico City. During the campaign on land he was cited several times for bravery. In November, 1847, he was detached from the service and granted permission to return to "Prospect Hill," his plantation on the Perdido River, in Baldwin County, Alabama.

After the treaty of peace which terminated the Mexican War, or from 1847 to 1861, he was on waiting-order status of the U. S. Navy more than half the time, but during those years he served as Inspector of Provisions and Clothing at Pensacola Navy Yard. He also made a cruise on the U. S. S. "Flirt" to Yucatan, was on court martial duty at Pensacola, and served as Judge Advocate General on court martial duty at the Memphis Navy Yard.

During this period of more or less naval inactivity he wrote *Service Afloat and Ashore during the Mexican War,* which was published in 1851, and *The Campaign of General Scott in the Valley of Mexico* which came out in 1852. On November 27, 1852, he addressed the United States Government relative to the laxity of the Timber Agents in Alabama and their lack of knowledge in conservation. He made several constructive recommendations, but as the local agents were political appointees and not selected for their knowledge of forestry, his suggestions were not heeded.

On September 14, 1855, he was promoted to Commander. Alabama seceded from the Union on January 11, 1861, and on February 9, following, Jefferson Davis was named President of the Confederate States of America. Six days later Commander Semmes tendered his resignation and severed all relations with the United States Navy.

On March 26, 1861, he was appointed a Commander in the Confederate States Navy and was immediately sent North to purchase munitions and succeeded in securing large quantities of percussion caps and powder which were shipped South before the commencement of hostilities. Upon his return to Montgomery he was made Chief of the Lighthouse Bureau, but on April 8, 1861, he was relieved and given the first high-sea command in the Confederate Navy on the C. S. S. "Sumter," a commerce destroyer, taking many prizes. In the spring of 1862 the United States fleet blockaded him and the "Sumter" at Gibraltar, and realizing the impossibility of a naval escape, he laid her up on April 12, 1862, discharging his officers and crew.

On June 8, 1862, while he was planning his return to the South, he received orders to take command of the C. S. S. "Alabama," a cruiser of 1070 tons then being built at Birkenhead, England, for the Confederacy. On August 21, 1862, he was promoted to Captain and cited for "gallant and meritorious conduct in capturing and destroying the enemy's commerce on the high seas" and was voted the thanks of the Confederate Congress. On August 24, following, the "Alabama" was turned over to his command off the coast of the Azores, armed, stored, and manned. He sailed directly to the mid-Atlantic whaling grounds, where he subdued and burned ten prizes. On January 11, 1863, he engaged and sank the U. S. S. "Hatteras" off Galveston, Texas.

For twenty-two months the "Alabama" had been continuously at sea, unable to put into port because foreign countries were desirous of avoiding entanglements with the United States. But during those months Captain Semmes was able to sink 82 vessels of the United States and virtually succeeded in breaking the southern blockade. His powder which had been stored on board for the entire two years had suffered much deterioration by a variety of climates, besides a number of repairs were needed. In the early summer of 1864 Captain Semmes was lying off the port of Cherbourg, France, awaiting permission from the French Government to go to the Imperial Dockyard for overhauling. Repeated requests were made, but the vacillating French were playing on time and Napoleon III was no exception. In the meantime the U. S. S. "Kearsage" which had been pursuing the "Alabama" appeared off Cherbourg. Although realizing that his ship was in no condition to fight, Captain Semmes sailed out to engage her in battle on June 19, 1864.

Within the first half hour of the fight the "Alabama" had lodged a shell in the bow of the "Kearsage" which, if it had exploded, would have meant, according to naval authorities, the end of the "Kearsage." The "Alabama" struck the "Kearsage" time and time again, but the shells and powder had lost their effectiveness after many months in tropical seas. After a fierce engagement of nearly an hour and a half, Captain Semmes realized that victory was hopeless and the "Alabama" struck her colors. The commander of the "Kearsage," however, continued his firing, with five repeated blows. The "Alabama" sank proudly and gloriously. Captain Semmes and his surviving crew were picked up by the English yacht, "Deerhound," which carried them safely to England.

In London he was received with many honors and the officers of the British Army and Navy presented him with a sword to replace the one which he had cast into the sea from the deck of his sinking ship. From England he traveled to Switzerland where he underwent a brief but complete rest, then he sailed for Mexico from which place he arrived in Richmond during January, 1865.

On February 10, 1865, he was promoted to Rear Admiral. Eight days later he assumed command of the James River iron-clad squadron, and took his position in the final defense of the Confederate Capital. When it was hopeless to hold out any longer and it was necessary for the Confederate forces to evacuate Richmond, he burned his ships, turned his men into a land naval brigade, and marched with the Army in its retreat from Richmond. He participated in the capitulation of General Joseph E. Johnston at Greensboro, North Carolina.

On April 28, 1865, he was paroled and returned to his home in Mobile, where his family had been living for the greater part of the conflict. Seven and a half months after he had received the guaranty of General Sherman, at Greensboro, that he should not be molested by the United States authorities he was arrested on order of Gideon Welles, Secretary of the United States Navy, without the process of any court, carried to Washington and imprisoned for nearly four months. His letters to President Johnson were brilliant constitutional treatises upon the illegality of his imprisonment and undoubtedly had much to do with his subsequent release which followed the quarrel between President Johnson and Congress respecting the reconstructon of the Southern States.

After his release he returned to his home in Mobile, where he engaged in the practice of law and compiled his memoirs. In 1869 was published his *Memoirs of Service Afloat, or the Remarkable Career of the Confederate Cruisers Sumter and Alabama during the War Between the States.*

The city of Mobile, in recognition of his heroic and devoted service to States' Rights and the principles of the Confederacy, presented him, through popular subscription, a house still standing on Government Street which he and his family occupied as a town residence.

He died at his home, Point Clear, Mobile, on August 30, 1877. His widow died at Mobile on March 7, 1892. Both are buried in Mobile. His statue guards the approach to the city of Mobile from the under-water tube constructed under Mobile Bay. No citizen in the past or present has received more homage than Admiral Semmes—a native Marylander who sought the charm and way-of-life in the Deep South.

SAMUEL MIDDLETON SEMMES[6]

1811–1867

SAMUEL MIDDLETON SEMMES, son of Richard Thompson and Catherine (Middleton) Semmes, was born March 9, 1811, at "Effton Hills," Charles County. He married in Washington, D. C., on May 14, 1840, Eleanora Nelson Guest. The notice of their marriage appeared in the Baltimore *Sun* on May 19th. She was born on December 20, 1820, in Philadelphia, the daughter of Jonathan

Guest and Mary Stoughton his wife. He became a prominent lawyer of Cumberland and was one-time Judge of the Court of Appeals. He died at his country seat "Glennora" near Cumberland, Maryland, on October 14, 1867. His widow died in Baltimore on January 14, 1875. Her obituary was printed in the Baltimore *Sun* on January 19, 1875.

Children of Samuel and Eleanora (Guest) Semmes

1. Mary Guest Semmes, born 1841, died 1842.
2. Richard Thompson Semmes, born Jan. 2, 1843, married Clementine Schlater. *q.v.*
3. Mary Guest Semmes, born Aug. 1844, died Nov. 18, 1866, at New Orleans, married Sept. 24, 1865, Hiram J. Grover, of New Orleans.
4. Kate Middleton Semmes, born Mar. 10, 1846, married Dec. 26, 1865, Rev. Frederick Gibson, of Baltimore.
5. Nora Semmes, born Mar. 26, 1848, married Nov. 11, 1866, William Johns Read, of Cumberland; later of Elkins, W. Va.
6. Middleton Semmes, born 1849, died 1852.
7. John Edward Semmes, born July 1, 1851, married Frances Hayward. *q.v.*
8. Samuel Middleton Semmes, born 1859, died 1872.

MAJOR BENEDICT JOSEPH SEMMES, C. S. A.[6]
1823–1902

BENEDICT JOSEPH SEMMES, oldest son of Raphael and Matilda (Jenkins) Semmes, was born June 15, 1823, in Georgetown, D. C. He followed mercantile pursuits in Washington until 1859, when he removed to Memphis and for years conducted a large and successful wholesale establishment.

In New York City on April 25, 1849, he married Jorantha Jordan, born February 19, 1829, daughter of Lawrence Pallette Jordan and his wife Mary Ann Lanckenau, of New York City.

Children of Benedict Joseph and Jorantha (Jordan) Semmes

1. Mary Julia Semmes, born May 23, 1850, at Georgetown, died Aug. 16, 1879, at Grayson Springs, Ky., reinterred 1880 at Memphis, married Oct. 10, 1877, at Memphis, Thomas F. Tobin, son of Edward Sarsfield and Bridget de Leon (Fogerty) Tobin; he died Sept. 28, 1900.
2. Joseph Malcolm Semmes, born July 24, 1852, at Georgetown, married Eleanor Martin. *q.v.*
3. Raphael Eustace Semmes, born Sept. 20, 1854, married Maude Duval. *q.v.*

4. Marianna Semmes, born June 12, 1857, at Washington, married Feb. 9, 1875, at Memphis William J. McGavock; removed to Mexico City.
5. Mary Jorantha Semmes, born Aug. 19, 1860, at Memphis.
6. Matilda Semmes, born and died 1865.
7. Thomas Jenkins Semmes, born Feb. 13, 1867, at Memphis, married Dec. 2, 1903, at Memphis Margaret Wiltshire, later of Mexico City.
8. Clara Augusta Semmes, born Oct. 12, 1869, at Memphis.
9. Ada Florence Semmes, born and died 1875.

On March 8, 1862, he enlisted as a sergeant in Co. L, 154th Tennessee Regiment under Col. Preston Smith, of Maynard Riflemen, and was wounded at the Battle of Shiloh on April 6, 1862. Upon his recovery he was commissioned a Captain of the Army of Tennessee on September 1, 1862, and assigned to duty as Chief Depot Commissary of that Army on July 12, 1863. He was promoted to Major on February 5, 1865, and surrendered on May 4, following. He was paroled at Gainesville, Ala. He died at Memphis on January 29, 1902.

HON. THOMAS JENKINS SEMMES, C. S. A.[6]
1824–1899

THOMAS JENKINS SEMMES, the second son of Raphael and Mary Matilda (Jenkins) Semmes, was born December 16, 1824, at Georgetown. At Montgomery, Ala., on January 8, 1850, by the Rev. James Ryder, S. J. D. D., he married Myra Eulalia Knox. She was born December 3, 1831, at Winchester, Tenn., the daughter of William Knox and Anne Octavia Lewis his wife, her father being one-time president of the Central Bank of Alabama.

Children of Thomas Jenkins and Myra (Knox) Semmes

1. William Knox Semmes, born Feb. 14, 1851, died 1851.
2. Myra Eulalia Semmes, born Sept. 6, 1865, married Sylvester Pierce Walmsley. *q. v.*
3. Cora Matilda Semmes, born Aug. 26, 1867, married Albert Sidney Ranlett, *q. v.*
4. Thomas Ignatius Semmes, born July 19, 1869, at Warrenton, Va.
5. Francis Joseph Semmes, born May 28, 1871, at New Orleans.
6. Hubert Vincent Marie Semmes, born July 19, 1873, at Warrenton, died Dec. 31, 1887, at New Orleans.
7. Charles Lewis Semmes, born Aug. 23, 1875, at Warrenton, Va.

THOMAS JENKINS SEMMES

United States District Attorney under President Buchanan, Attorney General for Louisiana, Member of Confederate Congress from Louisiana.

He settled in New Orleans immediately after his marriage and in June, 1858, by President Buchanan he was appointed the United States District Attorney for that area. On January 26, 1860, he was elected the Attorney General of Louisiana, and represented Louisiana in the Confederate Congress. He died at New Orleans on June 22, 1899, and was universally regarded as one of the most brilliant legal minds of the country.

ANN AMERICA (SEMMES) PAYNE [6]

1826–1862

ANN AMERICA SEMMES, daughter of Raphael and Mary Matilda (Jenkins) Semmes, was born July 3, 1826, at Georgetown, D. C. By license secured in the District of Columbia on January 3, 1848, she married Rice Winfield Payne, of Warrenton, Virginia. He was born in that town on October 7, 1818, son of Daniel and Elizabeth Hooe (Winter) Payne.

Children of Rice Winfield and Ann America (Semmes) Payne

1. Charles Borromeo Payne, born 1848, died 1853.
2. Elizabeth Winter Payne, born June 1, 1850, married Thomas Marshall Jones. *q.v.*
3. Matilda Jenkins Payne, born 1852, died 1853.
4. Cora Bernard Payne, born Nov. 2, 1853, married Christopher Columbus Shriver, of Baltimore, on Feb. 12, 1889.
5. John Carroll Payne, born Sept. 24, 1855, married Nov. 25, 1885, in Atlanta, Helen Fairlie, daughter of W. Rhode and Laura (Nance) Hill. Issue: Laura Hill, born Dec. 9, 1886 (*q.v.*); Helen Hill, born Apr. 7, 1890, John Carroll, born 1893, died 1895.
6. William Gaston Payne, born May 26, 1858, entered Catholic priesthood.
7. Raphael Semmes Payne, born June 3, 1860, married June 5, 1905, Mary Dunlap Thomas.
8. Mary Virginia Semmes Payne, born 1862, died 1869.

She died in Warrenton on January 29, 1862. Her husband married on April 4, 1864, her sister Mary Virginia Semmes. One child was born, America Semmes, on February 22, 1865, who died December 17, 1917. He died in Warrenton on September 25, 1884; his widow died there on November 18, 1897.

DR. ALEXANDER IGNATIUS SEMMES, C. S. A.[6]
1828–1898

ALEXANDER IGNATIUS SEMMES, son of Raphael and Mary Matilda (Jenkins) Semmes, was born December 17, 1828, in Georgetown, District of Columbia. He was educated at Georgetown and Columbian College, now George Washington University, as well as in Paris. After the completion of his medical studies he joined his brother in New Orleans, where he became the resident physician at Charity Hospital. At the outbreak of the War Between the States he joined the Louisiana Volunteers and later served as surgeon of Hay's Louisiana Brigade, Stonewall Jackson's Corps and Lee's Army of Northern Virginia. After the war he settled in Savannah, Georgia, where he practiced medicine and taught at the Savannah Medical College as professor of physiology.

He married the daughter of the Attorney General in the first cabinet of President Andrew Jackson. After her death he continued his medical endeavors until the age of fifty, when he forsook medicine entirely and was ordained a priest in the Roman Catholic Church. Besides performing the duties of a parish priest, he lectured, taught and did missionary work throughout the State of Georgia until 1895, when he became incapacitated by a paralytic stroke. In 1898 he died at Hotel Dieu in New Orleans, nursed during his last months by the Sisters of Charity who had been in charge of the nursing staff at Charity Hospital when he was resident physician in his youth.

CORA MATILDA (SEMMES) IVES[6]
1834–1916

CORA MATILDA SEMMES, daughter of Raphael and Mary Matilda (Jenkins) Semmes, was born June 26, 1834. By license obtained in the District of Columbia on June 15, 1855, she married Lieutenant Joseph Christmas Ives, U. S. A. He was born in 1829, and died in 1868. She died in New York City on January 27, 1916.

Children of Joseph and Cora (Semmes) Ives

1. Edward Ives, died a bachelor.
2. Francis Ives married Mildred Megeath. *q. v.*
3. Eugene Semmes Ives, born Nov. 11, 1859, married Ann Maria Waggaman. *q. v.*

MAJOR BENEDICT JOSEPH SEMMES, C. S. A.[6]
1833–1879

BENEDICT JOSEPH SEMMES, sixth child of Dr. Benedict Joseph and Emily (Edelen) Semmes, was born May 15, 1833, at Piscataway, Prince George's County. At the age of 14 years he entered Georgetown College from which he was graduated in 1853. After the study of law, he was admitted to the bar and began the practice of law in Chicago. There on December 27, 1857, he married Sallie F. Reynolds, of Kentucky ancestry, who died in Chicago on September 22, 1859. One son was born, but died in infancy.

At the outbreak of the War Between the States, he left Chicago and went South to offer his services to the Confederacy.

In 1864 near Gainesville, Sumter County, Alabama, he married his cousin, Jane Semmes, the daughter of Thomas and Catherine (Winter) Semmes, of Georgia.

Children of Benedict Joseph and Jane (Semmes) Semmes

1. Emily Edelen Semmes, born May 18, 1865, Sumter Co., Ala.
2. Catherine Winter Semmes, born 1866, d. 1867.
3. Jane Semmes, born Mar. 24, 1869, married Stanhope Joseph Posey.
4. Alice Semmes, born Aug. 10, 1871, took Holy Orders.
5. Catherine Winter Semmes, born Sept. 30, 1872, married Carnot A. Posey.
6. Celestia Semmes, born Aug. 1, 1874.
7. Mary Matilda Brawner Semmes, born Sept. 24, 1875.

In 1865 he settled in Canton, Mississippi, and resumed the practice of law where he gained great prominence. There he died on May 29, 1879, his wife having died in Atlanta, Georgia, on July 18, 1878.

JAMES HALL SEMMES[6]
1844–1913

JAMES HALL SEMMES, son of Thomas Felix and Mary Olivia (Edelen) Semmes, was born December 26, 1844, in Washington. On October 1, 1881, he married Minnesota Dennison, a native Washingtonian, the daughter of Major William Wallace Dennison, U. S. A., and his wife Ann Maston. The son, John Hall Semmes, was born August 29, 1882, and married Agnes Johnson; their daughter, Mary Olivia Semmes, was born March 31, 1884, but died unmarried.

THOMAS SEMMES[6]

1802–1862

THOMAS SEMMES, the only son of Roger Semmes by his wife Jane Sanders, was born January 19, 1802, in Georgia. On June 19, 1829, by the Rev. Nathan Hoyt, he married Harriet Shepherd Beall, of Columbus, Georgia, the daughter of Thomas and Polly (Maddox) Beall.

Children of Thomas and Harriet (Beall) Semmes

1. Alphonso Thomas Semmes, born Apr. 28, 1830, married Mary Sabina Semmes. *q. v.*
2. Roger Leonidas Semmes, born Oct. 26, 1831, married Sarah Ann Griffin. *q. v*
3. William Maddox Semmes, born 1834, died 1836.

His wife died in Georgetown, D. C., and was buried in the Roman Catholic cemetery of Georgetown College. Her headstone reads " Harriet Shepherd Beall wife of Thomas Semmes of Washington, Georgia, Died April 26, 1835, in her 21st year."

On November 9, 1837, at the home of her uncle, Raphael Semmes, of Georgetown, he married his cousin, Catherine Taliaferro Hooe Winter, the daughter of Richard Hooe and Mary Charlotte (Semmes) Winter.

Children of Thomas and Catherine (Winter) Semmes

1. Mary Charlotte Semmes, born Nov. 13, 1838, married Apr. 28, 1862, Sherrod Gustus Luckett.
2. Richard Winter Semmes, born Dec. 25, 1839, died 1856.
3. Virginia Elizabeth Semmes, born Aug. 8, 1841, married Lieut. Henry Bradford Luckett, of Canton, Miss.*
4. Thomas Semmes, born Nov. 8, 1842, *d. s. p.* 1864.
5. Raphael Semmes, born 1844, died 1853.
6. Jane Semmes, born June 28, 1845, married Benedict Joseph Semmes. *q. v.*
7. William Augustus Semmes, born Nov. 9, 1847, married Pamella Harrison.
8. Julia Semmes, spinster.
9. Henry Fenton Semmes, born 1851, died 1853.
10. Catherine Semmes, born Jackson, Miss., 1853, died 1854.
11. Ophelia Semmes, born near Augusta, Ga., spinster.

---

* See, Newman's *The Lucketts of Portobacco.*

On August 1, 1839, he and his wife, Catherine T. H. Semmes, of Wilkes County, Georgia, conveyed to William P. Golding, of Charles County, Maryland, "Effton Hills" on Burdit's Creek, containing 270 acres, which was the plantation inherited by the said Catherine T. H. Semmes as the only heir of her father Richard H. Winter, deceased.

At Washington, Georgia, he maintained a large and successful merchandise business, with a large plantation on the outskirts of the town, but about 1852 he removed to the newer and more fertile lands in Mississippi purchasing three large plantations in Madison County. While his home "Kalorama" was being constructed near Canton, he and his family resided in Jackson. In 1853 he occupied his new home and from then on he devoted his entire time to the cultivation of cotton. He was a staunch secessionist, but was prevented from entering the Army by a stroke of paralysis, but at his own expense he equipped completely a Mississippi company called the Semmes Rifles. He died at his home "Kalorama" near Canton in May, 1862, and was buried in the Catholic cemetery at Sulphur Springs.

THOMAS JAMES ANDREW SEMMES [6]
1808–1839

THOMAS JAMES ANDREW SEMMES, son of Andrew Green and Frances (Herbert) Semmes, was born August 7, 1808, at the Sand Hills near Augusta, Georgia. On October 23, 1832, he married Antoinette Tate [Toit, Tait].

Children of Thomas and Antoinette (Toit) Semmes

1. Frances Semmes, born Jan. 16, 1837, died Feb. 20, 1893, married Robert Pierce Coleman.
2. James Minor Toit Semmes, born June 25, 1839, married twice. *q.v.*
3. Thomas Andrew Semmes, born 1842, died 1853.

After his graduation from the University of Georgia, he settled in Mississippi, where he was killed on July 15, 1839, by the explosion of his gun while dismounting his horse after a fox hunt. His widow married secondly Samuel Smith, and removed from her home in Columbus, Mississippi, and settled at Hernando, De Soto County.

JUDGE ALBERT GALLATIN SEMMES[6]

1810–18–

ALBERT GALLATIN SEMMES, son of Andrew Green and Frances (Herbert) Semmes, was born August 18, 1810, at the Sand Hills near Augusta, Georgia. He was graduated from the University of Georgia, read law and was admitted to the bar. He removed to Florida, where he became the Associate Justice of the Supreme Court of that State 1851-1853.

On February 22, 1834, he married his cousin, Isabella V. Semmes, only daughter of James R. Semmes and his wife Mary Powell. Only one child, Frances, who married —— Sherwood, lived to maturity. He died in the city of New Orleans.

GENERAL PAUL JONES SEMMES, C. S. A.[6]

1815–1863

PAUL JONES SEMMES, son of Andrew Green and Mary (Robertson) Semmes, was born June 4, 1815, at Montford's Plantation, Wilkes County, Georgia. On June 14, 1836, he married in Athens, Georgia, Emily J. Hemphill, daughter of Thomas Hemphill, Esq., of that town.

Children of Paul Jones and Emily (Hemphill) Semmes

1. Mary Jane Semmes, born Apr. 26, 1837, died a spinster 1867, in Monroe Co., Ark.
2. Pauline Semmes, born Mar. 28, 1839, married Samuel Spencer Semmes. *q.v.*
3. Cleveland Porter Semmes, born Mar. 17, 1841, died 1842.
4. Thomas Hemphill Semmes, born 1842, died 1844.
5. Andrew Green Semmes, born and died 1845.
6. Andrew Green Semmes } twins, born Nov. 19, 1832, at Wynston, near
7. Thomas Hemphill Semmes } Columbus, Ga.

He lived at one time in Russell County, Alabama, where several of his children were born. For many years he was a prominent banker of Columbus, Georgia, and operated an extensive plantation nearby. He was interested in the militia of his State and was captain of the Columbus Guards, and also a member of the Board of Visitors for West Point Military Academy. In 1861 Governor Joseph E. Brown appointed him Brigadier-General of Georgia

Volunteers, but he resigned in order to serve with the regular State regiments. On May 7, 1861, he accepted the colonelcy of the 2d Georgia Regiment, and on March 11, 1862, he was advanced to Brigadier General. He conducted himself with great distinction in many battles of the war with the Army of Northern Virginia. While leading his brigade at the battle of Gettysburg, he was mortally wounded on July 2, 1863. He died seven days later at Martinsburg, Virginia, where he was interred. Later his remains were removed to his home near Columbus, Georgia. His widow died March 9, 1884, in Monroe County, Arkansas.

JOHN ROBERTSON SEMMES [6]
1817–1864

JOHN ROBERTSON SEMMES, son of Andrew Green and Mary (Robertson) Semmes, was born August 27, 1817, at his father's plantation on Williams' Creek in Wilkes County, Georgia. In Washington, Ga., on October 24, 1839, he married Lucy Sophia Stone, born September 20, 1819, in Wilkes County. Of two children born to this union, Andrew, the oldest died without issue, while Mary, born December 25, 1841, in Wilkes County, maried on January 15, 1863, at Canton, Mississippi, Nicholas Cromwell Orrick, born October 27, 1836, in Morgan County, Virginia, a descendant of the Cromwell and Orrick families of Maryland. John Robertson Semmes became a wealthy planter and died on November 6, 1864, in Washington County, Mississippi.

THOMAS MIDDLETON SEMMES [7]
1840–1904

THOMAS MIDDLETON SEMMES, son of Thomas and Elizabeth (Bernard) Semmes, was born September 4, 1840, in Alexandria. He became a professor of modern languages at the Virginia Military Institute, Lexington, Virginia. On November 16, 1863, he married Louise Gardner Brockenbrough, daughter of Judge John White Brockenbrough and Mary Carpenter Bowyer his wife. His death occurred on November 27, 1904.

Children of Thomas and Louise (Brockenbrough) Semmes

1. Bernard Semmes, born Sept. 22, 1864, married Frances Lewis. *q.v.*

2. Mary Bowyer Semmes, born Aug. 2, 1869, married Rev. Howard Jones.
3. Elise Vivian Semmes, born Mar. 12, 1873, married Montgomery Corse.
4. Lulu Semmes, born July 26, 1877, married William Archer Roberts.
5. Thomas Meredith Semmes, born Sept. 6. 1883.

ROBERT DOYNE SEMMES[7]

1835–1891

ROBERT DOYNE SEMMES, son of Robert and Mary (Worthington) Semmes, was born April 11, 1835, at Rose Hill, Charles County. His wife was Julia Egerton. His death occurred at Baltimore on December 17, 1891. Two children were born—Clara Egerton, born February 26, 1862, who married December 9, 1884, John Dozier Byrd, of Baltimore; and Rebecca born 1863, died 1865.

ALEXANDER HARRISON SEMMES[7]

1861–1923

ALEXANDER HARRISON SEMMES, son of John Beatty and Edmonia (Edelin) Semmes, was born December 7, 1861, in the District of Columbia. On April 15, 1891, in Washington, D. C., he married Mary Hodges, born June 6, 1861, at La Grange, Ga., daughter of Henry Hodges and Anna Elizabeth his wife. They had children, Henry Hodges, born January 18, 1892 (*q. v.*) and Helen Edelin who died an infant in 1901. Mr. Semmes died in Washington on November 12, 1923; his widow died on March 25, 1946.

CAPTAIN SAMUEL SPENCER SEMMES, C. S. A.[7]

1838–1912

SAMUEL SPENCER SEMMES, eldest son of Admiral Raphael Semmes and Anne Spencer his wife, was born March 4, 1838, in Cincinnati. On October 17, 1863, at Washington, Georgia, he married his cousin Pauline, born March 28, 1839, daughter of General Paul Jones Semmes, C. S. A.

Children of Samuel Spencer and Pauline (Semmes) Semmes

1. Paul Jones Semmes, born July 11, 1865, married Margaret Murray. *q.v.*
2. Raphael Semmes, born Mar. 31, 1867, married Lula Sullivan. *q.v.*
3. Marie Oliver Semmes, born Aug. 10, 1868, Monroe Co., Ark., ordained

priest of the Catholic Church, June 28, 1901, at Woodstock, Md., died Kingston, Jamaica, 1948, and buried there.

4. Mary Electra Semmes, born Nov. 29, 1871, married Sept. 3, 1895, Spencer S. Roane, and secondly M. A. Martin, of Henrico, Ark,; no issue of either marriage.
5. Anna Hemphill Semmes, born Sept. 21, 1873, married William Tipton Uzzelle. *q. v.*

His first wife died on December 6, 1877, in Osceola, Arkansas. On August 28, 1881, at Memphis he married secondly Frances Harding Morris, born May 25, 1860, in Mississippi County, Arkansas. She was the only daughter of the Rev. Frank Calvin Morris and his wife, Sarah Ann Alexander McFeat, who was born August 13, 1829, at "Oak Grove," Iredell County, North Carolina, and died September 20, 1866, at Osceola, daughter of William and Elizabeth (Plume) McFeat. The Rev. Mr. Morris was born April 8, 1825, in Morgan County, Alabama, the son of Taylor Morris and his wife, Susan McCrosky, and was an ordained minister of the Presbyterian Church, having studied at the Presbyterian Seminary of Columbia, South Carolina. The church at Osceola was his first charge. He died on April 14, 1876.

Children of Samuel Spencer and Frances (Morris) Semmes

6. Eulalia Spencer Semmes, born June 20, 1882, at Osceola, married Frank G. Gibson; no issue.
7. Francis Morris Semmes, born May 21, 1884, married Minnie Harrington. *q. v.*
8. Catherine Margaret Semmes, born Nov. 8, 1886, Osceola, Ark., entered convent; died at St. Cecilia Academy, Nashville, Tenn., 1953.
9. Electra Elizabeth Semmes, born Sept. 2, 1889, married twice. *q. v.*
10. Myra Felicia Semmes, born Nov. 18, 1891, Osceola, Ark., entered convent, died Jan. 26, 1914, at St. Cecilia Academy, Nashville, Tenn.
11. Lyman Alexander Semmes, born Dec. 29, 1893, at Osceola, Ark., died Jan. 29, 1929.
12. Samuel Prewitt Semmes, born Dec. 12, 1895, married Valerie Walker Danehower. *q. v.*
13. Charles Middleton Semmes, born May 28, 1898, married Jan. 12, 1924, Martha Tidwell. Issue: George Tidwell Semmes, born Jan. 13, 1925, married June 6, 1948, Juanita Hamilton.

While his father went North on a purchasing commission for the Confederate States, he offered his service to the State of Louisiana and was mustered in at New Orleans on April 3, 1861, as a 2d Lieut. of Co. E, 1st Regt. of Louisiana Infantry, Gibson's Brigade, Clayton's Division, and General Stephen D. Lee's Corps, Army of Tennessee. On December 20, 1862, he was the Assistant Paymaster of the 1st Louisiana Regiment, and was later promoted to captain and as Paymaster was attached to headquarters. He sustained all the vicissitudes of the 1st Louisiana and participated in the Georgia campaign when Sherman made his march to the sea. At the time of the final surrender he was at Augusta where he capitulated on April 28, 1865.

He settled ultimately in Mississippi County, Arkansas, where he died at Osceola on January 24, 1912. His widow died at Osceola on December 30, 1924.

MAJOR OLIVER JOHN SEMMES, C. S. A.[7]

1839– ——

OLIVER JOHN SEMMES, second son of Admiral Raphael Semmes and his wife, Anne Spencer, was born August 29, 1839, at the Norfolk Navy Yard. From Alabama he was appointed to West Point and had completed three years when he resigned to offer his services to the South. He was in New York City when his father arrived to purchase supplies for the Confederacy, and on March 22, 1861, his father addressed letters to the Hon. L. P. Walker, Secretary of War, and President Davis introducing his son, " This will be handed you by my son Oliver J. Semmes, late a cadet at West Point."

He was immediately appointed a 2d Lieut. of Infantry, but in February 1862, at Baton Rouge he organized the Semmes Battery, a mounted light artillery unit attached to the Trans-Mississippi Department, and saw extraordinary service throughout the war.

At the battle of Franklin, La., on April 14, 1863, while commanding the steamer " Diana," he was captured and taken to New Orleans, where the Provost Marshal delivered him and about fifty other officers of the Confederacy to Major J. W. Burgess of the 6th N. Y. Regt. to be conveyed to Fortress Monroe. While being transferred on June 10, 1863, from Fortress Monroe to Fort Delaware, Del., with other prisoners, most of whom were officers, they overpowered the guards on board the steamer " Maple Leaf " and made their escape. At great hazard he passed through the lines, crossed the Mississippi, and joined his command.

All his superior officers recommended him highly to the War Department at Richmond, including General Kirby Smith. Col. James P. Major writing to the Secretary of War stated " His coolness and bravery on the field of battle won for his battery the name of one, if not, the very best battery west of the Mississippi River. . . . Captain Semmes is a perfect gentleman and an educated soldier. . . ." Brig. Gen. Thomas Green likewise wrote " I know him to be eminently worthy of promotion . . . he is a worthy son of a noble sire." General Mouton addressing the Hon. Thomas J. Semmes, a member of the Confederate Congress from Louisiana, who was his cousin, stated that Captain Semmes had been under his command for 14 months and had been continually in the presence of the enemy and had " no superior in the Confederate Service."

On November 7, 1863, he was promoted to major of the Louisiana Artillery and held that commission when he received his parole at Mobile on May 9, 1865, a member of the staff of General R. Taylor.

On December 17, 1873, at Mobile, he married Amante Gaines, who was born September 18, 1849, and died October 27, 1889, daughter of Dr. Edmund Pendleton Gaines and his wife Mary Toalmine, the latter's mother being Amante de Juzon. The issue of Major Semmes and his wife were: Amante Electra, born October 2, 1877; Oliver John, born August 7, 1879; Raphael, who died in January, 1910; and Electra.

ELECTRA LOUISA (SEMMES) COLSTON [7]

1843–——

ELECTRA LOUISA SEMMES, daughter of Admiral Raphael Semmes and Anne Spencer his wife, was born January 29, 1843. On February 17, 1864, she married Pendleton Colston who was born at Martinsburg, Virginia, son of Josiah and Eliza Pendleton (Tutt) Colston. His forbears had settled early on the Eastern Shore of Maryland. He died at Mobile December 8, 1867. Two children were born: Raphael Semmes Colston, born May 13, 1865, married July 1901 at New Orleans Marguerite Ohio Tarrant; and Pendleton Colston, born August 19, 1866 at Mobile, died October 22, 1900, married Esther, daughter of Matthew and Fannie (Travis) Turner.

CATHERINE MIDDLETON (SEMMES) WRIGHT[7]
1845–1937

CATHERINE MIDDLETON SEMMES, daughter of Admiral Raphael Semmes and Anne Spencer his wife, was born April 9, 1845. On December 15, 1869, she married Luke Edward Wright, of Memphis, who was born August 15, 1846, at Memphis, son of Archibald and Elizabeth (Eldridge) Wright.

Children of Luke and Catherine (Semmes) Wright

1. Eldridge Wright, born July 25, 1871, at Mobile, died Jan. 22, 1912, married Dec. 18, 1895, Mignon Petus, of Memphis. Issue: William Folkes Wright, born Jan. 16, 1897, at Memphis, married ———, and had William and Luke Eldridge Wright.
2. Ann Spencer Wright, born Jan. 7, 1873, at Memphis, married Nov. 20, 1895, John Watkins; no issue.
3. Luke Edward Wright, born June 4, 1877, at Memphis; no issue.
4. Raphael Edward Wright, born June 4, 1877, at Memphis; no issue.
4. Raphael Semmes Wright born Apr. 23, 1879, married Maud ———. *q.v.*
5. Katrina Wright, born Apr. 29, 1886, at Memphis, married Charles Stancell. Issue: Dianna who married Eugene Coleman.

In 1870 Luke Wright was elected attorney general of Shelby County, Tenn., and on April 1, 1900, he was appointed one of the commissioners for the Philippine Islands. On February 1, 1904, he was appointed Governor General of the Islands serving until 1906. From 1906 to 1907 he was United States Minister to Japan, and in the latter year he was appointed Secretary of War by President Theodore Roosevelt. Mrs. Wright died in 1937, at the age of 94 in Surrey, England, at the home of her daughter, Mrs. Charles Stancell, being the last surviving child of the Admiral.

Electra lived to be 98+.

RAPHAEL SEMMES[7]
1849– ——

RAPHAEL SEMMES, youngest son of Admiral Raphael Semmes by his wife, Anne Spencer, was born April 17, 1849. In November, 1881, he married Marion Adams, of Clarksville, Tennessee, daughter of William and Eunice (McDaniel) Adams.

Children of Raphael and Marion (Adams) Semmes

1. Raphael Semmes, born Dec. 29, 1882, married Louise T. Semmes. *q.v.*
2. Aubray Middleton Semmes.
3. Richard C. Semmes.
4. Eunice McDaniel Semmes.

RICHARD THOMPSON SEMMES [7]

1843–1924

RICHARD THOMPSON SEMMES, son of Samuel Middleton and Eleanor (Guest) Semmes, was born January 2, 1843, near Cumberland, Maryland. On February 28, 1871, at Homestead Plantation, Plaquemine Parish, Louisiana, he married Clementine Schlater, born November 25, 1859, the daughter of Jervais Schlater and Mary Clement his wife. Richard Thompson Semmes was graduated from Yale, and became a member of the Maryland Bar. After the death of his first wife, he married Elizabeth Morgan Haff, widow. His death occurred on August 22, 1924.

Children of Richard Thompson and Clementine (Schlater) Semmes

1. Mary Grover Semmes, born Dec. 9, 1871, married at Cumberland Sept. 18, 18, 1894, Richard Gambrill, son of James H. Gambrill and Antoinette F. Staley, his wife, of Frederick County.
2. Clementine Schlater Semmes, born May 4, 1873.
3. Richard Middleton Semmes, born Sept. 19, 1874.
4. Eleanora Guest Semmes, born Nov. 1, 1876.
5. Jervais Schlater Semmes, born Aug. 29, 1883.
6. Edwin Douglas Semmes, born 1886, died 1890.

JOHN EDWARD SEMMES [7]

1851–1925

JOHN EDWARD SEMMES, son of Samuel Middleton and Eleanor (Guest) Semmes, was born "Tuesday the 1st day of July at half past 6 o'clock A. M. in the year 1851 . . . third son and seventh child," near Cumberland, Alleghany County, Maryland. On June 22, 1880, he married Frances Carnan Hayward, daughter of Peabody and Prudence (Carnan) Hayward, of Baltimore.

Children of John Edward and Frances (Hayward) Semmes

1. John Edward Semmes, born Apr. 15, 1881, at Baltimore, married Alice Canby Robinson.

2. Frances Carnan Hayward Semmes, born Nov. 12, 1882, unmarried.
3. Elizabeth North Semmes, born 1883, died 1884.
4. Raphael Semmes, born Aug. 25, 1890, died unmarried 1952.

John Edward Semmes studied first at the University of Virginia, was graduated in 1874 from the Maryland Law School, and ultimately became one of the leading lawyers of the Maryland Bar. He was City Solicitor from 1897 to 1899 and a member of the Water Board from 1903 to 1907, when he resigned to become president of the School Board. Among his clubs were the Maryland, University, and the Baltimore Athletic, being one of the organizers of the last named. He died at the residence of his son, John, in Guilford, Baltimore, on May 17, 1925.

JOSEPH MALCOLM SEMMES [7]

1852-—

JOSEPH MALCOLM SEMMES, eldest son of Benedict Joseph Semmes and his wife Jorantha Jordan, was born July 24, 1852, at Georgetown, District of Columbia. At Columbia, Tennessee, on December 20, 1877, he married Eleanor Wingfield Martin, daughter of Thomas Granville Martin, of that town, and Mary Mayes Wingfield his wife.

Children of Joseph Malcolm and Eleanor (Martin) Semmes

1. Joseph Malcolm Semmes, born Jan. 12, 1879, married Elsye ———. Issue: Iorantha Semmes married Burt Carle and had Kathleen, Eileen and Christine Carle.
2. Eleanor Julia Semmes, born May 22, 1881, married 1903 Edwin Haynes Humphrey, of Detroit. No issue.
3. Benedict Granville Semmes, born Aug. 26, 1882, at Memphis, married Gertrude Orrick. No issue.
4. Laura Ensley Semmes, born Feb. 13, 1884, at Memphis.
5. Iorantha Mary Semmes, born Aug. 15, 1885, married Frederick Sutton Stoepel. *q.v.*
6. Benedict Joseph Semmes, born Feb. 5, 1887, married Amy Lardner *q.v.*
7. George Wingfield Semmes, born Feb. 7, 1889, married Anne Ray.
8. Harriette Ensley Semmes, born Aug. 25, 1890, married Lewis Bruce Anderson. *q.v.*
9. Katherine Thompson Semmes, born May 2, 1895, married Francis C. Van Dyke. *q.v.*
10. Thomas Jenkins Semmes, born July 4, 1897, married Elise Humphries. *q.v.*

RAPHAEL EUSTACE SEMMES [7]

1854– ––

RAPHAEL EUSTACE SEMMES, son of Benedict Joseph and Jorantha (Jordan) Semmes, was born September 20, 1854, in Georgetown, D. C. On January 30, 1883, at Memphis, he married Maude Duval, born June 25, 1860, at Pass Christian, Miss., and died April 25, 1893, in Memphis, daughter of George W. Duval and his wife Margaret K. LaValette.* He resided at Memphis where all of his children were born.

Children of Raphael Eustace and Maude (Duval) Semmes

1. Julia Semmes, born Dec. 8, 1883.
2. Raphael Eustace Semmes, born Aug. 15, 1885, married Mary Alice Graves. *q. v.*
3. Mary Anita Semmes, born May 29, 1887.
4. Maude Duval Semmes, born Jan. 2, 1889, married Branner Gilmore.
5. Alberta LaVallette Semmes, born Mar. 20, 1891.
6. LaVallette Duval Semmes, born Apr. 13, 1893.

MYRA EULALIE (SEMMES) WALMSLEY [7]

1865– ––

MYRA EULALIE SEMMES, daughter of Thomas Jenkins and Myra (Knox) Semmes, was born September 6, 1865, at Montgomery, Alabama. She married on November 18, 1885, Sylvester Pierce Walmsley who died July 22, 1930, in Los Angeles.

Children of Sylvester and Myra (Semmes) Walmsley

1. Sylvester Pierce Walmsley married twice. *q. v.*
2. Myra Eulalie Semmes Walmsley married David Cartan Loker. *q. v.*
3. Thomas Semmes Walmsley married Julia Caroline Havard. *q. v.*
4. Caroline Gratia Walmsley, born Aug. 8, 1890, at Canandaigua, N. Y., married June 1, 1933, Leon Irwin who died Sept. 21, 1942. No issue.
5. Robert Miller Walmsley married Dorothy Jackson. *q. v.*
6. Byrd Greer Walmsley married Ennals Waggaman Ives. *q. v.*
7. Carroll Beard Walmsley, born Apr. 3, 1895, died a bachelor Aug. 24, 1943.

---

* For the genealogy of the Maryland Duvalls, see, Newman's "*Mareen Duvall of Middle Plantation.*"

8. Raphael Semmes Walmsley, born and died 1896.
9. William Knox Walmsley, born May 10, 1897, died Sept. 27, 1954, married Germaine Marie Doussan. No issue.
10. Mary Lucille Walmsley, born June 10, 1898, spinster.
11. Hughes Philip Walmsley married Arthemise Marie Avrill. *q.v.*
12. Miriam Louise Walmsley, born May 3, 1903, died Jan. 7, 1919.
13. George Penrose Walmsley, born 1906, died 1907.

CORA MATILDA (SEMMES) RANLETT [7]

1867–——

CORA MATILDA SEMMES, daughter of Thomas Jenkins and Myra (Knox) Semmes, was born August 26, 1867, at Warrenton, Virginia. On May 7, 1889, she married Albert Sidney Ranlett, of New Orleans, son of David Low Ranlett, of Augusta, Maine, and Eleanor Gittings Stone his wife, reputed to be of Maryland ancestry. He was born February 5, 1862, in New Orleans, and died March 28, 1918, in New York City.

Children of Albert S. and Cora Matilda (Semmes) Ranlett

1. Myra Eulalie Semmes Ranlett married Carroll P. Curtis. *q.v.*
2. Albert Sidney Ranlett married Kathryn Walsh. *q.v.*
3. Thomas Jenkins Semmes Ranlett married Adele Olive White. *q.v.*
4. David Low Ranlett, born June 11, 1893, died Jan. 26, 1944, married Elizabeth Holmes.
5. Cora Mary Ranlett married Alexander Torrence Thomson. *q.v.*
6. Eleanor Stone Ranlett, born Mar. 3, 1898, married May 19, 1927, George Randolph Kantzler.

ELIZABETH WINTER (PAYNE) JONES [7]

1850–——

ELIZABETH WINTER PAYNE, daughter of Rice Winfield and Ann America (Semmes) Payne, was born June 1, 1850, in Warrenton, Virginia. On June 23, 1880, in Warrenton, she married Dr. Thomas Marshall Jones, born October 1838, in Fauquier County, son of James FitzGerald Jones and his wife Ann Lewis Marshall. They made their home in Alexandria, Virginia, where all of their children were born.

Children of Thomas Marshall and Elizabeth (Payne) Jones

1. Winfield Payne Jones, born May 22, 1881, married Florence Hendricks Hobbs. *q.v.*

2. Anna Lewis Jones, born Apr. 7, 1882, unmarried.
3. John Marshall Jones, born May 16, 1884, married Mary Jeannette Shriver. *q.v.*
4. Elizabeth Winter Jones, born Dec. 7, 1886, married Harry Carter Beverley. Issue: Marshall Jones; Harye Carter; William Welby; Columbus Shriver.
5. James FitzGerald Jones, born Dec. 2, 1888, married Mabel Monteath. Issue: John Monteath; Gerald Marshall.
6. Cora Shriver Jones, born July 2, 1891, married Robert Webb Davis. Issue: Fitzgerald Jones; Robert Jones.
7. Gabriel Jones, born 1893, died 1896.

MAJOR FRANCIS JOSEPH IVES, U. S. A.[7]
1857–1908

FRANCIS JOSEPH IVES, son of Joseph Christmas and Cora Matilda (Semmes) Ives, was born July 19, 1857, at Dorchester, Massachusetts. On November 22, 1887, at Omaha, Nebraska, he married Mildred Elizabeth Megeath, born July 17, 1862, at Omaha, daughter of Samuel Addison and Judith (Carter) Megeath. He died in Washington, D. C., on Novehmber 27, 1908.

Children of Francis and Mildred (Megeath) Ives

1. Judith Carter Ives, born July 27, 1890, married Rudd Lowry, born Jan. 24, 1892. *q.v.*
2. Mildred Ives, born Feb. 14, 1889, married Edward Gibbons. Issue: Mary Virginia Gibbons married N. Scotty Webb; Joseph Edward; James; Helen married Will Hilstrom.
3. Joseph Christmas Ives, born Aug. 30, 1896, married Lorraine Holden. Issue: Joseph Semmes Ives.

EUGENE SEMMES IVES[7]
1859–1917

EUGENE SEMMES IVES, son of Joseph and Cora Matilda (Semmes) Ives, was born November 11, 1859, in Washington, D. C. On June 5, 1889, at Washington, he married Ann Maria Waggaman, born May 23, 1870, daughter of Thomas Ennals and Jane (Lenthall) Waggaman, of Washington. He died in 1917; his widow died in 1951.

Children of Eugene and Ann Maria (Waggaman) Ives

1. Annette Clara Ives, born Mar. 22, 1890, in New York, died 1929.
2. Cora Matilda Ives, born Mar. 26, 1891, in New York.
3. Jane Lenthall Ives, born and died 1892.
4. Helen Virginia Ives, born Aug. 12, 1894, married Russell Malone. *q. v.*
5. Miriam Lenthall Ives, born Jan. 27, 1897, Phoenix, Ariz., died 1927.
6. Thomas Ennals Waggaman Ives, born Oct. 12, 1898, Santa Barbara, Calif., married 1930 Byrd Greer Walmsley, born Aug. 6, 1893, New Orleans. Issue: Thomas Ennals Waggaman, born Oct. 7, 1932, Los Angeles.
7. Eugene Semmes Ives, born Dec. 27, 1903, at Tucson, Ariz.
8. Elinor Randolph Ives, born Nov. 29, 1906, at Tucson, Ariz.

DR. ALPHONSO THOMAS SEMMES [7]
1830–1895

DR. ALPHONSO THOMAS SEMMES, eldest son of Thomas and Harriett Shepherd (Beall) Semmes, was born April 28, 1830, at Washington, Georgia. On September 20, 1856, in Washington, D. C., he married his cousin Mary Sabina Semmes, daughter of Raphael Semmes and his wife Matilda Jenkins. He was graduated from Georgetown University with honors, delivering the valedictory, and then studied medicine in New Orleans. In 1855 he began the practice of medicine in Canton, Miss., and continued to do so until his death on January 9, 1895. His widow died July 25, 1908, in Canton.

Children of Alphonso and Mary Sabina (Semmes) Semmes

1. Raphael Thomas Semmes, born July 27, 1857, married, Kate Flannery. *q. v.*
2. Catherine Winter Semmes, born Apr. 16, 1859, at Canton, Miss., died July 14, 1881, at Brown's Valley, Minn., married Sept. 30, 1880, Stuart D. Cobb.
3. Roger Joseph Semmes, born Sept. 21, 1860, at Canton, Miss., died a spinster Nov. 17, 1906.
4. Virginia America Semmes, born and died 1862.
5. Mary Sabina Semmes, born Jan. 14, 1864, in Sumter Co., Ala.
6. William FitzGerald Semmes, born 1866, died 1878.
7. Alphonso Thomas Semmes, born and died 1868.
8. Joseph Mastai Ferretti Semmes, born 1871, died 1884.
9. Mary Dolores Semmes, born Aug. 23, 1873, married Nov. 5, 1894, Marquis de la Fayette Shelly.
10. Francis Xavier Semmes, born Sept. 3, 1874, married Marie Stella Griffin. *q. v.*

DR. ROGER LEONIDAS SEMMES [7]

1821–1855

ROGER LEONIDAS SEMMES, son of Thomas and Harriett Shepherd (Beall) Semmes, was born October 26, 1831, in Washington, Georgia. His wife was Sarah Ann Griffin, born January 4, 1836, daughter of Mortimer Griffin, of Taliaferro County, Georgia, but a native of County Carlow, Ireland. The latter's wife was Elizabeth Teresia Luckett, daughter of Thomas Hussey Luckett and Elizabeth Semmes his wife.* Dr. Semmes died in Canton, Mississippi, on September 25, 1855. His daughter Harriet Regena Semmes married Dr. Sylvester Craten, of Sulphur Springs, Mississippi.

JAMES MINOR TATE SEMMES [7]

1839–1899

JAMES MINOR TATE SEMMES, son of Thomas James Andrew and Antoinette (Tate) Semmes, was born June 25, 1938. On March 8, 1860, he married Mary Oliver Dorgherty, of Hernando, Mississippi.

Children of James and Mary (Dorgherty) Semmes

1. John Dorgherty Semmes, born June 1, 1862.
2. David Oliver Semmes, born Oct. 20, 1865.
3. Lemuel Banks Semmes, born Nov. 2, 1867, died Sept. 10, 1898.
4. Pearl Rivers Semmes, born May 12, 1869, died 1870.
5. James Bright Morgan Semmes, born June 9, 1871.

On October 22, 1874, he married secondly Mary Katherine Short, daughter of Colonel Monroe Short. He died March 27, 1899.

Children of James and Mary (Short) Semmes

6. William Short Semmes, born Mar. 9, 1875.
7. Janie Bird Semmes, born Aug. 4, 1877.
8. Katherine Semmes, born July 9, 1879.
9. Alice Monroe Semmes, born July 27, 1883.

---

* For the genealogy of the Luckett family, see, Newman's *The Lucketts of Portobacco.*

BERNARD BROCKENBROUGH SEMMES [8]

1864–1917

BERNARD BROCKENBROUGH SEMMES, son of Thomas Middleton and Louise Gardiner (Brockenbrough) Semmes, was born September 22, 1864, in Lexington, Virginia. On June 3, 1890, he married Frances Stuart Lewis, daughter of Benjamin and Ellen Elizabeth (Wilkins) Lewis, of Brunswick County, Virginia. He was graduated from the Virginia Military Institute and the Law School of Washington and Lee University. He was one-time Mayor of Newport News, Virginia, and died there in 1917.

Children of Bernard and Frances (Lewis) Semmes

1. Bernard Brockenbrough Semmes Jr., died young.
2. Benjamin Warner Lewis Semmes, born Feb. 14, 1893, in Brunswick Co., Va., married Alva Helen Durring Sept. 14, 1928. Issue: Benjamin Warner Lewis Semmes Jr., born Feb. 5, 1933, Brooklyn, N. Y., fourth successive generation to graduate from V. M. I.
3. Frances Stuart Semmes, born Apr. 15, 1900, at Newport News, Va., married Thomas Custis Parramore; Issue: Lt. Com. Douglas Semmes Parramore, U. S. N.; Custis Parramore, Jr.

BRIGADIER-GENERAL HARRY HODGES SEMMES [8]

1892–19–

HARRY HODGES SEMMES, son of Alexander Harrison and Mary (Hodges) Semmes, was born January 18, 1892, in Washington, D. C. On August 25, 1917, he married Juanita Hopkins.

Children of Harry and Juanita (Hopkins) Semmes

1. Harry Hodges Semmes married June 23, 1948, Luette Goodbody. Issue: Harry Hodges, III, born Jan. 18, 1950; Guy Hopkins, born Jan. 18, 1952; Thomas Goodbody, born Feb. 1954.
2. Raphael Semmes married June 1946, Carmel Benito. Issue: Alexander, born Feb. 24, 1948; Christina, born Oct., 1951; Andrew, born Apr. 3, 1953; Raphael, born Apr. 30, 1955.
3. John Gibson Semmes, married 1949 Elizabeth Keating. Issue: Suzanne, born Mar. 30, 1951; Mark Tabb, born May 5, 1953.
4. David Hopkins Semmes, married 1950 Dudley Nicolson. Issue: Stratton, born Nov. 24, 1953.

A successful and prominent attorney in Washington, D. C., he served with distinction in both World Wars, and also the Korean

Campaign. In World War I he received the Distinguished Service Cross and the Oak Leaf Cluster. For heroism in World War II he received for the second time the Distinguished Service Cross with Oak Leaf Cluster, the Bronze Star, Legion of Merit, Croce el Marito (Italian), and Medalha de Guerra (Brazilian).

All four of his sons saw active service in the Second World War, with two of them receiving decorations. First Lieut. Harry Hodges Semmes, Jr., received the Distinguished Service Cross, the Presidential Unit Citation, and the Purple Heart, while First Lieut. John Gibson Semmes received the Silver Star Medal (twice), the Purple Heart, Distinguished Unit Badge, and the Victory Medal.

PAUL JONES SEMMES [8]
1865–1915

PAUL JONES SEMMES, eldest son of Samuel and Pauline (Semmes) Semmes, was born July 11, 1865, at Washington, Georgia. He died on April 11, 1915, at Asheville, North Carolina. On December 29, 1885, at Osceola, Arkansas, he married Margaret Murray, daughter of Joseph B. Murray, of Osceola, and Elizabeth Griffin his wife.

Children of Paul Jones and Margaret (Murray) Semmes

1. Joe Murray Semmes, born Aug. 2, 1887, at Osceola, Ark., married Jan. 10, 1910, Virginia Irvin, born Jan. 31, 1892, at New Orleans, and married secondly Jan. 6, 1923, Ernestine Currie, born Mar. 12, 1898, at Arcadia, La. Issue: Mary Elizabeth, born Aug. 26, 1911, at Osceola.
2. Margaret Catherine Semmes, born Aug. 10, 1890, at Osceola, Ark., married Arthur Robert Barbiers, born Feb. 10, 1888, at Albany, N.Y. Issue: Anne Semmes Barbiers, born Sept. 3, 1920, at Osceola, married Thomas Pearson Berry, born Feb. 15, 1913, at Fayette, Ala.; Arthur Robert Barbiers, born Feb. 10, 1924, at Osceola, married Judith Marion McLusky, born Dec. 24, 1924, at Syracuse, N.Y., and have Linda Anne Barbiers, born Nov. 16, 1946, at Syracuse, and Nancy Jill Barbiers, born Jan. 11, 1951, at Bowling Green, Ohio.
3. Paul Jones Semmes, born Dec. 1, 1900, at Osceola, married first Velma Elizabeth Howell, born May 1, 1907, at Jones, La., and married secondly Elizabeth Lenora Brown, born Feb. 2, 1920, at Plaquemine, La. Issue: Margaret Elizabeth, born Oct. 27, 1927, at Shreveport, La., who married James Mitchell Lampton, born Aug. 23, 1927, at Aberdeen, Miss.; Paul Jones Semmes, III, born July 29, 1950, at Baton Rouge, La.

RAPHAEL SEMMES [8]

1867–1899

RAPHAEL SEMMES, son of Samuel Spencer Semmes and his wife, Pauline Semmes, was born March 31, 1867, at Mobile, and died September 28, 1899, at Osceola, Arkansas. On June 6, 1887, at Osceola, he married Lula Sullivan, daughter of Robert Sullivan and Clara Roussan, his wife.

Children of Raphael and Lulu (Sullivan) Semmes

1. Clara Semmes, born Oct. 14, 1890, married Joseph Alexander. Issue: 1. Spencer Alexander, married Mary Elizabeth Borum and have Mary Roussan Alexander and Henrietta Semmes Alexander; 2. Joseph Otto Alexander, married Melvina Hays; 3. John Leon Alexander, married Bennye Annette McCutcheon and have Bennye Annette Alexander and John Leon Alexander.
2. Spencer Semmes, born Feb. 4, 1892.
3. Louise Semmes, born Dec. 12, 1893, married Dr. William J. Sheddan, of Osceola. Issue: Billy Fain.

ANNA HEMPHILL (SEMMES) UZZELLE [8]

1873– ––

ANNA HEMPHILL SEMMES, daughter of Samuel Spencer Semmes and Pauline Semmes his wife, was born September 21, 1873, at McIntosh's Bluff, Washington County, Georgia. On October 10, 1893, at Osceola, Arkansas, she married William Tipton Uzzelle, son of John W. Uzzelle and Lavinia Evans, his wife.

Children of William and Anna (Semmes) Uzzelle

1. Spencer Semmes Uzzelle, born Dec. 28, 1894, at Osceola, Ark., died Oct. 1, 1942, at Chicago.
2. Nina Marie Uzzelle, born July 3, 1897, at Bardstown, Ark.
3. Pauline Frances Uzzelle, born Aug. 14, 1901, at Osceola, Ark.
4. Helen Semmes Uzzelle, born Nov. 14, 1907, at Osceola, married Jesse Patrick Farrell, Dec. 29, 1924, at Memphis. Issue: 1. Anne Semmes Farrell, born July 29, 1925, Memphis, married Lloyd Belmont Abernathy Feb. 14, 1953, at Germantown, Tenn.; 2. Martha Xavier Farrell, born July 15, 1927, at Memphis; 3. Mary Patricia Ferrell, born Sept. 25, 1937, at Sioux Falls, S. D.

FRANCIS MORRIS SEMMES [8]

1884–1932

FRANCIS MORRIS SEMMES, eldest son of Samuel Spencer Semmes by his second wife Frances Morris was born May 21, 1884, at Osceola, Arkansas. On June 12, 1909, he married Mary Claire [Minnie] Harrington. He died November 18, 1932.

Children of Francis and Mary Claire (Harrington) Semmes

1. William Harrington Semmes, born May 21, 1910, married Feb. 21, 1941, Mary Helen Bracken. Issue: 1. Susan Frances, born Mar. 11, 1942; 2. Mary Helen, born Feb. 27, 1944; 3. Janet Evelyn, born Jan. 12, 1949; 4. William Bracken, born July 3, 1953.
2. Raphael Semmes, born Sept. 13, 1913, married Sept. 3, 1936, Evelyn Marie Wilson. Issue: 1. William Raphael, born Feb. 7, 1938; 2. Frank Wilson, born Aug. 17, 1941.
3. Buford Bolger A. Semmes, born Jan. 30, 1915, married June 26, 1946, Shelby Fletcher McAllister. Issue: 1. Thomas McAllister, born Nov. 23, 1947; 2. Francis Bolger, born Dec. 3, 1953; 3. John Spencer, born Dec. 3, 1953, died Dec. 19, 1953.
4. Francis Morris Semmes, born Sept. 10, 1916, married Oct. 30, 1948, Charlie Sue Brock.
5. Oliver Marie Semmes, born Mar. 8, 1918, married Aug., 1945, Cynthia Ward.
6. Edward Martin Semmes, born Jan. 25, 1920, married Sept. 7, 1944, Gwendolyn Lucille Stanley. Issue: Catherine Martin, born Dec. 8, 1951; Michael Harrington, born Apr. 18, 1953; Richard Stanley, born Mar. 20, 1954.

ELECTRA ELIZABETH (SEMMES) BUCK PERRIN [8]

1889–19–

ELECTRA ELIZABETH SEMMES, daughter of Samuel Spencer and Frances (Morris) Semmes, was born September 2, 1889, and on June 10, 1909, married Walter Hale Buck.

Children of Walter and Electra (Semmes) Buck

1. Electra Semmes Buck, born June 29, 1910, married Sept. 14, 1942, Edward Earle Neff.
2. Spencer Eulalia Buck, born Aug. 18, 1912, married Dec. 16, 1932, William Volney Alexander. Issue: William Volney, born Jan. 16, 1934; Spencer Buck Alexander, born Nov. 17, 1935.

On October 26, 1926, she married Claude Baldwin Perrin.

Issue of Claude and Electra (Semmes) Perrin

3. Frank Gibson Perrin, born Dec. 13, 1927, married June 2, 1951, Ann Marie Ryon. Issue: Suzanne, born June 10, 1952; John Allison, born Aug. 10, 1953.

SAMUEL PREWITT SEMMES [8]

1895– —

SAMUEL PREWITT SEMMES, son of Samuel Spencer and Frances (Morris) Semmes, was born December 12, 1895, at Osceola, Arkansas. He was graduated from Georgetown University with the degree of LL. B. in 1920, and removed from Memphis to Detroit in 1925, where he was actively engaged in the practice of law until his retirement in 1945. He now makes his home in Grosse Pointe, Michigan. He is a member of the New Jersey Society of the Cincinnati, Descendants of Lords of the Maryland Manors, The Society of the Ark and the Dove, and Sons of the American Revolution.

On December 28, 1915, at Osceola he married Valerie Walker Danehower, daughter of Justus Danehower, of Mississippi County, Arkansas and his wife, Johanna Liddon, whom he married on August 19, 1889. Mr. Danehower was born in Tennessee on January 15, 1869, and died at Osceola on August 2, 1921.

Mrs. Semmes through her maternal great-grandmother, Mary Ann (Merrill) Liddon, is of old Maryland ancestry through the Merrill, Holland, and Aydolette families which settled early on the lower Eastern Shore. Joseph Merrill, great-grandson of William Merrill, the emigrant, of Somerset County, left Maryland before 1800 and settled near Louisville, where he married Mildred Hooper, of Virginia forbears. The mother of Mrs. Semmes, Johanna Liddon, was born September 18, 1871, the daughter of William Abraham Liddon and his wife, Francis E. Harding, who was the daughter of John Harding and his wife, Cynthia Motherall. Benjamin Liddon, great-great-grandfather of Mrs. Semmes, supported the cause of the Colonies during the Revolutionary War while residing in Wilmington, North Carolina. After the war he removed to Shelby County, Tennessee, where he died at Camp Springs in 1815. Through her motner, Frances E. Harding, who was born July 10, 1846, and died July 22, 1904, she is descended from the Hardings who were prominent in the settlement of Goochland County, Virgina, and the Giles and Knowles—two families which were active in affairs of early Henrico County and the upper James River settlements.

Still another distinguished ancestral family of Mrs. Semmes is the Routledge which was active in the early tidal settlements of the Carolina coast. Judge Thomas Routledge had both judicial and military service in the colonial period and his son, Lieutenant William Routledge, was an officer in the North Carolina Continental Line during the Revolution—both of whom are direct ancestors of Mrs. Semmes.

Children of Prewitt and Valerie (Danehower) Semmes

1. Valerie Danehower Semmes, born Sept. 2, 1920, married Harvey Monroe Smith, Jr. *q.v.*
2. Mary Martin Semmes, born Nov. 9, 1925.
3. Samuel Prewitt Semmes, Jr., born Oct. 10, 1927, married Faith Van Clief. *q.v.*

RAPHAEL SEMMES [8]

1882–19–

RAPHAEL SEMMES, son of Raphael and Marion (Adams) Semmes, was born December 29, 1882. His wife, Louise, was born on March 9, 1888; they now reside (1955) in Huntsville, Alabama.

One son, Raphael Semmes, was born on January 18, 1916, and married Juanita Runyon, born July 17, 1917. He was graduated from the United States Naval Academy in 1939, and now holds the rank of Commander. Two children were born to him and his wife, namely, Raphael Semmes, III, born August 17, 1943, and James Oliver Semmes, born July 17, 1947.

RAPHAEL SEMMES WRIGHT [8]

1879–19–

RAPHAEL SEMMES WRIGHT, son of Luke and Catherine Middleton (Semmes) Wright, was born April 23, 1879, at Memphis. His wife was Maud ———.

Children of Raphael and Maud Wright

1. Katherine Wright married Fred Wymer. Issue: Georgia who married James Skeen; Katherine who married Cris Arnoult.
2. Electra Semmes Wright married James T. Larkin. Issue: James Semmes; Jill Anna; Katherine.
3. Mary Semmes Wright married John Edgar. Issue: John and Ann.

IORANTHA (SEMMES) STOEPEL [8]

1885- ---

IORANTHA MARY SEMMES, daughter of Joseph Malcolm and Eleanor (Martin) Semmes, was born August 15, 1885, at Memphis. She married Frederick Sutton Stoepel, of Detroit, Michigan.

Children of Frederick and Iorantha (Semmes) Stoepel

1. Mary Anne Stoepel, entered Holy Orders.
2. Iorantha Jordan Stoepel, entered the Carmelite Order.
3. Ellen Semmes Stoepel.
4. Fredericka Josephine Stoepel.
5. Frederick Christopher Stoepel, U. S. N., World War II, married Margaret Davis. Issue: Frederick Christopher; Martha MacMillan; Anne Wingfield.

BENEDICT JOSEPH SEMMES [8]

1887- ---

BENEDICT JOSEPH SEMMES, son of Joseph Malcolm and Eleanor (Martin) Semmes, was born February 5, 1887, at Memphis. He maried Amy Lardner.

Children of Benedict and Amy (Lardner) Semmes

1. Benedict Joseph Semmes, Capt., U. S. N., married Katherine Ainsworth. Issue: Walden; Raphael; Joseph.
2. James Lardner Semmes, Capt. U. S. N., married Elizabeth Burbank. Issue: Robert.
3. Gilmore Semmes married Henry C. Donnelly. Issue: Clare, died Sept. 20, 1954; Henry.
4. Granville Semmes, Ensign, U. S. N., World War II, married Jane Pfiester. Issue: Granville; Donna.

HARRIETTE ENSLEY (SEMMES) ANDERSON [8]

1890– ——

Harriette Ensley Semmes, daughter of Joseph Malcolm and Eleanor (Martin) Semmes, was born August 25, 1890, at Memphis, and on January 27, 1916, married Lewis Bruce Anderson.

Children of Lewis and Harriette (Semmes) Anderson

1. Eleanor Martin Anderson married Selden Humphries. Issue: Eleanor Martin; Selden; Lewis.
2. Harriette Semmes Anderson married David Steege, Major, U. S. Air Force, World War II and Korean War. Issue: Bruce; Joseph; Keith.
3. Lewis Bruce Anderson, M. D.; married Jean Riley. Issue: Jeffrey; Cynthia; Katherine.
4. Arthur Jeffrey Anderson.

KATHERINE (SEMMES) VAN DYKE [8]

1895– ——

Katherine Thompson Semmes, daughter of Joseph Malcolm and Eleanor (Martin) Semmes, was born May 2, 1895, and on October 2, 1917, married Francis G. Van Dyke.

Children of Francis and Katherine (Semmes) Van Dyke

1. Marie Katrina Van Dyke married John Smillie. Issue: Jonathan; Francis; Philip Van Dyke.
2. George Semmes Van Dyke.
3. Joseph Semmes Van Dyke, 1st Lieut. U. S. Air Force, killed in action World War II.

THOMAS JENKINS SEMMES [8]

1897– ——

Thomas Jenkins Semmes, son of Joseph Malcolm and Eleanor (Martin) Semmes, was born July 4, 1897, and married Elise Humphreys.

Children of Thomas and Elise (Humphreys) Semmes

1. Elise Semmes married Alec Dann. Issue: Alec; Thomas Semmes; Elise Selden.

2. Thomas Semmes, died young.
3. Flournoy Semmes.
4. Anne Semmes.

RAPHAEL EUSTACE SEMMES, M. D.[8]

1885– ——

RAPHAEL EUSTACE SEMMES, son of Raphael Eustace and Maude (Duval) Semmes, was born August 15, 1885, in Memphis. He entered the medical profession and is one of the outstanding neurological surgeons in the United States and a member of many learned medical societies. He married Mary Alice Graves. Both he and his children maintain their home in Memphis.

Children of Raphael Eustace and Mary Alice (Graves) Semmes

1. Raphael Eustace Semmes married Joan Lovell, of Brookhaven, Miss. Issue: Victoria Lovell Semmes.
2. Mary Alice Semmes married Pat S. Martin, of Memphis. Issue: Stephen Semmes; Benjamin Duval; and Patrick Raphael Martin.

SYLVESTER PIERCE WALMSLEY[8]

1886– ——

SYLVESTER PIERCE WALMSLEY, son of Sylvester and Myra Eulalie (Semmes) Walmsley, was born August 11, 1886, in Canandaigua, New York. On October 7, 1908, at Sardis, Mississippi, he married Stella Mather Hyman.

Children of Sylvester and Stella (Hyman) Walmsley

1. Sylvester Pierce Walmsley, III, born July 3, 1909, married Aug. 16, 1938, in New Orleans, Allie Rhodes. Issue: Sylvester Pierce Walmsley, IV, born July 27, 1940, at Richmond, Va.; Philip Lee Walmsley, born Feb. 2, 1949, at Richmond.
2. Philip Mather Walmsley, born Aug. 25, 1919.

MYRA EULALIE SEMMES (WALMSLEY) LOKER[8]

1888– ——

MYRA EULALIE SEMMES WALMSLEY, daughter of Sylvester Pierce and Myra (Semmes) Walmsley, was born April 8, 1888 in New

Orleans. On November 18, 1911, she married David Cartan Loker, of St. Louis. He died August 1, 1951.

Children of David and Myra (Walmsley) Loker

1. Myra Semmes Walmsley Loker, born Aug. 16, 1912, married Dr. John Gilmer Menville May 6, 1939. Issue: John Gilmer, born June 4, 1940; Myra Walmsley Loker, born May 21, 1947.
2. Kathleen Cartan Loker, born Dec. 14, 1913, married Feb. 7, 1934, John F. Gibbons, Jr. Issue: John F., born Oct. 20, 1934; Kathleen Cartan Loker, born July 17, 1936; David Cartan Loker, born June 24, 1938.
3. Margaret Carroll Loker, born Nov. 13, 1914, married June 7, 1938, David Cottrell, Jr. Issue: Margaret Carroll Loker, born and died 1939; David, III, born May 1, 1942; Albert Peyton, born Mar. 1, 1945.
4. David Cartan Loker, born Apr. 27, 1916, married Sept. 6, 1941, Sheelah Rafferty. Issue: Leslie Sheelah, born Nov. 14, 1944; Sharon Walmsley, born Apr. 23, 1946.
5. Miriam Walmsley Loker, born Sept. 12, 1919, married Dr. Henry Duplessis Ogden Oct. 16, 1939. Issue: Miriam Loker, born Aug. 10, 1940; Marie Louise, born July 16, 1941; Marie Lucille Walmsley, born Oct. 10, 1942; Henry Duplessis, born May 21, 1945; Charles Barry, born Oct. 4, 1947; Peter Voorhies, born July 5, 1950.
6. George Hannibal Loker, born Oct. 20, 1921, married Apr. 21, 1952, Elsie Vantreight, Victoria, B. C., Canada. Issue: Helen Vantreight, born Feb. 1, 1952; George Hannibal, born Apr. 14, 1953; Caroline Gratia Walmsley, born Nov. 5, 1954.
7. Sylvester Pierce Walmsley Loker, born Apr. 5, 1923, married July 14, 1951, Carrol Jean Reagan. Issue: Sylvester Pierce Walmsley, born June 14, 1952; David Cartan, born Feb. 19, 1954.
8. Thomas Semmes Loker, born Mar. 19, 1924.
9. Janet Lilburn Loker, born Aug. 14, 1926, married Sept. 3, 1946, Donald M. Coleman, and secondly Oct. 29, 1954, William Banks Barbee.
10. Adele Penrose Loker, born June 16, 1928.

THOMAS SEMMMES WALMSLEY [8]
1889–1942

THOMAS SEMMES WALMSLEY, son of Sylvester Pierce and Myra (Semmes) Walmsley, was born June 10, 1889, in New Orleans. On April 15, 1914, he married Julia Caroline Havard. He died at Randolph Field, Tex., on June 17, 1942.

Issue of Thomas and Julia (Havard) Walmsley

1. Celeste Augusta Walmsley, born Sept. 12, 1915, married Apr. 15, 1942, Frederick J. King. Issue: Thomas Semmes Walmsley, born Nov. 6, 1943; Frederick J., Jr., born Jan. 27, 1945; Julia Carolyn, born Jan. 11, 1949; Katherine Havard, born Sept. 23, 1950.

ROBERT MILLER WALMSLEY [8]
1891–1953

ROBERT MILLER WALMSLEY, son of Sylvester Pierce and Myra (Semmes) Walmsley, was born September 14, 1891, in New Orleans, and died on November 17, 1953. He married on October 26, 1914, Dorothy Jackson.

Children of Robert and Dorothy (Jackson) Walmsley

1. Robert Miller Walmsley, married Apr. 10, 1943, Virginia Johnston, of Birmingham, Ala. Issue: Robert Miller, born Oct. 28, 1946; Gordon Semmes, born Sept. 1, 1949; Clara, born May 21, 1953.
2. John Norcom Walmsley, born May 5, 1917.
3. Peter Hamilton Walmsley, born Dec. 16, 1925, married Amelie Landry, Sept. 24, 1949. Issue: Phoebe Anne, born Nov. 1, 1951; Amelie, born Feb. 3, 1954.

BYRD GREER WALMSLEY [8]
1893– ——

BYRD GREER WALMSLEY, daughter of Sylvester Pierce and Myra (Semmes) Walmsley, was born August 6, 1893, in New Orleans. On August 28, 1930, she married Ennals Waggaman Ives, of Los Angeles. They had one son, Ennals Waggaman, Jr., born October 7, 1932.

HUGHES PHILIP WALMSLEY [8]
1902– ——

HUGHES PHILIP WALMSLEY, son of Sylvester Pierce and Myra (Semmes) Walmsley, was born May 13, 1902, in New Orleans. On May 12, 1931, he married Arthemise Marie Avrill.

Children of Hughes and Arthemise (Avrill) Walmsley

1. Arthemise Marie Walmsley, born Oct. 20, 1934.
2. Miriam Louise Walmsley, born Mar. 5, 1936.
3. Hughes Philip Walmsley, born Aug. 24, 1945.

MYRA EULALIE (RANLETT) CURTIS[8]

1890– ——

MYRA EULALIE SEMMES RANLETT, daughter of Albert Sidney and Cora Matilda (Semmes) Ranlett, was born February 23, 1890, in New Orleans. In New York City on April 9, 1913, she married Carroll P. Curtis, born March 20, 1889, in Warrenton, Virginia. He died in New York City on February 11, 1946.

Children of Carroll and Myra (Ranlett) Curtis

1. Carroll P. Curtis, born Feb. 26, 1918, died Sept. 28, 1921.
2. Cora Semmes Ranlett Curtis, born Mar. 1, 1921, N.Y.C., married in N.Y.C. Jan. 8, 1946, Virgil Hillman Jordan, born Nov. 7, 1920, at Little Rock, Ark. Issue: Cora Semmes, born Nov. 13, 1946, in New Mexico; Susan McLean, born at Charlottesville, Va., Oct. 27, 1948; Virgil Randolph, born at Baltimore, Aug. 26, 1952.

ALBERT SIDNEY RANLETT[8]

1891–1948

ALBERT SIDNEY RANLETT, son of Albert Sidney and Cora Matilda (Semmes) Ranlett, was born in New Orleans on May 21, 1891, and died in Baltimore, Maryland, on November 12, 1948. At New York City he married in October, 1923, Kathryn Walsh.

Children of Albert Sidney and Kathryn (Walsh) Ranlett

1. Helen Elizabeth Ranlett, born May 5, 1924, married Richard Aaron Noyes Apr. 30, 1945. Issue: Emily Susan, born Oct. 7, 1946; Timothy Jay, born Oct. 18, 1948; David Duer, born Apr. 2, 1951.
2. Jay Duer Ranlett, born Oct. 1925.

THOMAS JENKINS SEMMES RANLETT[8]

1891–1936

THOMAS JENKINS SEMMES RANLETT, son of Albert Sidney and Cora Matilda (Semmes) Ranlett, was born May 21, 1891, in New Orleans. In that city on April 27, 1911, he married Adele Olive White, born Aug. 31, 1892, also a native of New Orleans. He died in his native city in August, 1936.

Children of Thomas J. S. and Adele Olive (White) Ranlett

1. Adele Olive Ranlett, born July 7, 1912, married Apr. 13, 1946, Ralph Ferguson. Issue: Daryl Earl, born Aug. 12, 1954.
2. Thomas Jenkins Semmes Ranlett, born May 21, 1891, married Mary Lenore Diaz, and secondly, Nov. 2, 1944, Marjorie Prevost. Issue: (first) Patricia, born Jan., 1942; (second) Catherine Adele, born Jan. 10, 1946; Thomas Jenkins Semmes, III, born Dec. 30, 1946; David Harry, born Mar. 22, 1951; Christopher George, born Nov. 26, 1952.
3. Cora Ranlett, born Sept. 4, 1918, married 1939 Eugene Blankenship. Issue: Eleanor, born May 4, 1940; Jean Marie, born June 6, 1942; Thomas Jenkins Semmes, born Feb. 22, 1945; Cora, born Nov. 8, 1949; Lynne, born Aug. 31, 1950; Barbara, born May 31, 1953.
4. Albert Sidney Ranlett, born Jan. 4, 1920, married 1954 Maria Mirando.
5. Theodora Ranlett, born Aug. 14, 1922, married Mar. 19, 1942, Howard Schmalz. Issue: Karen, born Jan. 20, 1943; Howard, born Aug. 13, 1946.
6. Marie Ranlett, born Mar. 9, 1924, married John Hutsler. Issue: Margaret Ellen, born Sept. 1950; Frank, born Dec. 1951; Shelly Elizabeth, born Dec. 1953.

CORA MARY (RANLETT) THOMSON [8]

1895- ––

CORA MARY RANLETT, daughter of Albert Sidney and Cora (Semmes) Ranlett, was born September 5, 1895, in Warrenton, Virginia. In New York City on July 21, 1923, she married Alexander Torrence Thomson, son of Henry Torrence Thomson and Jessie Bryce, of Edinburgh, Scotland. He was born in Edinburgh on January 7, 1875, and died in Warrenton on October 27, 1947.

Issue of Alexander and Cora (Ranlett) Thomson

1. Eleanor-Torrence Thomson, born N. Y. C. Sept. 15, 1924, married June 12, 1948, at Warrenton, Douglas Harcourt Lees, born Oct. 14, 1921, son of Douglas Harcourt and Mary Stone Lees. Issue: Douglas Harcourt, III, born Washington, D. C., Feb. 12, 1950.

WINFIELD PAYNE JONES [8]

1881–1953

WINFIELD PAYNE JONES, son of Thomas Marshall and Elizabeth (Payne) Jones, was born May 22, 1881, and died on October 20, 1953. He married on June 1, 1909, Florence Hendricks Hobbs.

Children of Winfield and Florence (Hobbs) Jones

1. Carroll Payne Jones, born Mar. 26, 1910, married June 20, 1936, Marjorie Grove Gould. Issue: Marshall Gould, born Apr. 26, 1940; Carroll Payne, born June 3, 1944; Marjorie Dougherty, born June 17, 1946.
2. Arthur Hendricks Jones, born 1913, died 1916.
3. Winfield Marshall Jones, born Dec. 11, 1916, married Oct. 14, 1939, Eloise Robinson Dickey, and May 15, 1953, Evelyn Elizabeth Brown. Issue: Winfield Payne, born Apr. 20, 1941.
4. Florence Hobbs Jones, born Aug. 10, 1919, married Aug. 15, 1941, Hugh Willett Lester, Jr. Issue: Arthur Goff, born May 20, 1943; Anne Lewis, born June 17, 1946; Elizabeth Hendricks, born May 2, 1950.
5. Helen Hendricks Jones, born Mar. 6, 1923, married Aug. 15, 1941, Patman Moore Dobbins. Issue: Beverly Blythe, born July 26, 1946; Helen Hendricks, born Mar. 3, 1949.

JOHN MARSHALL JONES [8]
1884–1948

JOHN MARSHALL JONES, son of Thomas Marshall and Elizabeth (Payne) Jones, was born May 16, 1884, at Alexandria, Virginia. He studied at George Washington University and after a brief career in banking in Washington he removed to Baltimore where he became identified with several industrial concerns. At the time of his death in Baltimore on March 22, 1948, he was director of the Standard Wholesale Phosphate and Acid Works.

He married Mary Jeannette Shriver, daughter of Franklin and Helen (MacSherry) Shriver, of Carroll County, Maryland. Their children were: John Marshall; Helen MacSherry; Frank; Elizabeth Payne; Thomas Carbery; Raphael Semmes; Jeannette Shriver; Anna Lewis; and James Fitzgerald.

JUDITH CARTER (IVES) LOWRY [8]
1890– ––

JUDITH CARTER IVES, daughter of Francis Joseph and Mildred (Megeath) Ives, was born July 27, 1890, and married Rudd Lowry, born January 24, 1892.

Children of Rudd and Judith (Ives) Lowry

1. Elizabeth Judith Lowry, born Feb. 25, 1920, married Frank T. Lee, Jr. Issue: Francis Norvell, born Dec. 13, 1948; Judith Carter, born Sept. 16, 1950; Nancy Cochrane, born Sept. 3, 1953.

2. Samuel Addison Lowry, born Dec. 22, 1922, married Ellen Carey. Issue: Kathleen Marie, born Oct. 8, 1950; William Rudd, born Apr. 16, 1952.
3. James Rudd Lowry, born Dec. 12, 1924, married Donna Clepper. Issue: Diana Christine, born Jan. 25, 1951; Gloria Judith, born Apr. 6, 1953.
4. George Windsor Lowry, born July 13, 1926, married Barbara Whalen.
5. John Fenton Lowry, born July 13, 1926.
6. Thomas Carter Lowry, born May 20, 1928.
7. Ann Harrington Lowry, born Sept. 11, 1929, married Francis E. Mahoney. Issue: Deborah Ann, born May 3, 1951.
8. Raphael Semmes Lowry, born Oct. 1, 1931.
9. Martha Adams Lowry, born May 22, 1934.

HELEN (IVES) MALONE[8]
1894- ---

HELEN VIRGINIA IVES, daughter of Eugene and Ann Maria (Waggaman) Ives, was born August 12, 1894, at Spring Valley, New York, and in 1920 married Russell Malone, born January 13, 1881, in New York City.

Children of Russell and Helen (Ives) Malone

1. Joseph Eugene Ives Malone, born Mar. 19, 1921, Los Angeles, married 1945 Margaret Catherine Hartlein. Issue: Marian, born Jan. 28, 1946; Martha Francis, born July 9, 1949; Eugene Ives, born Nov. 28, 1952.
2. Elizabeth Ann Malone, born July 26, 1923, at Los Angeles, married 1948 Clifford Daniel Sweet, born Feb. 17, 1915, at Fresno, Calif. Issue: Clifford Daniel, born July 25, 1949; Thomas Ives, born Oct. 18, 1951; Mary Judith, born Mar. 18, 1953.

RAPHAEL THOMAS SEMMES[8]
1857–1916

RAPHAEL THOMAS SEMMES, son of Alphonso and Mary Sabina (Semmes) Semmes, was born July 27, 1857, at Canton, Mississippi. He was educated at private schools in Canton and the Christian Brothers' College in Memphis. On April 30, 1891, he married Kate Flannery, born July 10, 1868, in Savannah, Georgia, daughter of Captain John Flannery who was Captain of the Irish Jasper Greens of Savannah which fought in the service of the Confederate States of America.

He became a successful wholesale business man of Savannah, being president of the Semmes Hardware Company until failing health compelled him to release his holdings in the firm and withdraw from active service. He died at his home in Savannah on September 4, 1916, and was buried from the Cathedral of St. John the Baptist, of which he was a communicant. He rests in the Flannery lot in the Cathedral Cemetery.

It was he who became the first historian of the Semmes family and who devoted his private funds to the great research into many families of Southern Maryland. Death prevented his completion of the Semmes genealogy which he planned, but it was published posthumously in 1918 under the direction of his widow. His research, all meticulously documented, though not put together genealogically speaking, was presented to the Maryland Historical Society, Baltimore, and now known as the Semmes' Manuscripts are among the most valuable genealogical data found at that institution. This collection was consulted and used unsparingly in the writing of this genealogical history.

FRANCIS XAVIER SEMMES[8]

1874–19–

FRANCIS XAVIER SEMMES, son of Alphonso Thomas and Mary Sabina (Semmes) Semmes, was born September 3, 1874, at Canton, Mississippi. On February 10, 1901, at Sulphur Springs, Mississippi, he married Marie Stella Griffin, born November 2, 1880, at Sulphur Springs, daughter of George B. and Margaret E. (Herring) Griffin.

Children of Francis and Marie (Griffin) Semmes

1. Raphael Thomas Semmes, born Dec. 5, 1902.
2. George Griffin Semmes, born and died 1908.
3. Martha Elizabeth Semmes, born Feb. 5, 1910.
4. William Wilkes Semmes, born Oct. 27, 1912.
5. Alphonso Thomas Semmes, born Aug. 13, 1915.
6. Joseph Flannery Semmes, born Mar. 9, 1917.

LAURA HILL (PAYNE) SMITH[8]
1886- ——

LAURA HILL PAYNE, daughter of John Carroll and Helen (Hill) Payne, was born December 9, 1886, at Atlanta, Georgia. On November 18, 1911, she married Alexander Wyly Smith.

Children of Alexander Wyly and Laura (Payne) Smith

1. Helen Hill Smith, born Oct. 25, 1912, married Apr. 4, 1932, George Francis Willis. Issue: Charlotte Alexander Willis, born Feb. 6, 1933, married Aug. 16, 1952, Norman Douglas Courter and had Charlotte, born Feb. 2, 1954; Helen Hill, born Oct. 23, 1934; George Francis, born Aug. 19, 1941; John Payne, born Feb. 20, 1943.
2. Laura Payne Smith, born Apr. 11, 1914, married Nov. 23, 1935, Thomas Moore Clarke. Issue: Laura Payne, born Nov. 9, 1935; Thomas Moore, born May 20, 1940; William Walton, born Jan. 9, 1943; Theodore Smith, born Sept. 16, 1947; John Logan, born Sept. 8, 1950.
3. Emily Kendrick Smith, born Aug. 10, 1917, married June 9, 1838, Benjamin Harvey Hill. Issue: Benjamin Harvey; Charles Dougherty; Alexander Smith; William Roderick; Frank Ridley.
4. Alexander Wyly Smith, born June 9, 1923, married Aug. 31, 1946, Betty Rawson Haverty. Issue: Elizabeth Rawson, born Sept. 28, 1947; Alexander Wyly, born Mar. 30, 1949; Clarence Haverty, born Dec. 12, 1950; Laura Payne, born Jan. 17, 1952; James Haverty, born Aug. 9, 1954.
5. Carroll Payne Smith, born May 12, 1925, married July 30, 1946, Edward Scott Gay, Jr. Issue: Carroll Payne, born May 9, 1947; Edward Scott, born Dec. 3, 1948; Arthur Hobbs, born Dec. 6, 1949.
6. Joan Payne Smith, born May 12, 1925, married Jan. 20, 1954, Walter Hardie Zillessen, Jr.

VALERIE (SEMMES) SMITH[9]
1920- ——

VALERIE SEMMES, daughter of Prewitt and Valerie (Danehower) Semmes, was born September 2, 1920, at Osceola, Arkansas. On December 28, 1940, at Grosse Pointe, Michigan, she married Lieutenant Harvey Monroe Smith, Jr., U. S. N. He was born February 2, 1917, at Syracuse, New York, was graduated from Yale, and is the son of Harvey Monroe Smith, born January 13, 1888, and died

1949, and his wife, Dorothy Elizabeth Snow, born April 11, 1893; grandson of Monroe Clayton Smith, born April 28, 1861, died 1914, and his wife, Emma Jones, born April 30, 1870; great-grandson of Lewis Stevens Smith, born November 29, 1820; died March 1, 1890, and his wife, Eliza Hurlburt; and great-great-grandson of William Smith, born 1777.

Dorothy Elizabeth Snow, the mother of Mr. Smith, is the daughter of Nelson Powers Snow, born December 9, 1868, Syracuse, New York, died June 17, 1893, and his wife, Fanny Bray Bates, born Deecmber 18, 1865, New York City, died April 22, 1941; and the granddaughter of Charles Wesley Snow and his wife, Harriet Lavinia Powers.

Children of Harvey Monroe and Valerie (Semmes) Smith

1. Valerie Semmes Smith, born March 24, 1945, at Oxnard, Calif.
2. Dorothy Snow Smith, born Apr. 25, 1948, at Grosse Pointe, Mich.

SAMUEL PREWITT SEMMES, JR.[9]

1927– ––

SAMUEL PREWITT SEMMES, JR., son of Samuel Prewitt and Valerie (Danehower) Semmes, was born October 10, 1927, at Detroit. On August 14, 1950, he married Faith Van Clief, of Charlottesville, Virginia, the daughter of Courtlandt and Eleanor (Cameron) Van Clief. A daughter, Faith Cameron Semmes, was born on March 26, 1952.

JOHN SEMMES [2]

AND

HIS DESCENDANTS

JOHN SEMMES, who wrote his name Simes, was the third son of Marmaduke Semmes and Fortuna his wife. According to his father's will, he received 219 acres of "St. George's" upon the death of his mother. He married Mary, daughter of John and Millicent Higton, of Charles County. By the will of his father-in-law, dated and proved in 1723, his wife Mary Simes received a cow and calf; he is identified as the John Simes who witnessed the instrument.

Children of John and Mary (Higton) Semmes

1. Thomas Semmes, died young.
2. Clebourne Semmes married thrice. *q. v.*
3. Anne Semmes married William Cooksey.
4. Rebecca Semmes.
5. Mary Semmes, born March 28, 1724, married Abraham Davenport, born May 17, 1714.*

Between the writing of his will and its probation some 21 months later, or on March 28, 1724, was born a daughter, Mary, who with her husband Abraham Davenport settled in the Upper District of Frederick County, now Washington County. Her husband in 1757 approved the inventory of the estate of Anthony Sims, who died in Prince George's County.

The will of John Simms was dated April 15, 1723, being probated in Charles County on January 12, 1724/5, by Benedict Leonard Boarman, John Higton, Jr., and Benjamin Higton.

* The births of husband and wife with those of their children are taken from an old picture-chart used by the Germans of Western Maryland and Pennsylvania. They are grouped in circles around a central symbolical design—Elizabeth Davenport, born Feb. 13, 1747; Stephen Davenport, born Nov. 24, 1749; Abram Davenport, born Feb. 9, 1752; John Davenport, born Dec. 14, 1753; Marmaduke Davenport, born Apr. 23, 1755; Anthony Simms Davenport, born May 19, 1757; Adrian Davenport, born Apr. 26, 1759; Mary Davenport, born May 23, 1763; Samuel A. Davenport, born Aug. 3, 1765; Ariet Davenport, born Sept. 9, 1767; Catherine Davenport, born Aug. 5, 1769.

To son Thomas Simes the dwelling-plantation with 110 acres.
To son Cleburne Simes 110 acres of "St. Thomases" being part of "St. George's."
To daughters Ann and Rebecca 125 acres of "St. George's" equally.
To cousin Marmaduke Simes 100 acres with the plantation he then lived on called Simes Settlement being part of "St. George's."
To cousin Anthony Simes 100 acres of "St. George's" called Simes Settlement.
To cousin Elizabeth Simes the plantation where the testator's brother Marmaduke Simes lived being 100 acres of "St. Georges."
To cousin Elinor Simes 100 acres of "St. George's" where the testator's brother Marmaduke lived.
To cousin Ruth Simes 100 acres of land joining the 200 acres given to her two sisters.
To son Cleburne Simes his riding horse and was to be declared of age.
Residue of personal estate equally among four children—Thomas, Cleburn, Anne and Rebecca.
Executors—two sons.

CLEBORNE SEMMES [3]

17– –1750

CLEBORNE SEMMES, only son of John and Mary (Hidgon) Semmes to mature, received from his father's estate a portion of "St. George's" which he sold in 1726 to Henry Wathen. In 1736 he purchased another portion of "St. George's" from his cousin Marmaduke Semmes consisting of 230 acres on which he established his dwelling-plantation.

He married first a daughter of Andrew Simpson who predeceased her father, but her son, John Semmes, shared in his grandfather's will of 1744, styling him as grandson and son of Cleborne Semmes.

Issue of Cleborne and ——— (Simpson) Semmes

1. John Semmes.

After the death of his first wife he married Eleanor, only child of John Lemaster, who likewise predeceased her father who died in 1740. At a court held in Prince George's County in 1744 "Cleburn Semmes an infant under 21 years, the only son and issue of Eleanor Semmes who was the only daughter and issue of John Lemaster, late of Charles County, deceased, who died intestate, by Cleburn Semmes, the father and guardian of the said Cleburn Semmes" instituted action against Christian Lemaster, of Charles County, the widow of John Lemaster. After the death of John Lemaster it was stated that Cleburn Semmes, Sr., often requested of Christian Lemaster his son's portion of his grandfather's estate as the heir-at-law and until then she had refused to make delivery. The court thereupon ordered that Christian Lemaster pay unto Cleburn Semmes, Sr., for his son two-thirds of the balance of the estate including the slave Nan mentioned in the inventory.

Issue of Cleborne and Eleanor (Lemaster) Semmes

1. Cleborn Semmes.

In 1738 Cleborn Semmes sold to John Wathen his seated plantation on "St. George's" and in the same year bought a portion of "Market Overton" in Prince George's County from Zephanieh Wade. The latter remained his seat until 1748 when he sold "Market Overton" and removed farther west on the frontier in Frederick County.

By November, 1736, he had married thirdly Mary ———, who waived dower at the time he alienated his Charles County holdings.

His two sons were placed under Richard Johnson, for at a court held in Charles County in November 1744, John Symes, Cleborn Symes and Ignatius Sanders petitioned the bench, stating that they were misused by their master Richard Johnson. They lost their case, as the court decreed that they continue to serve their master according to the terms of their indenture.

He died intestate in Frederick County, when on June 20, 1750, letters of administration were issued to his widow, Mary Semmes. At the appraisement of the personalty, Elizabeth Jones and Richard Semmes, of Frederick County, approved as the next of kin. In September, 1758, his widow, Mary Semmes, of Frederick County made a deed of gift of certain household articles to her son-in-law James Barrance.

On September 8, 1758, Mary Simms, of Frederick County, widow, for natural love and affections which she held for her daughter, Mary Simms, and the further consideration of 5 shillings deeded her a gray mare and certain articles of household furniture, some of which had been shipped to Baltimore. She signed the deed in the presence of Ignatius Simms and Jacob Duckett.

From the casual manner in which the estate of Cleborne Semmes was administered, it is impossible to prove a correct list of his children. John, Cleborne, and Mary are definitely proved, but members of the family living at that time in Frederick County certainly fit somewhere into the group pattern, especially Richard Simms and Elizabeth Jones who approved the inventory of the estate. The following are therefore inferred children—1. Richard Simms, approved inventory, in 1778 took the oath in Washington County. 2. Elizabeth, who married a Jones and approved the inventory. 3. Ignatius Semmes witnessed the two deeds of gifts of Mary Simms to her daughter and son-in-law. 4. Miss Semmes who married James Barrance . 5. Thomas Simms, who died testate in Washington County in 1777, providing for his wife Ann and a possible posthumous child, and cancelling the debt of his brother Ignatius Simms. The widow later married John Lee.

His widow or daughter Mary married James Conn of Thomas, for on April 22, 1760, the Sheriff of Prince George's County ordered that the goods of James Conn of Thomas, of Baltimore County, be attached to the value of £283/3/½ plus 5,000 lbs. tob. for the use of Christopher Lowndes unless " he the said James Conn and Mary his wife otherwise lately called Mary Simms of Frederick County " made a settlement.

MARMADUKE SEMMES[2]

AND

HIS DESCENDANTS

MARMADUKE SEMMES, youngest son of Marmaduke and Fortuna Semmes, was born in what is now the vicinity of Newport, Charles County. Being the youngest son he was given the dwelling-plantation on " St. George's " at the death of his mother. He married Elizabeth, daughter of William and Ruth Clarkson and the granddaughter of the Hon. Benjamin Rozer, Esq.

Children of Marmaduke and Elizabeth (Clarkson) Semmes

1. Ruth Semmes married John Biggs.
2. Francis Semmes married Lucretia Chapman. *q. v.*
3. Eleanor Semmes married Henry Cooke.
4. Elizabeth Semmes married Abel Carrico.

The will of Marmaduke Semmes, of Newport, Charles County, was dated May 11, 1717, and probated on July 29, following.

To eldest daughter Ruth Sims tract of land in Prince George's Co., at head of Broad Creek and personalty to be delivered to her at 16 years or marriage.

To son Francis, daughter Ellanor, and unborn child the dwelling-plantation in equal division.

To son Francis and daughter Ellanor and Mr. James Haddock personalty.

To wife Elizabeth the residue of the personal estate.

Trustees—William Boarman and William Clarkson; in case his wife should die or remarry the trustees were to deliver the legacies to the legatees.

Letters of administration were issued to the widow, with James Semmes and George Brett as her sureties. At the appraisement on July 29, 1717, of the personal effects John Semmes and Marmaduke Semmes approved as the kinsmen. At the final accounting on January 22, 1722, the widow had married William Smith.

In 1734 Henry Cook and Eleanor his wife sold to John Biggs of Charles County for £3 all their rights and interests to " St. George's " left to Eleanor Cook by her father, Marmaduke Simms " and after John Sims uncle to the aforesaid Eleanor imagined that his brother's rights vested on him after his brother's death left the aforesaid land by his last will and testament to the aforesaid Eleanor " containing 106 acres.

FRANCIS SIMMS [3]

17– –1771

FRANCIS SIMMS, only son of Marmaduke and Elizabeth (Clarkson) Semmes, was born in Charles County. He married according to the rites of the Episcopal Church Lucretia Chapman on January 14, 1733/4. The births of eight of their ten children were registered in Trinity Parish, all of which indicate that he left the Catholic faith of his parents. The orthography used in the register was for most part Seemes.

Children of Francis and Lucretia (Chapman) Simms

1. Elizabeth Simms, born Oct. 24, 1734, married James Murphy.
2. Jane Simms, born June 28, 1736.
3. Joseph Simms, born Mar. 3, 1738/9, married Elizabeth Dent. *q.v.*
4. Marmaduke Simms, born May 23, 1741, married Susanna Burtles. *q.v.*
5. Chloe Simms, born Oct. 2, 1743.
6. Ignatius Simms, born Sept. 5, 1745, married Sabrit ———.
7. Francis Simms, born Oct. 28, 1747, married Mary Burtles. *q.v.*
8. Williamson Simms, *d.s.p.* 1774.
9. Ann Simms.
10. Eleanor Simms.

His mother-in-law, Jane Chapman, a widow, of Charles County on May 12, 1744, by deed of gift gave one-sixth of her personal estate to her son William Chapman, and the other five-sixths to her grandchildren—one-sixth going to her daughter " Lucretia's three daughters," namely, Elizabeth, Jane, and Chloe. She signed the deed in the presence of Daniel of St. Thomas Jenifer and Mathew Williamson.

On June 1, 1736, Francis Simms, of Charles County, Planter, " son and heir of Elizabeth Simms formerly Elizabeth Clarkson and daughter of William Clarkson, deceased," conveyed to William Clarkson, of Prince George's County, for £19 and 2,000 lbs. tobacco. " Stony Hill " which William Clarkson, deceased, had bought of Notley Rozer. His wife, Lucretia, acknowledged the sale.

On November 11, 1736, he bought of Marmaduke Semmes, of

Charles County, for 600 lbs. tobacco 103 acres of "St. George's," beginning at the line of Henry Wathen. Mary Semmes, wife of Marmaduke, waived her thirds.

On December 10, 1748, he conveyed to Hudson Wathen for 2,000 lbs. tobacco a 103-acre portion of "St. George's," at which time his wife waived dower rights. On September 19, 1767, he deeded to Bennett Wathen, of Charles County, for 20,000 lbs. tobacco another portion of "St. George's" known as "Simes' Fragments," beginning at the line of Mary Ann Boarman and also that of John Simes. At this time no wife waived dower.

On February 1, 1764, he purchased from Benjamin Fendall, of Charles County, Gent., for 20,000 lbs. tobacco 100 acres of land in Zachia Swamp, being part of "Charles Borough" and adjoining Westwood Manor.

His last will and testament was dated December 24, 1770, and probated in Charles County on January 10, 1771, in the presence of Joseph Semmes, the heir-at-law who consented to the probate.

> "A piece of cloth at the talors to make for my son Francis a coate & for my son Williamson a Jaccote."
> To children Ann, Williamson, Eleanor, Jean negroes.
> To daughter Elizabeth Murphey negro woman Lucy.
> To all children moveable estate equally.
> All land to be sold after all children come of age, son Williamson to be of age at 21 and daughters at 16, that is, daughters Ann and Eleanor, all to be raised on the plantation whereon I now live.

On January 1, 1772, Joseph Simms, Marmaduke Simms, Ignatius Simms, and Francis Simms, the sons of Francis Simms, late of Charles County, deceased, conveyed to Christopher Haw, of Charles County, Gent., for £400 "Charles Borough" of 100 acres lying on the north side of Zachia Swamp. Elizabeth wife to Joseph Simms, Susannah wife to Marmaduke Simms, Sabrid wife to Ignatius Simms, and Mary wife to Francis Simms relinquished their right of dower.

His youngest son, Williamson Simms, died intestate and without issue. His personal estate was inventoried on October 22, 1774, with Joseph Simms as the administrator and Ignatius Simms of Francis, and Francis Simms approving as the kinsmen. Distribution was made on December 2, 1775, when the balance of £65/17/6 was distributed to the eight brothers and sisters—all of whom were noted as of age.

JOSEPH SIMMS[4]
1739–1783

JOSEPH SIMMS, son of Francis and Lucretia (Chapman) Simms, was born March 3, 1738/9, in Trinity Parish, Charles County. On September 8, 1763, he married Elizabeth Dent who may not have been his first wife.* He established his seat at Port Tobacco.

Children of Joseph Simms

1. Francis Simms.
2. Victoria Simms married Ambrose Deakins.
3. Catherine Simms.
4. ——— Simms.
5. ——— Simms.
6. ——— Simms.

In 1772 as Joseph Simms of Francis he purchased lots in "Charleston commonly called Portobacco." In 1778 he subscribed to the Oath of Allegiance to the State of Maryland before Judge Warren Dent. He served as a private in the militia of Charles County under Captain Benjamin Lusby.**

His will, dated December 8, 1782, was proved in Charles County on January 25, 1783. His entire landed estate was to be sold at the expiration of 12 months and the money placed with interest for the benefit of his children and to be divided equally, each receiving their share upon majority. His wife, Elizabeth, however, was to have use of the estate during her widowhood only. He appointed his wife and her brother, Joseph Dent, as the executors.

At the probation the widow renounced the will and demanded her thirds and at the same time, Joseph Dent refused to act as executor. The inventory of the personal estate was approved by Anne Simms and Ellender Simms as the next of kin.

About 1789 Lawson Speake, Thomas McAtee, Francis Speake, and Franklin B. Franklin gave their bond to the Orphans' Court with the permission to take possession of the estate of Joseph Simms, late of Charles County, deceased, then in the custody of Elizabeth Simms, the acting executrix.

* For the Dent family, see, *Charles County Gentry*, by Newman.

** Militia List, p. 39, Maryland Historical Society.

On October 28, 1790, Ambrose Deakins and Victoria his wife and Catherine Simms, all of Prince William County, Virginia, the women being daughters and legatees of Joseph Simms, late of Charles County, deceased, appointed their brother, Francis Simms, the son and heir, their lawful attorney to make over to John Maddox, of Charles County, all their rights and interests to "Partner's Mistake" of $163\frac{1}{2}$ acres and which Joseph Simms directed to be sold within one year after his death. His executrix not having sold the land, her power under the will had then ceased. Furthermore, they gave their brother power to sell the land and to dispose of the money to the heirs, three of whom were minors under their patronage.

On September 20, 1791, Francis Simms, of Prince William County, Virginia, son and heir of Joseph Simms, late of Charles County, deceased, on behalf of himself and his sisters, Victoria Deakins and Catherine Simms, conveyed to John Maddox, of Charles County, for £62/10/– "Partner's Mistake," being part of a tract originally granted to Samuel Gray in 1745 for 362 acres except 150 acres the dower belonging to the widow. No wife of Francis waived her third.

MARMADUKE SIMMS [4]

17– –1774

MARMADUKE SIMMS, son of Francis and Lucretia (Chapman) Simms, was born May 23, 1741, in Trinity Parish, Charles County. His wife was Susannah Burtles who was made an heiress in the will of her father William Burtles, Sr., in 1789. His wife joined him with his brothers and sisters on January 1, 1772, in a deed upon the settlement of his father's estate.

Children of Marmaduke and Susanna (Burtles) Simms

1. Aloysius Simms, born Mar. 10, 1770.
2. Sarah Simms, born circa 1772.
3. Marmaduke Simms, born 1774.

The will of Marmaduke Simms, dated July 8, 1774, was proved in Charles County on August 26, 1774, by James Simpson and Basil Knott.

Wife Susannah all that part of tract of land called "St. Thomases" which I hold of James Simpson for a term of years; personalty, including the use of two Negroes.

To children Aloysius and Sarah and unborn child the Negroes at decease of wife, and other personalty.

To son Aloysius, daughter Sarah, and unborn child the residue of the personal estate and what was due from James Simpson on certain land.

Executors—wife Susannah and friend Joseph Townslin.

His personal estate was appraised on August 26, 1774, and approved by Francis Simms and Joseph Simms as the kinsmen, with William Burtles as a bondsman. The widow married secondly Mark Semmes, her deceased husband's kinsman. Before her marriage, however, or on August 12, 1776, she deeded to her children Marmaduke and Sarah for natural love and affections each a Negro slave.

At the August term of the court for 1789 Elexius [Aloysius] a minor aged 19 on March 10 last made choice of his step-father as guardian and at the same time Marmaduke aged between 14 and 15 made choice of his step-father. In 1791 Mark Simms was cited by the court for his failure to file an account upon the estates of his wards. At this time the mother of the orphans was deceased, for Mark Simms in August, 1791, had married the Widow Simpson.

The guardianship and the administration of their father's estate were ultimately taken away from Mark Simms and placed with William Burtles who in December, 1799, petitioned the court to sell the effects of Marmaduke Simms, deceased, and to distribute the proceeds among the representatives. On July 26, 1800, William Burtles delivered to Aloysius Simms £11/12/3. Before the final settlement, however, William Burtles died and his widow, Sarah Burtles, assumed the administration and on October 9, 1802, delivered a Negro woman appraised at £50 to Aloysius Simms.

FRANCIS SIMMS[4]

1747–18–

FRANCIS SIMMS, son of Francis and Lucretia (Chapman) Simms, was born October 28, 1747, in Trinity Parish, Charles County. He married Mary Burtles, who as Molly Simms was named in the will of her father, William Burtles, in 1789.

Children of Francis and Mary (Burtles) Simms

1. James B. Simms married Alluzer Tompkins. *q.v.*
2. Eleanor Simms married William B. Simpson. *q.v.*
3. Elizabeth Simms married William Keech.
4. Bennett Simms married Martha Craycroft. *q.v.*

During 1778 Francis Simms subscribed to the Patriot's Oath of Allegiance in Charles County before Judge John Parnham.

He died intestate. His widow likewise died intestate, for on January 14, 1812, letters of administration upon her estate were issued to James Simms and William Burtles Simpson on January 14, 1812. The final account was rendered on April 3, 1813, when the filial shares were delivered to James Simms, William B. Simpson in right of his wife Eleanor, William Keech in right of his wife Elizabeth, and to Martha Simms in right of her husband Bennett Simms deceased.

JAMES BURTLES SIMMS[5]
17- -1845

JAMES BURTLES SIMMS, son of Francis and Mary (Burtles) Simms, was born in Charles County. He married Alluzer, the daughter of John Tompkins.

Children of James and Alluzer (Tompkins) Simms

1. John Francis Simms married Elen ———. *q.v.*
2. James William Simms married twice. *q.v.*
3. Mary Ann Simms married William Tompkins (license D.C. Jan. 13, 1829), William Yeatman and William Rogers.

On August 7, 1818, "Tompkins Purchase" which began at "Hope's Bite" containing 295 acres was divided into four parts for the following–Zachariah Penn and Ann his wife, James Simmes and Alluzer his wife, Thomas Norris and Mary his wife, and Levin Watson and Catherine his wife. In 1825 James Simms, of Charles County, purchased from Levin Watson and Catherine his wife their share of a tract of land which John Tompkins "father of Catherine Watson died seized" called "Tompkins's Purchase." On March 28, 1825, he bought the share of John Penn.

The will of James B. Semmes, dated November 29, 1844, was probated in Charles County, on June 10, 1845.

To son John Francis Semmes the plantation on which I now live called "Tompkins' Purchase" of 270 acres and negroes.

To son James William Semmes plantation on which he lives called "Horse Shoe" of 200 acres on condition that he conveys all his rights of "Tompkins' Purchase" to my son John Francis Semmes, and Negroes.

To daughter Mary Ann Rogers $240 on condition that she conveys all her rights to "Tompkins Purchase."

To grandson James Richard Tompkins the lot of land on which his mother now resides called "Tompkins' Purchase" of 20 acres; and Negroes; if he died without issue then to my two sons.

His daughter, Mary Ann, married thirdly William Rogers. With his consent she drew up her will on September 8, 1846, it being proved in 1849 in Charles County. She appointed her husband the guardian of her son, James R. Tompkins, and devised the latter "Peale's Gift" on which she resided as well as Negroes and $300 for his education. In the event of his death without issue, then the estate was to revert to the "kin of my deceased husband William Yeatman."

On July 27, 1850, William Rogers, of Charles County, conveyed to John F. Semmes of the same county, the interest of the late Margaret [Mary] A. Rogers "one of the children of James B. Semmes, deceased, in a tract in Cobb Neck which belonged to the mother of the said Margaret and wife of James B. Semmes" and furthermore it was decreed by the court that John F. Semmes pay William Rogers $278.60 for the portion due his wife.

JOHN FRANCIS SIMMES[6]

1808–18–

JOHN FRANCIS SIMMES, son of James and Alluzer (Tompkins) Simmes, was born about 1808 in Charles County. At the 1850 census he was domiciled in Allen's Fresh District, aged 42, with realty appraised at $2,160. In his household were Elen Simmes (*sic*) aged 37; James aged 14; John aged 13; Benjamin aged 9; Ann aged 6; Nabler (?) aged 4; and Luisa aged 2.

His son, Benjamin Simms, with his wife Salome G. joining him in the deed, conveyed to James R. Tompkins his one-sixth interest in the 260-acre tract called "Tompkins' Purchase" which had been the property of the late John F. Simms.

JAMES WILLIAM SIMMS [6]

1809–18–

JAMES WILLIAM SIMMS, son of James and Alluzer (Tompkins) Simms, was born about 1809 in Charles County, being aged 41, at the 1850 census. He married twice. On July 31, 1852, he and his wife Mary Adeline Simms conveyed to John F. Simms, of Charles County, for $5.00 " Horse Shoe " in compliance with their father's will. In 1850 he was domiciled in Allen's Fresh District with realty appraised at $2,000 with the following members of his household at home—Mary A. Simmes (*sic*) aged 24; Charles aged 11; Jane aged 9; Margaret aged 6; Sylona aged 3; and James aged 3 months.

BENNETT SIMMS [5]

17– –1812

BENNETT SIMMS, son of Francis and Mary (Burtles) Simms, was born in Charles County. He married Martha, the daughter of Thomas and Charity (Green) Craycroft, of Charles County. She shared in the estate of her father who died in 1783, and was named as an heir in the will of her mother, Charity Craycroft, in 1792.

Children of Bennett and Martha (Craycroft) Simms

1. Joseph M. Simms, born May 19, 1808.
2. Martha Simms.

In 1790 as Bennett B. Simms he was the head of a family in Charles County with one female and six slaves.

He died intestate during 1812, the inventory of his personal estate being appraised on May 6 of that year. Joseph Green and Giles G. Craycroft were the bondsmen for the widow, and the court awarded her the custody of her two children—Joseph M. Simms, aged 4, and Martha, no age given. At the settlement of her mother-in-law's estate on April 3, 1813, her attorney, Charles Craycroft, acknowledged the receipt of $233.51 for her portion of her husband's estate. The final settlement of her husband's estate was not made until July 13, 1819, when it was divided among the widow and the two children—Joseph M. Simms and Martha Simms.

PARENTAGE NOT IDENTIFIED

Alexander Semmes. He died intestate in Charles Co., Md. Personal estate appraised on Apr. 10, 1766, at £35/8/3, with Benjamin J. Clark as the kinsman. At final account in 1767, an overpayment was declared by Walter Hanson, the administrator.

Anthony Simm. On Dec. 4, 1790, he secured license in Frederick Co., Md., to marry Christianna Smith; on April 28, 1800, he secured license to marry Mary Smith. In 1790 he was the head of a family in Frederick Co., with two males over 16, one female, and 10 slaves. His estate was settled on Jan. 30, 1810, by Henry Koontz, Jr., showing a balance of £685/12/6. Distribution was made to the widow and the following children–Ann, Catherine, Joseph, Christianna, Mary, Thomas, and Harriott. On Feb. 8, 1810, Mary Simm was made the guardian of Christianna, Mary, Thomas, and Harriott, with Middleton Smith and Walter Smith as her sureties.

Catherine Simms. Her will, dated Apr. 24, 1796, was proved in Charles Co., Md., on June 15, 1802. She named her son-in-law, Ignatius Ward, the husband of her daughter Sarah Simson Ward, and two grandsons–John Simms Ward and Samuel Ward.

William Simmes. He married Sarah Boone, the relict of Thomas Luckett, who had died intestate 1734 in Charles Co., Md. William Hagan and William Middleton, who had been the sureties for the widow, were apprehensive of her husband who had assumed administration of the estate and requested the court to have Simmes give security. His bond was recorded at court on Aug. 9, 1737, with Thomas Hawkins and Mr. Pidgeon as his sureties.

GREENE FAMILY

THOMAS GREENE, one of the " twenty gentlemen of very good fashion " who sailed on the *Ark* and the second Provincial Governor of Maryland, was one of the most interesting characters of early Maryland and one whose history has been quite neglected. He had invested in the adventure to a minor extent, so consequently its success was of more than casual interest. He was always styled by Governor Leonard Calvert " my well beloved friend," but the tradition that he was a kinsman of Leonard Calvert has not been proved and the oft repeated statement that he married Helen, a daughter of George, Lord Baltimore, is merely a myth of genealogy, His brother, Robert Greene, Esq., emigrated to Maryland, but being the son and heir to the parental estates in England he returned to the mother country, but before departing he assigned his land rights to his brother Thomas.

Governor Thomas Greene was a member of the Catholic faith, like most of the gentlemen on the *Ark*, a Royalist in politics, a supporter of the Stuart dynasty, and for his loyalty to the Crown he was castigated figuratively before his death by the radical elements which were then gaining strength in the Province—principally the Puritans who had been outlawed in Virginia and virtually driven out and to whom Lord Baltimore offered a haven in his Province.

His marriage to Mistress Ann Cox, a spinster,* who was among the few gentlewomen on the initial voyage of the *Ark* and the *Dove*, was undoubtedly the first Christian marriage to have been celebrated on Maryland soil. She died within a few years, but was living as late as April, 1638. He married secondly Mistress Winifred Seybourne [Seaborne] who arrived in Maryland some time during 1638.

The mother of his children has been the subject of much discussion, but of the two younger sons there is no question of their being the issue of Winifred his last wife. When he applied for

* Mistress in the 17th century was the title given to an unmarried woman of gentle birth who had acquired an estate and independent status. The statement that she was the widowed sister of Thomas Gerard is wholly unfounded.

land rights on September 15, 1647, among the claims was " 100 acres more being the right of his wife Mrs. Winifred Seyborn for Transporting herself into the Province 1638." It is therefore proved that she emigrated and financed her passage in 1638. At the same time he proved rights for 50 acres each for his children " 100 more for Transporting 2 children in the year 1644 vizt Thomas and Leonard Green." From the strict construction of the wording, there is no implication that Mistress Seyborne brought them over or was their mother. Mistress Seyborne came in 1638 and the boys came six years later. This point is important. They were less than 18 years of age in 1650 and they came out of England in 1644. There is no record of Thomas Greene returning to England, so the only inference that can be placed on the matter is that two older children were born in Maryland and had at one time been sent to England, presumably for a year of two of schooling.

Children of Thomas Greene, Esq.

1. Thomas Greene, *d. s. p.*
2. Leonard Greene married Anne ———. *q. v.*
3. Robert Greene married Mary Boarman. *q. v.*
4. Francis Greene married Elizabeth ———. *q. v.*

Before sailing from England, or shortly thereafter, Thomas Greene was granted a large manor of 10,000 acres, for Father Copley writing to Cecilius, Lord Baltimore on April 3, 1638, cautioned him against the excessive taxation imposed on the *manor lords* " An accordingly Mr. Green one of the Gentlemen that came in the Arke, reflecting that besydes the losse of his halfe share of trucks [harvest] he was now to pay tenne barrels of Corne for his 10,000 acres and that only he had three men to raise that and maintaine himself and his wyfe confidently told me that he must necessarily deserte the Colonye." As no further record has been found for this manor, he probably permitted it to escheat to the Lord Proprietary being in those difficult times more of a burden than an asset.

After the manor of Richard Thompson on Popely Island in the Bay was forfeited by treason against the Lord Proprietary, Lord Baltimore granted the manor to Thomas Greene, though the letters patent were apparently among those papers burned by Ingle on his raid into Maryland during 1645. The manor consisted of 500 acres on the tip of Kent Isle not far from Fort Kent Manor of Giles Brent and the entire Isle of Popely of 1,000 acres on which Thompson was seated and which was the scene of the entire massacre of his wife and children by Indians during his absence. If Thomas Greene maintained a steward on his manor, no record has come down, but leases were made for records exist of a Gersom Cromwell being a tenant on the portion on Kent. Greene gave the name of Bobing to his island manor and held it until February 8, 1650/1, when he sold for 10,000 lbs. tobacco to Thomas Hawkins, of London, Mariner, " all rights and interests in my whole Mannor."

He received other land grants, one of which was a warrant for 2,500 acres, but he died before the patent was issued. Consequently, in 1665 it was surveyed and granted to his three sons who gave it the name of " Green's Inheritance." His seat, however, was on "Green's Rest " within the environs of St. Mary's City and bordering St. Mary's River.

He took a serious interest in all the affairs of the Province and became one of the leading factors in the early political developments. He attended the early General Assemblies to whom all freeholders were summoned. When the legislature became representative and the Upper House or Privy Council developed, he was one of the first to be appointed by the Lord Proprietary to that body which was virtually a counterpart to the British House of Lords. He was also appointed one of the Justices of the Provincial Court at its inception. He retained his seat in the Council until 1647 when he succeeded to the governorship by the death of Leonard Calvert, the first Provincial Governor. His term of office lasted until April 26, 1649, when Lord Baltimore commissioned Captain William Stone, of Virginia, and for a short period thereafter acted as governor when Stone was on a business trip to Virginia.

On November 18, 1650, he negotiated a document whereby he assigned his entire estate in trust under certain conditions to his friends, Henry Adams and James Langworth, for the benefit of his wife, Winifred, and sons—Thomas, Leonard, Robert, and Francis. He desired his wife to have full possession of the estate during life except for a certain amount of tobacco which was bequeathed to his friend Thomas Copley. His widow was to grant his sons the designated shares in succession as they came of age, " . . . be Sufficiently maintained and Provided for . . . both for Subsistance and Education answerable to their quality until each of them respectively come to *eighteen years of age*." * In the event of his widow's decease and the death of his sons without issue, then three-fourths of his estate were to be distributed to charity and the residue to Henry Adams and James Langworth.

He died before January 20, 1651/2, the day on which Henry Adams appeared in court as the trustee of the estate. His widow married secondly Robert Clarke, Gent., one-time Surveyor-General of the Province, and became the mother of at least two children—Robert and Thomas. On November 16, 1654, Robert Clarke on behalf of his wife Winifred Clarke " late wife of Thomas Greene deceased and her children by the said Greene " demanded 400 acres of land for the transportation of four servants by Thomas Greene on June 10, 165–.

In 1658 William Hewes instituted action against Robert Clarke for repairs on "Green's Rest " before Clarke married the widow of Thomas Greene. At that time Madam Greene-Clarke was deceased. Hewes claimed that Captain William Stone engaged him for the work and that the overseers of the estate of Thomas Greene should be responsible for the expenditures.

LEONARD GREEN, GENT. [2]

163– –1688

LEONARD GREEN, second but first surviving son of Governor Thomas Greene, was under age on November 18, 1650, when his father drew up the instrument which provided for his four children and widow in the event of his death. Accordingly 13 years after his death, his widow was to deliver " unto son Leonard Green the fourth part of all such clear estate in kind as shall then and at that time be in her possession." Leonard Green was born before 1644. inasmuch as he and his older brother were brought into the Province in that year and inasmuch as he and his brother Thomas were less than 18 years of age in 1650 (for in that year his father placed the estate of the four sons in trust with Henry Adams and James Langworth " untill each of them respectively come to eighteen years of age "), he was therefore born sometime after 1634 and before 1644.

* The fact that his two older sons were less than 18 years of age in 1650 disproves the statement often made that the two sons were conceived of a marriage contracted in England before his sailing in 1633.

He was a godson of Governor Leonard Calvert and was bequeathed personalty in the nuncupative will of the Governor in 1644. He was the only son of Governor Greene to manifest any interest in civil and military affairs. He participated in the Nanticoke Indian War, and in November, 1678, he was voted 400 lbs. tobacco by the General Assembly for his service.* On April 24, 1679, he was commissioned a Deputy Sheriff for St. Mary's County, and served as a delegate to the Lower House from St. Mary's County from 1682-1684.** And in 1683 he was appointed on the commission for the advancement of trade in the Province.†

His wife was Ann ——.

Children of Leonard and Ann Green

1. Thomas Green, *d. s. p.*
2. Winifred Green married Aug. 28, 1690, Francis Wheeler.
3. Mary Green married Francis Marbury.
4. Margaret Green married Joseph Alvey.

Inasmuch as his only son, Thomas, though married, died without issue, the line of Leonard Green was carried on only through his three daughters. His will, dated January 10, 1687/8, was proved in St. Mary's County on July 4, 1688.

> To wife Ann "Green's Rest" during life.
> To son Thomas said plantation at the death of his mother, also 200 acres at Panguya in Charles Co., being part of "Greene's Inheritance" patented by testator and his two brothers—Francis and Robert.
> To eldest daughter Wynyfred 200 acres of "Greene's Inheritance."
> To daughter Mary 200 acres of the same tract.
> To daughter Margaret 200 acres of the same tract.
> Children to be under the care of their mother; executors—brothers Francis Greene and Thomas Clarke.

On January 10, 1688/9, his widow married Charles Evans. On September 8, 1692, Francis Wheeler in right of his wife Winifred instituted action in court against Charles Evans and Ann his wife "the relict of Leonard Green deceased" for a portion of his wife's inheritance. The bill of complaint stated that Leonard Green died

* Archives, vol. 7.

** Archives, vol. 51, p. 246, *passim.*

† Archives, vol. 7, p. 610.

possessed of a personal estate in excess of 100,000 lbs. tobacco, sufficient to cover all indebtedness.

The son and heir, Thomas Green, as a matured bachelor, married a widow. His will, dated January 9, 1749/50, bequeathed the entire estate to his wife, Mildred Green. Her will was written three days later, when she devised all realty to her grandson Joseph Raley, but in the event that he died without issue then to her grandson Henry Sheirclif. One shilling was bequeathed to her daughter, Telca Green, and a legacy to her grandson Henry Miles. Both wills were probated in St. Mary's County on February 6, 1749/50.

ROBERT GREEN, GENT. [2]

1646–171–

ROBERT GREEN, third son of Governor Green and his wife Winifred Seyborne, was born at "Green's Rest," St. Mary's County. His birth occurred in or about 1646, according to a deposition made on January 29, 1676/7. His wife was Mary, one of the older daughters of Major William Boarman by his first wife Sarah.

A land transaction by Robert Green and his wife in 1713 proves definitely that Major William Boarman "gave" Mary, the wife of Robert Green, on July 16, 1679, 450 acres of "Boarman's Manor" which they called "Green's Rest." The deed of gift is not recorded in Charles County, but probably in St. Mary's County, now destroyed, as that part of Charles was St. Mary's in that day. Although the deed in 1713 does not state that Mary Green was his daughter, Major Boarman about that time was making deeds of gift to his older children, and it is difficult to believe that Major Boarman would have made a gift of so large an acreage if the wife of Robert Green were not his daughter.*

Additional proof that his wife was Mary Boarman developed in 1755 over the bounds of "Hall's Place," a portion of Boarman's Manor. Joseph Jameson swore that a stump was the bound tree of "Mr. Green's land." That it was the dividing tree "between the

* For many years this compiler has been wanting to identify the wife of Robert Green, for she was definitely a lady of high birth. The education of Robert Green had been neglected by his mother and step-father, for he always made his mark, yet his wife Mary wrote her name on legal documents. And only maidens of the best houses in that day were taught to read and write.

two Sisters" and that when it stood "there was a large blase on which was designed to have Put the Two first Letters of the Two Sisters names on, And that this deponant Apprehends was Mrs. Green and Mrs. Mudd and that the afsd Thomas Mudd told him that a Place neare Henry Jameson Tob° House, which was at that time Proved to be a dividing tree between the Two Sisters, was not the dividing tree." As it is proved that Mrs. Mudd was born Sarah Boarman and was then the wife of Thomas Mudd, and inasmuch as Mrs. Green and Mrs. Mudd were the two sisters, it is therefore evident that Major Boarman gave "Green's Rest," a freehold on Boarman's Manor, as a dowry to his daughter Mary about the time of her marriage to Robert Green.

There are evidences of financial reverses during the life of Robert Green, one of which is the re-purchase of "Green's Rest" by his father-in-law. The settlement of his estate does not prove a complete list of his children, but in 1709 Thomas Federick, of Prince George's County, by his will devised his godsons, James and Thomas Green, each 100 acres of "Strife," and 200 acres to Mary Green. At the death of his widow, Mary Federick, the personal estate was to pass to Jane Green, Jr., Thomas Green, and Elizabeth Green.

Children of Robert and Mary (Boarman) Green

1. Thomas Green married Telca Shirtcliff. *q.v.*
2. Elizabeth Green married Andrew Simpson. *q.v.*
3. Mary Green married John Thompson.
4. Sarah Green married Patrick McAtee.
5. Ann Green married [——— Clark].
6. William Green, born Dec. 28, 1694.
7. Robert Green, *d.s.p.* 1749.
8. James Green married Elizabeth Dyer and Eleanor ———. *q.v.*

In 1660 he was named as kinsman in the will of James Langworth, his guardian or trustee, according to the terms of his father's legal instrument of 1650, though the relationship between the Green and Langworth families is not known. By an Act of the General Assembly of May-June, 1676, he received 1,500 lbs. tobacco for services to the Province which are believed to have been for participation in an Indian expedition.*

On November 9, 1702, Robert Green conveyed to Andrew Sympson, of Charles County, in consideration of a marriage about to take

* Archives of Maryland, vol. 2, p. 551.

place between the said Andrew Sympson and his daughter, Elizabeth, 100 acres of land lying on Port Tobacco Creek. On June 8, 1703, he deeded to his daughter, Mary the wife of John Thompson, of Charles County, " that portion of the tract called Thompson's Rest being a portion of Robert Green's third of Green's Inheritance."

On August 25, 1703, he and Mary his wife sold to Richard Combs for 7,000 lbs. tobacco a portion of " Green's Inheritance " which had been patented in the name of Leonard Green, Robert Green, and Francis Green.

On June 25, 1713, he, his wife Mary, and the son and heir Thomas Green conveyed to William Boarman, the son and heir of Major William Boarman, deceased, a portion of " Green's Rest." On the same day they conveyed to Francis Ignatius Boarman for £50 Green's Rest " or 450 acres of Major William Boarman's Manor which " said land was formerly given to the said Mary Green and her heirs by the said Major William Boarman deceased as by conveyance dated 16 July 1679." The 1713 assignment stated that Major Boarman in his life time " purchased again of the said Robert Green " the plantation, but apparently had not made payment. By Major Boarman's will of 1709 he had devised the land to his youngest son Francis Ignatius Boarman. The present deed was therefore to clarify the title as it stated " but nothing appearing upon record from the Thomas Green to the said William Boarman is the cause of this present indenture." Robert Green made his mark, but his wife and son both signed the instrument.

No will nor administration account on his estate is available at Annapolis. He was undoubtedly deceased by 1718, for on August 30, 1721, Thomas Green, Planter, was summoned to court by Patrick Macatee and Sarah his wife to answer for an unpaid debt of £6/12/– which had been owing them since 1718. In the bill of complaint Sarah Macatee declared herself to be " late Sarah Green sister to the said Thomas Green."

His son, Robert Greene, died intestate; letters of administration were issued on October 14, 1749, to Thomas Greene, with William Thompson and John Maccatee, of Charles County, as the sureties. The inventory of the estate was approved by Bennett Green, Joshua Green, Anne Clark, and Thomas Green, Jr. The account showed no distribution to the heirs.

FRANCIS GREEN, GENT.[2]

1648–1707

FRANCIS GREEN, son of Governor Thomas Greene and Winifred his wife, was born about 1648 at "Green's Rest" near St. Mary's City. He established his seat on "Green's Inheritance" in Port Tobacco Hundred, Charles County. Ignatius Causine, of Port Tobacco, writing his will on May 4, 1695, named his cousin, Francis Green, one of the overseers of his estate.* His wife was Elizabeth.

Children of Francis and Elizabeth Greene

1. Leonard Green married (1) Mary Sewell and (2) Prudence Cooper. *q.v.*
2. Verlinda Green, born Aug. 16, 1692, married Thomas Sanders.
3. Francis Green, born Apr. 23, 1694, married Elizabeth Wheeler. *q.v.*
4. Clare Green married Jacob Clements.
5. Giles Green. *q.v.*

His will, dated September 16, 1706, was probated in Charles County on May 7, 1707.

To son Leonard 100 acres of land bought of Leonard Brooke, 800 acres of "Greene's Inheritance" lying between main road to Piscataway and the Rowling Road of "brother Robert Greene."
To son Francis all land on "The Old Woman's Branch."
To son Giles all land between that of sons Leonard and Francis.
To daughter Clare personalty.
Residuary of personal estate to all children after wife's thirds.
Executors—wife and son Leonard.

THOMAS GREEN[3]

1683–1760

THOMAS GREEN, son of Robert and Mary (Boarman) Green, was born in or about 1683, according to his deposition in 1743, when he declared himself to be 60 years of age and referred to his deceased father Robert Green.

* Apparently there was no blood relationship between Ignatius Causine and Francis Green unless it was through their respective wives whose paternity is unknown. Ignatius Causine's step-father, Robert Clark, was also a step-father to Francis Green, the said Robert Clark having married first Winifred (Seyborne) Green and secondly Jane (Cockshutt) Causine.

Although it has been stated that he married first Sarah, daughter of William and Jane (Neale) Boarman, no proof or inference can be found. Sarah, the daughter of William Boarman 2d, was styled Sarah Boarman in his will of April, 1720, thereby, indicating that she was unmarried at that time. On January 9, 1719/20, the wife of Thomas Green was Telca, who waived dower on the sale of 140 acres of "Green's Inheritance" to Samuel Hanson. She was the daughter of William and Mildred Shirtcliff and as a maiden was devised unnamed land in the will of her father on March 25, 1707/8. Her mother married secondly Thomas Green of Leonard, and dying testate in 1750, she bequeathed her daughter, Telca Green, one shilling. Consequently, Telca was the wife of Thomas Green as early as 1719 and was alive at his death in 1760.

Children of Thomas Green

1. Bennett Green married Anne ———. *q.v.*
2. Joseph Green married Jane ———, *d.s.p.* 1748, widow married Ignatius Simpson. *q.v.*
3. Thomas Green married Henrietta ———. *q.v.*
4. Nicholas Green married Susannah ———. *q.v.*
5. Raphael Green married Elizabeth ———. *q.v.*
6. Thomas Dudley Green married Mary Semmes. *q.v.*
7. Peter Green married Appolonia ———. *q.v.*
8. William Green married Eleanor ———. *q.v.*
9. Thomas Melchizedeck Green. *q.v.*
10. Mary Green.

On August 30, 1721, he was summoned to court to answer the complaint of Patrick Macatee and Sarah his wife "late Sarah Green sister to the said Thomas Green" in action of trespass growing out of the settlement of the estate of their father Robert Greene.

On September 11, 1747, he conveyed to Joseph and William Green, no relationship stated, 134 acres of "Green's Inheritance" for 5 shillings, with his wife Telca waiving her third interest.

His will, dated August 27, 1759, was proved in Charles County on March 12, 1760.

To sons Thomas, Nicholas, Raphael, Dudley, Peter, William, and Melchizedeck equal portions of "Green's Inheritance."

If my beloved son, Bennett Green "shall get no right nor property in a parcel of land being part of Boarman's Manor then he shall have an equal share of "Green's Inheritance" with his 7 brothers."

To son Bennett all "my rights, title, property and interest to a parcel of land being part of a tract of land called Boarman's Manor" and likewise to all other lands by me unwilled as my proper heir at law provided his brothers have an equal share with him.*

To son Melchizedeck a Negro.

To wife Telca during life the use of a Negro woman and also her increase after her death to be equally divided among my children except Melchizedeck.

Residuary estate equally to 8 sons and daughter Mary.

Executors—Sons Bennett, Nicholas, and Ralph (*sic*).

At probation his widow, Telca Green, accepted the legacies, but demanded her third of the landed estate.

The claims of the son and heir, Bennett Green, to a portion of "Green's Rest" on "Boarman's Manor" was recognized, for on August 30, 1762, Bennett Green conveyed to William Boarman, Jr., Gerrard Boarman, and William McPherson for a consideration of 20,000 lbs. tobacco "for the docking, barring, and extinguishing all estates tail and all reversions . . . in Green's Rest" being part of a greater tract of land called "Content" and containing 450 acres. Anne Green, the wife of Bennett, relinquished her third interest.

The division of "Green's Inheritance" possessed by Thomas Green at his death was made to the seven brothers on August 23, 1765, each son receiving 57 acres. All seven sons signed the agreement, with Leonard Green and Edward Green as the witnesses.

The son, Joseph Green, died testate in 1748, leaving a wife, Jane, to whom he bequeathed his entire estate including a portion of "Green's Inheritance." The inventory of the personalty was taken on February 22, 1748/9, and approved by William Green and Bennett Green as the kinsmen. At the final account in 1750 his widow had married Ignatius Simpson. On April 2, 1764, Ignatius Simpson and Jane his wife conveyed to Bennett Green for 4,000 lbs. tobacco 66 acres of "Green's Inheritance."

* The testator's interest in the manor was as the son and heir or the eldest son of his father, Robert Green, and was the property entailed or otherwise which his mother Mary Boarman brought his father as the heiress of her father Major William Boarman.

JAMES GREEN [3]

17– –1776

JAMES GREEN, placed as the son of Robert and Mary (Boarman) Green, was born apparently at "Green's Rest" in Charles County. In 1709 he inherited from his godfather, Thomas Federick, 100 acres of "Strife" in Piscataway Hundred, Prince George's County, on which he settled at maturity.

His first wife was Elizabeth, daughter of Patrick and Comfort (Barnes) Dyer, who was born January 22, 1711/12, and to whom he was married on July 26, 1727, by the Rev. Henry Whitehall, of St. John's Piscataway Parish. The births of their seven children were recorded in the register of the Established Church of Maryland in St. John's Piscataway Parish. His wife was the step-daughter of the affluent Thomas Edelen who died testate in Prince George's County in 1749 and bequeathed silver plate to his step-daughter, Elizabeth Green. Her mother, Comfort Dyer-Edelen, died testate in 1760 and named her daughter, Elizabeth Green, and her grandson, Thomas Edelen Green.

Children of James and Elizabeth (Dyer) Green

1. Catherine Green, born Feb. 16, 1729/30.
2. Mary Green, born Mar. 30, 1732, married ——— Bowling.
3. Elizabeth Green, born May 7, 1734.
4. Charity Green, born Oct. 5, 1736.
5. James Green, born Oct. 4, 1738, married Elizabeth ———. *q.v.*
6. Rebecca Green, born Apr. 4, 1741.
7. Thomas Edelen Green, born Mar. 9, 1745/6; subscribed to Patriot's Oath Jan. 27, 1778, before Judge Thomas Clagett; removed to Washington Co., Ky., before 1800.
8. Basil Green married Mary Ann Lanham. *q.v.*
9. John Green.

His wife, Elizabeth, was living as late as 1760. However, he married secondly Eleanor ——— who survived him. All his children, except John, are proved as issue of his wife, Elizabeth, and inference is quite strong that John was likewise.

His will, dated November 15, 1774, was probated in Prince George's County on August 23, 1776.

To wife Eleanor, executrix, "Strife" whereon he lived during life and the personal estate, and at her death to be divided among all children unnamed.

To son John 10 acres in Mattawoman Swamp.
To son Thomas Edelen Green "my gun."
To son Basil the plantation "Strife" after the death of the widow.

On May 29, 1776, the widow renounced the administration and requested that letters be issued to her son-in-law, Basil Green, and at the same time refused to abide by the will and demanded her third.

The personal estate was appraised at £220/13/7½ on November 21, 1776, and approved by Thomas Edelen Green and Mary Bowling as the kinsmen. At an account filed on May 6, 1777, nine unnamed children of the deceased were noted as the heirs.

His widow died intestate, when her administrator, Thomas Edelen Green, filed the inventory of her estate, appraised at £68 at court on November 13, 1783. At final account on March 23, 1790, distribution of the balance went to Joseph Blandford and Thomas Edelen Green.

LEONARD GREEN [3]
1691–1733

LEONARD GREEN, son to Francis Green and Elizabeth his wife, was born May 30, 1691, at "Green's Inheritance" near Port Tobacco, Charles County. He married Mary, the daughter of John Sawell [Seawell], of St. Mary's County, by his wife Anne, a family of no immediate connection with Henry Sewell, Esq., one-time Secretary of the Province.

On February 4, 1720/1, citations were issued by the sheriff to Mary Green, for her appearance at court relative to the execution of the will of her brother John Sewell. Leonard Green, husband to Mary, appeared during September, 1721, and stated that his wife Mary had lately been delivered of a child and was not capable of traveling to court. Cuthbert Sewell by his will proved in St. Mary's County on March 7, 1723/4, devised his sister, Mary Green, his interest in "Fenwick Manor" and "Cuthbert's Fortune" and the "Addition to Cuthbert's Fortune," appointing his brother, Leonard Green, the executor.

Children of Leonard and Mary (Sawell) Green

1. Leonard Green. *q.v.*
2. Cuthbert Green. *q.v.*

3. John Green, *d.s.p.*
4. Teresa Green married ——— Milstead.

His first wife died early in life and after June 4, 1725, he married secondly Prudence, daughter of Nicholas and Penelope Cooper, but then the widow of Charles Sanders. Prudence had been born April 11, 1692, in Charles County "of ye River side."

Issue of Leonard and Prudence (Cooper) Green

1. Francis Green married Charity Hagan. *q.v.*

He wrote his will on October 11, 1733, it being probated in Charles County on November 8, following. He devised his son, Leonard, all realty in St. Mary's County, and to his other sons—Cuthbert, John, and Francis—his portion of "Green's Inheritance." His wife, Prudence, was willed one-third of the personal estate, with the residue being divided among all his children.

Letters of administration were issued to the widow, with Thomas Sanders, Jr., and Robert Doyne as her bondsmen. Francis Green and Leonard Green approved the valuation of the personal effects as the kinsmen.

The will of his widow, Prudence Green, dated September 27, 1757, was probated in Charles County on November 21, same year. Negroes and other chattels were bequeathed to her daughter Jane, wife of Robert Doyne; to her son Francis Green; but the bequests to her daughter, Mary Livers, were exclusive of her husband, James Livers, and were by no means to be used for the payment of his debts. Other heirs were her grandchildren—Mary Saunders, Jane Saunders, Elizabeth Saunders, Mary Simms, Sarah Doyne, and Jane Doyne.

FRANCIS GREEN[3]
1694–1761

FRANCIS GREEN, son of Francis Green and Elizabeth his wife, was born near Port Tobacco on April 23, 1694, according to court records. At a young age he married Elizabeth, the daughter of Benjamin Wheeler.*

* The marriage according to family records is given as "anno 1711" which would make him about 17 years of age. The year of Elizabeth's birth is given as 1693, making her one year older than her husband. The marriage, her

Children of Francis and Elizabeth (Wheeler) Green

1. Leonard Green, born Nov. 8, 1712, married Clare ———. *q.v.*
2. Elizabeth Green, born Jan. 24, 1713/4.
3. Francis Green, born Nov. 5, 1716, married Elizabeth ———. *q.v.*
4. Anastatia Green, born Sept. 29, 1718.
5. Eleanor Green, born June 28, 1720.
6. Susanna Green, born May 10, 1722.
7. Anne Green, born Jan. 24, 1724, married Patrick Hamilton.
8. Henry Green, born Feb. 24, 1726, married the Widow Thomas. *q.v.*
9. Henrietta Green, born Oct. 13, 1728.
10. Benjamin Green, born Jan. 15, 1730/1, married Elizabeth Thomas *q.v.*
11. Ignatius Green, born Jan. 19, 1732/3.
12. Clement Green, born Apr. 11, 1735, married Hannah Thomas. *q.v.*
13. John Green, born Oct. 28, 1737, married Elizabeth Beaven.

On July 20, 1758, Francis Green assigned the plantation on which he was living, being 200 acres of " Green's Inheritance " to Leonard Green for a consideration of 5,443 lbs. tobacco. No wife waived dower.

He died intestate. Letters of administration were issued to Leonard Green who filed the inventory on March 28, 1761, with William Clements and Thomas Green approving. The final account was passed by the court on April 11, 1764, reporting a balance of £38/13/3 to be distributed to the heirs. The heirs were not listed in account, which stated that the representatives were " all of age."

parentage, and birth of their children are all from copies of family papers which have been examined personally. They are now in the possession of Mrs. Harry M. Ullmann, of Bethlehem, Penna., a direct descendant. From the script, watermark, and style of stationery, the papers are judged to be well over 150 years of age, and look as if the births were copied from an old family prayer-book. I believe it was the custom of the Catholic families to place the births of their children in a prayer-book rather than the family Bible. Then there seems to have been a journal kept of certain facts such as the recording of a member of the family going to Kentucky. " Leonard Green and wife took their leave of their friends 29th Septe. 1790 from thence to go down to Kentucky. Adieu, adieu, my children forever." Signed " Elizabeth Green 1790." Then there is the record of another Leonard Green " & family went out to the back country December ye 2d 1785." It is my earnest opinion that these papers are authentic, genuine and should be recognized as definite proof of parentage, etc.

GILES GREEN [3]

17– –1792

GILES GREEN, son of Francis and Elizabeth Green, was born at "Green's Inheritance," Charles County. His dwelling-plantation lay in the West Hundred of Port Tobacco, where he was a tithable in 1775. His wife has not been identified. It is not known whether he nourished Tory sympathies during the Revolution, but no record of his taking the Oath of Allegiance in 1778 can be found. In 1790 he was living alone with 11 Negro slaves.

Children of Giles Green

1. Edward Green. *q.v.*
2. Charles Green, *d.s.p.* 1808.
3. Giles Green married Elizabeth Craycroft. *q.v.*
4. Clare Green.
5. Eleanor Green married ——— Macatee.
6. ——— Green married ——— Thomas.

On March 28, 1765, he deeded to his son, Edward, for natural love and affections the portion of "Green's Inheritance" which was then occupied by his son Edward. No wife waived dower.

He drew up his will on May 2, 1792, it being probated in Charles County on June 18, following, by Leonard Neale, Wilfred Green, and Lewis Green.

To grandson Joseph Green of Giles all land including the dwelling-plantation and the mansion house; Negroes.
To sons Giles and Charles Negroes.
To grandchildren Elizabeth Green, Sarah Green, and Giles Thomas.
To daughters Clare Green and Elianore Machatee £50 each.
To Leonard Clements £50.
Residue to two sons and two granddaughters, namely Giles Green, Charles Green, Elizabeth Green, and Sarah Green.
Executor—sons and grandson Joseph Green of Giles.

The sons apparently refused to act, for letters of administration were issued solely to Joseph Green.

Charles Green, the son, although married twice, died without issue. By 1769 he had married Jane, the daughter of Anthony Simms, of Charles County, who named daughter Jane Green and son Charles Green in his will. Green later married Eleanor ——— who was a sister to Sarah, the wife of Hezekiah Berry. His will, dated August 4, 1804, was proved in Charles County on April 12, 1808, by which he devised his estate to his wife, Eleanor, with the land being possessed by her during life and at her death reverting to his wife's sister "Sarah Berry wife of Hezekiah Berry" during her life, and then the latter's son William Marbury Berry. At the final account in 1810, there was a reference to a law-suit instituted by Joseph Greene—apparently his nephew.

BENNETT GREEN [4]

1710–17–

BENNETT GREEN, son and heir of Thomas Green and his wife, was born about 1710 at "Green's Inheritance." His father in his will of 1760 mentioned his son Bennett's rights to certain land in "Boarman's Mannor" which was apparently entailed property which had come through Bennett's grandmother Mary Boarman. Accordingly, on August 30, 1762, Bennett Green, of Charles County, after docking, barring and extinguishing all reversions conveyed to William Boarman, Jr., Gerard Boarman, and William McPherson, in consideration of 20,000 lbs. tobacco "Green's Rest" of 450 acres in Charles County, being part of a greater tract of land called "Content." Ann Green, wife, waived all dower rights.

On April 2, 1764, he bought of Ignatius Simpson and Jane his wife 66 acres of "Green's Inheritance" for 4,000 lbs. tobacco which he, Bennett Green, in 1772 sold to Samuel Hanson. Ann Green, wife of Bennett, again waived all dower interest. On May 11, 1773, being of Prince George's County, he conveyed an additional 7 acres of "Green's Inheritance" to Samuel Hanson, with his wife Ann waiving her legal third.

THOMAS GREEN [4]

17– –17–

THOMAS GREEN, son of Thomas and Telca (Shirtcliff) Green, was born at "Green's Inheritance." On August 31, 1767, he conveyed to his brother, Peter, his share of the parental plantation or 57 acres at which time his wife, Henrietta, relinquished her third. In 1775 a Thomas Green, Sr., and Thomas Green, Jr., were tithables in

Upper Hundred of Port Tobacco. He did not subscribe to the Oath of Allegiance in Charles County in 1778, nor was he a tithable in Charles County during 1783.

NICHOLAS GREEN[4]

17– –1802

NICHOLAS GREEN, son of Thomas and Telca (Shirtcliff) Green, was born at "Green's Inheritance," 57 acres of which he received at the death of his father and where he established his dwelling-plantation. In 1775 he was domiciled in the Upper Hundred of Port Tobacco Parish, and there in 1778 he took the Oath of Allegiance to the State of Maryland before Judge Samuel Hanson. In 1790 he was the head of a family with 2 males over 16 years, 4 females, and 2 slaves. He died testate in Charles County, his will being dated July 31, 1800 and proved on March 16, 1802. He devised to his son, Solomon, the dwelling-plantation "Green's Inheritance" and bequeathed certain legacies to his daughters–Dorothy, Eleanor, and Mary.

RAPHAEL GREEN[4]

17– –17–

RAPHAEL GREEN, son of Thomas and Telca (Shirtcliff) Green, was born at "Green's Inheritance." On March 5, 1768, he mortgaged 57 acres of "Green's Inheritance" and Negress Moll to Samuel Hanson, and on March 13, 1772, he conveyed the 57 acres to his brother, Thomas Melchizadeck Green, being his inheritance as one of the seven sons of Thomas Green. Elizabeth Green, his wife, acknowledged the conveyance. Within a short time, or on March 13 following, he deeded to his brother Thomas for £100 the same or another portion of "Green's Inheritance" of 57 acres. Elizabeth his wife likewise waived dower. He apparently removed elsewhere, for he was not listed in the 1775 census for Charles County nor did he subscribe to the Oath of Allegiance in that county during 1778. Furthermore, he was not a tithable of Charles County in 1783.

THOMAS DUDLEY GREEN [4]

17– –1794

THOMAS DUDLEY GREEN, sixth son of Thomas Green and Telca Shirtcliff his wife, was born at "Green's Inheritance," Charles County. He married in 1765 Mary Simms, born March 1747, daughter of Alexius Simms and Verlinda his wife. In 1804 Edward Simms, of the District of Columbia, bequeathed his sister, Mary Green, a legacy of $100.00. The births of his children are taken from his extant Family Bible.

Children of Thomas Dudley and Mary (Simms) Green

1. Jesse Green, born June 6, 1766, married twice *q. v.*
2. Sarah Green, born June 14, 1767.
3. Thomas Green, born Dec. 25, 1768, died young.
4. Catherine Green, born 1770.
5. Bennett Green, born June 5, 1772, died young.
6. Bennett Green, born Apr. 25, 1774.
7. Teasely Green, born Apr. 24, 1776, died young.
8. Winfred Green, born Jan. 11, 1778.
9. Thomas Green, born Jan. 2, 1781.
10. Mary Green, born Jan. 18, 1783.

On September 27, 1768, of Charles County, he sold to Basil Spalding, of Prince George's County, his share of "Green's Inheritance" or 57 acres, at which time his wife, Mary, waived dower. After disposing of his landed estate in Charles County, he removed to Baltimore Town, where his wife, Mary, died on Febraury 2, 1786. He died on September 22, 1794, and was buried in Old St. Peter's churchyard, then the only Roman Catholic church in Baltimore.

PETER GREEN [4]

17– –18–

PETER GREEN, seventh son of Thomas and Telca (Shirtcliff) Green, was born at "Green's Inheritance." In 1765 he received his share or 57 acres of the parental plantation, and on August 31, 1767, he purchased from his brother, Thomas, the latter's share of "Green's Inheritance." In 1775 he was a tithable in the Upper Hundred of Port Tobacco Parish where he took the Oath of Allegiance in 1778 before Magistrate Samuel Hanson. In 1783 he was seized of 114 acres of "Green's Inheritance." On August 17, 1787, he sold to Samuel Hanson 57 acres of the plantation, at which time his wife, Appolina, waived all dower rights.

On August 24, 1787, Brooke Beall, of Montgomery County, conveyed to Elizabeth, daughter of Peter Green, of Charles County, for 5 shillings and other considerations all the household furniture which had been conveyed to him by Peter Green. In 1790 he had in his household himself and another male over 16 years of age, three males under 16, five females, and seven slaves.

There is no record of his conveying his ownership in "Green's Inheritance," nor are there any estates administered in Charles County for a Peter Green in the early Federal period.

A namesake married Allalu Mudd, daughter of Richard and Jane (Gardiner) Mudd, and settled in Washington County, Kentucky. In 1829 Allalu Green, wife of Peter Green, of that county and State, was an heir through her mother, Jane Gardnier, to the estate of Cornelius Boarman, late of Prince George's County. In 1830 Peter Green, of Washington County, was the head of family. He and his wife were both between the ages of 60 and 70.

WILLIAM GREEN [4]

17-- ?

WILLIAM GREEN, son of Thomas and Telca (Shirtcliff) Green, was born at "Green's Inheritance." On September 4, 1765, he assigned his rights in the parental plantation of "Green's Inheritance" to his brother Edward Green, at which time his mother, Telca Green, joined him in waiving her dower. His wife was Eleanor ——— who brought him a portion of "Pye's Chance," for on December 17, 1768, he and his wife, Eleanor, sold to the Rev. George Hunter for £54 the westernmost moyety of "Pye's Chance" of 77 acres which lay on the road leading from Newport to Port Tobacco. On January 7, 1775, they conveyed another portion of the same tract for £30. Inasmuch as he was not a tithable at the 1775 census for Charles County, and did not take the Oath of Allegiance in Charles County during 1778, it is assumed that he removed elsewhere.

THOMAS MELCHIZADECK GREEN [4]

17-- ?

THOMAS MELCHIZADECK GREEN, son of Thomas and Telca (Shirtcliff) Green, was born at the parental plantation near Port Tobacco. His share of "Green's Inheritance" at his father's death was 57 acres, and on March 13, 1772, he bought the share of his brother, Raphael Green, and on December 2, 1773, sold it to Edward Green. On September 2, 1777, he and Joseph Green Thompson were sureties for George Thompson when the latter administered on the estate of his brother Samuel Thompson. Ann Thompson and Elizabeth Thompson approved the inventory as the next of kin. In 1778 he subscribed to the Oath of Allegiance in Charles County before Judge Samuel Hanson. In 1790 he was the head of a family with one male under 16 years of age, six females, but no slaves.

JAMES GREEN [4]

1738–1777

JAMES GREEN, son of James and Elizabeth (Dyer) Green, was born October 4, 1738, in St. John's Piscataway Parish, Prince George's County . He died intestate. His personal estate was inventoried on August 10, 1777, and appraised at £378/19/5, including four Negroes. Thomas Edelen Green and Joseph Clarke approved the valuation and the administratrix, Elizabeth Green, filed the papers at court on October 21, 1777. The final account was made on October 14, 1780, when the balance of £454/10/11 was distributed to the following heirs—the widow, and three children—Terry Green, James Ramon Green, and Mary Elizabeth Green.

BASIL GREEN [4]

17--1782

BASIL GREEN, son of James Green and his wife, was born in Piscataway Hundred ,Prince George's County. On January 18, 1780, he secured license in his native county to marry Mary Ann Lanham. On January 27, 1778, Basil Green subscribed to the Oath of Allegiance in Prince George's County before Judge Thomas Clagett.

He died intestate, when his personal estate was appraised on May 16, 1782, at £226/6/6 including six slaves. Thomas Edelin Green and William Langworth Bowling approved as the kinsmen, while Eleanor Green and Walter Boone aproved as the creditors. The papers were filed at court on June 11, 1782, by his administratrix Mary Ann Green. The final account and distribution of the estate were made on October 16, 1787, when the balance or £116/3/8 was divided among the widow and son James Green, the latter receiving a two-thirds share. At that time the administrators were William Langworth Bowling and Mary Eleanor his wife.

The son and heir, James Fairfax Green, was made an heir in the estate of his maternal grandmother, Mary Lanham, who died testate in Prince George's County in 1782. In the event, however, that he died before the age of 21, his share was to revert to the testatrix' daughter Mary Green.

LEONARD GREEN [4]

17– –1755

LEONARD GREEN, son of Leonard and Mary (Sewell) Green, was born at "Green's Inheritance," Charles County, and was a minor at the death of his father in 1733, but old enough to select a guardian—his uncle Giles Green. (14 yrs. law)

Children of Leonard Greene

1. Benedict Leonard Doyne Green, died intestate 1777.
2. Robert Green.
3. Martha Green.
4. Mary Anne Sewell Green.

His will, dated April, 18, 1755, was probated in Charles County on April 28, 1755. He devised to his son, Leonard, 100 acres of "Fenwick Manor" in St. Mary's County, and 75 acres of "Green's Inheritance." To his son, Robert, and the testator's brothers, Cuthbert and Francis Green, all the remaining part of "Green's Inheritance," also 100 acres of "St. Matthews," and 18 acres of "The Mount." The residuary estate was bequeathed to his four children—Leonard, Robert, Martha, and Mary Anne Sewell Green. He appointed Joseph Doyne the executor.

Joseph Doyne died soon afterwards and the administration of the estate fell first to Robert Doyne and Jane Doyne and then to Jesse Doyne and Jane Doyne, and apparently some irregularities resulted. Mrs. Teresia Milstead, the paternal aunt, championed the cause of the four orphans. At the January court of 1761 at her request citations were issued against Jesse Doyne and Jane Doyne concerning the concealment of sundry effects belonging to the estate of Leonard Green.

In March, 1762, Teresia Milstead, the guardian to Benedict Leonard Doyne Green and Robert Green, requested that the wardship be granted to Thomas and Daniel McPherson and reported that the orphans were seized of 100 acres of "St. Matthews" 18 acres of "The Mount," and 133 acres of "Green's Inheritance," all of which were in her possession.

Leonard Green, the son and heir, died intestate in 1777, apparently without issue, as letters of administration were issued to his sister, Martha Green, on May 22, 1777, with Henry McAtee and Edmund McAtee as her bondsmen.

CUTHBERT GREEN [4]

17-- ?

CUTHBERT GREEN, son of Leonard and Mary (Sewell) Green, was born at "Green's Inheritance," Charles County. On June 21, 1755, he sold to William Clements for 15,000 lbs. tobacco 147 acres of "Green's Inheritance," but no wife waived dower. By March 5, 1762, he had removed to Kent County, Delaware, when he disposed of his remaining interest in "Green's Inheritance," being an undivided third of "Green's Inheritance" which formerly belonged to Francis Green, deceased. No wife waived dower at this alienation.

FRANCIS GREEN [4]

17--1759

FRANCIS GREEN, son of Leonard and Prudence (Cooper) Green, was born at "Green's Inheritance" near Port Tobacco, Charles County. He married Charity, the daughter of Thomas and Mary Hagan.

Children of Francis and Charity (Hagan) Green

1. Clothida Green married Arnold Elder.
2. Benedict Green married Catherine ———. *q.v.*

On April 19, 1759, he conveyed to Robert Doyne for £50 a 200-acre portion of "Green's Inheritance," 400 acres of which was devised by his father, Leonard Greene, to his three sons, Cuthbert, John, and Francis, but John dying without issue in his minority he, Francis Greene, became possessed of 200 acres or one-half of the plantation. No wife waived dower.

His will, dated April 20, 1759, was probated in Charles County on July 10, same year. He bequeathed his daughter, Clothilda, slaves and livestock at 16 or marriage, but in the event that she died before that age then the legacy was to go to the testator's niece and nephew, Robert Doyne and Elizabeth Brent Doyne, children of Robert Doyne. In the event that his wife died, then his sister, Mary Livers, and Robert Doyne were to be guardians of his daughter. Furthermore, if his daughter died before 16 years or marriage other legacies were to go to the testator's two sisters (half) Jane Doyne and Mary Livers.

By an indenture made on January 15, 1781, by Arnold Elder and Clothilda his wife, of Frederick County, when they conveyed a portion of "Green's Inheritance" to Francis Edelen, of Charles County, it was shown that Robert Doyne, uncle to Clothilda Elder, and daughter of Francis Green, by said Doyne's will devised his portion of "Green's Inheritanec" to Clothilda Elder, then Clothilda Green, at the age 21 years, but in the event that she died without issue before that age, then "Green's Inheritance" was to be divided between Robert Doyne, the testator's son, and Benedict Green, the son of Francis Green.

LEONARD GREEN [4]
1712–1777

LEONARD GREEN was assigned the parental plantation "Green's Inheritance" in 1758 by his father Francis Green. His birth according to family papers occurred on November 8, 1712, at "Green's Inheritance." His wife was Clare ———.

Children of Leonard and Clare Green

1. Bennett Green.
2. Leonard Green, died intestate 1779.
3. Edward Green.
4. Elizabeth Green.
5. Henry Green married Sarah Coombs. *q.v.*
6. Eleanor Green married Charles Ferrall.
7. Verlinda Green, died spinster 1779, naming mother Clare and sister Clare.
8. Clare Green married 1781 Richard Coombs by Father Ignatius Matthews.
9. Jane Green.
10. Charles Green, *d.s.p.*

Leonard Green dated his will January 11, 1777, it being probated at court in Charles County on February 13, following. He devised his wife and his three daughters Linder, Clare, and Jean, as long as they remained single, his plantation " Green's Inheritance." The heir-at-law, Bennett Greene, was present at the probation and offered no objections to the instrument.

The inventory of the personal estate was signed by Verlinda Green and Henry Green as the kinsmen, and at the final distribution on February 7, 1778, it was shown that Charles Greene, a son of the deceased, had died before his father, but the son's personal effects were inventoried with those of the father. The balance or £718/10/6 was distributed to the widow Clare Green, and the following children all of age—Bennett, Leonard, Edward, Elizabeth, Henry, Eleanor, Virlinda, Clare, and Jane. Bennet Hanson Clements and Giles Green were sureties for the widow.

The personal estate of the son, Leonard Green, Jr., was inventoried on July 5, 1779, and appraised at £62/12/4, with Edmund Macatee as the administrator. Leonard Hamilton and Ann Hamilton approved as the kinsmen.

His widow, Clare Green, died testate in Charles County. Her will, dated December 23, 1793, was proved in Charles County on November 30, 1795. She named her son-in-law, Charles Ferrall and his wife, Eleanor; granddaughter Ann Ferrall; son-in-law Richard Coomes and his wife Clare, and their children Richard and Clare Coomes; grandson Francis Green; and her son Henry Green whom she appointed executor.

FRANCIS GREEN [4]

1716–1772

FRANCIS GREEN, son of Francis and Elizabeth (Wheeler) Green, was born November 5, 1716, at "Green's Inheritance," Charles County. The name of his first wife and the mother of his children is not known, but after 1756 he married Elizabeth ———, the widow of Anthony Simms. On October 19, 1768, as a resident of Prince George's County, he purchased 100 acres of "Atchison's Pasture" from Joseph Green Thompson and Leonard Thompson which they had bought from James Atchison on December 14, 1753.

Children of Francis Green

1. Benedict Green, born 1742, married Margaret Ann ———. *q.v.*
2. Philip Green.
3. Sarah Green married Simon Reeder.
4. ——— Green married Charles Sanders.
5. ——— Green married Arnold Elder.
6. ——— Green married William Waters.
7. David Green born 1756.

He died intestate. His personal effects were inventoried on April 22, 1772, and approved by Benedict Green and Samuel Green the kinsmen. His widow and administratrix filed the papers at court on August 28, same year.

The will of his widow was probated in Prince George's County on May 8, 1777, having been written on April 17, preceding. She appointed her brother-in-law Marmaduke Simms, the executor, and willed him all "land I hold or have any claim thereto." Legacies were made to the following: Mary Athy, wife of Elijah Athy, Margaret Naylor Simms, Mary Anne Simms, Rev. Benjamin Rules, Samuel Tills, Jacobus Clementina Bathilda Spalding, and the following widows–Anne Connor, Darkey Simms, and Mary Bowling.

Marmaduke Simms completed the administration of the estate of Francis Green on March 5, 1790, when it was distributed to the following heirs–Philip Green, Sarah Green who had married Simon Reeder, Charles Sanders in right of his unnamed wife, Arnold Elder in right of his unnamed wife, William Waters for the use of Anne Waters, and to Simon Reeder the guardian of David Green.

HENRY GREEN[4]

1726–1797

HENRY GREEN, son of Francis and Elizabeth (Wheeler) Green, was born February 24, 1726, at "Green's Inheritance." He removed to the Deer Creek settlement in Baltimore County, and there he married Elizabeth, the widow of David Thomas, sometime after September 20, 1746 and before July 2, 1748, when he and Elizabeth his wife filed an account upon the estate of David Thomas, late of Baltimore County, deceased.

On July 11, 1768, he and his wife Elizabeth sold to David Thomas, the son and heir of the said Elizabeth Green, for £150 a 200-acre portion of "The Three Sisters," which had been bought by David Thomas, the deceased father of the said grantee, from Isaac Butterworth.

Children of Henry and Elizabeth Green

1. Ann Green married Bennett Bussey.
2. [Son], predeceased his father.

By his will which was proved in Harford County on May 16, 1797, having been made on April 10, 1795, he devised his dwelling-plantation to his daughter, Ann wife of Bennett Bussey. Realty, Negroes and other personalty were willed to the following grandchildren—Mary wife of Henry Cooper, Jr., Elizabeth Green, Martha Green, Sarah Green, and Susannah Green. Bennett Green and Henry Cooper, Jr., were named as executors.

BENJAMIN GREEN[4]

1730–1808

BENJAMIN GREEN, son of Francis and Elizabeth (Wheeler) Green, was born January 15, 1730/1, near Port Tobacco, Charles County. He was a member of that Catholic emigration from southern Maryland to Baltimore County, now Harford, which began around 1747, when the Rev. Bennett Neale, S. J., established a mission on Deer Creek.

On June 18, 1763, he and his brother, Henry, purchased from Edward Mattingly, of St. Mary's County, several contiguous tracts, namely, "Francis's Delight," "Bond's Choice," "Bond's Beginning," "Good Neighborhood," and "Bond's Fortune," in all 603 acres.

In Baltimore County he married his brother's step-daughter, Elizabeth, daughter of David Thomas, who was born September 14, 1736.

Children of Benjamin and Elizabeth (Thomas) Green

1. Henrietta Green, spinster.
2. Leonard Green married Mary Wheeler; emigrated to Kentucky.
3. Elizabeth Green married Benjamin Wheeler of Thomas. License Feb. 4, 1793, Harford Co.
4. Benjamin Green married Mary Reynolds.
5. Mary Green married John A. Durkee.
6. John David Green married Rachel A. Clements.
7. Francis Green, *d. s. p.*
8. Anastatia Green married Bernard Croskey.
9. Clement Green married Rebecca Todd.
10. Sarah Green, spinster.
11. Teresa Green married Leonard Wheeler.
12. Eleanora Green married Edward Beaven; removed to Washington Co., Ky., before 1800.

His wife died on November 23, 1803. His will, dated April 4, 1808, was probated in Harford County, on April 26, same year. He devised his son, Benjamin, the dwelling-plantation "Good Neighborhood," and the residuary landed estate, but the testator's daughters, Henrietta and Sarah, were to enjoy the dwelling for three years after his death. Negroes and cash legacies were willed to the following children—Henrietta Green, Leonard Green, Ann Croskey, Clement Green, Sarah Green, Teresa Wheeler. Other bequests were made to his grandchildren—Michael and Frances Wheeler, with the residue of the estate to be divided equally among all children. Benjamin Green and Clement Green, his sons, were appointed executors.

CLEMENT GREEN [4]

1745–1796

CLEMENT GREEN, son of Francis and Elizabeth (Wheeler) Green, was born on April 11, 1735, at "Green's Inheritance," near Port Tobacco. He settled in that part of Baltimore County which in 1775 became a part of Harford County. He married Hannah Thomas, but died without issue in 1796. By his will he devised his wife, Hannah, a life interest in "Brooke's Cross," lying along the Little Falls of Gunpowder; then to his nephew, Clement Green, the third son of his brother Benjamin, who also received his uncle's favorite gun and violin. Other bequests were made to his niece Henrietta and nephew Benjamin, children of his brother Benjamin. Personalty was willed to Clement Bussey, son of Bennett, of Harford County, but no relationship was stated.

EDWARD GREEN [4]
17– –1789

EDWARD GREEN, son of Giles Green and his wife, was born at "Green's Inheritance" and in 1765 he augmented his seat by the purchase of 57 acres of the ancestral tract from William Green. During 1778 he took the Oath of Allegiance in Charles County before Samuel Hanson.

Children of Edward Green

1. Elizabeth Green, died spinster 1797.
2. Sarah Green, *d.s.p.* before 1799.
3. Wilfred Green, died intestate 1805.
4. Lewis Green.
4. Susanna Green married Richard Basil Edelen.
5. Matthias Green.
6. Joseph [Josias] Green, *d.s.p.* 1804.
7. Edward Green *d.s.p.* before 1799; wounded severely at battle of White Plains from which he never recovered.
8. Thomas Green.
9. John Green.
10. Mary Green married Vernon Smith.

His will, dated September 14, 1788, was admitted for probate in Charles County on January 26, 1789. He devised his son, Wilfred, the dwelling-plantation containing the home, while son, Lewis, received the other portion of the plantation. His daughters, Elizabeth and Sarah, were granted permission to use and dwell upon his plantation during their lives. Minor bequests were made to his children–Susanna, Matthias, Joseph, and Edward.

Letters of administration were issued to his daughter, Elizabeth Green, with John Clements of Jacob and Basil Edelen as her bondsmen. The final account was rendered on September 26, 1791, but no distribution was noted.

His daughter, Elizabeth Green, died intestate, when an inventory of her personal effects was taken on February 27, 1798, with Susanna Edelen and Lewis Green approving as the kinsmen. Distribution was made in 1799 to the following six brothers—Thomas, John, Matthias, Josias, Wilfred, and Lewis—also to Vernon Smith in right of his wife Mary, a sister of the deceased, and to Basil Edelen in right of his wife Susanna, another sister of the deceased.

The son, Joseph Green, died testate in 1804, and willed his brother, Wilfred, the house and lot in Georgetown, and minor legacies to his brother Lewis, and nephew Isadore Green, and referred to his uncle, Giles Green.

The estate of the bachelor son, Wilfred Green, was distributed in Charles County on August 4, 1814, to the following brothers and sisters of the deceased: Thomas Green; Mary, the wife of Vernon Smith; Susan, the wife of Richard B. Edelen; Matthias Green; and Lewis Green.

GILES GREEN [4]

17– –1802

GILES GREEN, son of Giles Green and his wife, was born at "Green's Inheritance." His dwelling-plantation was in the Upper Hundred of Port Tobacco Parish where he was a tithable in 1775. He subscribed to the Oath of Allegiance in 1778 before Judge Samuel Hanson. The tax list for 1783 listed him as domiciled on 96 acres of "Durham."

He married Elizabeth, daughter of Thomas Craycroft and Charity his wife. Their son "Joseph son of Young Giles Green" was made an heir in the will of his uncle, Benjamin Craycroft, of March 10, 1772. His wife, Elizabeth Green, shared in the final distribution of the estate of her mother, Charity Craycroft, on July 30, 1792.

Children of Giles and Elizabeth (Craycroft) Green

1. Joseph Green married Sarah Clements. *q. v.*
2. Benjamin Green.
3. Francis Green.

On August 7, 1780, as Giles Green, Jr., he and Charles Green received from Henry Neale for 5 shillings 243 acres of "Durham" lying in Charles County.

His will, dated September 29, 1802, was probated in Charles County on December 28, following. To his son, Joseph, he devised the dwelling-plantation "Durham." Other children so named were Benjamin, Joseph, and Francis.

MAJOR-GENERAL JESSE GREEN [5]
1766–1831

JESSE GREEN, son of Thomas Dudley and Mary (Simms) Green, was born June 6, 1766, presumably after his father settled in Baltimore Town. He removed to the State of Delaware, and from his journal and private books which were extant in 1910, it appeared that he was the first genealogist of the Green family, though some of his early assumptions were definitely inaccurate, for it was he who was the author of the statement that Governor Thomas Green married Helen Calvert, the daughter of George, 1st Baron.

It is stated in his journal that he was the personal friend of George Washington and "bore arms in defense of his Government during the Whiskey Rebellion of 1794." At this time he was apparently a resident of Alexandria, Virginia, for on May 24, 1796, as Jesse Green, of Sussex County, Delaware, he purchased lots in Alexandria from Jesse Semmes, of Fairfax County, Virginia.

He married first on July 16, 1790, Sarah, the widow of James Buchanan. She died on July 11, 1793.

Issue of Jesse and Sarah Green

1. William Green, born Aug. 8, 1791.

On May 11, 1797, he married Betsy Gunby, of Sussex County, Delaware, a daughter of James and Mary Gunby, the latter being a brother to Colonel John Gunby, a distinguished Maryland officer of the Revolution.

Children of Jesse and Betsy (Gunby) Green

1. James Gunby Green, born 1800, died 1814.
2. Molly Green, born 1802, married Jan., 1822, George Hall.
3. Emeline Green, born Mar. 1804, married ——— Long.
4. Jessie Green, born Jan. 21, 1806.
5. Alfred Green, born Apr. 4, 1808.

6. Thomas Green, born Mar. 4, 1809.
7. Julian Green, born Jan. 23, 1812.
8. Clarissa Green, born Jan. 13, 1814.
9. George Washington Green, born June 23, 1818.
10. Susanna Green, died infancy.
11. Catherine Roach Green, born Sept. 30, 1821.

His seat was on the Deep Creek tract near Concord. He served in the Delaware Legislature for a number of terms, and was once nominated for governor of the State. In 1808 he was appointed the Adjutant General of the State Militia, and during the War of 1812 he participated at the bombardment of Lewes. In 1827 he was commissioned Brigadier General of the Third Brigade, and on May 30, 1828, was promoted to Major General. During one of General LaFayette's visits to this country, he was a guest at the entertainment in Alexandria, Virginia. He died at his seat at Concord, Delaware, in 1831.

BENNETT GREEN [5]
1759– 18–

BENNETT [BENEDICT] GREEN, presumably the posthumous son of Francis Green and Charity his wife, was made an heir in the will of his uncle, Robert Doyne, in 1760. He removed to Harford County, Maryland, where on February 5, 1796, he conveyed to William Penn Ford, of Charles County, for £300 "Green's Inheritance" of 200 acres where "Francis Green now deceased formerly dwelt." Catherine Green, his wife, waived her dower interest.

HENRY GREEN [5]
17– –1813

HENRY GREEN, son of Leonard and Clare Green, was born at "Green's Inheritance" and was the executor of his mother's estate in 1795. He married Sarah, daughter of William Coombes. In 1790 he was the head of a family in Charles County with himself and another male over the age of 16, six males under 16, four females, and 10 slaves in his household. In 1778 he subscribed to the Oath of Allegiance in Charles County before Walter Hanson.

Children of Henry and Sarah (Coombes) Green

1. Sarah Green married ——— Murray.
2. Henry Green.
3. Jane Green married [Charles] Wills.

His father-in-law, William Coombes, Sr., dying in 1783, willed the latter's daughter Sarah Green " the plantation she liveth on and with my fense to the road which leads to George Boswell during her life then to her son Henrye."

On July 1, 1789, Joshua Coomes, of Charles County, conveyed to Henry Green for £17/11/10 the tract of land willed him by his grandfather, William Coomes, deceased, to Sarah Green wife of the said Henry Green, being 118 acres of "Coomes Hunting Place." On the same day Henry Green sold to George Lee 118 acres of " Friendship " and to Bennett Hamilton 82 acres of " Friendship," at which time his wife, Sarah Green, waived dower rights.

His widow died testate in Charles County and by her will, dated August 6, 1822, and proved on November 4, following, she bequeathed her estate to her three children—Sarah Murray, Henry Green, and Jane Wills—appointing Charles Wills the executor.

BENEDICT GREEN[5]

1742–1——

BENEDICT GREEN, son of Francis Green, of Prince George's County, settled in the Lower District of Frederick County, where he was domiciled at the 1776 census as follows: himself aged 34, his wife Margaret aged 35, with their children—Cloe aged 7, Francis 4, and Jean 6 months. With him was also his brother, David, aged 20. In 1778 he subscribed to the Oath of Allegiance before His Worshipful Oneas Campbell, of Montgomery County.

On November 16, 1779, Bennett [Benedict]Green, of Montgomery County, as the "heir of Francis Green, late of Prince George's County, deceased " conveyed to Marmaduke Simms, of Prince George's County for £20 "Atchison's Pasture " of 100 acres and also " Providence " of 36 acres of which his father died seized. On August 23, 1780, his wife, Margaret Ann Green, of Montgomery County, waived her dower rights on the two tracts.

JOSEPH GREEN[5]

1760–1826

JOSEPH GREEN, son of Giles and Elizabeth (Craycroft) Green, was born January 5, 1760 at the parental seat in Charles County. On December 27, 1792, he married Sarah, the daughter of John Clements.

Children of Joseph and Sarah (Clements) Green

1. Alexander Green, born 1793, died 1794.
2. Francis Caleb Green, born Apr. 27, 1795.
3. Maria Green, born Dec. 14, 1796, married ——— Coombes.
4. Elizabeth Green, born 1797, died 1829.
5. Joseph Green, born 1800, died 1803.
6. Sarah Green, born and died 1802.
7. John Alexander Green, born 1802, died 1803.

Joseph Green of Giles and Francis T. Clements on December 19, 1805, agreed to a division of their interest in the following tracts of land—"The Mount," "Clement's Addition," "Reformation," "William and Joseph" and portions of "St. Matthews," "Green's Inheritance," and "Thomas and Henry."

His wife died on September 10, 1803, in her 40th year, according to a Bible record. He and General Jesse Green, of Delaware, were interested in the genealogy of the family and correspondence dated 1822 was extant a few years ago between the two in which he was addressed as Colonel Joseph Green.

He died on January 4, 1826, according to his family Bible. By his will he devised his daughter, Elizabeth Green, all land that he had inherited from his father-in-law John Clements. The residue of the landed estate was devised to his son, Francis C. Green, and a minor bequest was made to his grandson Joseph W. Coombes.

SIMPSON FAMILY

Several members of the Simpson family were early settlers in Southern Maryland, but this history deals with Thomas Simpson, of St. Thomas, Charles County, who was in the Province as early as October 26, 1658. On the latter date he entered his hog and cattle mark at the county court. He transported his wife Elizabeth into the Province, and on April 26, 1662, he proved his rights to 50 acres of land for her transportation. At the same time he claimed 300 acres by an assignment from John Medcalfe. Among his land grants was a large tract of 1,180 acres patented in 1671 which he called "St. George's" on which several members of the Semmes family later established their plantations.

At a session of the Provincial Court held on October 7, 1665, Thomas Simpson and Elizabeth his wife were unable to travel to court, inasmuch as they were "soe weake that they are not able without great danger of their Bodyes to travayle to St. Mary's" to acknowledge a deed of conveyance of 100 acres of "Simpson's Supply" to John Smyth. They were literate, for both signed their names to the instrument.

In some manner he was related to Mr. Richard Willan, Gent., Lord of Snow Hill Manor, and one-time secretary to Governor Leonard Calvert and later a prominent attorney of the Province. On May 28, 1662, he appointed his "loving kinsman Mr. Richard Willan his attorney" to sue Francis Batchelor at the Provincial Court in the matter of debt.

Two sons have been proved, but that there were some daughters is highly possible.

Children of Thomas and Elizabeth Simpson

1. Thomas Simpson married Mary Matthews. *q.v.*
2. Andrew Simpson married Elizabeth Green and Juliana Goodrick. *q.v.*

On December 14, 1685, styling himself Thomas Simpson, Sr., of St. Mary's County, he deeded to his son, Thomas, Jr., for natural love and affections and the further consideration of 5 shillings "St. Thomas," a plantation in St. Mary's [now Charles] County, then in his possession and which adjoined Mr. Gerard's Manor of Westwood. On April 20, 1687, he conveyed to Robert Hagan, of St. Mary's County, for 5,000 lbs. tobacco, "St. George's" of 100 acres beginning at a bound tree of Mr. Marmaduke Simms.

No administration of his estate is available from the extant records, but he was living as late as January 14, 1688/9, when as Thomas Simpson, Sr., he made George Plater his attorney.

On November 9, 1708, Robert Hagan, Sr., of Charles County, Planter, and Elizabeth his wife, and Robert Hagan, Jr., eldest son of the said Robert Hagan, Sr., sold to Richard Edelen, of Charles County, for £50 plus 2,400 lbs. tobacco three tracts of land lying in Charles County, being three portions of "St. George's" adjoining the plantation of Mr. Marmaduke Simmes. One portion contained 100 acres which the said Robert Hagan, Sr., had purchased of Thomas Simpson, of St. Mary's County, Planter, by a deed of conveyance on April 29, 1687. The second parcel of 40 acres had been purchased of Thomas Simpson on March 9, 1695/6, and was bounded on an oak of Andrew Simpson which stood between the land of the said Andrew Simpson and Mr. Thomas Clark, and the third portion of 50 acres adjoined the dwelling-plantation of Robert Hagan, Sr., which was a moiety of the 100 acres of "St. George's" which had been given by Thomas Simpson to his son Andrew Simpson and which Robert Hagan had purchased from Andrew Simpson by deed of January 10, 1699/00. Both Robert, Sr., and Robert, Jr., signed the deed of conveyance to Richard Edelen, but Elizabeth Hagan made her mark.

THOMAS SIMPSON [2]

16– –173–

THOMAS SIMPSON, son of Thomas Simpson and Elizabeth his wife, was born in old St. Mary's County. On December 14, 1685, he received by deed of gift from his father the "St. Thomas Plantation" then in St. Mary's County, but later in Charles, which lay north of "Westwood Manor" of Mr. Gerard. No wife waived dower. About this time he had apparently attained his majority, for the next year he gave power of attorney to William Dent.

His wife was Mary Matthews, the youngest daughter of Thomas Matthews II and Sarah Boarman his wife. He and his wife shared in the lawsuit over the plantation "Hall's Place" which Major William Boarman had given his daughter in 1678. On September 30, 1703, he and his wife Mary with the other claimants conveyed their interests to Thomas Jameson.

Children of Thomas and Mary (Matthews) Simpson

1. Thomas Simpson, born 1695, married twice. *q.v.*
2. William Simpson, born 1700, married Rachel ———. *q.v.*
3. Ignatius Simpson, born 1708, married Elizabeth Mudd. *q.v.*
4. Mary Simpson [married James Williams].
5. James Simpson.

On October 24, 1706, he sold to Benjamin Hall for 3,500 lbs. tobacco a 50-acre portion of "St. Thomas" which had been granted to "Thomas Simpson father of the said grantor on June 10, 1671." On June 2, 1707, he conveyed 10 acres of the same tract to John Wathen, at which time his wife, Mary Simpson, waived dower.

On May 4, 1710, Raphael Neale and Mary his wife and Thomas Simpson and Mary his wife conveyed to Patrick Callahan for 3,800 lbs. tobacco a portion of "St. Matthews" which lay on the east side of Mattawoman Run or St. Thomas' Creek, extending to the land of John Sanders and then to the 100 acres formerly sold by Leonard Brooke to Francis Green.

On March 10, 1710/1, Thomas Simpson and Mary his wife deeded to Leonard Green for 2,000 lbs. tobacco a tract of land formerly taken up by Thomas Matthews called "St. Matthews" which had been sold and conveyed by Leonard Brooke and Ann his wife to Francis Green, father of the aforesaid Leonard Green, but by some defect in the will of Thomas Matthews, the patentee, the tract had become the right and property of Thomas Simpson and Mary his wife.

On June 9, 1713, Thomas Sympson conveyed to Richard Edelen two tracts of 200 acres which had been granted the said Thomas Sympson by his father. No wife waived dower.

On June 8, 1714, Thomas Simpson, Sr., in order to meet a debt of 4,000 lbs. tobacco placed a mortgage on his dwelling-plantation consisting of 50 acres of "St. Thomas" with Richard Edelen and Alexander Willson, Gent. The next year Alexander Willson died testate in Charles County and bequeathed his entire estate to William, Ignatius, James, and Mary Simpson, with Richard Edling (Edelen) as the executor. Thomas Simpson was one of the witnesses.

On March 4, 1718/9, he deeded 46 acres of "St. Thomas" which lay between his dwelling house and Pile's Fresh Swamp to Thomas Simpson, Jr., for 1,000 lbs. tobacco. On February 17, 1719/20, he and Thomas Simpson, Jr., conveyed to Gilbert Lewis for 5,000 lbs. tobacco "Hucklebury Swamp," of 100 acres. Sarah wife to Thomas Simpson, Jr., waived all dower rights, but no wife of Thomas Simpson, Sr., relinquished her third.

On December 1, 1730, Thomas Simpson, Sr., and Thomas Simpson, Jr., deeded to James Simpson for 1,000 lbs. tobacco 63 acres of "St. Thomas" which had been patented to Thomas Simpson, deceased, and which had been resurveyed for Thomas Simpson, Jr. Sarah Simpson, wife of Thomas Simpson, Jr., waived all rights.

No court administration of the estate of Thomas Simpson 2d has been found. From various conveyances it looked as if his plantation "St. Thomas" was entailed, so therefore he did not feel the necessity of a will. He was living as late as 1733 when he appears as a tithable in Newport Upper Hundred.

ANDREW SIMPSON [2]

16– –1744

The parentage of ANDREW SIMPSON is proved by the deed of Robert Hagan in 1708. Hagan in the deed conveyed the portion of "St. George's" which he purchased in 1699 from Andrew Simpson, it having been given "to Andrew by his father Thomas Simpson." His early life was spent at the head of the Wicomico, but after his marriage he settled in the Port Tobacco area where his descendants continued to live for several generations.

He married Elizabeth Green, the daughter of Robert Green. On November 9, 1702, his father-in-law, Robert Green, made him and his wife, Elizabeth, a gift of 100 acres on the main run of Portobacco Creek adjoining the plantation of John Thompson in consideration of a marriage already "had and solemnized" between his daughter Elizabeth and Andrew Simpson.

His wife died prior to May 19, 1718, for on that day he entered into a nuptial agreement with Madam Juliana Price, inasmuch as a marriage was shortly to be solemnized between him and the said Madam Price. He negotiated a bond to the value of £60, as witnessed by Charles Varner, Mary Simms, and Marmaduke Simms, and agreed to give Mary Price, the youngest daughter of Madam Price, for her education a Negro boy valued at £30. Robert Price, the father of Mary, had died in 1715.

Children of Andrew Simpson

1. Thomas Simpson. *q.v.*
2. Joseph Green Simpson married Elizabeth Keech. *q.v.*
3. Ann Simpson married ——— Clarke.
4. Mary Simpson married James Semmes. *q.v.*
5. ——— Simpson married Cleborne Semmes. *q.v.*
6. Clare Simpson, died spinster 1770.

His will was dated November 2, 1744, being proved in Charles County on December 2, following. He bequeathed Negroes and other personalty to his sons Thomas and Joseph Green Simpson, and to his daughters Anne Clarke, Mary Simpson, and Clare Simpson. To his grandson, John, son of Cleborne Semmes, he left 5 shillings. To his wife, Julianna, he willed three Negroes and bequeathed her the residue of the personal estate. Letters of administration were issued to his widow, with Joseph Milburn Semmes and William Hagan as her sureties.

By a deposition of 1745 Madam Juliana Simpson stated that she was 63 years of age and that her father was the late Robert Goodrick and that her former husband was Robert Price. Her daughter Clare Simpson died unmarried in 1770, willing Negroes and other personalty to her mother, Clare, and at her death they were to revert to the four sons of James Semmes.

THOMAS SIMPSON [3]
1695–1761

THOMAS SIMPSON, son of Thomas and Mary (Matthews) Simpson, was born about 1695, according to deposition. By 1719 he had married Sarah ——— who waived dower when he and his father assigned a portion of "St. Thomas." She is placed as the granddaughter of Thomas Jenkins who by will, dated November 1, 1726, bequeathed "unto my Granddaughter Sarah Simpson my Negro Woman Mary to her and her assigns." The account made by the widow of Thomas Jenkins on May 5, 1729, showed that the legacy left Sarah Sympson, appraised at £15, had been delivered to Thomas

Sympson, per his receipt. His wife, Sarah, was living as late as April, 1743, when she waived dower on the conveyances of her husband Thomas Sympson, Sr.—250 acres to Peter Wood and 190 acres to Richard Edelen.

After February 11, 1745/6, but before May 19, 1747, he married Mary, the widow of John Fanning, late of St. Mary's County. On the latter date, "Thomas Simpson and Mary his wife executors of John Fanning" closed the estate, reporting a balance of £147/6/8 to be divided accordingly to the will of the deceased. The ages of his children would indicate that they were all issue of the first wife.

Children of Thomas and Sarah Simpson

1. Andrew Simpson. *q.v.*
2. James Simpson.
3. Mary Ann Simpson married ——— Thompson.
4. Thomas Simpson married Charity ———. *q.v.*
5. Ignatius Simpson. *q.v.*

On April 6, 1730, Thomas Simpson, Jr., of Charles County, conveyed to the heirs of James Williams, late of Charles County, that is, John Williams, Thomas Williams, James Williams, Daniel Short and Catherine his wife, Justinian Williams, William Williams, and Gilburtus Simpson and Elizabeth his wife, for 5 shillings "all the interest Thomas Simpson has in a tract of land called "St. Thomas" containing 50 acres. No wife waived dower.

On October 16, 1760, Thomas Simpson, Sr., and Thomas Simpson, Jr., sold to Jacob Clements for £110 a portion of "St. Thomas" or 69 acres which adjoined the land of John Corry. Both grantors signed the deed of conveyance, while Charity Simpson, wife to Thomas Simpson, Jr., waived dower.

His will, dated September 14, 1760, was probated in Charles County on March 21, 1761.

To wife Mary Negroes and other personalty.
To son Andrew Simpson that part of the dwelling plantation whereon he was then living, but not to extend farther from the main road that leads from Piles Plantation to chapel.
To son James remaining portion of the dwelling-plantation on which "I now dwell" being part of "St. Thomas."
To daughter Mary Ann Thompson one shilling.
To son Thomas one shilling, having already received his share.
To son Ignatius one shilling.
Executors—Wife and son James Simpson.

The sureties for the widow and her son James were Justinian Burch and Thomas Ash. William Simpson and Ignatius Simpson signed the inventory as the next of kin.

WILLIAM SIMPSON [3]

1700–1784

WILLIAM SIMPSON, son of Thomas and Mary (Matthews) Simpson, was born in or about 1700, being aged 52 in 1752. His widow was Rachel ——, who is not believed to have been the mother of his children.

Children of William Simpson

1. Mary Simpson married Baker Brooke.
2. Charity Simpson married Thomas Lamaster.
3. Eleanor Simpson married —— Clements.
4. Elizabeth Simpson married Francis Posey.

On February 18, 1750, William Sympson, Gent., deeded 100 acres of " Keeth's Rest " to Baker Brooke, of St. Mary's County, in consideration for a marriage already contracted and solemnized between Baker and his daughter Mary. No wife waived dower.

At court on December 27, 1766, Mary Hagan, aged about 50 years, swore that seven years ago she lived at the home of Mr. William Simpson for about ten months and that he had a Negress named Bess " big with child and further sayeth that about six months after she left the house she came to see Mr. Simpson and the Negro had given birth to a boy called Tom who was a suckling at her breast." Furthermore, she was told by Mrs. Simpson, the wife of William Simpson, and Eleanor Clemens and Elizabeth Simpson, daughters of William Simpson, that Tom at his birth had been given to Elizabeth Simpson by her father.

Ann Jones, aged more than fifty years, of Fairfax County, Virginia, deposed that she was present when Bess was delivered of a Negro boy by Mrs. Posey, and that it was to be given to his daughter Elizabeth.

At the 1775 census William Simpson was domiciled in Newport West Hundred of Charles County, and in 1778 he subscribed to the Patriot's Oath before Judge John Parnham. His undated will was proved in Charles County on December 11, 1784, by James Simpson,

William Nally, and Walter Winter. He devised his entire estate to his wife, Rachel, during life and at her death the plantation "St. Thomas" was to revert to his daughter Elizabeth Posey. He signed the instrument as William Simpson, Sr. At the 1790 census his widow was living alone in Charles County without slaves.

At the August court of 1785 Rachel Simpson, executrix of the estate of William Simpson, had citations issued against Elizabeth Posey, relict of Francis Posey, and Thomas Lamaster and Charity his wife to show cause why they refused to approve the appraisement of the personal estate. The inventory was ultimately signed by Elizabeth Posey and Thomas Lamaster as the kinsmen on December 31, 1785.

IGNATIUS SIMPSON [3]
1708–1768

IGNATIUS SIMPSON, placed as a son of Thomas and Mary (Matthews) Simpson, was born about 1708, deposing in 1752 to be 44 years of age. On December 31, 1730, he purchased a 60-acre portion of "St. Thomas" from Thomas Simpson, Sr., and Thomas Simpson, Jr. His wife was Elizabeth, daughter of Henry and Elizabeth (Lowe) Mudd. By the will of her father, dated June 30, 1736, she received a two-year old heifer. She was likewise made an heir in the will of her mother Elizabeth Mudd in 1761.

Children of Ignatius and Elizabeth (Mudd) Simpson

1. Henry Simpson. *q.v.*
2. John Lowe Simpson. *q.v.*
3. Charles Simpson married Sarah Burtles. *q.v.*
4. Henrietta Simpson.
5. Monica Simpson.
6. Elizabeth Simpson, died spinster 1783.
7. William Simpson.
8. Ignatius Simpson married Thomasa Mollohan. *q.v.*
9. Mary Simpson married Richard Varden [Vanden].

On March 5, 1760, Ignatius Simpson, Sr., sold to Dr. John Corry 60 acres of "St. Thomas" which adjoined the land sold to Richard Edelen by Thomas Simpson, Sr. and Thomas Simpson, Jr. His unnamed wife waived dower rights.

He drew up his will on August 9, 1767, it being probated in Charles County on February 24, 1768. He bequeathed his entire estate to his wife, Elizabeth, during life, but if she remarried, then only her third. At her death the estate was to be divided equally among his children, that is, Henry Simpson, John Low Simpson, Charles Simpson, Mary Verden, Henrito Simpson, Moneca Simpson, Elizabeth Simpson, William Simpson, and Ignatius Simpson.

His widow lived until September 17, 1794, and was buried on the 21st, according to the register of Bryantown Catholic Church.

THOMAS SIMPSON [3]
1704–1766

THOMAS SIMPSON, son of Andrew and Elizabeth (Green) Simpson, was born at "St. Thomas," Charles County, about 1704, deposing to be 48 years of age in 1752. The name of his wife is not known. She predeceased him, for he made his eldest daughter the executrix of his estate.

Children of Thomas Simpson

1. Elizabeth Simpson.
2. Mary Simpson.
3. Eleanor Simpson.
4. Ann Simpson.
5. James Simpson, born Feb. 1747, married twice. *q.v.*
6. Henry Simpson. *q.v.*
7. Ignatius Simpson. *q.v.*
8. Thomas Simpson, born 1752.

On November 16, 1764, as Thomas Simpson, Sr., he conveyed to Abraham Cox a portion of "Green's Inheritance," lying on the main branch of Port Tobacco Creek and adjoining the land of Abraham Cox. The land had come to him as the eldest son of his mother Elizabeth Green. No wife waived dower. The conveyance was made to satisfy a judgment as recorded at the April Term 1765 of the Provincial Court. "Abraham Cox recovered against Thomas Simpson of Charles County, Planter, his Seisin of 100 acres of plantable land in Charles County which a certain Robert Green of the County aforesaid conveyed unto his Daughter Elizabeth Simpson by Deed of Gift."

His will was drawn up on March 31, 1765, and proved in Charles County on May 14, 1766. He bequeathed legacies to his four unmarried daughters—Elizabeth, Mary, Eleanor, and Ann. The residue of the estate was to be divided among all of his unnamed children. He named his daughter, Elizabeth Simpson, as the executrix.

The personal estate, appraised at £293/3/7, was approved by Mary Semmes and Charles Simpson as the kinsmen. The final distribution was made on August 19, 1767, by his executrix, Elizabeth Simpson, to the following representatives—the accountant, Mary Simpson, and Eleanor Simpson, all of age, to James Simpson aged 21 years February next, Thomas Simpson aged 15 years, and to Henry Simpson and Ignatius Simpson whose ages were unknown to the court. Thomas Hussey Luckett and George Jenkins were the sureties.

JOSEPH GREEN SIMPSON [3]

17– –1750

JOSEPH GREEN SIMPSON, son of Andrew and Elizabeth (Green) Simpson, was born near Port Tobacco, Charles County. At manhood he removed to Prince George's County, and there he married Elizabeth (Keech) Aulder, the widow of George Aulder who had died on August 28, 1737, according to the register of St. John's Church, Piscataway Parish.* On March 5, 1738, he and his wife closed the estate of her deceased huhband, George Alder (*sic*), when they reported a balance of £214/10/11 due to the three children of the deceased, namely, James, Bowles, and Ruth Hawkins Alder.

Children of Joseph and Elizabeth (Keech) Simpson

1. Thomas Simpson, born 1741, *d.s.p.* 1769, as his brother John inherited the landed estate.
2. John Simpson. *q.v.*
3. Sarah Simpson.
4. Andrew Simpson.

He died intestate in Prince George's County. The personal estate was inventoried on August 3, 1750, with his widow, Elizabeth Simpson, as the administratrix. Thomas Simpson and Ann Clark, iden-

* George Aulder was married to Elizabeth Keech on Dec. 16, 1729, by the Rev. John Fraser, rector of St. John's, Piscataway Parish. The births of their four children, as follows, were registered in the parish books: James, born Oct. 7, 1730; Bowles, born Jan. 5, 1723/3; Ruth Hawkins, born Mar. 24, 1735/6; and Mary Lindzy, born Oct. 12, 1737.

tified as brother and sister of the deceased, approved the valuation as the next of kin.

The estate was settled on August 23, 1751, showing £143 due to the heirs of George Alder, the late husband of the administratrix. The balance was distributed to the widow of Joseph Simpson and the following children—Thomas, John, Sarah, and Andrew—the "eldest about ten Yeares old."

On October 28, 1769, the widow and her son, John Simpson, who were seized of an undivided moiety of "Locust Thickett" of 500 acres agreed to a division. Both signed the agreement before George Hardy, Jr., and Fraser Hawkins.

The widow, Elizabeth Alder-Simpson, died testate in Prince George's County, her will being dated August 30, 1786 and proved on November 21, following. She devised her grandson, George Alder, 125 acres of "Locust Thickett" and the residue of the plantation was to be divided among her unnamed children. Wearing apparel was bequeathed to her two daughters unnamed. She appointed her son, John Simpson, and grandson James Latimer Alder as the executors.

ANDREW SIMPSON [4]

17— -18—

ANDREW SIMPSON, son of Thomas and Mary (Matthews) Simpson, was born at "St. Thomas," and in 1775 was domiciled in Newport East Hundred. In 1778 he took the Oath of Allegiance and Fidelity to the State of Maryland before John Parnham. He was not the head of a family in Maryland during the first census.

THOMAS SIMPSON [4]

17— -18—

THOMAS SIMPSON, son of Thomas and Sarah Simpson, was born in Charles County. In 1760 he joined his father in the conveyance of 69 acres of "St. Thomas" to Jacob Clements which would indicate that he was the son and heir and therefore had rights under the common law in the plantation. His wife at that time was Charity ——— who waived dower. By the will of his father, however, he received one shilling. In 1778 he subscribed to the Patriot's Oath in

Charles County before Joshua Sanders whose bailiwick was in Port Tobacco Parish. He is placed as one of the three Thomas Simpsons who were the heads of families in Charles County at the 1790 census, but he was definitely not the head of a family in that county at the second census. He was probably the Thomas Simpson who removed to Washington County, Kentucky, but who was deceased by 1800. In that year the heirs of Thomas Simpson were listed as tithables in the 1800 tax list.

IGNATIUS SIMPSON [4]

17– –1793

IGNATIUS SIMPSON, son of Thomas and Sarah Simpson, was born at "St. Thomas," Charles County. He settled in Port Tobacco Hundred, and there about 1750 he married Jane, the childless widow of Joseph Green. The latter had devised his wife his entire estate which included a portion of "Green's Inheritance." His wife, Jane [Joan], was living as late as March 11, 1773, when she waived her dower interest on a portion of "Green's Inheritance" which her husband, Ignatius Simpson, conveyed to Bennett Green.

Issue of Ignatius and Jane Simpson

1. Joseph Simpson.

He married secondly Anne Semmes, daughter of Ignatius and Mary (Doyne) Semmes. In 1788 Mary Semmes, widow, deeded two Negroes to her daughter Ann Simpson, and in 1798 Negroes to her granddaughter Mary Anne Pye, the wife of Edward Pye, but the Negroes were to remain in the possession of Ann Simpson, daughter to the grantor, during life.

Children of Ignatius and Ann (Semmes) Simpson

1. Robert Simpson.
2. Mary Ann Simpson married Edward Pye.

During the Revolutionary War he subscribed to the Patriot's Oath of Allegiance before Judge Richard Barnes. He is also placed as the Ignatius Simpson who served as a sergeant in the militia company of Captain Sinnett who lived in Port Tobacco Hundred.*

* Militia List, p. 59, Maryland Historical Society.

In 1790 he was the head of a family in Charles County with himself and another male over 16, one male under 16, three females, and eight slaves.

His will, dated September 6, 1793, was probated in Charles County on November 23, following. He bequeathed personalty to his son, Joseph, valued at £17, and the residue of his estate real and personal to his wife Ann during life, authorizing her to convey, to George Clements a lot in Port Tobacco whereon stood a store house. His two children, Robert Simpson and Mary Ann Simpson, were to possess the estate in fee equally but "if either of them died before their mother" then the survivor was to inherit the whole.

The widow married secondly Richard Mason, of Charles County, but before the marriage was solemnized they both agreed to maintain their separate estates. Mason was possessed of a large and valuable estate, whereas that of Madam Simpson consisted of a lot in Charles Town which she had bought of David Luckett, Negroes, and various effects. The contract was signed and dated February 18, 1800.

HENRY SIMPSON[4]

17– –18–

HENRY SIMPSON, son of Ignatius and Elizabeth (Mudd) Simpson, was born at "St. Thomas," Charles County. In 1775 he was a tithable in Newport West Hundred and there in 1778 he took the Oath of Allegiance to the State of Maryland under Magistrate John Parnham. During the war he served as a private in the militia company of Captain Benjamin Lusby Curry.* In 1783 he administered upon the estate of his sister Elizabeth Simpson. He was not the head of a family in Charles County at the first census. He probably was among the Catholic families which went west at the close of the Revolutionary War, for a Henry Simpson was a tithable in the 1800 list for Washington County, Kentucky.

* Militia List, p. 59, Maryland Historical Society.

JOHN LOWE SIMPSON [4]

17– –18–

JOHN LOWE SIMPSON, son of Ignatius and Elizabeth (Mudd) Simpson, was born in Newport Hundred, Charles County. In 1775 he was domiciled there and in 1778 he took the Oath of Allegiance before Magistrate John Parnham. In 1790 he was the head of a family in Charles County with four females and four slaves; at the second census he was likewise the head of a family, himself over 45 years of age, one male under 10 years, and female between the ages of 26 and 45 years.

CHARLES SIMPSON [4]

17– –1794

CHARLES SIMPSON, son of Ignatius and Elizabeth (Mudd) Simpson, was born at " St. Thomas " and was named in the will of his father in 1767. He married Sarah, the daughter of William Burtles who died testate 1789 in Charles County. Her share of the estate of her father was five shillings. The marriage was performed on November 19, 1786, by Father Henry Pile.

Children of Charles and Sarah (Burtles) Simpson

1. Joseph Simpson married Catherine ———. *q.v.*
2. William Burtles Simpson. *q.v.*

In 1778 he subscribed to the Oath of Allegiance in Charles County before John Parnham, and he also served in the county militia during the Revolution in the company of Captain Benjamin Lusby Curry.*

He died intestate in Charles County. The inventory of his personal estate was taken on September 17, 1794, listing four slaves and a total value of £267/9/6. Richard Varden and Ignatius Varden approved as the next of kin. Sarah Simpson his administratrix filed an account on September 29, 1796, and the final account and distribution were made on July 26, 1797, when the balance was divided among the widow and the two minor children—Joseph and William Burtles Simpson. The widow married Jeremiah Skinner.

* Militia List, p. 39, Maryland Historical Society.

IGNATIUS SIMPSON [4]

17– –1782

IGNATIUS SIMPSON, son of Ignatius and Elizabeth (Mudd) Simpson, was born at "St. Thomas," Charles County. In 1778 he took the Oath of Allegiance in Charles County before Magistrate John Parnham, and also served as a private in the militia company of Captain Benjamin Lusby Curry.* About 1788 he married Thomasa Mollohan, widow.

Children of Ignatius and Thomasa Simpson

1. Williamson Simpson, born Feb. 16, 1779.
2. Wilfred Simpson, born Feb. 9, 1781.

He died intestate. Letters of administration were issued to his widow, Thomasa Simpson; the inventory of the personal estate was approved by Henry Simpson and Elizabeth Simpson.

The widow died a few months after her husband. Her will was probated in Charles County on October 12, 1782. With the exception of Negroes which she bequeathed her son Wilfred, the entire estate real and personal was devised to her mother Mary Sinclair during life then to be divided among her children "as well as those by my first husband Mollihan and those by my second husband Simpson." The witnesses were Charles Simpson and Bennett Wathen. The appraisement of her estate was signed by Luke Huntington and John Huntington as the next of kin.

The estate of Ignatius Simpson was settled on November 27, 1784, when the balance of £67/1/6 was divided between the two heirs—Williamson and Wilfred Simpson. The estate of Thomasa Simpson was distributed the same day or £8/2/1 to the following heirs all minors—William John Mollohan, Mary Mollohan, Williamson Simpson and Wilfred Simpson.

JAMES SIMPSON [4]

1747–1789

JAMES SIMPSON, son of Thomas Simpson and his wife, was born February, 1747, being aged 21 in February, 1768. He married first a daughter of Fedelmus Simms who was deceased by 1776, for the

* Militia List, p. 39, Maryland Historical Society.

latter named three of his Simpson grandchildren in his will of that date, leaving them each one shilling and no more.

Children of James and ——— (Simms) Simpson

1. Thomas M. Simpson, married Judith ——— *q.v.*
2. Charity Simpson.
3. Mary Simpson.

He married secondly Catherine ——— who is placed as the mother of his four minor children at the time of his death.

Children of James and Catherine Simpson

4. Catherine Simpson, not an heir in mother's estate.
5. James Simpson, not an heir in mother's estate.
6. Benedict Simpson, heir in mother's estate 1833.
7. Gustavus Simpson, heir in mother's estate 1833.

On January 2, 1773, he leased to Duke Simms, Jr., of Charles County, for £100 and for the maintenance of his younger child for the term of 5 years and the yearly rent of one turkey a farm with tenement lying in Charles County except that part which was last year leased to Basil Knott.

In 1778 he took the Oath of Allegiance in Charles County before John Parnham. He also served in the county militia as a private in the company of Captain Benjamin Lusby Curry.*

He died intestate. Letters of administration were issued on August 11, 1789, to Catherine Simpson and Thomas Mathias Simpson, with James Simms and John Winter as the sureties. Charity Simpson as the kinswoman approved of the inventory. On August 9, 1791, his widow married Mark Simms. The final account on his estate was rendered on August 12, 1793, when the personal estate was divided among the widow and seven children of the deceased, namely Thomas M., Charity, Mary, Catherine, James, Benedict, and Gustavus, the last four being under age.

On November 5, 1801, Thomas M. Simpson conveyed to Joseph Green for £100 his portion of "St. Thomas" or 150 acres which he had possessed since the death of his father James Simpson. The conveyance did not include "one-third part thereof which Catherine Simpson widow of the said James Simpson had her right of dower in and which Mark Simms who intermarried with said widow now

* Militia List, pp. 39, 59, Maryland Historical Society.

dwells on." Thereupon, Joseph Green re-conveyed the land to Thomas M. Simpson.

HENRY SIMPSON [4]

17– –18–

HENRY SIMPSON, son of Thomas and Sarah Simpson, was born in Charles County. In 1775 he was domiciled in Port Tobacco West Hundred, and in 1778 he took the Patriot's Oath before Magistrate Walter Hanson. During the war he served as a corporal in the militia company of Captain Sinnett.* He was not the head of a family in Charles County at the 1790 census.

JOHN SIMPSON [4]

17– –18–

JOHN SIMPSON, son of Joseph Green and Elizabeth Simpson, was born in Prince George's County. He shared in his father's estate in 1751, and was made the executor of his mother's estate in 1786. As John Simpson of Green he subscribed to the Oath of Allegiance in Prince George's County before Judge Thomas Clagett. On January 4, 1794, he conveyed to Thomas Latimer, of Loudoun County, Virginia, for £275 a portion of "Locust Thickett" of 125 acres, beginning at the line of Elizabeth Alder's land, and also the portion which he, John Simpson, had bought of George Alder. No wife waived dower.

JOSEPH SIMPSON [5]

17– –1816

JOSEPH SIMPSON, son of Charles and Sarah (Burtles) Simpson, was born in Charles County. He was under age as late as February 15, 1799, when his stepfather and mother, Jeremiah Skinner and Sarah Skinner, filed an account with the Orphans' Court. If he be the Joseph Simpson who married Catherine ——— and begot seven children, he therefore married no later than 1800. On February 8, 1803, he filed accounts with the Orphans' Court of Charles County

* Militia List, p. 59, Maryland Historical Society.

as the guardian of John, Thomas G., Mary, William, and Clare Ann Hopewell.

Children of Joseph and Catherine Simpson

1. Eliza Simpson married Horatio Dyer, Jan. 15, 1819, per register of Bryantown Catholic Church.
2. Louisa Simpson.
3. Grace Simpson.
4. Alexander Simpson.
5. Caroline Simpson.
6. Mary Jane Simpson, born Feb. 1, 1807, baptized Feb. 8, Teresa Boone, godmother.
7. Maria Simpson married ——— Green, died Apr. 22, 1840, per register of Bryantown Catholic Church.

He died intestate in Charles County. Letters of administration were issued to his widow Catherine Simpson. The personal estate, listing 26 slaves, was appraised on October 4, 1816. The final account was filed on April 10, 1821, with the widow and the following as the representatives of the deceased—Horatio Dyer in right of his wife Elizabeth, Louisa Simpson, Grace Simpson, Alexander Simpson, Caroline Simpson, Jane Simpson, and Maria Simpson.

At the October term of the court in 1825 Alexander Simpson, Maria Simpson, and Mary J. Simpson gave their receipts to "Catherine Simpson administratrix of Joseph Simpson her husband as portions of their estates due from their father."

His widow died April 4, 1840, and was buried two days later from the Catholic Church at Bryantown.

WILLIAM BURTLES SIMPSON [5]

17– –1815

WILLIAM BURTLES SIMPSON, son of Charles and Sarah (Burtles) Simpson, was born at "St. Thomas," Charles County. He was a minor at the death of his parents and was placed under the guardianship of Ignatius Ryan, being a minor as late as June, 1808. Before 1813 he had married Eleanor, the daughter of Francis and Mary (Burtles) Simms, when he shared in the estate of his mother-in-law. His last wife and widow was Anne W. ———.

Children of William B. and Eleanor (Simms) Simpson

1. Robert Simpson.
2. Alemeida Simpson.

He died intestate, and the appraisement of his personal estate was filed at court on November 14, 1815, with his widow Ann W. Simpson as the administratrix. His widow married secondly William Murdock. No account was filed until June 18, 1823, when she accounted for a balance of $4,264.44, and after various disbursements, $2,807.42 remained for distribution to the heirs. On November 15, 1824, the balance was divided among the widow, Mrs. Ann Murdock and the two children—Robert and Alemeida Simpson.

THOMAS MATHIAS SIMPSON [5]
17— –1805

THOMAS MATHIAS SIMPSON, son of James Simpson by his wife Miss Simms, was born in Charles County. He died intestate in Charles County, when the inventory of his personal estate was filed at court on September 10, 1805, with Judith Simpson as his administratrix. James Simpson and Ben Simpson approved as the kinsmen. An account was filed by Judith Simpson on May 30, 1809, reporting a balance of $389.19, but no distribution to the heirs.

BOARMAN FAMILY

WILLIAM BOARMAN, the founder of the Maryland family of that name, arrived in the Province as a youth of not more than 15 years of age. His coming timed with the Civil Wars in England, when Royalists, Catholics and Anglicans were the subject of prosecution by the militant Puritans. His adventure to Maryland at 15, for he deposed to be aged 20 on May 28, 1650, and financing his own passage stir the imagination and create a desire to know the reason of his leaving the parental roof at so young an age. He was a scion of old Catholic house, for at a Puritan court in 1655 it was recorded that "William Boreman confesseth in court that he's a Roman Catholick and that he was borne and bred so." He was in the Province as early as 1645, for in that year he was on board a pinnace in St. Inigoe's Creek when certain clothing belonging to Cuthbert Fenwick who lived at the Crosse House was stolen.

From the Lord Proprietary he received a number of land patents, the total acreage amounting to more than 17,000. His most conspicuous grant was a lordship on "Boarman's Manor," of 3,333 acres, with all the prerogatives of a baronial court in accordance with the ancient feudal laws of England. The village of Bryantown in Charles County now embraces part of his manorial domain. Another large grant was "Brother's Gift" of 3,000 acres lying in St. Mary's County.

William Boarman was intimately associated with the Calvert family. And it is within the realm of possibility that he or his first wife, Sarah, in some manner was related to the Lord Proprietary. His 3,000-acre tract in St. Mary's County was given the significant name of "Brother's Gift" granted in 1674 during the reign of Cecilius, and only the Lord Paramount had the power to give or even grant land.

Upon Charles Calvert's, later 3d Baron, initial coming to Maryland in 1661, he was a guest in the manor house of William Boarman until he found suitable quarters. At that time his half-uncle, Philip Calvert, was in Maryland residence. In Calvert's retinue was an Irish servant wench, Nell Butler, who became attracted to one of

Major Boarman's black African slaves and insisted upon marrying him much against the entreaties of Calvert and Boarman who finally gave their consent. About 100 years later her issue who had remained slaves in the Boarman family sued for their freedom which resulted in an interesting court case and legal decision.

Prior to the rebellion of 1689 William Boarman was one of the outstanding men in the Province—an officer of the provincial militia, a magistrate of the local courts, High Sheriff for Charles County from 1679 to 1681, and a delegate to the Lower House of the Assembly from 1671 to 1675.* He acquired a thorough knowledge of the Indian tongue and was usually the official interpreter during political conclaves and other intercourse.

He fought on the side of law and order at the disastrous battle of the Severn in 1654, when the Proprietary forces were defeated by the usurping Puritans, with the result that the leaders were captured, condemned and several shot in cold blood by the insurgents. Somehow his life was spared, but the Puritan court which sat in judgment fined him 1,000 lbs. tobacco.

When Lord Baltimore regained his Province after a despotic rule of about eight years by the local Cromwellians, William Boarman received due recognition and on October 12, 1661, was commissioned a captain of the provincial militia. In the same year "four men out of Captain William Boreman's company" were called for Indian service. On February 8, 1667/8, the Council ordered Captain William Boarman to raise 20 men out of his company for an expedition against the Indians. By 1676 he had been promoted to major, for as Major William Boreman, he was ordered to purchase provisions for the army. In the same year he was summoned to St. Mary's City for a council of war which apparently resulted in the declaration of war against the Nanticoke Indians on the Eastern Shore for their atrocities. In 1678 he received 2,000 lbs. tobacco for his participation in that punitive expedition. At the time of the radical uprising of 1689 he held the rank of major and thereafter was always addressed as Major William Boarman. Being disenfranchised he retired to his seat on Boarman's Manor and late in life he sustained deafness, for on May 8, 1700, he was referred

* *Archives of Maryland*, vol. 3, pp. 490, 503, 553; vol. 49, p. 565; vol. 15, p. 153; vol. 17, p. 379; vol. 51, p. 344; vol. 2, pp. 239, 439; vol. 51, 246; vol. 15, p. 232, 402-404; vol. 17, p. 47.

to as a "deafe old man," but was commissioned by the Council to direct the laying out of the lands belonging to the Piscataway Indians.

He transported his first wife, Sarah, into the province, but her family name and with whom she came has not been proved. It was not until May 11, 1658, however, that he claimed land rights for her, stating that he had transported her about 1651. From time to time he transported a number of servants and free men and women to Maryland, for whom various land rights were accorded him in conformity with the decrees of Lord Baltimore to compensate those who financed the passage of prospective inhabitants. And it was not until April 1, 1662, that he claimed his 100 acres for his own personal emigration—some 22 years after the event.

His first wife, Sarah, was accordingly the mother of the older children. He failed to name all his children in his will of 1709, consequently there is the possibility of other issue, especially daughters whose names have not come down to posterity. There was a daughter Eleanor, for in 1695 Madam Elizabeth Young bequeathed property to "her goddaughter Ellinor Boreman daughter of Major William Boreman." On November 10, 1668, his wife Sarah waived dower when he conveyed land on Nanjemoy Creek, but on April 12, 1669, when he sold 150 acres of "The Hunting Quarter," no wife came. The estimated death date for his first wife can therefore be placed between those two events, and the marriage span of his first union as about 17 years.

Children of William and Sarah Boarman

1. William Boarman married twice. *q.v.*
2. Sarah Boarman married Thomas Mathews, Jr., and later Thomas Mudd. *q.v.*
3. George Boarman, probably *d.s.p.*
4. Mary Boarman, the Elder, married Robert Green. *q.v.*

By 1674 William Boarman had married Mary, the daughter of Dr. Thomas Mathews, of Charles County, who held baronial prerogatives on St. Thomas' Manor. Dying in 1676, Dr. Mathews devised his daughter "Mary wife of Captain Boreman" a portion of a 700-acre plantation on the Mattawoman and "Hill Freehold" of 225 acres in St. Mary's County. She was living as late as July 1, 1681, when Boarman and "Mary his wife one of the daughters of Thomas Mathews late of Charles County, Gent., deceased "conveyed to the

Hon. Philip Calvert, Esq., and Jane, his wife, for 15,000 lbs. tobacco Town Land commonly called "St. Mary's Freehold" on a branch of St. Inigoe's Creek which had been willed by Dr. Thomas Mathews to his son Thomas Mathews, since deceased, and to his daughter Mary Boarman.

Issue of William and Mary (Mathews) Boarman *

1. Anne Boarman married Leonard Brooke.

Before 1687, being again a widower, he married thirdly Mary Jarboe, daughter of Colonel John Jarboe, a French Catholic from Dijon, Burgundy, who had settled in Maryland and was allied with the conservative Proprietary Party. She was a maiden at the time her father made his will on March 4, 1664/5, for in the instrument he bequeathed his daughter, Mary Jarboe, personalty and mentioned land which had been given her by Marke Cordea. In 1687 Major Boarman claimed this land and prevented a sale of the estate of Mark Cordea by rights of Cordea's gift to his wife, when she was Mary Jarboe, thus proving his marriage to the Jarboe heiress.

Children of William and Mary (Jarboe) Boarman

1. Benedict Leonard Boarman, born 1687, married Anne ———. *q.v.*
2. John Baptist Boarman, born 1689, married Elizabeth Edelen.** *q.v.*
3. Francis Ignatius Boarman, born 1701, married Anne Slye. *q.v.*
4. Mary Boarman married (1) John Gardiner and (2) Gerard Slye.
5. Clare Boarman married (1) Richard Brooke and (2) Richard Shirbin.
6. Elizabeth Boarman married ——— Hammersley.

In the course of a lawsuit between Thomas Mudd and John Sanders, William Williams in 1693 deposed that he had been a retainer of Major William Boarman and recalled that Major Boarman offered 400 acres of "Boarman's Rest" as a dowry for his daughter, Sarah, if an engagement were announced between her and Joseph Pile. The latter did not materialize, so the 400 acres of

* It is reasonable to assume that there were other children born to Mary Mathews and that perhaps one or more of the daughters whom his widow, Mary Jarboe, named in her will of 1739 may have been actually step-daughters. Major Boarman was still married to Mary Mathews in 1681, and by depositions we have the approximate births of his three younger sons, all definitely the issue of the last wife, but if Francis Ignatius were born in 1701, Major Boarman was fully 71 years of age.

** For the history of the Edelen family, see, Newman's *Charles County Gentry.*

land were offered to Thomas Mathews, the son and heir of Dr. Thomas Mathews, of Portobacco. Williams at the time questioned Major Boarman, for he understood that the land had been promised to Boarman's son, George, but Major Boarman replied that he had other lands for his son. William Williams sailed for England and did not return to Maryland for six or seven years, at which time Thomas Mathews had married Sarah Boarman. He visited them at "Boarman's Rest" where they were living and he spent the night. It was the same plantation on which Thomas Mudd was then living with his wife Sarah.

By a land conveyance in 1713, it was shown that on July 16, 1679, William Boarman made a deed of gift of 450 acres of "Boarman's Manor" to Mary, the wife of Robert Greene, which they called "Greene's Rest."

Major William Boarman drew up his will on May 16, 1708, but it was not probated in Charles County until January 17, 1708/9, after the addition of a codicil on June 17, 1708. The witnesses were Joseph Pile, John Mudd, who is identified as a grandson, and John Wathen.

To his wife Mary whom he appointed executrix he bequeathed personalty and devised the dwelling-plantation "Boarman's Rest," but she was to pay his daughter Clare certain money due by debt from Ephraim Leverton of North Carolina.

To his son Benedict he devised the dwelling-plantation "Boarman's Rest" provided he kept it in repair especially the Catholic Chapel on the place; if he failed to do so, the dwelling was to pass to the next heir.

To his son John Baptist he devised the plantation "Lanterman" and the rents due from Edward Benson who held it under lease.

To his daughters Mary and Clare he bequeathed personalty and 400 acres where the Negro quarters were, being part of the manor.

To his daughter Ann Brooke he devised 500 acres of land which was to be taken up by his widow and executrix.

In the event of the death of his sons John Baptist and Francis Ignatius during minority or without issue, the survivor was to inherit the deceased's portion, and both dying without issue or during minority their estates were to revert to son Benedict, and the latter dying a minor and without issue, his lands were to pass to the other two sons aforesaid.

Overseers—son Benedict Boarman, Benjamin Hall, and Raphael Neale.

By April 7, 1711, the widow and executrix had married John Sanders and with him an account was filed at court; thereby legacies were paid to Benedict Boarman, John Baptist Boarman, Francis Ignatius Boarman, Clare Boarman, and to the following poor persons—Robert Green and Douzabell Semmes. To Leonard Brooke and his wife, Anne, £25 were paid.

His widow, Mary Sanders, died testate in Charles County, and by her will dated March 12, 1739 and probated on December 17, following, she bequeathed her personal estate to her sons—Benedict, John Baptist, and Francis Boarman; also to her daughters May Sly, Elizabeth Hamozley, and Clare Shirbin. Bequests were made to the priest who would officiate at her last rites and to the poor of the parish.

At a session of the Provincial Court in 1767, Thomas Bowling, aged 63, stated that "He knew Leonard Brooke who he always understood married Major Boarman's daughter and [he knew] Richard Brooke and his wife Clear which Clear was the Daughter of Major Boarman."

WILLIAM BOARMAN, GENT.[2]

1654–1720

WILLIAM BOARMAN, son and heir of Major William Boarman and Sarah his wife, was born about 1654 at his father's plantation in St. Mary's County. His father failed to mention him in his will, but as the son and heir according to the feudal law he acquired his father's lordship of 3,333 acres with all manorial prerogatives. He discovered, however, some surplus land or faulty boundaries, so before his death he petitioned the Lord Proprietary for a correction and the permission to add surplus land to his manor. The resurvey, however, was not made until after his death.

His first wife was Jane, daughter of Captain James Neale and Anne Gill his wife, whose father held lordship on Wollaston Manor. Captain James Neale dying in 1683 made his daughter one of the residuary heirs and bequeathed personalty to his granddaughter, Jane Boarman, but her father, William Boarman, was to retain possession until her marriage or coming of age.

Children of William and Jane (Neale) Boarman

1. William Boarman married Monica Turner. *q.v.*
2. Jane Boarman, died young.
3. Henrietta Boarman married Marsham Waring.
4. Ann Boarman married Joshua Guybert.
5. Sarah Boarman, unmarried in 1720.

After January 16, 1691/2, but before October 11, 1701, he married secondly Mary Pile, the daughter of Joseph Pile and Mary his wife, who was granted manorial rights on "Sarum." Mary Pile by the will of her father probated in St. Mary's County in 1692 was devised "Baltimore's Gift" of 110 acres. At an account filed at court on October 11, 1701, by Anthony Neale, one of the executors of Joseph Pile, deceased, William Boarman received one-fifth of the balance in right of his wife, Mary, a daughter of the deceased.

Children of William and Mary (Pile) Boarman

1. Joseph Boarman, *d.s.p.* 1730, naming mother and brother Thomas James.
2. Jane Boarman, born 1694, married James Neale. *q.v.*
3. Thomas James Boarman married Jane Edelen. *q.v.*
4. Mary Boarman married Luke Gardiner.

On July 17, 1712, in consideration of a marriage already solemnized between Joshua Guibert and Ann his wife, and for the love which he held for his daughter, Ann Guibert, William Boarman, Sr., made a deed of gift of 250 acres of "Ann's Delight" then occupied by Peter Montgomery.

In 1714 he deposed that he was 60 years of age and that he had heard Abraham Lemaster say that his father, William Boarman, Sr., had bought the rights of William Williams in the warrant for "Lanternum."

On November 3, 1719, he and Mary his wife sold to Benedict Leonard Boarman for 5,000 lbs. tobacco the tracts "Hardshift" of 115 acres which adjoined "Calvert's Hope" and also "Boarman's Rest" of the same acreage. He and his wife both signed the deed of conveyance.

The following is an abstract of the will of William Boarman, Jr., dated April 8, 1720, and probated in Charles County on May 23, same year.

To son William personalty and the land between the run and Thomas Jameson's great run where his mill stands, reserving the use of said land to the testator's wife Mary and the dwelling plantation during her life and then to son William in fee.

To son Joseph the tract between the lines of son-in-law Marsham Warran and son Josua Giurbert, and personalty.

To son Thomas James tract beginning at foot of run and running to the line of the manor, personalty.

To daughter Sarah personalty and use of orchard with 60 acres where Betty Prockter lived during her single life.

To daughter Jean personalty, 30 acres in possession of cousin Thomas Turner in fee and use of 60 acres of her brother Joseph's tract while unmarried.

To daughter Mary personalty and use of 60 acres of her brother Thomas James's tract during her single life.

To sons Joseph and Thomas James tract between son-in-law Josua Giurbert's and Joseph's great run equally. The upper part with plantation where John Glass lives to son Joseph. Said sons to be of age at 18, should either die during minority deceased's portion to survivor; should both die and without issue, their lands to three daughters—Sarah, Jane, and Mary equally.

To wife Mary the residuary estate and executrix.

His widow died testate in 1733, and left her estate to her children –Jane Neale, Mary Gardiner, and Thomas James Boarman, with a few bequests to the poor and the Church.

BENEDICT LEONARD BOARMAN [2]
1687–1757

Benedict Leonard Boarman, son of Major William Boarman and Mary Jarboe his wife, was born about 1687 in Charles County, deposing to be 58 years of age in 1745. Statements have been made that he married Anne, daughter of Baker and Katherine (Marsham) Brooke and the granddaughter of Colonel Baker Brooke and Anne Calvert his wife, but no documentation has been cited except perhaps that Richard Marsham, father to Katherine (Marsham) Brooke, in 1713 named a granddaughter Mary Boarman. A child of Benedict Leonard Boarman would actually be a great-granddaughter.

In 1698 Baker Brooke devised his daughter, Ann, the tracts

"Brooke Forest," "Summersett," and "Westfield" at which time it was evident that she was unmarried. About 1705, according to the rent roll, the latter two tracts were possessed by John Miles.

As Benedict Boarman was born in 1687, he probably did not marry until 1710 or thereabouts. In 1724 Benedict Boarman and John Parnham approved the inventory of the estate of Joseph Pile, 2d, as next of kin. Joseph Pile, 2d, left only minor children and named John Parnham as "brother" in his will. John Parnham had married Elizabeth Pile, a sister of Joseph Pile, 2d. Furthermore, two sons of Benedict Boarman in 1758 approved the inventory of Joseph Pile, 3d, as kinsmen. There was definitely some relationship between Benedict Boarman and the Pile family.

Children of Benedict Leonard Boarman

1. Benedict Leonard Boarman married Elizabeth ——. *q.v.*
2. Richard Basil Boarman married Anne Gardiner. *q.v.*
3. George Boarman married Mary Gardiner. *q.v.*
4. Joseph Boarman, *d.s.p.* before 1763.
5. Mary Boarman.
6. Eliner Boarman, died spinster 1795.
7. Jane Boarman, died spinster 1783.

His will, dated July 28, 1754, was probated in Charles County on March 11, 1757.

> To wife Ann the dwelling house and plantation during her widowhood; if she remarried, then only one-third.
> To four sons—Benedict Leonard, Richard Basil, George, and Joseph all landed estate; Benedict was to have part of "Boarman's Rest" where he was then living; Richard was to have the Quarters, being portions of "Rest" and "Enlargement"; George was to have "Standford's Field" being a part of "Boarman's Rest"; and Joseph was to have the dwelling-plantation after the death or marriage of his mother.
> Daughters Mary, Eliner, and Jane were to have 100 acres of land, if they remained unmarried.
> One-third of personal estate to wife, and certain Negroes to four sons.

On March 17, 1763, the three sons—Leonard, Richard, and George—agreed to the division of the land, being portions of several tracts which their father, Benedict Leonard Boarman, left them by will and testament. The divisions were recorded at court on February 23, 1769.

Jane Boarman died a spinster, and by her will dated September 20, 1779, proved in Charles County on April 26, 1783, she named the following heirs: sister Eleanor Boarman; nephews Francis Gardiner, Joseph Gardiner, Charles Gardiner, Charles Boarman, Benedict Boarman, Silvester Boarman, and Aloysius Boarman; nieces Elizabeth Boarman, and Elizabeth Boarman, Elinor Boarman and Mary Boarman, the latter three being children of her brother George; and the two children of Richard Boarman, that is, Catherine and Teresa, but of no stated relationship.

Elinor Boarman likewise died unmarried and testate, her will being dated July 22, 1794, and proved on October 12, 1795. Her estate which consisted chiefly of Negro slaves was bequeathed to the following: nieces Elizabeth Boarman, Eleanor Edelen, Mary Boarman, Catherine Gardiner, Monica Edelen, Ann Gardiner, Catherine Thomas, Teresa Boarman, and nephews Charles Boarman, John Francis Gardiner, Joseph Gardiner, Charles Gardiner, Benedict Boarman, Joseph Boarman, and Sylvester Boarman; to Hetta Edelen daughter of John Edelen; and to Newport Chapel. At an account filed on August 23, 1798, it was shown that William Thomas accepted the legacy willed to his wife.

JOHN BAPTIST BOARMAN, GENT.[2]
1689–1750

JOHN BAPTIST BOARMAN, son of Major William Boarman and Mary Jarboe his wife, was born in or about 1689 in what is now Charles County. His wife was Elizabeth, the daughter of Richard Edelen, Gent., and Sarah Hagan his wife. She apparently predeceased her father, Richard Edelen, who died testate in 1760 and who provided for numerous grandchildren—among whom was Raphael Boarman.*

Children of John Baptist and Elizabeth (Edelen) Boarman

1. Henrietta Boarman married Thomas Jenkins and Richard Thompson. *q.v.*
2. Richard Bennett Boarman married Mary Ann Hoskins. *q.v.*
3. Joseph Boarman, born 1733, married Mary ———. *q.v.*

* For the Edelen family, see, *Charles County Gentry*, by Newman.

4. Raphael Boarman, born May 1736, married twice. *q.v.*
5. Richard Boarman, born Dec. 1743, *d.s.p.* 1785, married Mary Ann ——.

On April 12, 1743, he deeded to his son, Richard Bennett Boarman, Gent., for love and 5 shillings three tracts of land—one called " Boarman's Intention " of 52 acres, " Boarman's Low Ground " of 50 acres, and " Boarman's Rest " of 233 acres. Elizabeth Boarman, his wife, waived all dower claims.

The will of John Baptist Boarman was dated April 25, 1747, but was not probated at court in Charles County until August 15, 1750.

> To wife Elizabeth the plantation purchased from Charles Smoot whereon I now live during life, then to son Richard.
>
> To sons Joseph and Raphael " Calvert's Hope " equally; Joseph to have the first choice, also the tract on Zachaiah Swamp near the old bridge called " Hazard " of 70 acres; if he died without issue or before coming of age, then to be divided equally between his brothers Raphael and Richard.
>
> To daughter Henrietta Thompson " Simpson's Supply " of 150 acres.
>
> To wife Elizabeth certain Negroes, and in the event that wife remarries, then son Bennett and Richard Thomson to be guardians of sons Joseph and Raphael until they attained 16 years; said sons Joseph and Raphael were to live with Richard Thomson to learn their trade.
>
> To son Bennett 1 shilling.
>
> To the poor 2,000 lbs. tobacco, and 1 guinea to the priest.

The administration bond of the widow and executrix was dated February 1, 1750/1, with Richard Edelen, presumably her father, and Richard Bennett Boarman as her sureties. At the valuation of the personal estate Benedict Boarman and Richard Bennett Boarman signed as the next of kin.

By February 8, 1752, the widow had married Barton Warren, who with her filed an account with the court showing a balance of £713/19/2. Distribution was made on July 31, 1752, by Barton Warren and his wife, to Joseph Boarman of age, born 1733; to Raphael Boarman aged 16 years May last; and Richard Boarman aged 8 years old December last.

Her will, dated July 3, 1769, was probated in Charles County on March 14, 1771, by Edward Edelen, John Smoot, and Charles Bradley, with the consent of Joseph Boarman, Sr., the heir-at-law.

> To son Richard Boarman tract called " Widow's Discovery," Negroes and other personalty.

To son Joseph Boarman Negroes and other personalty.
To daughter Henrietta Thompson Negroes and other personalty.
To granddaughters Elizabeth Thompson and Jane Thompson Negroes.
To great-granddaughter Ann Bradford Negroes and in the event that she died without issue, then to the next oldest sister or brother that may be living by her own mother Eleanor Bradford.
To grandson John Baptist Boarman £20 at 21 years.
To son Raphael Boarman Negroes and other personalty.
To the poor 1,000 lbs. tobacco.

The son, Richard, though married, died without issue and testate in 1785. He devised his wife, Mary Ann Boarman, the use of the dwelling-plantation during her life, then it was to revert to Raphael Thompson who was to pay Joseph and John Baptist Boarman, sons of Raphael Boarman, £193 each. His wife was also bequeathed one-third of the personal estate. Other bequests were made to Sarah Boarman, daughter of Raphael Boarman; to his niece, Henrietta Simms during life and then to her son Richard Thompson Simms; to his nephew, John Baptist Thompson; to Matilda, daughter of John Boarman; to his sister [sister-in-law] Eleanor Boarman; and others including the Church. His widow was apparently displeased with the provisions, refused to abide by them and demanded her " thirds."

FRANCIS IGNATIUS BOARMAN [3]

1701–1743

FRANCIS IGNATIUS BOARMAN, the youngest son of William and Mary (Jarboe) Boarman, was born in 1701, deposing to be aged 41 in 1742. He married Anne Slye, daughter to Gerard Slye by his first wife, —— van Swearingen. Her father dying in 1733 named his daughter, Ann Boarman.

Children of Ignatius and Anne (Slye) Boarman

1. Ignatius Gerard Boarman married Susanna Sewell. *q.v.*
2. William Boarman married Dorothy Sewell. *q.v.*
3. Francis Boarman married Beatrice ——. *q.v.*
4. John Boarman.

The will of Ignatius Boarman, Gent., dated June 19, 1743, was probated in Charles County on March 15, 1743/4. He devised his entire estate to his sons, Gerard, William, Francis, and John, at 18 years of age, with the liberty to dispose of their respective shares at the age of 21. He named Richard Brooke and Willeford Gremer as the executors.

At the taking of the inventory of the personal estate on April 27, 1744, John Boarman and Benedict Boarman approved as the kinsmen. On September 19, 1745, Richard Brooke, of St. Mary's County, the surviving executor, filed an account and reported a balance of £497/12/9.

WILLIAM BOARMAN[3]

16– –1729

WILLIAM BOARMAN, the son and heir of William and Jane (Neale) Boarman, was born at Boarman's Manor, Charles County. He married Monica Turner, the daughter of Thomas Turner and Elizabeth his wife, of St. Mary's County. Her father dying in 1696/7 devised her " St. Dorothies " of 300 acres lying on the west side of St. Clement's Bay, and also several slaves to her and her brother, Thomas, to be divided at the marriage of his daughter Monica. On June 25, 1714, " St. Dorothy " was resurveyed for William Boarman, Jr., and Monica, his wife, and was found to contain only 263 acres.

Children of William and Monica (Turner) Boarman

1. William Boarman, born 1710, married Winifred Edelen. *q.v.*
2. James Boarman married Mary Pile. *q.v.*
3. Elizabeth Boarman married as his 2d wife Roger, son of Roger and Elizabeth (Hutchins) Brooke.

The will of William Boarman was dated February 26, 1728/9, and proved in Charles County on June 30, 1729.

To son William and heirs " St. Dorothys " on St. Clement's Bay in St. Mary's Co., portion of tract devised by his father where his mother-in-law now lives; personalty.

To son James and heirs part of tract had from his father including dwelling-plantation where mother-in-law now lives, also 50 acres of " Coventry " and personalty.

To daughter Elizabeth personalty; tract near uncle Benjamin's to be sold and proceeds invested for said daughter.

To cousin Raphael Neale, Jr., personalty.

Residue to three children, with two sons as executors.

THOMAS JAMES BOARMAN [3]
17— -1785

THOMAS JAMES BOARMAN, son of William and Mary (Pile) Boarman, was born at Boarman's Manor, Charles County. During 1778 he subscribed to the Patriot's Oath before Judge Joshua Sanders. His first wife was Jane, daughter of Richard Edelen, of Lanterman, Gent., but she predeceased her father. The latter dying in 1760 devised 180 acres of "Boarman's Manor" to an unnamed granddaughter, the wife of Charles Boone and the daughter of Thomas James Boarman.

Issue of Thomas and Jane (Edelen) Boarman *

1. Mary Boarman, married Charles Boone.

It is also stated that he married secondly Jane Neale. The only Jane Neale who would fit into the picture seems to be the daughter of James and Jane (Boarman) Neale, who was unmarried at the death of her father in 1731.

Other Children of Thomas James Boarman

1. John Chrisostrom Boarman, 1742-1797, took Holy Orders.
2. Thomas James Boarman married Susannah Semmes. *q.v.*
3. Joseph Boarman. *q.v.*
4. Edward Boarman. *q.v.*
5. Sarah Boarman.
6. Raphael Boarman, born 1749, married Mary Boarman. *q.v.*

His will, dated December 19, 1784, was proved in Charles County on June 15, 1785.

To son Thomas James Boarman a parcel of land near his dwelling-plantation.

To son Joseph Boarman land between Marsham Waring and the line of Boarman's Manor.

To sons Edward and Raphael Boarman realty, Raphael to have the dwelling-plantation at the death of his mother; Negroes.

---

* It has been stated that Thomas and Raphael were likewise issue of his first wife Jane Edelen, and it was repeated in *Charles County Gentry*, but after careful study, only one issue of his wife, Jane Edelen, can be proved. Thomas Boarman spoke of Raphael as the son of his last wife. Furthermore, in his will, according to the English custom, he named or provided for his sons in the order of seniority by naming Raphael last.

To daughter Sarah Boarman Negroes.
To grandchildren Nicholas Boarman, Thomas Boarman, Rachel Boarman and Henry Boone Negroes.
To wife Jean Negroes and residue of personal estate.
Residuary real estate to four sons—Thomas, Joseph, Edward and Raphael.
" Son Raphael to pay unto His brother hence my son the priest John C. Boarman 500 lbs. tob. yearly."

In June, 1787, at court it was stated that Thomas James Boarman, Sr., died heavily in debt and permission was asked to sell his realty at public vendue. From 1789 through 1791 citations were issued to Thomas James Boarman and Raphael Boarman to show cause why they failed to file an account upon the estate of their deceased father.

His widow died testate. Her will, dated August 26, 1796, was proved in Charles County on January 27, 1801, with her son Raphael Boarman as the sole legatee.

LEONARD BOARMAN [3]
17- -1794

BENEDICT LEONARD BOARMAN, son of Benedict Leonard and Anne Boarman, was born near the present village of Bryantown, Charles County. During 1778 he subscribed to the Oath of Allegiance in Charles County before John Parnham. His wife was Elizabeth ———.

Children of Leonard and Elizabeth Boarman

1. Sylvester Baker Boarman took Holy Orders.
2. Joseph Boarman married Sarah Jameson. *q. v.*
3. Charles Boarman married Mary Edelen. *q. v.*
4. Catherine Boarman married Henry Gardiner.
5. Ann Boarman married Ignatius Gardiner.
6. Monica Boarman married John Edelen.*
7. Leonard Boarman, *d. s. p.*

On April 23, 1763, Benedict Leonard Boarman assigned to his brother, George, for 9 pistoles all the land which had been willed him by his father, Benedict Leonard, namely, portions of " Boarman's Rest," " Assenton," and " Boarman's Enlargement." Elizabeth his wife waived all dower rights. On May 13, 1785, he made a

* For the Edelen family, see, Newman's *Charles County Gentry.*

deed of gift to his son Leonard for three tracts of land namely " Calvert's Hope," " Hardshift," and " Boarman's Rest," all comprising 250 acres.

His will, dated October 14, 1791, was probated in Charles County on February 3, 1794.

> To wife Elizabeth one-third of the land and Negroes during life, then to his daughter Catherine Gardiner, the children of his daughter Monica Edelen, and Anne Gardiner.
>
> To son Joseph one-third of " Boarman's Rest," " Calvert Hope " and " Hardshift."
>
> To son Charles Boarman " Cold Turner's Addition."
>
> To daughters Catherine Gardiner, Monica Edelen's children, and Anne Gardiner " Boarman's Folly " and 20 acres at head of Holy Bush Branch called " Boarman's Rest " equally.
>
> Legacy to the poor of the congregation.
>
> To daughter Monica Edelen a slave called Mark.
>
> Executor—son Joseph Boarman.

On January 1, 1794, Henry Gardiner and Catherine his wife, John Edelen and Monica his wife, and Ignatius Gardiner and Ann his wife, all of Charles County, sold for £82/10/– to Joseph Boarman of Leonard their 3/6 undivided portion of all those tracts which had been conveyed by their father Leonard Boarman, Sr., to his son Leonard Boarman, Jr., by deed of 1785.

The will of his widow, Elizabeth Boarman, was proved in Charles County on October 10, 1794, having been dated June 30, previously. She bequeathed her son, Sylvester Baker Boarman, £5, with the residue to her children–Joseph Boarman, Charles Boarman, Catherine Gardiner, Ann Gardiner, and Monica Edelen. Other heirs were her granddaughter, Hester Edelen, and the poor of Newport Chapel congregation. Her son-in-law, Henry Gardiner, was named executor.

Their son, the Rev. Sylvester Boarman, died in 1812. His estate was distributed on December 3, 1814, to the following: brothers Charles and Joseph Boarman; the children of his deceased sister Catherine Gardiner; the children of his deceased sister Monica Edelen; and to Ignatius Gardiner in right of his wife Ann.

RICHARD BASIL BOARMAN [3]

17--1782

Richard Basil Boarman, son of Benedict Leonard and Ann Boarman, was born at the parental plantation near where the village of Bryantown now stands. He married Ann Gardiner, the daughter of Clement and Eleanor Gardiner, whose sister Mary had married his brother George. Clement Gardiner died intestate in St. Mary's County during 1746, but his widow, Eleanor, dying in 1760 willed 7 slaves each to her daughters, Ann Boarman and Mary Boarman, and appointed Richard Boarman the executor.

Children of Richard and Ann (Gardiner) Boarman

1. Catherine Boarman, born 1760, died 1812, buried at St. Joseph's, St. Mary's Co., married Major William Thomas, Jr., and became the mother of Governor James Thomas, of Maryland.
2. Teresa Boarman.
3. Ann Boarman, died unmarried before 1789.

It was Richard Boarman who had inherited some of the issue of the children born to his grandfather's black slave Charles who had married Nell Butler, an Irish woman. She had been brought to Maryland by Charles, later Lord Baltimore, who was living at the home of Major Boarman. Apparently, Major Boarman had been assigned the indentureship of the Irish servant, for she was referred to as a serving woman in Major Boarman's household.

In 1764 at the Provincial Court two slaves who called themselves William Butler and Mary Butler sued Richard Boarman, of St. Mary's County, alleging that he had detained them in perpetual slavery and that they were free born. A number of interesting depositions was made.

Edward Edelen, aged 50, deposed on May 27, 1767, that he had heard his father, Richard Edelen, say a few years before he died, which was seven years the next fall, that he was 89 years old and that he had heard his father say that the latter went to Major Boarman one morning and when he arrived Lord Baltimore was there "and then lived there," and he heard Lord Baltimore ask for Eleanor Butler, a servant woman. When the servant came, Lord Baltimore said, "I understand you are going to be married to Day to negro Charles. What a pity so likely a young girl as you are should fling herself away, so as to marry a Negro. You will make slaves of your children." To which the Irish wench replied, "I rather marry Charles than your Lordship." Other remarks by the wench were quoted which were not very complimentary to Charles Calvert. Richard Edelen, Sr., did not remain for the wedding, which Edward Edelen, the deponent, understood occurred that day. He furthermore stated that his sister, who had married one of the Boarmans, possessed some of the descendants of Nell Butler.

John Jordan Smith on September 12, 1787, then aged 85, swore that he was acquainted with Ellener Butteler, an Irish woman, and negro Charles, and that they lived together for several years and had three children—John, Sarah, and Catherine. That they all lived on the plantation of Major Boarman and that the woman used to come to his father's house to wash for the family.

Jane Howard, aged about 70, deposed that when she was a girl, she frequented the home of Major Boarman whose wife was her godmother and knew two mulatto slaves, Jack about 20 years of age, and a "well grown young husky wench named Kate." She always understood that they were the children of a slave Charles and an Irish woman Nell.

The court decided in favor of the complainants. While issue sired by a free man of a slave woman were declared to be slave, those sired by a slave of a free woman were not decreed to be in bondage. William and Mary Butler were not only declared free, but the court ordered Richard Boarman to pay damages.

Richard Boarman's will, dated April 12, 1777, was not probated in St. Mary's County until August 8, 1782.

To wife Ann £50 over and above what she is entitled to and one mare.

To daughters Catherine and Teresa Boarman personalty.

To daughter Ann Boarman one horse at the age of 12 years.

To sisters Eleanor Boarman and Jane Boarman during life tract of land then in their possession, being part of "Boarman's Rest" and at their death to my nephew Benedict Boarman son of my brother George Boarman, deceased.

To nephew Benedict Boarman of George "The Enlargement Amended."

In event that his daughters died without issue then their land to revert to their aunt, Mary Boarman's daughters—Elizabeth, Elener, and Mary Boarman.

To St. Joseph's Chapel £20.

The final distribution of the legacies was made on December 22, 1789, at which time it was shown that the daughter, Ann, had died, and also the horse which had been willed to his daughter Teresa. The legatees were the widow, and the daughters, Teresa Boarman and Catherine who was the wife of William Thomas.

The widow died within a few years thereafter, for her estate was settled on February 22, 1792, in St. Mary's County by her son-in-law and administrator, William Thomas, when the balance was divided equally between the two heirs – Catherine, the wife of William Thomas, and Teresa Boarman.

GEORGE BOARMAN [3]
17– –1768

GEORGE BOARMAN, son of Benedict Leonard and Ann Boarman, was born near Bryantown in Charles County. He married Mary, the daughter of Clement Gardiner.

Children of George and Mary (Gardiner) Boarman

1. Benedict Boarman. *q.v.*
2. Aloysius Boarman *d.s.p.* 1796.
3. Elizabeth Boarman died spinster 1825.
4. Eleanor Boarman married Edward Edelen,* Feb. 12, 1782, by Rev. John Bolton.
5. Mary Boarman died spinster 1807.

Dying in 1768, his will was dated April 7 of that year and proved in Charles County on July 5, following, by Leonard Boarman, Eleanor Boarman, and James Boarman.

To wife Mary Boarman one working Negro above her third.
To son Benedict parts of the dwelling-plantation " Boarman's Rest " and " Hard Shift."
To son Aloysius part of " Richlands " in St. Mary's Co. bought of the testator's brother Richard Basil Boarman.
To daughters Elizabeth Boarman, Eleanor Boarman, and Mary Boarman Negroes.
Residuary estate to five children equally—Benedict, Aloysius, Elizabeth, Eleanor, and Mary.
To the poor of the parish, 1,000 lbs. tobacco.

---

* For Edelen family, see, Newman's *Charles County Gentry*.

His spinster daughter, Mary Boarman, willed at her death in 1807 her moiety of "Indian Quarter" to her sister, Elizabeth Boarman, and bequeathed a legacy to her nephew Elston Edelen. Her brother, Benedict Boarman, was appointed executor.

Aloysius, their son, died without issue in 1796, his will being dated 1786. He devised a portion of "St. John's" in St. Mary's County to his mother during life then to his sister Elizabeth Boarman. Other heirs were his brother Benedict and his three sisters.

Elizabeth Boarman, the unmarried daughter, drew up her will on April 18, 1825, it being probated in Charles County on November 10, with her nephew George Edelen as the executor. She devised her nephew, Elston A. Edelen, 89 acres of "Indian Quarter," lying on the east side of Gilbert Swamp. To her nephew Elston A. Edelen's children, namely, Joseph and Elizabeth Edelen, and her nephew Richard B. Boarman she willed "Simmes Fragments," formerly a part of "St. George's," containing 103 acres. In the event that her nephew, Richard Boarman, should inherit certain land belonging to his sister, Catherine Boarman, then Richard's share was to go to the testatrix' nephew, Aloysius I. Edelen. Her carriage and horses were bequeathed to her nephew, George Edelen. For the education of Jane Edelen, the daughter of her nephew, George Edelen, she left $200. She named her nephew, Aloysius I. Edelen, and Mrs. Mary Fenwick as the executors, but they evidently refused to act, as letters of administration were issued to George Edelen.

RICHARD BENNETT BOARMAN [3]

17--1758

RICHARD BENNETT BOARMAN, son of John Baptist and Elizabeth (Edelen) Boarman, was born in Charles County. His wife was Mary Ann Hoskins, daughter of Bennett and Eleanor (Neale) Hoskins, and the granddaughter of Raphael Neale. He and his wife as the heirs of her deceased mother shared on July 10, 1754, in the partition of Raphael Neale's portion of Wollaston Manor among the six coheiresses or their representatives.

Children of Bennett and Mary Ann (Hoskins) Boarman

1. Raphael Boarman married twice. *q.v.*
2. Eleanor Boarman, born 1745, married Henry Bradford.
3. Elizabeth Boarman married James Neale. *q.v.*

4. Richard Bennett Boarman, *d.s.p.* testate 1785.
5. Mary Ann Boarman.
6. John Hoskins Boarman married Sarah Teresia Neale. *q.v.*

His will was drawn up on September 14, 1752, and probated at court in Charles County on July 8, 1758.

> To wife Mary Ann during life half of the dwelling-plantation being portions of "Calvert's Hope," "Boarman's Rest," and "Boarman's Low Ground."
>
> To brothers Joseph and Raphael Boarman all right to land left them by my father John Baptist Boarman.
>
> To wife and daughters Eleander Boarman and Elizabeth Boarman and son Raphael Boarman Negroes.
>
> To son Richard Bennett Boarman Negroes and the dwelling-plantation.
>
> To son Raphael Boarman 150 acres of "Calvert's Hope" where Thomas Reed formerly lived and also 110 acres of "St. George's," also 150 acres of land in possession of Richard Thompson whereon James Short then lived.
>
> Residue of estate equally to four children—Raphael, Eleanor, Elizabeth, and Richard Bennett.

At the probation the widow, Mary Ann Boarman, renounced the provisions and demanded her thirds. It was furthermore stated that the heir-at-law was a minor and not present at the probate. The final distribution of the personal estate was made on July 21, 1767, by his widow, Mary Ann Boarman, with legacies paid to the following children—Eleanor Bradford, Raphael Boarman, Elizabeth Neale, and Richard Bennett Boarman.

On May 5, 1779, Mary Ann Boarman, the widow of Richard Bennett Boarman, made a deed of gift to her son, Richard Bennett, of "Boarman's Help" and "Boarman's Enlargement."

Their bachelor son, Richard Bennett Boarman, dated his will November 18, 1776, it being proved in Charles County on November 3, 1785. He devised his mother, Mary Ann Boarman, the use of his plantations "Boarman's Rest," "Calvert's Hope" and "Boarman's Enlargement," and in the event that his sister, Mary Ann Boarman, was not married at the death of his mother then his sister was to enjoy the plantation during her single life. Other heirs were brothers Raphael Boarman and John Hoskins Boarman, nieces Eleanor Bradford and Eleanor Neale, and schooling was provided for his godson Joseph Boarman. The witnesses were Gerard Boarman, Henrietta Thompson, and Raphael Boarman. At the probation Henrietta Thompson was then Mrs. Henrietta Semmes.

Their son, Richard Bennett Boarman, though he married, died without issue in 1785, making the following bequests:

> To wife Mary Ann during widowhood the dwelling-plantation and at her death to Raphael Thompson who was to pay Joseph and John Baptist Boarman, sons of Raphael, £193 each.
>
> To wife one-third of personal estate before payment of debts and legacies.
>
> Personalty to godson James Neale of James, Sarah Boarman, daughter of Raphael Boarman, chapel at Cobb Neck, priest who buried him, niece Henrietta Semmes, nephew John Baptist Boarman, Matilda Boarman, daughter of John Boarman, sister Eleanor Boarman.

At the probation by the executors, John Baptist Boarman and the widow of the deceased, the latter claimed her third in the landed estate.

The will of Mary Ann Boarman, widow of Bennett, was dated January 4, 1792, and probated in Charles County, on May 7, following. To her son, John Hoskins Boarman she devised one-half of the tract " Boarman's Enlargement " which was not conveyed to her by her son Richard Bennett Boarman. A number of Negro slaves were bequeathed to her children, namely, John Hoskins Boarman, Mary Ann Boarman, Eleanor Bradford, and Elizabeth Neale; also to her grandchildren, namely, Polly Bradford, Nancy Bradford, Eleanor, daughter of John Hoskins Boarman, Nancy, daughter of Ralph Boarman, Polly Neale, and Elizabeth Neale. The residuary estate was willed to her children—Raphael Boarman, Elinor Bradford, Elizabeth Neale, John Hoskins Boarman, and Mary Ann Boarman.

JOSEPH BOARMAN [3]

1733–180–

JOSEPH BOARMAN, son of John Baptist and Elizabeth (Edelen) Boarman, was born 1733 at " Boarman's Manor," Charles County. He settled in Prince George's County, and at the census of St. John's Parish in 1776 he was aged 44 years with males in his household aged 21, 18, 15, and 10 respectively. His wife Mary was aged 40. Fourteen slaves were listed. In that county he subscribed to the Oath of Allegiance in 1778 before Magistrate William Lyles, Jr.

Children of Joseph and Mary Boarman

1. Joseph Boarman.
2. Raphael W. Boarman.
3. Richard Bennett Aloysius Boarman, married Eleanor Pile Boarman. *q.v.*

On December 19, 1758, as of Prince George's County, he conveyed to John Bowling, of Charles County, for £70 a 175-acre portion of "Piscataway Manor." Mary, his wife, waived dower. On January 1, 1759, he sold to John Hoskins Boarman, of Charles County, for love and natural affections and the further consideration of 5 shillings a 200-acre portion of "Calvert's Hope" which had been willed him by his father. Mary, his wife, waived her interest.

At the 1800 census with 28 slaves he was the only Boarman the head of a family in Prince George's County. He was deceased by August, 1803.

On August 6, 1803, Joseph Boarman, Raphael Boarman, and Richard Bennett Aloysius Boarman, sons of the late Joseph Boarman, Sr., all of Prince George's County, and Joseph Boarman and John Baptist Boarman, sons of the late Raphael Boarman, of Charles County, conveyed to William Barton Smoot an undivided portion of "Boarman's Hazard." Their fathers had agreed to sell this tract of land to Smoot, but had died before the formal conveyance.

On September 15, 1808, Joseph Boarman and Raphael Boarman of Prince George's County negotiated a bond with Richard Boarman for £1,000, setting forth that, whereas Joseph Boarman, the father of the above Joseph and Raphael, died intestate and whereas the estate descended to his three sons—Joseph, Raphael, and Richard—they agreed to a division of the realty namely "The Point" and "The Ridge" bought of Catherine Cox and which had not been fully paid at the time of their father's death. It was stated that the personal estate had already been divided equally among them.

RAPHAEL BOARMAN [3]

1736–1781

RAPHAEL BOARMAN, son of John Baptist and Elizabeth (Edelen) Boarman, was born May, 1736, being 16 in 1752. The name of his first wife is not known. He married secondly Eleanor, daughter of William and Ann (Brooke) Neale, and the widow of John Holme, by whom there was no issue. In 1778 he subscribed to the Oath of Allegiance in Charles County before Magistrate John Parnham.

Children of Raphael Boarman

1. Elizabeth Boarman married ——— Underwood.
2. Rebecca Boarman married 1790 George Edelen.*
3. Julianna Boarman.
4. Sarah Boarman married ——— Barrett.
5. Joseph Boarman married Jean Cordelia Edelen. *q.v.*
6. John Baptist Boarman, *d.s.p.* D.C. 1813.

His will was drawn up on June 25, 1781, and probated in Charles County on December 11, following:

To wife Eleanor Boarman one-third of the personal estate.

To children—Elizabeth, Rebecca, Julianna, Sarah, Joseph, and John Baptist Boarman one slave each at 16 years of age.

To sons Joseph and John Baptist parts of " Calvert's Hope " and " Boarman's Hazard " equally.

In the event that court action be brought by the orphans of Mr. Holmes or any person for them for " my wife's dower or third part of Mr. Holmes' estate " executors were to draw sufficient money and tobacco from estate to maintain a suit according to equity and justice.

Residuary estate to his six children when the eldest daughter attained 16; sons to have their estates at 18, with his brothers Joseph Boarman and Richard Boarman as guardian to his children.

Executors—Wife and brothers Joseph and Richard Boarman.

At the probation the widow, Eleanor Boarman, refused to act as executrix and demanded her " thirds " in the landed estate. Her will, dated December 24, 1800, was probated in Charles County on January 20, 1801; she left her entire estate to her children–Richard, Mary, and William Holmes.

The bachelor son, John Baptist Boarman, resided in Washington City, where he died testate. His will, dated February 10, 1813, was proved on May 15, following.

To his friend and cousin Raphael W. Boarman, of Georgetown, two tracts of land in Charles Co., " Addition to Comree " and " Bachelor's Hope " purchased of George R. Leiper, of

* For the Edelen family, see, Newman's *Charles County Gentry.*

Prince George's Co., provided that the said Raphael Boarman would deliver to " my nephew Raphael Horace Boarman, of Chas. Co." his bond dated Nov. 30, 1811, to be destroyed and provided that Raphael W. Boarman exonerates " my heirs " from all claim from George R. Leiper.

To nephew Raphael Boarman lot on Bridge St. in Georgetown.

To sister Rebecca Edelen personalty.

To sister Sarah Barrett legacy and also to her four children—Francis Barrett, Catherine Barrett, Sarah Ann Maria Barrett, and Julian Barrett.

To sister Elizabeth Underwood of Charles Co. and her children unnamed legacies.

Executor—friend and cousin Raphael W. Boarman.

IGNATIUS GERARD BOARMAN [3]
1728–1799

IGNATIUS GERARD BOARMAN, son of Francis Ignatius and Ann (Slye) Boarman, was born about 1728 in Charles County, deposing to be 45 years of age in 1773. During 1778 he subscribed to the Oath of Allegiance in Charles County before Magistrate John Parnham.

His wife was Susanna Sewell, daughter of Clement and Mary (Smith) Sewell. Madam Mary Sewell, his mother-in-law, by will of 1761, bequeathed her daughter, Susanna Boarman, one-half of her wearing apparel and one-half of all household and kitchen furniture. And to her grandson, Clement Boarman, she bequeathed 3,500 lbs. tobacco to purchase a Negro girl, but her son-in-law, Gerard Boarman, was to enjoy the use of her services until the grandson attained legal age.

Children of Gerard and Susanna (Sewell) Boarman

1. Clement Boarman, apparently predeceased his father.
2. Ann Boarman married Francis Queen.
3. Mary Boarman married ——— Wight.
4. Gerard Sewell Boarman married twice. *q.v.*

His will, dated December 11, 1799, was probated in Prince George's County, on December 31, same year. Other than several legacies to the poor and the Church, he bequeathed his entire personal estate to his son-in-law Francis Queen, and his three children—Ann Queen, Mary Wight, and Gerard Boarman.

WILLIAM BOARMAN [3]

17– –1780

WILLIAM BOARMAN, son of Francis Ignatius and Anne (Slye) Boarman, was born in Charles County. He married Dorothy, daughter of Clement and Mary (Smith) Sewell. His mother-in-law, Madam Mary Sewell, by her will dated and proved in 1761 bequeathed her daughter, Dorothy Boarman, a gold ring, one-half of her wearing apparel and kitchen furniture.*

Children of William and Dorothy (Sewell) Boarman

1. William Boarman, born 1760, migrated to Kentucky, *d.s.p.* 1800.
2. Ignatius Boarman married Rebecca Conyers Harding, widow. *q.v.*
3. Mary Smith Boarman.
4. Susanna Boarman.
5. Clement Boarman served under Capt. Belain Posey, in the Revolutionary War.
6. Gerard Boarman served as private under Capt. Benjamin Lusby Curry, in the Revolutionary War.

In 1778 he subscribed to the Oath of Allegiance in Charles County before Magistrate John Lancaster.

His will, dated May 10, 1779, was probated in Charles County on April 8, 1780, with his widow, Dorothy Boarman, and son, William Boarman, as the executors.

> To wife Dorothy during widowhood the use of the entire estate except certain heads of livestock.
> Personalty to children—William Boarman, Ignatius Boarman, Mary Smith Boarman, Susannah Boarman.
> At the death of his widow, the residuary was to be divided equally among his three youngest sons—William, Clement, and Gerard.

His son, William, at the age of 16, being 5 ft. 4 in., enlisted July 12, 1776, in the Flying Camp under Captain Bowie. After the war he settled in Nelson County, Kentucky, where he died testate and

* Inasmuch as two daughters of Madam Sewell married two Boarman brothers and she named five Boarman grandchildren without reference to their father in her will, it has been difficult to place the following two grandchildren—Henry Boarman and Basil Smith Boarman. The latter aged 19, 5 ft. 3 in., was enlisted by Ensign William Shirtcliff on July 14, 1776, for the Flying Camp. Ref.: *Archives*, vol. 18, p. 36.

without issue in 1800. He bequeathed his estate to his mother, Dorothy, and at her decease it was to revert to the four children of Ignatius Boarman, that is, Elizabeth, John, Ignatius, and Mary. In the event that his brother, Clement, "should come from the settlement and make demands in person" then the inheritance of the four children of Ignatius should be cancelled except the girls "Elizabeth and Polly." He appointed Elizabeth Boarman the executrix.

FRANCIS BOARMAN [3]

17– –1773

FRANCIS BOARMAN, son of Francis Ignatius and Anne (Slye) Boarman, was born in Charles County. He married Beatrice ———, and settled in St. Mary's County. The births of three of his children were registered in St. Andrew's Episcopal Parish register.

Children of Francis and Beatrice Boarman

1. John Boarman, born Oct. 8, 1758.
2. Francis Ignatius Boarman, born March 14, 1762.
3. Sarah Boarman, born March 1, 1764.

His will was dated May 12, 1773, and probated in St. Mary's County on July 1, following. He devised his entire estate to his three orphan children, placing his son, Francis Ignatius Boarman under the guardianship of George Slye; his son, John Boarman, under Richard Boarman; and his daughter, Sarah, under Mrs. Henrietta Plowden. He appointed his friend, Enoch Fenwick, the executor.

WILLIAM BOARMAN, GENT.[4]

1710–1767

WILLIAM BOARMAN, son of William and Monica (Turner) Boarman, was born at "Boarman's Manor" about 1710, being aged 32 in 1742. He married Winifred, daughter of Richard Edelen.* The latter died in 1760 at an advanced age and provided for his granddaughter, Mary Ann Boarman, daughter of his daughter Winifred, with a plantation purchased from John and James Hill.

* For the genealogy of the Edelen family, see, *Charles County Gentry*, by Newman.

Children of William and Winifred (Edelen) Boarman

1. William Boarman married Elizabeth Gardiner. *q.v.*
2. Mary Ann Boarman born 1740, died 1820, married John Manning.
3. Edward Boarman married Elizabeth Boarman. *q.v.*

On February 26, 1744, he declared himself to be the great-grandson and heir-at-law of Major William Boarman and petitioned the court to resurvey " Boarman's Manor " of 3,333 acres and to add a surplus of 645 acres. The surplus had been discovered during the lifetime of his father, William Boarman, who had petitioned but the resurvey had never materialized.

His will was dated March 26, 1765, and proved in Charles County on April 6, 1767.

> To wife Winifred the dwelling-plantation during life then to son William, and Negroes.
>
> To daughter Mary Ann Boarman and son Edward Negroes and other personalty.
>
> To Marsham Queen he devised all that land which the " lines of my land takes from his," provided it did not exceed 25 acres.

His widow removed to Prince George's County and there she died testate in 1784. She bequeathed Negroes to her son William Boarman, her grandson Wilfred Boarman, and her granddaughter Anne Minta Manning. To her son-in-law, John Manning, she willed 2,400 lbs. tobacco.

JAMES BOARMAN [4]

17– –1756

JAMES BOARMAN, son of William and Monica (Turner) Boarman, was born in Charles County. His wife was Mary, the youngest daughter of Joseph Pile, of Sarum, and Elizabeth his wife. Her father dying testate in 1724 left his daughter, Mary, then a minor, 100 acres of the Manor of Sarum.

Children of James and Mary (Pile) Boarman

1. Henry Boarman married Teresa Edelen, *d. s. p.* 1800.
2. Elizabeth Boarman married Edward Boarman. *q.v.*

He died intestate leaving two minor children. Letters of administration were issued to his widow, Mary Boarman, on October 25, 1756, with Joseph Pile, William Bowling, and Joshua Sanders as her sureties. William Boarman, Sr., and Thomas James Boarman approved the valuation of the inventory, and the final account was rendered by the administratrix on April 26, 1748, showing distribution to the widow and two unnamed children.

On July 11, 1772, when his widow, Mary Boarman, and her son, Henry Boarman, conveyed her portion of Sarum for £202/10/– to Walter Dodson, of Charles County, Gent., she was addressed as " Lady " –a title in Maryland afforded only the great ladies of the Province. Inasmuch as her share consisted of 150 acres and her father had devised 300 acres of the manor to be divided among his three daughters, it is evident that one of the daughters had died without issue, as the survivors, in the event that the daughters died during their minority, were to inherit.

The will of his widow, Mary Boarman, dated November 14, 1790, was admitted to probate in Charles County, on January 24, 1791. She bequeathed her entire estate to her son, Henry Boarman, and then to her grandchildren, James Boarman and Harriet Boarman. Minor bequests were made to her niece, Helen Clements, and to her niece, Catherine Boarman, the wife of Edward Boarman.

The son, Henry, distinguished himself in the Revolutionary War as Captain of the Lower Battalion of militia in Charles County. He married Teresia, the daughter of Richard and Sarah (Harrison) Edelen, but died without issue. His last will and testament on the motion of his widow was declared null and void by the court. Letters on the estate were issued to her on November 4, 1800; the personal estate was appraised at $7,242.36, with James Boarman as one of the kinsmen. Raphael Boarman for his daughter, Harriet, approved as the other kinsman.

The widow died shortly afterwards, and her will dated November 10, 1801, was proved on the 27th instant. She left a large estate, having 28 slaves at the 1800 census, which were bequeathed to the following heirs–her sisters Rachel Gardiner, Jane Mudd, Doratha Gardiner, Elizabeth Edelen, and Araminta Edelen; and her brothers Philip Edelen, Samuel Edelen, and Richard Edelen. Legacies were willed to Joseph Harrison, son of the testatrix's uncle Samuel Harrison, and the Catholic clergy.

At her death an administration bond *d. b. n.* was issued on November 21, 1801, to James Boarman as administrator of the estate of Captain Henry Boarman, her deceased husband. On January 15, 1801, a second appraisement was made showing a value of $5,940.80.

A law suit ultimately developed, whereby it was stated that Henry Boarman died intestate in 1800, leaving a widow, Teresa Boarman, but no issue. Furthermore, that Henry Boarman had no brothers but an only sister, Elizabeth Boarman, who predeceased him. The sister had two children, James Boarman and Mary Boarman, the latter dying in the lifetime of her mother. She, Mary Boarman, however, by her husband, Raphael Boarman, left an only daughter, Harriet, then aged 14 years. Harriet was represented by her father, Raphael Boarman, who declared that his daughter was entitled to one-fourth of the estate, whereas James Boarman stated that he was entitled to one-half.

THOMAS JAMES BOARMAN [4]

17– –18–

THOMAS JAMES BOARMAN, son of Thomas James Boarman and his wife, was born in Charles County. He married Susanna, daughter of Marmaduke and Henrietta (Jenkins) Semmes. Marmaduke Semmes by his will of 1772 named his daughter, Susanna Boarman, and his granddaughter, Catherine Boarman.

Children of Thomas and Susanna (Semmes) Boarman

1. Catherine Boarman.
2. Joseph Milburn Boarman. *q.v.*
3. Marmaduke Boarman.
4. John Boarman married Monica Hagan. *q.v.*
5. Thomas Boarman married Catherine Edelen. *q.v.*
6. [Roswell Boarman married twice.] *q.v.*

During the Revolutionary War he served as a private in the militia company of Captain Alexander McPherson of Charles County.*

He can be placed in the censuses of 1790 and 1800 for Charles County, but not in 1810, yet he was living in that year, for in 1814 he conveyed land to his son.

* Militia List, p. 40, Maryland Historical Society.

JOSEPH BOARMAN [4]

17– –1797

JOSEPH BOARMAN, son of Thomas James Boarman and his wife, was born in Charles County. His wife was Rachel, the daughter of Henry Brooke, of Prince George's County, and Margaret his wife. She was unmarried at the writing of her father's will on September 25, 1751, her legacy being a Negro wench called Sarah. She was still a maiden at the final distribution of her father's estate on June 28, 1762. Before October 4, 1768, however, she had married and as Rachel Boarman, she was an heir in the will of her bachelor brother, Charles Brooke, of Prince George's County.

Children of Joseph and Rachel (Brooke) Boarman

1. Henry Boarman.
2. Michael Boarman.
3. John Chrisostrom Boarman. *q.v.*
4. Mary Boarman.
5. Margaret Boarman.
6. Rachel Boarman.

By his will, dated June 4, 1797, and probated in Charles County on July 12, following, he devised his entire landed estate to his sons, Henry, Michael, and John Chrisostrom, and his personal estate to his daughters–Mary, Margaret, and Rachel Boarman. The inventory was filed on November 24, 1797, with Michael Boarman as the executor.

ENSIGN EDWARD BOARMAN [4]

17– –18–

EDWARD BOARMAN, son of Thomas James Boarman and his wife, was born in Charles County. In 1778 he subscribed to the Oath of Allegiance before Judge Joshua Sanders. At the beginning of the war he served as a sergeant in the militia company of Captain Alexander McPherson, of Charles County, and on June 19, 1781, he was commissioned an ensign of the county militia.*

His wife was Catherine ———, a niece of Madam Mary (Pile) Boarman, who was made an heir in Madam Boarman's will of 1790.

* Militia List, p. 40; *Archives of Maryland*, vol. 45, p. 280.

On November 19, 1785, Edward Boarman of Thomas James, of Charles County, conveyed to Gabriel Moran for 30,600 lbs. tobacco the "Warren" and "Guiberd's" tracts of 204 acres. Catherine, his wife, waived all dower rights.

William Waters, of Charles County, obtained judgment against him at court, whereby he and his wife, Catherine, appealed the decision. On February 29, 1788, he deeded to John Neale and William Francis Neale, his sureties, five Negro slaves.

On June 13, 1787, styling himself the son of Thomas James Boarman, of Charles County, he sold to John Chapman, Sr., for £250 his dwelling-plantation called "Warren" of 1772 acres, lying on the east side of Zachia Swamp, adjoining the land of Gabriel Moran and his brother Raphael Boarman. Catherine, his wife, waived all dower rights.

In 1790 he was the head of a family in Charles County with himself and another male over 16 years, one male under 16, one female, and three slaves. He cannot be placed as the head of a family in Charles County in 1800.

RAPHAEL BOARMAN [4]
1749–1829

RAPHAEL BOARMAN, son of Thomas James Boarman by his last wife, was born in or about 1749, near Bryantown. During 1778 he subscribed to the Oath of Allegiance in Charles County before Judge John Parnham. He was a member of the militia company of Captain Alexander McPherson, serving first as a private and later as a corporal during the Revolutionary War.

He married his cousin, Mary, born 1765, daughter of Edward and Elizabeth (Boarman) Boarman. She died on August 6, 1786, aged 20, according to her tomb in the Catholic cemetery at Bryantown. He lived for many years thereafter and apparently did not remarry. At his death he was buried beside the remains of his wife, his tomb reading "Raphael Boarman Died May 19, 1829 aged 80 years."

A daughter, Harriet, was the only issue of this union. She was born on June 12, 1786, and at the age of 14 in 1800 was one of the heirs to the wealthy estate of her great-uncle, Captain Henry Boarman. She married Benjamin Lancaster and in her old age she was always known as the "Rich Old Mrs. Lancaster."

JOSEPH BOARMAN[4]

1755–1825

JOSEPH BOARMAN, son of Leonard Boarman and Elizabeth his wife, was born about 1755 near Bryantown, Charles County. His wife was Sarah, daughter to Benjamin and Sarah (Queen) Jameson. His father-in-law died testate in 1787 in Charles County and bequeathed personalty to his daughter Sarah Boarman. His mother-in-law, Sarah Jameson, died testate in 1795, willing her daughter, Sarah Boarman, £50.

Children of Joseph and Sarah (Jameson) Boarman

1. Benedict Leonard Boarman.
2. Joseph S. Boarman, died Aug. 6, 1854, aged 53, buried in Bryantown Cemetery, left entire estate to brother Walter F. Boarman.
3. Frederick M. Boarman, died bachelor.
4. Sarah E. Boarman, died July 2, 1854, in her 64th year; married Walter B. Posey.
5. Catherine M. Boarman.
6. Walter F. Boarman, born 1797, married Henrietta Thompson. *q.v.*
7. ——— Boarman married ——— Knott.

On July 8, 1776, he enlisted in Captain Belain Posey's company of the Flying Camp and saw active and bloody service in the campaign around New York. He was mustered out shortly before Christmas and returned to his home in Charles County. Later he served in the county militia.*

The notice of his death appeared in the *Baltimore Gazette* of December 5, 1825: "Died 21 November 1825 at his residence in Charles County in his 70th year Colonel Joseph Boarman of Leonard, a Revolutionary soldier."

His will which was dated November 14, 1825 was admitted to probate in Charles County on March 23, 1826.

> To sons Benedict L. Boarman and Joseph S. Boarman the plantation on Gilbert Swamp called "Simpson's Chance" of 168 acres which had been deeded to them.
>
> To son Frederick M. Boarman the plantation whereon I dwell with the use of the testator's two daughters—Sarah E. Posey and Catherine M. Boarman—during their single lives.

---

* *Archives of Maryland*, vol. 18, p. 32; Militia List, p. 40, Maryland Historical Society, Baltimore.

To son Walter F. Boarman Negroes.
To minor grandchildren Joseph A. Knott and Sarah Julia Posey personalty.
Executors—Walter F. Boarman.

Styled Colonel Joseph Boarman of Leonard, the inventory of his personal estate was filed at court on November 23, 1826, appraised at $2,708.50.

CHARLES BOARMAN [4]

1751–1819

CHARLES BOARMAN, son of Leonard and Elizabeth Boarman, was born 1751 near Bryantown, and in his youth was sent to Liege, Belgium, for his education. He returned before the Revolution and about 1775 he married Mary, the daughter of Philip and Jane (Gardiner) Edelen, of Charles County. In 1778 he subscribed to the Oath of Allegiance in Charles County before John Parnham. On February 1, 1796, he was appointed to a professorship at Georgetown College, where he continued to teach until his death. He died in 1819 and was buried on the college campus.

Children of Charles and Mary (Edelen) Boarman

1. Jane Boarman, born July 7, 1776, married Jan. 19, 1795, Samuel Jameson, of Charles Co.
2. Elizabeth Boarman married Samuel Queen.
3. Anne Boarman married Marsham Queen.
4. Thomas Courtney Boarman married July 16, 1810, Mary Louisa Boarman and Aug. 26, 1817, Polly Edelen.
5. Philip Aloysius Boarman married June 11, 1816, Catherine Gardiner.
6. Charles Boarman, born Dec. 24, 1795, died Sept. 1879, married Anna Abell. Appointed midshipman U.S.N. 1811 and rose to Rear Admiral.
7. Joseph George Boarman married Lucy Dyer. License Prince Georges Co., Feb. 7, 1812.
8. Sarah Boarman, spinster.

BENEDICT BOARMAN [4]

17– –1815

BENEDICT BOARMAN, son of George and Mary (Gardiner) Boarman, was born in Charles County.

Children of Benedict Boarman

1. Richard B. Boarman, *d. s. p.* 1838.
2. George S. Boarman.
3. Elizabeth Boarman married Henry Stonestreet.
4. Catherine Boarman [married R. L. Burch].
5. Mary Boarman married John Francis Gardiner.

His will dated May 26, 1815, was admitted to probate in Charles County on August 24, following.

To son Richard B. Boarman "Hardshift" and "Marsh Neck."
To son George S. Boarman "St. John's" in St. Mary's Co., near St. Joseph's Church.
To three daughters Elizabeth, Catherine, and Mary all land in Charles Co.
In consideration of the land given to son George and the three daughters, they were not to claim the land arising from their mother's estate which was given to son Richard.
To sister Elizabeth Boarman 50 acres adjoining her dwelling-plantation, and legacy.
Executors—all five children.

The inventory of the personal estate was filed at court on October 15, 1817, by George S. Boarman and Henry Stonestreet as "two" of the executors.

On December 3, 1819, Henry Stonestreet and Elizabeth his wife, of Charles County, conveyed to John Francis Gardiner portions of "Boarman's Rest," "Boarman's Meadows," "Boarman's Enlargement" and "Boarman's Low Ground" which had been devised by John Hoskins Boarman to his three sons, namely, Bennett, John, and Michael, and by the three sons deeded to Benedict Boarman. The latter by his will of 1815 had devised the tracts to his three daughters, Elizabeth, Catherine, and Mary. Consequently Elizabeth and her husband, Henry Stonestreet, were selling their portion to John Francis Gardiner.

His son, Richard B. Boarman, died without issue in 1838. His personal estate was appraised at $856 on February 13, 1838, with John F. Gardiner as the administrator. A reappraisement was made by Walter F. Boarman and R. L. Burch on December 19, 1845, at which time it had appreciated to $1,020.00. Lot no. 1 was drawn by Mrs. Elizabeth Stonestreet and lot no. 2 by R. J. Burch. The final account was passed on June 14, 1842, by John F. Gardiner and Mary his wife.

ENSIGN RAPHAEL BOARMAN[4]
17– 1807

RAPHAEL BOARMAN, son of Richard Bennett and Mary Ann (Hoskins) Boarman, was born near Bryantown, Charles County. He married between September 27, 1774, and March 21, 1775, Dorothy, the daughter of Basil and Anne (Wharton) Smith of Charles County. Basil Smith drew up his will on September 27, 1774, and devised his daughter, Dorothy Smith, considerable realty and other property. The final account was rendered the court on December 1, 1778, at which time "Dorothy Boarman formerly Dorothy Smith" was listed as one of the legatees.

On May 30, 1788, Raphael Boarman and Dorothy his wife "formerly Dorothy Smith," conveyed to Samuel Hanson the tract "Rinkle and Nephew" which had been willed by Basil Smith, late of Charles County, to his wife Ann and daughter Dorothy and the "longest liver of them."

Children of Raphael and Dorothy (Smith) Boarman

1. Elizabeth Harriet Boarman, entered convent.
2. Mary Ann Boarman married ——— Fenwick.
3. Eleanor Phebe Boarman married ——— Fenwick.
4. Dorothy Smith Boarman, died spinster 1857 leaving entire estate to brother Raphael.
5. Ann Wharton Boarman.
6. Raphael Hoskins Boarman, *d.s.p.* in D.C., 1861, married Ellen M. ———.

On February 26, 1776, as Raphael Boarman, Jr., he was appointed ensign of Captain Jonathan Yates' company of Charles County Militia by the Committee of Observation.*

He married secondly on December 27, 1802, Elizabeth Thompson, but no issue resulted.

His wife, Elizabeth Boarman, with his permission made a will on September 25, 1804, which was proved at court in Charles County on May 10, 1806. She mentioned her husband and her brothers—John Baptist Thompson and Raphael Thompson. Other heirs were her sisters—Jane Brooke, and Henrietta Semmes; and her nieces and nephews—Basil Brooke, Mary Ann Thompson, Richard Brooke,

* *Archives of Maryland*, vol. 11, pp. 186, 206.

Mary Teresa Thompson, Elizabeth Thompson, Charity Semmes, and Henrietta Semmes.

His will was dated May 29, 1807, being probated in Charles County on August 22 following, with his son, Raphael Hoskins Boarman, as the executor.

To daughter Elizabeth Harriet Boarman $300 having already paid the admission fee to the monastery of which she is a member.

To daughters Mary Ann Fenwick, Eleanor Phebe Fenwick, Dorothy Smith Boarman, and Ann Wharton Boarman all land in William and Mary Parish to the south of Allen's Fresh.

To son Raphael Hoskins Boarman "Calvert's Hope" where Easter Williams and William Hill formerly lived, and also "Boarman's Lot" and all land bought of William Barton Smoot, part of "Boarman's Meadows," and a lot in Carrollsburgh in Washington City, and all other land except the land under lease in Cornwallis Neck.

The gifts to his daughters Mary Ann Fenwick and Eleanor Phebe Fenwick, then widows, at the time of their marriages were confirmed, and he requested stones be placed at the graves of himself and his deceased wives.

JOHN HOSKINS BOARMAN[4]

17– –1804

JOHN HOSKINS BOARMAN, son of Richard Bennett and Mary Ann (Hoskins) Boarman, was born in Charles County. He married Sarah Teresa Neale, born September, 1752, daughter to William Neale who died testate during 1766. Her brother, John Neale, died testate in 1809 and named his sisters, Sarah Boarman and Catherine Boarman. In 1778 John Hoskins Boarman subscribed to the Patriot's Oath in Charles County before Magistrate John Parnham and likewise served in his militia company as a private.*

Children of John Hoskins and Sarah Teresa (Neale) Boarman

1. Mildred Matilda Boarman.
2. Mary Louisa Boarman married July 16, 1810, as his first wife Thomas Courtney Boarman.
3. Juliana Boarman married Michael, son of Joseph and Anne Neale (Smith) Mudd. License Prince George's Co., Apr. 19, 1819.
4. George Washington Boarman married Sophia ———.

---

* Militia List, Maryland Historical Society, p. 43.

5. Bennet Hoskins Boarman.
6. John Baptist Boarman.
7. Michael Boarman.
8. Eleanor Pile Boarman married Richard B. A. Boarman. *q.v.*

His will was dated January 1, 1804, and probated in Charles County on April 7, following.

To daughters Mildred Matilda Boarman, Eleanor P. Boarman, Mary Louisa Boarman, and Juliana Boarman personalty.

To son George W. Boarman part of " Calvert's Hope " as deeded to the testator by his uncle Joseph Boarman excepting that part which testator deeded to his brother Raphael Boarman.

To sons Bennet H. Boarman, John B. Boarman, and Michael Boarman portions of " Calvert's Hope," " Boarman's Rest," " Boarman's Meadows," " Boarman's Help " and " Boarman's Enlargement " and the whole of " Boarman's Low Ground "; son Michael to have his share at 18.

Executrix—wife Sarah Teresa Boarman and son Bennett H. Boarman.

The distribution of the slaves was made in August, 1809, to the widow, to the Misses Louisa and Juliana Boarman, and to Mrs. E. Pile Boarman.

His widow, Teresa Boarman, died testate in Charles County, her will dated June 16, 1813, was proved on August 17, following.

To daughter Julianna Boarman as much property as I gave my daughter Louisa Boarman when she married.

To granddaughters Matilda Boarman and Harriet Boarman, daughters of Eleanor P. Boarman, each a mourning suit.

To daughter Louisa Boarman and her daughter Sophia Ann Boarman each a mourning suit.

Executors—son Michael Boarman and daughter Juliana Boarman.

Her daughter, Juliana Boarman, filed the inventory of the personal estate on July 19, 1817. By license issued in Prince George's County on April 19, 1819, she married Michael Mudd, and with him she filed the final account upon the estate on April 10, 1821. They accounted for legacies due to the deceased from George W. Neale, the administrator of John Neale, and also from Alexander Matthews, the administrator *d. b. n.* of the said John Neale.

RICHARD BENNETT ALOYSIUS BOARMAN [4]

17– –1811

RICHARD BENNETT ALOYSIUS BOARMAN, son of Joseph and Mary Boarman, was born in Prince George's County. He married his cousin, Eleanor Pile Boarman, daughter of John Hoskins and Teresia Boarman.

Children of Richard and Eleanor (Boarman) Boarman

1. Harriett Boarman.
2. Matilda Boarman.
3. Francis Boarman.
4. Richard Boarman.
5. Joseph Boarman.

On August 6, 1803, he and his two brothers as heirs of their father, Joseph Boarman, figured in the conveyance of "Boarman's Hazard" to William Barton Smoot with their cousins, Joseph Boarman and John Baptist Boarman, who were also grantors in the deed.

His will which was dated April 4, 1811, was probated in the District of Columbia on May 20, following, by George Fenwick, Benedict Boarman, and Mary Ann Fenwick. He devised his wife, Eleanor Pile Boarman, during life his lot and house in Georgetown on Frederick Street where he lived, and at her decease it was to be divided among his heirs. Legacies were bequeathed to Bishop Neale and Father Francis Neale, with the residuary estate going to his wife and unnamed children.

His widow died before 1818, for in that year his children were placed by the Orphans' Court of the District under certain guardians. Harriet was placed under Mary Ann Hardy, Matilda under Charles Boarman, Jr., Francis and Richard were placed under Joseph Brigden, and Joseph under Robert Clarke.

JOSEPH BOARMAN [4]

17– 18–

JOSEPH BOARMAN, son of Raphael Boarman and his wife, was born in Charles County. He married Jane Cordelia Edelen, daughter of Richard and Sarah (Stonestreet) Edelen, of Prince George's

County.* His four children—Anna Maria, Raphael Horace, Carolina Matilda, and Catherine Aramentinia—were all bequeathed legacies in the wills of their unmarried Edelen aunts and uncles in 1805 and 1808.

Children of Joseph and Jean Cordelia (Edelen) Boarman

1. Anna Maria Boarman.
2. Raphael Horace Boarman.
3. Carolina Matilda Boarman married John Baptist Edelen. License Prince George's Co., July 29, 1819.
4. Catherine Aramentinia Boarman.

He was made the executor of the will of his brother-in-law, Christopher Edelen, of Prince George's County, in 1794, in which his wife, Cordelia Boarman, received several Negroes; he was bequeathed a mourning suit by the will of Electius Edelen, another brother-in-law, in 1808.

As Joseph Boarman of Raphael he was the head of a family in Trinity Parish, Charles County, in 1800, with a male less than 10 years of age, two females less than 10 years of age, and one female between 16 and 26. He died before the 1810 census, for his widow, Jane, was the head of a family in Charles County at that time. In November, 1825, Frances Edelen, of Prince George's County, bequeathed slaves for the " support of my sister Delia Boarman " and at her death to her daughter Catherine Aramentinia Boarman.

GERARD SEWELL BOARMAN [4]

17— –1840

GERARD SEWELL BOARMAN, son of Ignatius Boarman and Susanna his wife, was born in Charles County. He married first Elizabeth, the daughter of Joseph Queen, of Prince George's County. The latter died testate in 1802 and named his daughter Elizabeth, the wife of Jarred S. Boarman.

Children of Gerard and Elizabeth (Queen) Boarman

1. George Boarman married Rebecca Boarman.
2. Susan Boarman, born May 20, 1801, entered convent.
3. Mary Ann Boarman, entered convent.

---

* For her ancestry see *Charles County Gentry*, p. 192; the statement that her husband was son of John Baptist Edelen is hereby corrected.

His first wife died in young womanhood and he married secondly Catherine Neale with whom, according to tradition, none could live in peace. The two girls were placed in the Visitation Convent in Georgetown and the son was placed with his Queen kinsmen in Baltimore.

Issue of Gerard and Catherine (Neale) Boarman

1. Elizabeth Loretta Boarman married —— McWilliams.

The will of his widow, Catherine Boarman, dated July 22, 1843, was probated in Charles County on February 13, 1844. She named her daughter, Elizabeth Loretta McWilliams, and her grandchildren—Francis McWilliams, Mary Catherine McWilliams, and Mary Clementina McWilliams, appointing her friend, Dr. William Queen, as the executor.

IGNATIUS BOARMAN [4]

17— -18—

IGNATIUS BOARMAN, son of William and Dorothy (Sewell) Boarman, was born in Charles County. After December 11, 1776, but before July 31, 1779, he married Rebecca Conyers Harding, the widow of Joseph Harding, of St. Mary's County, and settled in the latter county. According to the 1790 census, he was the only Boarman living in St. Mary's County, at which time he had in his household besides himself, two males under 16, and four females; no slaves. In 1778 before Judge John Lancaster he subscribed to the Patriots's Oath in Charles County.

Children of Ignatius and Rebecca Conyers Boarman

1. Elizabeth Boarman, married —— Reynolds, of Bardstown, Ky. Their son, Ignatius Aloysius Reynolds, became Catholic Bishop of Charleston, S. C.
2. John Boarman.
3. Ignatius Boarman married Mary Kintz. *q.v.*
4. Mary Boarman married —— Cooms, of Ky.

His four children were named in the will of their uncle, William Boarman, of Kentucky, which is the only authority found for his issue. The two daughters settled in Kentucky, while Ignatius, one of the sons, removed to Baltimore.*

* The Rev. C. F. Thomas in his book on the Boarmans, published in 1934,

WILLIAM BOARMAN [5]

17– –1782

WILLIAM BOARMAN, son of William and Winifred (Edelen) Boarman, was born near Bryantown, Charles County. His wife was Elizabeth, the daughter of Luke Gardiner and Mary Boarman his wife. In 1778 he subscribed to the Patriot's Oath in Charles County.

He died in 1782 testate devising his estate to his only son, Cornelius, but in the event that he died without issue then to his [testator's] nephew Wilfred Boarman. Henry Boarman of James was named as guardian. Letters of administration were issued to Capt. Henry Boarman, whereas James Boarman and Edward Boarman as kinsmen approved the inventory.

In 1797 the son and heir, Cornelius, was declared *non compos mentis* by the court and placed under the guardianship of his aunt, Mrs. Mary Ann Manning, then aged 57, of Prince George's County. His next of kin at that time were, beside his aunt, James Boarman aged 38, a first cousin, of Charles County, and Harriet Boarman aged 11, a second cousin. No kinsmen on the maternal side were cited.

John Manning, the husband of his aunt, died in January, 1809, and the aunt died in November, 1820. Thereafter Ignatius and John H. Manning, sons of the aunt, assumed guardianship. Ultimately James Boarman, of Charles County, who declared himself to be a full cousin, accused the Mannings of improper care and depositions to that effect presented to the court bore out the allegations.

Cornelius Boarman died on November 17, 1828, aged about 54 years, seized of a portion of " Boarman's Manor " and a number of Negro slaves. Letters of administration were issued to James Boarman. At the lawsuit over the property it was stated that Mrs. Manning at her death left three representatives, but in 1828 only two were living–Ignatius Manning who resided in the District of Columbia and John H. Manning who was a widower with two children.

gives considerable space to this Baltimore branch. It stated that Ignatius' father died when he was a boy and that his mother married again in Washington a man named Harding. His mother was a Widow Harding with children whose husband had left her an affluent estate. It is possible, though not probable, that she did marry thirdly another Harding.

The personal estate was appraised at $10,140 including 53 Negro slaves. The balance or $9,537 was distributed on September 14, 1830, among the following heirs–Marsham Queen, Richard Gardiner, Peter Green, William Gardiner, Elias Mudd, Samuel Queen, Cornelius Manning and Ignatius Manning. Unfortunately the court did not cite the amount or relationship of each representative to the decedent.

Marsham Queen, of Charles County, deposed, however, that Elias Mudd, of Washington County, Kentucky was the son of Jennet Mudd, formerly Jennet Gardiner, who was a sister to Elizabeth Boarman, formerly Elizabeth Gardiner, of Charles County. On July 22, 1829, Edward Wheatley, of Washington County, Kentucky, deposed that Allalu Green, wife of Peter Green, was then living and that she was a daughter of Jennet Mudd, formerly Jennet Gardiner, who was a sister to Elizabeth Boarman, formerly Elizabeth Gardiner, who was the mother of Cornelius Boarman.

EDWARD BOARMAN [5]

17– –1785

EDWARD BOARMAN, son of William and Winifred (Edelen) Boarman, was born in Charles County. He married Elizabeth, his cousin, the daughter of James and Mary (Pile) Boarman.

Children of Edward and Elizabeth (Boarman) Boarman

1. Mary Boarman, born 1765, married Raphael Boarman. *q.v.*
2. Wilfred Boarman, *d.s.p.* before 1800.
3. James Boarman, born 1759, extant 1828; served in militia company of Capt. Alexander McPherson, Revolutionary War; nearest heir to Cornelius Boarman.

In 1778 he took the Oath of Allegiance in Charles County before Judge Joshua Sanders. As Edward Boarman, Sr., of Charles County, he on April 21, 1784, conveyed to James Boarman and Wilfred Boarman for the consideration of £1,000 all that tract of land on which he lived called "Boarman's Manor" including Bryantown and 11 Negroes.

His will dated November 5, 1784, was probated in Charles County in January, 1785.

To daughter Mary Boarman all Negroes, stock and other personalty I gave her when she married Raphael Boarman.

Whereas John Gardiner did by his will bequeath unto me all right to some Negroes that his father Luke Gardiner gave him at the time the said John Gardiner married his wife and that I have been at law for with the Mattinglys, my will is that my executors should sue for the said Negroes again and should they recover any part of them bequeathed to me by the said John Gardiner, then the costs of the suit be first paid out of the said Negroes, then one-third to be given to Mary Tiers' children, she being the daughter of the said John Gardiner, and to Monica Gardiner daughter of the said John Gardiner, and my two sons James and Wilfred the remaining third.

To son James and Wilfred the entire landed estate, and each one-third of the personal estate.

To wife Elizabeth all household goods and one-third of the residue.

Executors—wife and two sons—James and Wilfred.

At the probation the widow renounced the will and demanded her dower rights under the law.

JOSEPH MILBURN BOARMAN [5]

17--181-

JOSEPH MILBURN BOARMAN, son of Thomas and Susanna (Semmes) Boarman,, was born in Charles County. He appeared for the first time as the head of a family at the 1800 census, when he was between the ages of 26 and 45, his wife between 16 and 26, with a male and female under 10. On March 8, 1800, he bought of his father, Thomas James Boarman, for £80 a portion of "Boarman's Manor," lying on the side of the road leading from Joseph Simpson to Bryantown.

He died intestate, when letters of administration were issued to Henry Macatee. At the final account on February 27, 1816, a payment of $15.58 was made to Benjamin Lancaster and one of $204.00 to John Boarman as a result of a judgment against the estate. The balance or $205.67 was to be distributed according to law, but no heirs were named.

JOHN BOARMAN [5]

17--1813

JOHN BOARMAN, son of Thomas and Susanna (Semmes) Boarman, was born in Charles County. He married Monica, daughter of John and Mary Hagan. The latter in her will proved in Charles County during 1790 bequeathed her daughter, Monica Boarman, Negro slaves and other personalty. During the Revolutionary War he served as a private in Charles County Militia under Captain Benjamin Cawood.*

Children of John and Monica (Hagan) Boarman

1. Francis Xavier Boarman, died intestate 1824, Tobias Boarman, adm.
2. Aloysius Boarman, born Oct. 23, 1804.
3. Tobias Boarman, died intestate 1834, married Sarah Ann Edelen.
4. George Boarman, *d. s. p.*
5. Catherine Boarman, died spinster 1827.
6. Martha Boarman married Joseph Thompson.
7. Mary Ann Boarman married Thomas Bowling.
8. Mary Ann Teresa Boarman married May 18, 1807, at Bryantown Catholic Church Joseph Wathen, settled in Missouri.
9. Matilda Boarman, died spinster 1827.

Styling himself John Boarman of Thomas, he dated his will August 17, 1812, it being probated in Charles County on March 23, 1813. He devised his widow, Monica, until his youngest son attained 21 years, his plantation on Zachia Swamp, being a part of " Boarman's Manor " of 160 acres. She was to occupy it for the support of his unmarried children, and the land was to be divided among his four sons—Francis, Aloysius, Tobias, and George. Other children mentioned were his daughters—Catherine Boarman, Martha Boarman, Mary Ann Boarman, Mary Ann Teresa Wathen, and Matilda Boarman. He appointed his wife and son, Francis, the executors, both of whom refused to act at time of probation.

His daughter, Catherine, dying testate in 1827, named her niece Ann Marcellina Wathen and her nephew John Francis Boarman, appointing her brother, George Boarman, the executor. Matilda, another unmarried daughter, died the same year, but prior to her sister, Catherine, for the latter and the sister Martha were made heirs in her will.

* Militia List, Maryland Historical Society, p. 50.

The will of his widow, Monica Boarman, was dated May 5, 1830, being proved in Charles County on May 30, 1831.

To daughter Martha Thompson one-half of the plantation on which she lived called "Hagan's Addition."

To her four granddaughters the other half of the dwelling plantation—Elizabeth Isabella Wathen, Mary Henrietta Wathen, Ann Marcellina Wathen, and Letha Camilla Wathen.

To children Mary Ann Theresa Wathen, Martha Thompson, Tobias Boarman, George Boarman, and Aloysius Boarman personalty.

Residuary estate to son George Boarman and four above-named Wathen granddaughters.

Legacy to the Catholic congregation of the Lower Zachia Church.

THOMAS BOARMAN [5]

17– –18–

THOMAS BOARMAN, son of Thomas James and Susanna (Semmes) Boarman, was born on "Boarman's Manor," Charles County. Before October 1, 1813, he maried Catherine, daughter of James and Susanna (Gardiner) Edelen, one-time of Prince George's County, but later of the District of Columbia. His mother-in-law died testate, will proved November 15, 1813, providing for her daughter Catherine Bowman (*sic*). On October 19, 1815, the heirs of James Edelen, namely Thomas Boarman and Catherine his wife, and Alexius Edelen, of Charles County, Ignatius Edelen, and Thomas Craycroft and Nancy his wife, of Washington, D. C., sold to George Morton, of Charles County, 17 acres of "Boarman's Manor" which James Edelen on July 28, 1784, had purchased of Edward Boarman.

On October 24, 1814, his father conveyed to him for $100 a portion of "Boarman's Manor" which bordered the road leading past Joseph Simpson's house to Bryantown and which lay between his plantation (the grantee's) and that of the grantee's brother, John Boarman, then deceased, and which had been given them by their said father Thomas James Boarman.

On October 5, 1815, he deeded to Jesse Jamson for $1,050 a portion of "Boarman's Manor" or 75 acres which had been conveyed to him on February 10, 1792, by Thomas James Boarman. Catherine, his wife, waived dower.

He is placed as the Thomas Boarman, Jr., born between 1755 and

1780, at the 1800 census with a wife, one female between 10 to 16 years, three females under 10 years. In 1810 he was still less than 45 years, and besides his wife, he had two females between 16 and 26, one male and one female between 10 and 16, and a male less than 10.

ROSWELL BOARMAN [5]

1778–1854

ROSWELL BOARMAN, born 1778 in Charles County, was the son of Thomas and Catherine Boarman, of that county, according to Kentucky vital statistics recorded in 1854. It would seem therefore that he was a son of Thomas and Catherine (Edelen) Boarman, but from circumstances it would not seem possible for them to have a son born as early as 1778. As mistakes often happen at the recording of statistics at death, he was probably the son of Thomas James and Susanna (Semmes) Boarman, as the age brackets would be more logical, and his mother was incorrectly given as Catherine instead of Susanna. Furthermore, a complete list of the children of Thomas James Boarman has not been proved.

In 1810 he bought land in Charles County from Ann H. Wilkerson, according to the index, but the liber (1810-1813) for deeds is missing. In that year he appeared first as the head of a family in Charles County. In his household were himself and another male between 26 and 45 years, a female between 26 and 45, four males and two females less than 10 years, and four slaves. It is tradition that his first wife was ——— Macatee.

He settled in Washington County, Kentucky, where on December 19, 1812, he purchased a plantation on Shepherd's Run, a branch of Cartwright Creek. There on October 15, 1827, he secured license to marry his second wife Margaret Browning, with John Hughes as his surety.

He died in Marion County, Kentucky, and according to the record at Frankfort Statehouse "Roswell Boarman died July 15, 1854, in Marion Co., Ky., aged 76, born in Charles County, Maryland, son of Thomas and Catherine Boarman."

JOHN CHRISOSTROM BOARMAN [5]

17– –1844

JOHN CHRISOSTROM BOARMAN, son of Joseph Boarman, died testate in Charles County, during 1844, leaving his estate to his children—Joseph, Adeline, and John H. Boarman.

DR. WALTER FAIRFAX BOARMAN [5]

1797–1854

WALTER F. BOARMAN, son of Colonel Joseph Boarman and Sarah his wife, was born August 10, 1797, near Bryantown, Charles County. On January 17, 1823, according to the register of the Church at Bryantown, he married Henrietta Thompson, daughter of John Baptist and Eleanor (Middleton) Thompson.

Children of Walter and Henrietta (Thompson) Boarman

1. William I. Boarman.
2. John W. Boarman married Elizabeth Lancaster.
3. Richard Thomas Boarman.
4. Albert J. Boarman, born Mar. 14, 1845, died Apr. 22, 1897.
5. Mary Julia Boarman.
6. Eleanor Rose Boarman.
7. Sarah Emily Boarman.

His tombstone in Bryantown Cemetery reads "Our Father Dr. Walter F. Boarman born Aug. 10, 1797, died Oct. 2, 1854." The tombstone of his widow reads "Henrietta wife of Dr. Walter F. Boarman died Mar. 7, 1863, aged 56." Also "Elizabeth wife of John W. Boarman, and eldest daughter of the late Alexander Lancaster, died January 29, 1857, in the 30th year of her life."

The will of his widow, Henrietta Boarman, was dated March 7, 1863, and probated in Charles County on September 29, 1863. A Negro slave was placed in trust with her son, John W. Boarman, during the minority of his four daughters, whereas other servants were willed to her children, Mary Julia, Eleanor Rose, Sarah Emily, Richard Thomas, and Albert. Legacies were left to her sister, Elizabeth Bowling, niece Ann E. Holton, and to the Roman Catholic Church.

IGNATIUS BOARMAN [5]

17– –1852

IGNATIUS BOARMAN, son of Ignatius and Rebecca Conyers Boarman, was born in St. Mary's County. At the age of 16 he settled in Baltimore and became a contractor and builder. In 1830 he constructed the Convent of the Carmelites on Aisquith Street. On April 15, 1805, he married Mary Kintz at St. Peter's, the Pro-Cathedral of the Baltimore Catholic Diocese, she being a native of Pennsylvania.

Children of Ignatius and Mary (Kintz) Boarman

1. Rebecca Boarman, born Feb. 8, 1806, married Nov. 15, 1821, George Boarman.
2. William Boarman, born Mar. 26, 1808, removed to Missouri, but returned East and lived in Georgetown.
3. Ignatius Boarman, born Oct. 15, 1809, married Dec. 24, 1831, Sarah Ann Warner, of Baltimore; he died at St. Genevieve, Mo., May 18, 1872.
4. Mary Boarman, born Sept. 17, 1811.
5. Susannah Boarman, born Dec. 9, 1813.
6. Charles Sylvester Boarman, born Aug. 24, 1816, in 1880 living in Cooper Co., Mo.
7. John Athanasius Boarman, born July 5, 1818.
8. Jerome George Boarman, born July 25, 1820; to California in 1849.
9. Cecilia Agnes Boarman, born Mar. 2, 1822.
10. Frances Helen Boarman, born May 26, 1827.
11. Thomas M. Boarman removed to California and served in Mexican War 1849; died at Red Bluff, Calif. July 6, 1870, aged 46, according to Baltimore press.

In 1819 according to the city directory he was living opposite St. Mary's College on the east side of Paca Street, north of Franklin. About 1840 he settled in St. Genevieve County, Missouri, and it is traditional that all of his children removed with him except his daughter Rebecca who remained in Baltimore with her family.

Notice of the death of his wife appeared in the *Baltimore American* on October 24, 1845: "Died at St. Genevieve, Mo., 2 Oct., 1845, Mrs. Mary Boarman, wife of Ignatius Boarman, Sr., formerly of Baltimore." He died at St. Genevieve on December 9, 1852.

MATTHEWS FAMILY *

Thomas Mathews, Gent., emigrated to the Province of Maryland in 1638, four years after the arrival of the *Ark* and the *Dove*, with a retinue of servants even at that young age, for he was not more than 16 years old. In 1643 came his wife who transported herself into the Province and for whom he claimed 100 acres of land in 1650. He was born in or about 1622, having deposed in November, 1659, that he was 37 years of age.

He was one of the leaders of the early colony and was numbered among the so-called Calvert Party which was conservative in its political beliefs and affiliations. In religion he was a Catholic. He settled first in St. Mary's County, but later established his seat at Port Tobacco, still maintaining quarters or plantations in Old St. Mary's. He was conversant in jurisprudence, practiced law before the county and provincial courts, and while his parentage has not been proved on the other side, the fact that the inventory of his personal effects at his death listed a "silver seal" indicates that he was from an armorial family and a member of the English county gentry. Besides being an attorney at law he had been trained in the science of medicine or physic as it was called in that day, and he was addressed as Dr. Thomas Mathews.

Before his application for land, he had been assigned by Thomas Copley, Esq., a Jesuit, who had arrived or who had been responsible for the transportation of ten "Adventurers" on the *Ark* and the *Dove*, the latter's landrights. His claim to 3,500 acres was recognized and in 1649 Lord Baltimore granted him a manor which he called "St. Thomas," to "have hold use and Enjoy within the said Mannor a Court Leet and Court Baron with all things to the Said Courts or Either of them belonging by the law or Custome of England."

He attended the session of the General Assembly from January to March, 1647/8, opened to all freeholders, but at the elected As-

* The emigrant spelled his name consistently with a single *t*, but succeeding generations used both the single *t* and the double *tt*. In each history below an attempt has been made to use so far as possible the orthography of the respective member. Known descendants of today use the double *tt*.

sembly of April, 1650, he was chosen a delegate from St. Inigoe's Hundred, St. Mary's County. He, however, was fined 50 lb. tobacco for non-attendance on April 6, but upon his appearance on April 8 his fine was rescinded " for tht it was proved not bee voluntary or willful neglect . . . but justly occasioned through foule weather."

At the Battle of the Severn he fought with the Proprietary forces against the Puritan Rebels and was thus in jeopardy for several years during the Puritan supremacy. On October 5, 1655, he was fined £100 for his participation in " the late Rebellion of Capt. Stone."

After Lord Baltimore regained control of his Province, he was commissioned in 1658 a Justice of the Provincial Court, and in 1659 he was commissioned a Justice of the Peace for St. Mary's County. After his removal to Charles County he was appointed a magistrate for that county, and according to extant records he served from 1663 to 1674 in that capacity. In 1662 and 1664 he was the presiding justice of the Court held at Newtowne. In 1664 he was nominated for High Sheriff of Charles County, but failed to receive the confirmation. He, however, was appointed in 1666.

When he proved landrights for his wife in 1650, he failed to address her by her Christian name. It is assumed that she was the Mrs. Hester Mathews who was subpoenaed with him in a lawsuit between Ralph Crouch and Madam Jane Fenwick over the ownership of a colt.

Children of Thomas and Hester Mathews

1. Thomas Mathews married Sarah Boarman. *q.v.*
2. Mary Mathews married William Boarman. *q.v.*

Records show that Hester Mathews was alive on November 12, 1659. Sometime after that date she passed on and he married secondly Jane Cockshutt, a maiden much his junior. She was the second and youngest daughter and coheiress of John Cockshutt, Gent., and his wife, Jane. The latter as a widow married secondly Nicholas Causeen, a Frenchman, and as a third husband she married Robert Clarke, Surveyor General of the Province.

Children of Thomas and Jane (Cockshutt) Mathews

1. Ignatius Mathews married Mary Doyne. *q.v.*
2. Victoria Mathews married William Thompson. *q.v.*
3. Jane Mathews married Capt. Joshua Doyne.

4. Ann Mathews married Thomas Mudd and Philip Hoskins.
5. William Mathews, born 1674, married Jane ———. *q.v.*

Thomas Mathews died testate early in 1675/6. His last will and testament was dated January 9, 1675/6, and probated in Charles County on March 11, 1675/6. He failed to name all his children, and signed his name thus "Thos Mathews."

> To wife Jane personal estate at Port Tobacco for good of her and her children; 500 acres of Huckleberry Swamp in Charles Co.
> To son Thomas 700-acre portion of 1,000 acres on Mattawoman branches, including that part he had already [settled] upon, "and I give to my Daughter Capt. Borman's wife 300 acres of land which is remainder of that I give to my son Thomas"; also to son Thomas and daughter Mary Borman 255 acres of "Hill's Freehold" in St. Mary's Co., equally.
> To wife Jane 400 acres of "St. Ellin's called 'Mathews' Hope."
> To Captain Borman certain personalty on plantation at "St. Ellin's" and to wife all other personalty at "St. Ellin's."
> Executrix—wife Jane, but if she died then "my son" and Capt. William Boarman.

The inventory of his personal estate showed "chirurgeon's chest with instruments," 4 white servants and 3 Negro slaves.

On January 15, 1676/7, his widow deeded to her children—Ignatius, William, Victoria, Jane, and Anne—two fillies for natural love and affections. By October 3, 1677, the widow had married John Bread, Gent. On September 4, 1678, her husband, John Bread, made a deed of gift to his step-children "for ye good will and great affections I have and bear to my wife Jane Breade and unto Ignatius, William, Victoria, Jane, and Anne Matthews."

By 1681 there seems to have been some conflict in the household, for she appealed to the High Sheriff of Charles that "she hath been grievously and manifestly threatened by her said husband [John Bread] of her life and of Mutilation of her members."

No court administrations are found for the estate of John Bread, but his spouse was widowed by July 10, 1688, when as "Jane Bread, widow" she conveyed to her daughter, Victoria Thompson, wife of William Thompson, 300 acres of land formerly belonging to John Nevill and by him sold to her late husband Thomas Mathews. She married thirdly Judge Thomas Hussey, Gent., a widower. She was living as late as April 24, 1693, but died before February 6, 1699/00, the date of her third husband's will.

THOMAS MATHEWS[2]

16– –1677

Although THOMAS MATHEWS, SR., named his son, Thomas, in his will drawn up on January 9, 1675/6, the son predeceased his father, having been killed while on an expedition to the Susquehannock Fort at the head of the Chesapeake. On January 29, 1676/7, at a court held in St. Mary's County, Robert Green and William Boarman, Jr., deposed that " Mr. Thomas Mathews, of St. Mary's County, Gent., being in perfect health at the time before he went up a soldier to the Susquehannah Fort that his full intention was to dispose of his wordly estate equally to his wife and children."

His wife was Sarah Boarman, the daughter of Major William Boarman by his first wife.

Children of Thomas and Sarah (Boarman) Mathews

1. Ignatius Mathews, *d. s. p.*
2. Sarah Mathews married John Sanders.
3. Mary Mathews married Thomas Sympson. *q. v.*

After his death Major William Boarman on behalf of his grandson, Ignatius Mathews, instituted legal proceedings against William Guyther, Gent., for recovery of 400 acres of " Hawley's Manor " in St. Mary's County known as " Mathews' Hope " which Thomas Mathews, Sr., had purchased from William Hawley which by rights of inheritance became the property of Ignatius Mathews who was the son and heir of Thomas, Jr., who was the son and heir of Thomas, Sr. Major Boarman won his suit for his grandson.

Sarah, the widow of Thomas Mathews, Jr., became the first wife of Thomas Mudd, and died before 1690. After her death a lengthy lawsuit resulted over the inheritance of " Hall's Place," a portion of " Boarman's Manor " which her father had deeded to her and her heirs in 1678. The children of the first husband claimed it against Thomas Mudd, II, as the son and heir of his mother by her second husband Thomas Mudd, I. Ignatius Matthews, son and heir of the first spouse, died without issue and intestate, consequently his landed estate descended to his two sisters and coheiresses Sarah Sanders and Mary Sympson.

After much litigation a compromise was reached by September 30, 1703, when the claimants agreed to sell the plantation to Thomas

Jameson, Gent., Therefore, Thomas Mudd, Gent., of the first part, John Sanders, Gent., and Sarah his wife, of the second part, and Thomas Sympson, Gent., and Mary his wife of the third part conveyed their interests, whereby Thomas Jameson paid Thomas Mudd £33/6/– and £8, to John Saunders (*sic*) and Sarah his wife £30, and to Thomas Simpson and Mary his wife £30.

IGNATIUS MATHEWS [2]

16– –1698

IGNATIUS, the second son of Thomas Mathews, but first by his wife Jane Cockshutt, was born in St. Mary's County. He married Mary Doyne, daughter of Captain Joshua Doyne, Gent., by his first wife Barbara. By the will of Captain Doyne, dated March 10, 1697/8, he bequeathed property to his daughter Mary, the wife of Ignatius Mathews, and to his two grandchildren, Thomas and Jane Mathews.

Issue of Ignatius and Mary (Doyne) Mathews

1. Thomas Mathews married Mary Stone. *q.v.*
2. Jane Mathews.

His will was dated February 19, 1697/8, and proved in Charles County on July 21, 1698. Other than legacies to his wife, Mary, and his brother William Mathews, he willed the entire estate to his son, Thomas, including 1,200 acres of unnamed land on the east side of the Potomac.

His widow married shortly afterwards Thomas Jameson and had issue. Her will, dated May 28, 1755, was probated in Charles County on September 22, following. Her estate was bequeathed to the following children—Thomas, Joseph, and Benjamin Jameson, Mary Queen, Elizabeth Jameson, Martha Mathews, and Ann Spalding; grandchildren—Henry Spalding, Mary Spalding, and Mary Jameson. She appointed Marsham Queen and Benjamin Jameson the executors. She failed to name any of her grandchildren through her first marriage.

WILLIAM MATTHEWS [2]

1674–1725

WILLIAM MATTHEWS, son of Thomas and Jane (Cockshutt) Matthews, was born about 1674 in St. Mary's County. On November

28, 1721, he deposed that he was 47 years of age and was the son of a daughter of Jane Cockshutt, the latter being entitled to 2,200 acres of land at the time of her death. Furthermore, he deposed that the widow of John Cockshutt married Nicholas Causeen, a Frenchman, by whom she had a son Ignatius Causeen.

His wife was Jane ——— who joined him in 1717 when he sold 100 acres of "Marsh Land" to John Blee of Charles County. She predeceased him, as she was not mentioned in his will.

Children of William and Jane Matthews

1. Lucas Matthews married Martha Jameson. *q.v.*
2. Thomas Matthews.
3. Joseph Matthews married Susanna Craycroft. *q.v.*

His will, dated February 15, 1724/5, was probated in Charles County on March 24, 1724/5.

> To son Thomas and heirs ½ of "Mathews' Purchase" of 460 acres and personalty.
> To son Joseph and heirs the residue of "Mathews' Purchase" and personalty.
> To son Lucas and heirs "Second Addition" and land adjoining, now occupied by Joseph Chrismond; the dwelling-plantation and residue of estate real and personal.
> Sons to live with their brother, Lucas, until day of marriage or 21; should either son die before marriage his portion to be divided between the surviving brothers.

The inventory of his personal estate was approved by William Matthews, Thomas Matthews, and Ignatius Doyne as the kinsmen.

THOMAS MATHEWS[3]

16– –1749

THOMAS MATHEWS, the only son and heir of Ignatius Mathews by his wife, Mary Doyne, was born in Charles County. He married Mary Stone, daughter of Judge William Stone, of Poynton Manor, and Theodosia Wade his wife. He accepted the Episcopal faith of his wife, and his children established an Anglican branch in the family.*

* For the ancestry of Mary Stone, see, Newman's *The Stones of Poynton Manor.*

Children of Thomas and Mary (Stone) Mathews

1. Maximillian Mathews married Anne ———. *q.v.*
2. Mary Mathews.
3. Thomas Mathews *d.s.p.* 1762; in 1747 at age 15 was deputy clerk of Charles Co.
4. John Mathews.
5. Theodosia Mathews married John Short.
6. William Mathews married Elizabeth Barnes. *q.v.*

He dated his will as of January, 1747/8, it being proved in Charles County on March 9, 1748/9. He requested to be buried on his plantation and "on the hill near to where my shop now stands."

To son Maximillian slaves and the land on Mattawoman called "Argyle" of 156 acres, but if he died without issue to daughter Mary Matthews.
To sons William and Thomas slaves.
To son John slaves and plantation "White Haven Dock" of 200 acres; if he died without issue then to daughter Mary.
To daughters Theodosia Short and Mary Mathews slaves.
To wife slaves and residue of estate equally with children.
Executor—Son-in-law John Short.

His son, Thomas Mathews, died without issue in 1762, willing his estate to his nephew Thomas son of William Mathews, his brothers John and Maximillian, his sisters Mary Mathews and Theodosia Short, and his friends–Mrs. Mary Simms, Mrs. Christian Smith, Mrs. Sarah Chilton, and Mr. Johnstone Hawkins.

LUKE MATTHEWS [3]

17– –1734

LUKE [LUCAS] MATTHEWS, son of William and Jane Matthews, was born in Charles County. He married Martha, the daughter of Thomas and Mary (Doyne) Jameson, his wife's mother being his aunt by marriage, the widow of his uncle Ignatius Matthews. His father-in-law by his will of November 17, 1733, bequeathed legacies to his daughter Martha Matthews, his son-in-law Luke Matthews, and their children Elizabeth and Anne Matthews. Furthermore, Martha Matthews on September 22, 1765, then his widow, was named as sister in the will of Elizabeth Jameson, spinster.

Children of Luke and Martha (Jameson) Matthews

1. Jesse Matthews married Margaret Pye. *q.v.*
2. Elizabeth Matthews.
3. Ann Matthews.
4. Jane Matthews died spinster.
5. Mary Matthews married [Nicholas] Shirburn.

His will was probated in Charles County on April 2, 1734, having been written on January 3, preceding.

> To son Jesse one-half of "Cocksetts," one-half of "The Addition" and personalty.
> To unborn child, if a son, one-half of the above named land, but if a girl, then son Jesse to have entire tracts.
> To wife part of "Mathews' Purchase" and one-half of residuary personal estate, the other half of personal estate to be divided among daughters Mary and Jane and the unborn child.
> To children of brother Joseph Matthews, that is, William and Ignatius, the other half of "Mathews' Purchase."

His inventory was signed by John Causeen and Ignatius Doyne as the kinsmen.

On November 9, 1776, the division of the landed estate of Luke Matthews, deceased, was agreed upon in accordance with his will, whereby 230 acres of "Matthews' Purchase" were to be divided between his widow, Martha Matthews, and the children of his brother Joseph Matthews, that is, William and Ignatius. It seemed, however, at that time William Matthews of Joseph claimed or was entitled to his brother's portion. Martha Matthews, widow, made choice of the northern half where Mr. Nicholas Shirbin was then living. On November 9, 1776, Martha Matthews conveyed for £5 her rights to the tract of 115 acres to her daughter Mary Shirburn.

The estate of the unmarried daughter, Jane Matthews, was divided equally between Mary Shirburne and Luke Matthews in Charles County on March 28, 1792.

JOSEPH MATTHEWS [3]

17— –1734

JOSEPH MATTHEWS, son of William Matthews and Jane his wife, was born in Charles County. His wife was Susanna Craycroft, daughter of Ignatius and Sophia (Beadle) Craycroft. Susanna was a minor at the death of her father in 1707, and was to receive certain legacies upon her 18th birthday, but it was as late as 1741 before she finally inherited her bequests.

Children of Joseph and Susanna (Craycroft) Matthews

1. William Matthews married Mary Neale. *q.v.*
2. Ignatius Matthews, born Jan. 25, 1730, took Holy Orders, died at Newtown May 11, 1790.
3. Anne Matthews, born 1732, died a Carmelite nun, June 12, 1800.

His will, dated December 31, 1733, was probated in Charles County, on March 30, 1734. He devised his landed estate which included 230 acres of unnamed land and 115 acres of the moiety of the northernmost portion of " Matthews' Purchase " to his two sons – William and Ignatius – equally. One-half of the personal estate was bequeathed to his daughter, Anne Matthews, and the residue to his wife Susannah. At the inventory filed on July 2, 1734, Ignatius Doyne and Thomas Thompson approved the value as the next of kin.

On November 22, 1734, his widow Susanna Matthews received a portion of her inheritance from the widow and administratrix of her brother John Craycroft's estate who had been the executor of their father's estate. His widow later married Edward Clements and on September 29, 1741, as Susanna Clements she received another legacy or the final bequest from the estate of her father, Ignatius Craycroft, from her nephew Clement Craycroft who had assumed the administration of his grandfather's estate upon the death of his mother. The legacy was delivered to " Edward Clements who married one other of the said Deceased [Ignatius Craycroft] daughters in full discharge of her portion according to the will due to her."

It is said that no issue resulted from her marriage with Edward Clements who had likewise been married previously. He died testate in Charles County during 1751 and named his wife Susanna, his son William Clements, and his granddaughter Mary Ann Clements.

Benjamin Craycroft, brother to Susanna Matthews-Clements, died testate in Charles County during 1772, and by his will dated December 31, 1771, he bequeathed slaves to his nephew William Matthews, niece [great-niece] Susanna Matthews, nephew [great-nephew] William Matthews son of Ignatius, niece Ann Matthews "in France at the Nunnery of Poor Clares to be sent her by her brother, that is, my nephew William Matthews and if she died before the money is sent then to go to Ann Matthews daughter of William."

MAXIMILLIAN MATTHEWS [4]

17--1771

MAXIMILLIAN MATTHEWS, son of Thomas and Mary (Stone) Matthews, was born in Charles County. His wife was Anne ——.

Children of Maximillian and Anne Matthews

1. William Matthews.
2. Mary Matthews.

His will was probated in Charles County on March 2, 1771, having been written on December 31, preceding. He styled himself of Durham Parish, and named his wife Ann and his two children, William and Mary.

WILLIAM MATTHEWS [4]

17--1756

WILLIAM MATTHEWS, son of Thomas and Mary (Stone) Matthews, was born in Durham Parish, Charles County, but after his marriage he established his seat in Trinity Parish, where the births of his three children are recorded. According to family records, his wife was Elizabeth Barnes.

Children of William and Elizabeth Matthews

1. Catherine Matthews, born July 16, 1750, died Feb. 13, 1784, married Feb. 14, 1773, Samuel Amery.
2. Mary Matthews, born Oct. 18, 1752, married Dec. 9, 1773, Benjamin Burch.
3. Thomas Matthews, born June 3, 1755, married Anne Poston. *q.v.*

He died intestate. His personal estate was inventoried and passed at court in Charles County on February 24, 1757, with his brothers Maximillian and Thomas Matthews signing as the kinsmen. On March 12, 1757, according to the register of Trinity Parish, the widow married secondly Thomas Reed Cooksey, and they both filed an account on the estate on May 10, 1757.

JESSE MATTHEWS [4]

17– –1774

JESSE MATTHEWS, only son of Luke Matthews and Martha Jameson his wife, was born in Charles County. He married Margaret, daughter to Edward and Sarah (Edelen) Pye. Edward Pye died testate in Charles County and by his will of June 10, 1750, he named his daughter Margaret Pye. Her mother, Sarah Pye, who had been the widow of Samuel Queen at the time of her marriage to Edward Pye died testate in 1773 and among her bequests was one to her daughter Margaret Matthews.

Issue of Jesse and Margaret (Pye) Matthews

1. Luke Francis Matthews, born 1773, married Rose Causine. *q.v.*

His will, dated November 27, 1774, was probated in Charles County on January 30, 1775.

To his wife Margaret Matthews one-third of the entire estate.
To his nephew Richard Shirburn saddle and bridle.
To his mother Martha Matthews during her life the land in her possession and at her death to his sister Jane Matthews during her single life.
To son Luke Francis Matthews "Cockshett" and the "Addition," and 8 Negroes at age of 18 years; if he died without issue then to the testator's two sisters—Mary Shirburn and Jane Matthews.
If his widow married "imprudently" or died, then the guardianship of his child to the testator's uncle Benjamin Jameson, and if he died then to the testator's brother-in-law Walter Pye.

At the probation the widow renounced the instrument and all three named executors refused to serve. At a court held in Charles County in August, 1789, Luke Francis Matthews, aged 16 years made choice of Joseph Simms as his guardian.

WILLIAM MATTHEWS [4]

1728–1776

WILLIAM MATTHEWS, the son and heir of Joseph and Susanna (Craycroft) Matthews, was born about 1728 in Charles County. His wife was Mary Neale, daughter of William and Ann Neale.

Children of William and Mary (Neale) Matthews

1. Joseph Matthews, *d.s.p.* 1786.
2. Ignatius Matthews.
3. Mary Matthews.
4. Susanna Matthews, entered the Carmelite Order.
5. Margaret Matthews married William Duhurst Merrick.
6. William Matthews, born Dec. 1770, died 1854, one-time pastor of St. Patrick's Church, Washington.
7. Ann Teresa Matthews, entered the Carmelite Order.

His will was proved in Charles County on November 30, 1776, with no date of writing. He devised his son, Joseph, 340 acres of land and personalty, but his wife, Mary, was to have the use and benefit of the land during life. The residue of his estate was to be divided among his wife and the "rest of my children."

THOMAS MATTHEWS[5]
1755–1796

THOMAS MATTHEWS, son of William and Elizabeth Matthews, was born June 3, 1755, in Trinity Parish, Charles County. On December 2, 1780, he married Anne Poston, daughter of William and Priscilla Poston, of Charles County, born October 6, 1760, according to the register of Trinity Parish. His wife, Anne Matthews, shared in the landed estate of his mother-in-law, Priscilla Poston, by her will proved in Charles County on October 18, 1797. During the Revolutionary War he served as a sergeant in the militia company of Captain Benjamin Lusby Curry of Charles County.*

Children of Thomas and Anne (Poston) Matthews

1. William Matthews, born Dec. 2, 1781.
2. John Matthews, born Dec. 14, 1783.
3. Catherine Matthews, born Nov. 19, 1785.
4. Alexander Matthews, born Apr. 25, 1788.
5. Elizabeth Barnes Matthews, born Feb. 24, 1790.
6. Thomas Matthews, born Nov. 1, 1792.
7. Elias Poston Matthews, born Feb. 3, 1795.
8. Henry Cooksey Matthews, born July 29, 1799, died Apr. 29, 1862, married Sept. 28, 1820, Lucinda Stoddart Haw, born Nov. 11, 1800, died June 16, 1884.

* Militia List, p. 39, Maryland Historical Society.

Thomas Matthews died on December 25, 1796, and was buried in accordance with the rites of the Episcopal Church by the rector of Trinity Parish. His widow died in 1825.

MAJOR LUKE FRANCIS MATTHEWS [5]
1773–1815

LUKE FRANCIS MATTHEWS, son of Jesse and Margaret (Pye) Matthews, was born about 1773 in Charles County. At court in August 1789, he declared himself to have become 16 on December 16, last, and made choice of Joseph Simms as his guardian.

He married Rose, daughter of Gerard Blackistone Causine, a descendant of Nicholas Causine, a native of France, who held a lordship on Causine Manor. On April 24, 1790, Gerard Causine conveyed to his daughter Rose Causine for natural love and affections and to carry out provisions in the will of Rose Dade, of Stafford County, Virginia, various slaves. On May 8, 1800, he deeded to his daughter, Rose Matthews the wife of Luke Francis Matthews, certain slaves which had been bequeathed her by his aunt, Mrs. Rose Dade, of Stafford County, for his children.

Children of Luke Francis and Rose (Causine) Matthews

1. Maria Harriot Matthews married George W. Neale.
2. Jane Margaret Matthews.
3. George Washington Matthews.
4. Anna Causine Matthews.
5. Francis Matthews, born August 16, 1807, married Elizabeth Eleanor Neale.
6. Charles Henry Matthews, born July 23, 1809.
7. William Matthews, born Feb. 7, 1811.
8. Thomas Matthews, born April, 1813.

His will, dated August 2, 1813, was probated in Charles County on April 4, 1815.

> To wife Rose one-third of real and personal estate in lieu of and in bar of dower under same conditions had I died intestate; the residue of the estate for the support of my children—Maria Harriott Matthews, Jane Margaret Matthews, George Washington Matthews, Anna Causine Matthews, Francis Matthews, Charles Henry Matthews, William Matthews, Thomas Matthews, and such child or children as my wife is now big or instinct with.

When son George Washington attains 21 years, the estate to be sold and divided among the children.

On death of brother-in-law Nicholas Causine the whole estate placed in trust with the testator was to be divided equally among the testator's wife Rose, and his brothers-in-law Dr. Nathaniel Pope Causine and Gerard Newton Causine.

Friend Francis Digges, Esq., to act as administrator in the event of the death of his wife Rose.

His plantation in Charles County was known as "Mt. Air," and the inventory of his estate at his death recorded 44 Negro slaves.

The estate of his widow was settled on April 10, 1822, by William D. Merrick, her administrator, who likewise settled the estate of Major Luke Matthews on November 28, 1823. The heirs were George W. Neale in right of his wife, Anna C. Matthews, George W. Matthews, Francis Matthews, Charles H. Matthews, William Matthews, and Thomas Matthews.

THOMPSON FAMILY

WILLIAM THOMPSON, the ancestor of one of the several branches of the family in Southern Maryland, was in the Province as early as March 1641/2, for at the Assembly of all freeholders in that month he assigned his proxy to Thomas Green, Gent. At subsequent Assemblies he generally authorized a proxy, but in January 1647/8, he attended in person and held the proxy of Captain John Price. At first he was seated in St. Michael's Hundred, but later his dwelling-plantation was in New Towne Hundred, both in St. Mary's County.

In January, 1646/7, he proved land rights for 250 acres, 50 of which were for the service of his wife unnamed. His widow was Anne who was probably not the mother of his son and heir William; if so, they were married before 1640. In June, 1647, Robert Tuttley, of New Towne, by his will bequeathed legacies to " Mr. Thomson and his children," and appointed William Thomson as the executor. Only two sons, William (*q. v.*) and Andrew, have been proved, but it is quite possible that there were other children.

In April 1648 as " Mr. Willm Tompson," he was appointed High Sheriff of St. Mary's County and subscribed to the oath accordingly.* His under-sheriff was Philip Land.

Some libelous statements were transmitted to Lord Baltimore by persons unknown regarding his conduct during Ingle's Rebellion of 1645. The councilors and burgesses later disavowed them under their signatures, stating that they were " made out of hatred and spleen " and that " your Honour hath not a more faithful and cordial friend in the whole Province."

In his last will and testament he styled himself as William Thompson, of New Towne, dating the instrument January 8, 1649/50. He made his wife Anne the sole legatee and executrix and thus failed to name a single child. After his death some question occurred over the landed estate, thereupon his widow gave power of attorney to Lieut. William Evans, whom she later married. Robert Robins deposed that he saw William Thompson sign and seal the will and

* *Archives of Maryland*, vol. 4, p. 379.

made an acknowledgment of his plantation. Ralph Crouch, Gent., a Jesuit, deposed that he wrote the instrument and that William Thompson was of " sound and perfect understanding and memory " and that he made an acknowledgment under his hand touching upon his land.

On February 25, 1649/50, Lieut. William Evans and Anne his wife deeded to " ' Andrew Tompson the sonne of William Tompson of Little Brittain late deceased " a heifer and all her increase.

WILLIAM THOMPSON [2]

16– –1661

WILLIAM THOMPSON, son and heir of William Thompson, patented 100 acres of land on January 12, 1657/8, in New Towne Hundred, which he called " Thompson's Purchase." It adjoined the plantation of William Bretton, of Little Brittaine Manor on Bretton Bay, whose daughter and sole-heiress he married. The proof of the marriage was cited as late as 1743 in a deed of Cecil County, when Joseph Lowman and Elizabeth his wife conveyed land to John Kanken. The land so conveyed had been sold to Samuel Lowman by James Robinson. It had been taken up by William Bretton on September 9, 1659, and " fell to one William Thompson of Charles County, son and heir of Mary ye sole daughter and heir of ye William Bretton," and sold by William Thompson to John Sewall and by Sewall to James Robinson on April 13, 1696.

Children of William and Mary (Bretton) Thompson

1. William Thompson married thrice. *q.v.*
2. Elizabeth Thompson married Robert Brooke and Thomas Cosdin.

His father-in-law, William Bretton, Gent., emigrated to Maryland in 1637 and was for many years clerk of the Lower House. He married after his settlement in the Province Mary, the daughter of Thomas Nabbs, who had likewise emigrated in 1637. Other civil offices held by him were " register " of the Provincial Court and in 1664 he was commissioned a Justice of the Peace for St. Mary's County. He died after May, 1671.

William Thompson died suddenly, making a nuncupative will on January 21, 1660/1. It was proved at court on February 21, following, by the oaths of Walter Pakes and Frances his wife. He desired that his entire estate go to his wife, Mary, and his unnamed children, and requested his father-in-law, William Bretton, to assist his wife in the administration.

WILLIAM THOMPSON [3]

1655–1740

WILLIAM THOMPSON, son of William and Mary (Bretton) Thompson, was born in St. Mary's County about 1655, deposing in November, 1721, that he was 66 years of age. He married Victoria, the daughter of Dr. Thomas Matthews and his second wife Jane Cockshutt. Her father died in 1677, and her mother married secondly before September, 1678, John Bread. As his widow, Madam Jane Bread on July 10, 1688, made a deed of gift to her daughter Victoria, the wife of William Thompson, for 100 acres of land which had been surveyed for John Nevill and by him sold to her late husband Thomas Matthews.

Children of William and Victoria (Matthews) Thompson

1. Thomas Thompson, born Sept. 12, 1682, married twice. *q.v.*
2. William Matthews Thompson, born Mar. 5, 1684, married Katherine Queen. *q.v.*
3. Victoria Thompson, born May 20, 1687.
4. Jane Thompson, born Nov. 13, 1689, married Henry Brent and ——— Watts.
5. Cuthbert Thompson, born Sept. 12, 1692, married Elizabeth ———. *q.v.*
6. Mary Thompson, born Feb. 12, 1694.

He established his seat first in Charles County, but after the death of his wife and his remarriage he removed to St. Mary's County. By September 21, 1720, he had married Eleanor, daughter of James Pattison, but then the widow of William Herbert and John Angel.

On February 6, 1723, he made a deed of gift to his two children, Jane Brent and William Matthews Thompson, both of Charles County, giving them a plantation called "Thompson's Chance," lying on the road between Port Tobacco and Piscataway. They were to enjoy it jointly during the widowhood of his daughter, but at her death the son was to gain complete possession in fee. Eleanor Thompson, his wife, waived all dower rights.

By February 3, 1734/5, his second wife had died and he had married thirdly Ann, the widow of Colonel John Baker, of St. Mary's County, who died intestate leaving an only son and heir.

On May 17, 1735, he gave his granddaughter, Ann Thompson, the daughter of Thomas Thompson, a mulatto slave but her father was to enjoy possession until Ann came of age.

His will was dated January 10, 1736/7, being probated in St. Mary's County, on June 25, 1740.

> To son Thomas Thompson Negro during life then to grandson Henry Thompson.
>
> To grandsons Joseph Thompson, Richard Thompson, son of Thomas, and Richard Matthews Thompson, son of Matthews, personalty.
>
> To kinsman William Compton personalty.
>
> To wife Ann during life the residue of estate and at her death to the daughters of John Baker—Ann and Mary Baker.

The value of his personal estate was approved by Thomas Thompson and Elizabeth Angel as the kinsmen. By August 26, 1740, the widow and executrix had married John Dossey.

THOMAS THOMPSON [4]
1682–1749

THOMAS THOMPSON, son of William and Victoria (Matthews) Thompson, was born September 12, 1682, in Charles County, and was the only child to survive his father. There is evidence of at least two marriages, but the name of his first wife and apparently the mother of his children is not known.* His last wife had had two previous husbands and was his senior, inasmuch as her father, Colonel John Douglas, had died in 1678. Yet in 1745, they speak of " our son Henry " which would indicate that he was an issue of the last wife.

Children of Thomas Thompson

1. Thomas Thompson.
2. Mary Thompson married ——— Carberry.
3. Elizabeth Thompson married (1) ——— Angel and (2) ——— Taylor.

---

* It is generally stated that his first wife was Jean, daughter of Madam Margaret Tant, but when the latter died testate in 1726, her son-in-law was Richard Thompson and not Thomas Thompson.

4. Richard Thompson married Henrietta Boarman. *q.v.*
5. Henry Thompson married Margaret Howard. *q.v.*
6. Joseph Thompson married Sarah Douglas. *q.v.*
7. Ann Thompson married Thomas Sanders.

After October, 1728, he married Elizabeth, the daughter of Colonel John Douglas and Sarah Bonner his wife, and one who had buried previously two husbands, Charles Brandt and Thomas Howard.

On January 28, 1745, Thomas Thompson, Sr., and Elizabeth his wife made a deed of gift to "our son Henry Thompson of Charles County for love and effections" of a portion of "Three Brothers" of 130½ acres lying on the Potomac with the exception of the "burying place and grave yard." On January 24, 1746, for love and natural affections he held for his son Richard he deeded him 100 acres being of "High Cliffs" on the Potomac, but reserving the use of the timber for himself during his life.

He drew up his will on November 13, 1749, it being probated in Charles County on January 1, 1750.

To daughters Mary Carbery, Elizabeth Angel, and Ann Sanders personalty.
To grandchildren Thomas Carbery and Jane Angel personalty.
To sons Thomas Thompson and Richard Thompson personalty.
To son Henry Thompson one shilling, having received his share.
To son Joseph Thompson land including three tracts all adjoining called "High Clifts," "Thompson's Delight," and "Haply."
To wife her "thirds," with the residue to son Joseph.

WILLIAM MATTHEWS THOMPSON [4]
1684–1728

WILLIAM MATTHEWS THOMPSON, son of William and Victoria (Matthews) Thompson, was born March 5, 1684, at the head of the Wicomico in Charles County. He married Katherine, the daughter of Samuel and Katherine (Marsham) Queen. She shared in the personal estate of her father who died testate in St. Mary's County in 1711, and also in the estate of her maternal grandfather Richard Marsham, of Prince George's County, in 1713.

Issue of William Matthews and Katherine (Queen) Thompson

1. Richard Matthews Thompson married Sarah Douglas. *q.v.*

He died suddenly, making a nuncupative will on March 24, 1727/8, before William Thompson and Ignatius Doyne. He left his entire estate to his wife and child, and in the event that his child died before the age of 18 years, his widow was to inherit the entire estate. William Thompson and Thomas Thompson signed the inventory taken on December 28, 1728, as the kinsmen, and the widow, Catherine Thompson, filed the final account on July 7, 1729.

CUTHBERT THOMPSON [4]
1692–1725

CUTHBERT THOMPSON, son of William and Victoria (Matthews) Thompson, was born September 12, 1692, in Charles County. On December 5, 1722, he received by deed of gift from his father 189 acres of "Little Worth" lying on the south side of "Matthews' Purchase." He married Elizabeth ———. He died intestate. Letters of administration were issued to his widow, Elizabeth Thompson, with John Courts and William Middleton as her sureties. His brothers, Thomas and William Thompson, approved the valuation. By May 26, 1727, his widow had married Joseph Gwinn who filed the final account but showed no distribution to the heirs.

RICHARD THOMPSON [5]
17– –1763

RICHARD THOMPSON, son of Thomas Thompson, was born in Charles County. Prior to April 25, 1747, he married Henrietta Boarman, daughter of John Baptist and Elizabeth (Edelen) Boarman, but then the widow of Thomas Jenkins with an infant son, Raphael Jenkins, who died under age.

Children of Richard and Henrietta (Boarman) Thompson

1. Elizabeth Thompson married Raphael Boarman. *q.v.*
2. Jane Thompson married Raphael Brooke.
3. John Baptist Thompson, born Jan. 21, 1753, married (1) Mary Lancaster and (2) Eleanor Middleton. *q.v.*
4. Henrietta Thompson, born 1755, married Joseph Semmes. *q.v.*
5. Anna Maria Thompson, born July 18, 1757.
6. Richard Walbert Thompson, born Mar. 9, 1759.
7. Raphael Thompson, born Oct. 31, 1761.

He died intestate in Charles County. The administration bond of his widow was dated September 14, 1763, with Joseph Thompson and Raphael Boarman as her sureties. Joseph Thompson and Henry Thompson approved the evaluation of the personal estate.

His widow died testate in Charles County; her will dated March 20, 1772, was proved on May 1, following. She named her children John Baptist Thompson, Henrietta Thompson, Ann Thompson, and Raphael Thompson, and her son-in-law Raphael Brooke. To her son, Richard Walbert Thompson, she devised the land in St. Mary's County which had been given her by her grandfather Richard Edelen.

An account filed with the court on July 1, 1773, by Raphael Brooke, her executor, reported four children under age. At the November court of 1773 Richard Thompson made choice of John Baptist Thomson as his guardian.

The daughter, Elizabeth who married Raphael Boarman, died without issue in 1806. Her estate was closed on March 5, 1811, by her brother, John B. Thompson, with the following legatees—nephews Basil Brooke who as attorney received the share of Richard and Henrietta Brooke (his brother and sister); Joseph Semmes for his daugthter, Henrietta Semmes, a niece of the deceased; Mary Charity Semmes, a niece; John B. Thompson for his daughters, Elizabeth and Mary Ann Thompson, nieces of the deceased; Raphael Thompson " now in the West Indies, if alive," a nephew of the deceased; and Clement McWilliams.

HENRY THOMPSON [5]

17— -17—

HENRY THOMPSON, son of Thomas Thompson and possibly his last wife Elizabeth Douglas, received in 1745 a deed of gift to " The Three Brothers " from his parents. He was married by July 31, 1749, when Benjamin Fendall sold to him and his wife, Margaret, for £60 " Battin's Clifts " of 166½ acres. Thereupon on the same day he and his wife Margaret sold to Benjamin Fendall for £120 " The Three Brothers " of 130 acres. It is said that his wife was Margaret Howard. By September 24, 1768, he and his wife had disposed of their realty in Charles County. As he was not a tithable in the county at the 1775 census and disappeared from the rent rolls after 1747, it is assumed that he had his family removed elsewhere.

JOSEPH THOMPSON [5]

17- -1775

JOSEPH THOMPSON, son of Thomas Thompson, was born in Charles County. By December 7, 1751, he had married Sarah, the widow of his cousin Richard Matthews Thompson, and the daughter of Joseph Douglas.

Children of Joseph and Sarah (Douglas) Thompson

1. Joseph Thompson married twice. *q.v.*
2. Mary Thompson.
3. Jane Thompson, died spinster 1778; administration granted her brother Joseph Thompson.
4. Sarah Hanson Thompson.
5. William Matthews Thompson.

His will, dated December 22, 1774, was proved in Charles County on January 2, 1775.

To daughters Mary and Jane Thompson the use of the dwelling house during their single lives.
To daughters Mary Thompson, Jane Tant Thompson, and Sarah Hanson Thompson Negroes, silver plate, and other personalty.
To William Matthews Thompson Negroes and personalty, his estate to be under the management of his godparents William and Sophie Leigh.
To nieces Ann Philphott and Elizabeth Taylor personalty.
To sister Elizabeth Taylor personalty.
To son Joseph " High Cliffs," ' Thompson's Delight," and " Happily."

RICHARD MATTHEWS THOMPSON [5]

17- -1749

RICHARD MATTHEWS THOMPSON, only child of William Matthews and Katherine (Queen) Thompson, was born in Charles County. He married Sarah Douglas, the daughter of Joseph and Penelope (Morris) Douglas. Her father dying in 1756 made his daughter Sarah Thompson an heir in the residuary estate. His paternal grandfather, William Thomspson, willed him his gun in 1740.

Children of Richard and Sarah (Douglas) Thompson

1. William Matthews Thompson, born Sept. 7, 1746.
2. Catherine Thompson, born Sept. 2, 1749, married Hoskins Hanson.*

* For their descendants, see Newman's *Charles County Gentry*.

Richard Matthews Thompson died intestate in Charles County. The administration bond of his widow, Sarah Thompson, was issued on December 11, 1749, with Richard Marshall and Charles Courts as her sureties. The inventory of the personal estate was approved by Elizabeth Thompson [Elizabeth Hanson] and Joseph Thompson as the next of kin. By December 7, 1751, the widow had married her deceased husband's cousin, Joseph Thompson, who closed the estate on that date and named the two minor heirs–William Matthews Thompson and Catherine Thompson.

JOHN BAPTIST THOMPSON [6]
1753–1814

JOHN BAPTIST THOMPSON, son of Richard and Henrietta (Boarman) Thompson, was born January 21, 1753, in Charles County. On November 7, 1779, as Baptist Thompson he was married to Mary Lancaster by the Rev. John Bolton.

Issue of Baptist and Mary (Lancaster) Thompson

1. Mary Teresa Thompson married Clement McWilliams.

His wife died leaving an only child. He married secondly Eleanor Middleton, the daughter of James Middleton, the latter by will of 1790 bequeathed his daughter Eleanor Thompson 15 Negro slaves.

Children of Baptist and Eleanor (Middleton) Thompson

1. Ignatius Fielder Thompson.
2. Mary Ann Thompson married Jan. 26, 1817, Alexander Middleton.
3. Elizabeth Thompson married Jan. 19, 1818, William Holton.
4. Richard Aloysius Thompson.
5. Ann Thompson died spinster 1824.
6. Joseph Thompson.
7. Henrietta Thompson, born Oct. 12, 1805, married Jan. 17, 1823, Walter Fairfax Boarman. *q. v.*

In 1778 he subscribed to the Oath of Allegiance and Fidelity to the State of Maryland before Magistrate George Dent. The 1790 census shows him as the head of a family in Charles County with two males under 16, two females and 25 slaves.

On February 3, 1810, he bought from his son-in-law and daughter, Clement McWilliams and Mary Teresa his wife, then living in St. Mary's, a portion of "His Lordship's Favor" whereon his son-in-law formerly lived. The plantation adjoined the seat of Baptist Thompson and had been purchased by Joseph Lancaster, Sr., then deceased, from William Middleton and Elizabeth his wife, both then deceased.

JOSEPH THOMPSON [6]

17--1810

JOSEPH THOMPSON, son of Joseph and Sarah (Douglas) Thompson, was born in Charles County. In 1778 he subscribed to the Oath of Allegiance before Magistrate George Dent. The name of his first wife has not been proved, but he married secondly Elizabeth, the elder one of the daughters of James Middleton by his first wife, and who was apparently not named in her father's will of 1790. By 1795 Joseph Thompson had emigrated to Hancock County, Georgia, where he was a tithable in that year. Marriage licenses for several of his children were obtained in Warren County, but his domicile at his death was Wilkes County.

Children of Joseph Thompson

1. William Thompson married Sarah Scott. License May 12, 1800, Warren Co., Ga.
2. James B. Thompson married Priscilla Semmes. License May 1, 1813, Warren Co., Ga.
3. Teresa Thompson married George Hargraves. License Feb. 13, 1806, Warren Co., Ga.
4. Henry Bradford Thompson married Louisa Sophia Cratin. License Oct. 25, 1813, married Oct. 26, by rector of Trinity Church, Augusta.
5. Henrietta Thompson married Dr. Ignatius Semmes.

His will was dated December 9, 1809, and probated in Wilkes County, Georgia, on May 7, 1810.

To son William Thompson during life the use of the land I bought of Edward Short and Stephen Brown; at his death to my grandson Joseph Thompson of William.

To grandchildren William Thompson, Julia Thompson, Elizabeth Thompson, Anne Semmes, Henrietta Semmes, and George Hargraves, personalty.

To wife Elizabeth crops of every kind and all money on hand, and all bonds, notes, and accounts, and my dwelling-plantation during life, a parcel of land purchased from John Travis lying on the north side of spring branch near where it falls into Beaver Dam Creek, the whole of said land I bought of Johnson and a piece taken up by myself.

To son James B. Thompson personalty.

To son Henry Bradford Thompson all land whereon my wife has her estate.

To daughter Teresa Hargraves personalty, and son-in-law George Hargraves.

Executors—Wife and son Henry Bradford Thompson.

He also devised land for a priest's home, if established within two years. It was to be laid out by his son, Henry Bradford Thompson, to include the burying ground, chapel, and spring and the northern line was to be five yards from the grave of Ignatius Semmes. He also mentioned deeds of gifts from Ignatius Semmes to the latter's two daughters, Annie and Henrietta Semmes.

On November 5, 1810, William Thompson, Elizabeth Thompson, James B. Thompson, John Tarver and Andrew G. Semmes gave their receipts to Henry B. Thompson for their legacies.

The will of his widow, Elizabeth Thompson, was proved in Taliaferro County, Georgia, on November 1, 1830, having been written on February 8, preceding.

To James B. Thompson grandson of my late husband, tract of land no. 69 as drawn in Houston Co.

To Sarah Thompson, widow of William Thompson, personalty.

To grandchildren Benjamin Lancaster Thompson, Elizabeth Teresa Thompson, Elizabeth Hargraves, George Thompson Hargraves, Henry Bradford Thompson, and John Cratin Thompson, personalty.

To nieces Elizabeth Thompson, Henrietta Thompson, Elizabeth Ellen Posey, personalty.

To son-in-law George Hargraves personalty.

To brother-in-law Lawrence Posey personalty.

To sister Eleanor Thompson 17 acres of "Middleton's and Askin's Progress" which I bought of Uncle Marmaduke Semmes, deceased. Brother Francis Middleton and brother-in-law Lawrence Posey trustees for sister Eleanor.

To James H. A. Middleton, Joseph Thompson, and Ann Rosaly Middleton the residue of the unpaid debt due from Robert and Joseph Turner, also a judgment in Prince George's Co., Md., against Alexius Boone, now of Frederick Co., Md., also a judgment against Henry Hagan, deceased, near Port Tobacco.

To sister Eleanor Thompson all my shares in different banks and a tract called "Hard Struggle" near Beantown.

Executors and trustees—Francis Middleton and Lawrence Posey.

MIDDLETON FAMILY

The progenitor of the Middleton family of Southern Maryland was Robert Middleton, Gent., a member of the Established Church, who bore a name generally associated with the north of England. But giving such a wide variety of names to his plantations, not all of them could be from childhood or ancestral association. His first land grant which he called "Wickham," after a parish in County Cumberland, was obtained in 1680. Other grants were "Dalkeith," the name of a market place and parish near Edinburgh; "Appledore," a parish in both Devonshire and Kent, "Carrick Fergus" the name of a place in County Antrim, Ireland, and "Sanqwhar" for a borough and parish in Dumfrieshire.

Before 1673 he married Mary Wheeler, the Catholic maiden and daughter of Captain John Wheeler and Mary his wife. Although allied in marriage with a Catholic, and undoubtedly his children were raised in the strict tenets of the Roman Church, he retained his traditional faith, was a member of the vestry of St. John's Parish at Broad Creek, and two of his sons followed him as members of the Established Church. From the second generation a staunch Catholic branch developed as well as a branch equally as staunch in their adherence to the Anglican faith.

On February 30, 1684/5, John Wheeler, of Charles County, Gent., made a deed of gift to Robert Middleton and Mary the "daughter of the said John Wheeler" for love and affections of the plantation "Wheeler's Hope" of 365 acres lying on a fresh run which emptied into Piscataway Creek. It was there that he established his seat, then on the frontier of the Province.

His father-in-law, John Wheeler, rose from an ensign of the Provincial Militia in 1660 to Major, a commission he held at the time of the Revolution of 1689. Besides he served in a judiciary capacity in the county court of Charles:*

Children of Robert and Mary (Wheeler) Middleton

1. John Middleton, born 1673, married Mary ———. *q.v.*

---

* *Archives of Maryland*, vol. 60, pp. 108, 11, 119; vol. 2, p. 551; vol. 7, p. 611; vol. 8, p. 7, vol. 17, p. 380.

2. James Middleton married Sarah Smith. *q.v.*
3. Thomas Middleton married Penelope Hatton. *q.v.*
4. Robert Middleton, born 1682, married Elizabeth Smith. *q.v.*
5. William Middleton, born 1686, married Elizabeth Tears. *q.v.*

On July 1, 1681, at a meeting of the Council held at St. Mary's City, Robert Middleton was commissioned a cornet of a troop of horse under Captain Randolph Brandt. When Prince George's County was organized out of Charles and Calvert Counties in 1605, he was appointed a justice of the first court held in the County and also made one of the coroners.*

Robert Middleton died intestate in Prince George's County during 1708. The administration bond of his administrators, Mary Middleton and John Middleton, was dated May 6, 1708, but not recorded at court until January 16, 1708/9. His estate was casually administered. consequently from the court records a complete list of his children can not be proved. There were most likely daughters, for Benjamin Belt whose wife was Elizabeth ——— named a son, Middleton Belt, and the name Middleton was carried down for several generations in the Belt family.

CAPTAIN JOHN MIDDLETON, GENT.[2]

1673–174–

JOHN MIDDLETON, son and heir of Robert Middleton and Mary Wheeler his wife, was born in or about 1673, being aged 55 in 1728, according to deposition. As the eldest son of his father who died intestate, he inherited the entire landed estate under the Common Law which was applicable then in the Province.

He established his seat on "Wheeler's Hope" bordering a run of Piscataway Creek, but he maintained quarters as far west as the Eastern Branch [now Anacostia River] within the present city of Washington. He may be considered one of the early industrialists of the Province, for on his plantation he maintained a blacksmith's shop, a tannery, a shoemaker's shop, and a grist mill. With all these enterprises in his hands, he was granted in 1706 a license to operate an ordinary. From Great Britain he imported white indentured artisans who, aided by his Negro slaves, operated his various enter-

* *Archives of Maryland*, vol. 15, p. 385; vol. 20, pp. 425, 546.

prises. From his many interests he amassed quite an estate, but owing perhaps to such a limited market on the frontier and his generosity in going security for his friends, he sustained financial reverses and was forced to liquidate much of his holdings.

His wife was Mary ——— who was literate, quite an accomplishment for a matron of that period, but so far the name of her family has not been proved.

Children of John and Mary Middleton

1. Charity Middleton married William Luckett.*
2. Sarah Middleton married Thomas Hawkins.
3. Anne Middleton married Mar. 22, 1717, Ralph Marlowe, according to register of St. John's Parish.

He was frequently styled Captain Middleton in the records, so there are reasons to assume that he commanded a militia company, and further evidence of his military service is brought out by the fact that in the liquidation of his estate he sold among other things a "silver hilted sword." Documentation, however, as to his commission has not been found.

On February 2, 1705/6, he acquired from James Wheeler, of Prince George's County, 200 acres of land called "Wheeler's Purchase" lying on the east side of the Piscataway and the mouth of St. John's Creek at an Indian town called Pamunkey, adjoining the land of Luke Gardiner. It had been granted to John Wheeler, the grandfather of the grantor, who by his will of 1694 had devised portions to his three grandchildren—James, the party to the deed, John, and Ann Wheeler who later married Hillary Ball.

In November, 1725, John Middleton requested that a commission be appointed to define the boundaries of his plantation "Wheeler's Hope." Accordingly, on June 15, 1726, Francis Marbury, aged 65, deposed that about 20 years ago at the request of Hillary Ball and Francis Clarvoe he surveyed "Brother's Delight" which belonged to the said Ball and that a certain bound tree marked the beginning of "Wheeler's Hope." Francis Wheeler, aged 50, and John Wheeler, aged 40, swore to the boundary according to their knowledge, whereas Dorman Walker, aged 60, deposed that Mr. Robert Middleton showed him a bound tree which was the tree of "his son John

* For the genealogy of the Luckett family, see Newman's *The Lucketts of Portobacco.*

Middleton's land," and that about 26 years ago Mrs. Ann Scandell, aged 48, swore that her deceased husband, Hillary [Henry] Ball told her that a certain tree was the bound tree of Mr. John Middleton's land and that about 25 years ago Mr. Robert Middleton was running out his land called "Wheeler's Hope" and it began at a bound tree of "Brother's Delight."

On June 7, 1727, John Middleton and Mary his wife mortgaged to Richard Bennett, of Queen Anne's County, merchant, for £200 his dwelling-plantation "Wheeler's Hope" of 365 acres, also "Maiden's Bower" of 100 acres, "Nothing Worth" of 30 acres on the Eastern Branch of the Potomac, and one acre of "Leith" with a dwelling house and smith's shop, also tools, watermill house, dam, tan yard, shoemaker's tools, about 150 hides, three white servants "one mulatto girl Nan aged about 6 years born of a white woman to be free at 31 years," also household furniture at the dwelling-house and at his quarters on the Eastern Branch, and 90 heads of livestock.

On February 15, 1730/1, he conveyed to Thomas Middleton a number of items of personalty including one "silver hilted sword" and all his rum at the Eastern Branch quarters. On March 24, following, he granted power of attorney to his "brother" Thomas Middleton, of Prince George's County, to sell certain realty.

In 1732 it was shown that Josiah Wilson, then deceased, had been the executor of his father's will, Major Josiah Wilson, and that Samuel Magruder, of Prince George's, merchant, and John Middleton "then insolvent and living out of the Province" had been bondsmen for Josiah Wilson in the sum of £5,000.

On March 10, 1740/1, John Middleton and Mary his wife, of Prince George's County, conveyed to "our sone-in-law and daughter William Luckett and Charity his wife" the tracts "Thomas and Mary" and "Wilson's Enlargement," containing 95½ acres.

On May 28, 1748, "Captain John Middleton of Truro Parish, Fairfax County, Va., Gent." conveyed to Richard Marshall, of Charles County, certain land in Fairfax County. And on August 17, 1750, "John Middleton, of Cameron Parish, Fairfax County" deeded to Valentine Peyton, Gent., of Dettingen Parish, Prince William County, Va., land in Fairfax County. Both John Middleton and wife signed their names.

No formal administration of the estate of John Middleton or of his wife Mary's estate is found in Maryland, but he undoubtedly spent his last years with his daughter in Frederick County. By the sale of "Maiden's Bower" on June 27, 1781, it is proved that the tract had descended to the three co-heiresses and had remained undivided. At that time only one of the daughters was alive, namely, Charity the wife of William Luckett, of Montgomery County. The other heirs-at-law were Middleton Marlowe and John Hawkins, both of Prince George's County. It was recorded that John Middleton, late of Frederick County, deceased, died possessed of "Maiden Bower" then in Frederick County (but later in Montgomery County), containing 100 acres; and it is further recited that "whereas the said John Middleton in his life time made no will and left three daughters living, to wit, Charity the wife of the aforesaid William Luckett, Ann Marlowe the wife of Raphael Marlowe, and Sarah Hawkins the wife of Thomas Hawkins, which the said Ann Marlowe, then deceased, was grandmother to the aforesaid Middleton Marlowe, and the said Sarah Hawkins then deceased was the grandmother to the aforesaid John Hawkins and coheiresses to John Middleton, deceased." For £1,000 they sold the tract to William Davis.

JAMES MIDDLETON[2]

16– –1769

JAMES MIDDLETON, son of Robert and Mary (Wheeler) Middleton, was born in that part of Charles County which in 1695 became Prince George's County. He married Sarah, the daughter of John Smith, of the "Jordan" tract adjoining Zachia Swamp. Her father by his will, proved November 16, 1716, left her 300 acres of the tract lying on the south side of Jordan's Branch. Being deprived of his father's land, he established his seat on his wife's inheritance and thus became a resident of Charles County.

Children of James and Sarah (Smith) Middleton

1. Smith Middleton married Mary Hawkins. *q.v.*
2. Ann Middleton married (1) Thomas Jenkins of Edward and (2) Charles Beavin.
3. James Middleton, born Mar. 29, 1726, married thrice. *q.v.*
4. Mary Middleton married ——— Hawkins.
5. Ignatius Middleton married Ann Goodrick. *q.v.*
6. Sarah Middleton married Edward Jenkins of Edward.

7. Charity Middleton married Cornelius Davis.*
8. Martha Middleton married Marmaduke Semmes. *q.v.*

On February 8, 1758, he and his wife, Sarah, made a deed of gift of the "Jordan" plantation to their sons Smith and Ignatius. Both signed their names to the instrument.

His will was dated August 5, 1769, being proved in Charles County on October 6, following. He devised his son James the manor land which joined the west side of the land already given him by deed. A Negro was left to his son, Ignatius, after the death of his mother. To his wife, Sarah, he bequeathed the use of the personal estate and a number of Negro slaves during her widowhood, then three of the slaves were to go to his daughter Martha Middleton, and the residuary to be divided among his children—Smith Middleton, James Middleton, Ignatius Middleton, Mary Hawkins, Sarah Jenkins, Charity Davis, and Martha Middleton. The latter received also the remainder of the manor land.

At the September Court for Charles County in 1744 his daughter, Anne Jenkins, widow of Thomas Jenkins, had the sheriff issue citations against Susanna Jenkins, her mother-in-law for allegedly concealing effects which belonged to her [Anne's] deceased husband. Madam Susanna Jenkins aged 58 denied the charge, but declared that about two months before the marriage of her son, Thomas, with a daughter of James Middleton, she agreed that if James Middleton would give his daughter a Negro, she would give her son a Negro girl called Poll. Mr. Middleton, however, never complied with his agreement, so she was not obligated to keep her part of the bargain.

THOMAS MIDDLETON, GENT.[2]

16– –1745

THOMAS MIDDLETON, son of Robert and Mary (Wheeler) Middleton, was born in Charles County. He was a surety for his mother and brother when the court issued letters of administration of the estate of his father in 1708. Furthermore, he was named "brother" to John Middleton when the latter gave him power of attorney in

* For ancestry and descendants, see, Newman's *Mareen Duvall of Middleton Plantation.*

1730. He married Penelope, daughter of William and Mary Hatton. The births of four of their children are found in St. John's Parish register.

Children of Thomas and Penelope (Hatton) Middleton

1. Mary Middleton married William Hawkins.
2. Hatton Middleton, born Dec. 9, 1705, married Jane ———. *q.v.*
3. Thomas Middleton, born Jan. 29, 1707/8. *q.v.*
4. Benjamin Middleton, born Feb. 24, 1709/10.
5. Penelope Weston Middleton, born Mar. 29, 1712.
6. Sarah Middleton.
7. Elizabeth Middleton.
8. Eleanor Middleton.
9. Susannah Middleton.

William Hatton died testate in Prince George's County in 1712, and devised his daughter, Penelope Middleton, the portion of the dwelling-plantation which extended along the road to "cousin Gardiner's Neck." The other portion which seems to have been "Thompson's Rest" and "Rich Hill" was willed to his son, Joseph Hatton, but in the event that the latter died without issue then it was to revert to the testator's grandchildren, Hatton and Mary Middleton.

Mary Hatton, widow of William, and mother-in-law to William Middleton, died testate in 1731, and among her heirs were her grandson, Hatton Middleton, to whom she devised 100 acres of land willed her by her deceased husband, and at his death they were to be divided between Hatton's daughter, Penelope Hatton Middleton, and the testatrix' granddaughter, Susannah Middleton. Bequests were made to her grandchildren Elizabeth Middleton, who received a necklace, Hatton Middleton, and Thomas Middleton. Sarah Middleton and her sister, Susannah Middleton, were to have the use of her Negress Nan until the expiration of her servitude. The residue of her estate was to be divided into two parts–one portion to the four youngest children of her daughter, that is, Sarah, Elizabeth, Eleanor, and Susanna Middleton She named her son Joseph Hatton and grandson Hatton Middleton as the executors.

On March 26, 1729, Thomas Middleton, Gent., deeded for love and affections held for his son-in-law, William Hawkins, and his grandson Thomas Hawkins of William by Mary his late wife daughter of the said Thomas Middleton, "Long Point" of 60 acres of Prince George's County.

His daughters—Sarah, Elizabeth, Eleanor, and Susannah—were all unmarried and under age on March 25, 1735, when their inheritance from their maternal grandmother's estate was delivered to their guardians.

After the death of Thomas Smallwood, Thomas Middleton married Alice his widow, but the courtship and honeymoon were brief, for the will of Thomas Smallwood was probated on April 9, 1735, and when the inventory was filed on September 17, following, the widow, who had married Thomas Middleton, was then deceased.

After February 14, 1735/6, and before November 9, 1736, he married thirdly Susanna, the widow of George Brett, of Charles County.

He died intestate. His personal estate was appraised on January 4, 1745, with the approval of Holland Middleton and Thomas Middleton as the kinsmen and Francis Goodrick and James Middleton as the creditors. William Middleton was the administrator. No accounts with the court have been found among the archives, so it is not known if all of his children were living at his death or if any of his daughters were married at that time.

ROBERT MIDDLETON [2]

1682–17–

ROBERT MIDDLETON, son of Robert and Mary (Wheeler) Middleton, was born about 1682, being 48 years of age in 1730. Like his brother, James, he married a daughter of John Smith of the "Jordan" plantation on Zachia Manor. John Smith by his will, dated April 13, 1716, devised his daughter, Elizabeth, 300 acres of the manor adjoining the devise of her sister, Priscilla, then the wife of John Moore. On April 7, 1729, Robert Middleton, of Charles County, and Elizabeth his wife, the daughter and heiress to the lands mentioned in the will of John Smith, late of the county, conveyed to John Ebernethy for 8,000 lbs. tobacco 300 acres of "Jordan." The debt books which begin about 1753 show that he remitted no quit-rents to the Lord Proprietary, and no will nor administration is on record among the archives of the prerogative courts of the Province. He most likely died without issue, or removed from the Province after his conveyance of "Jordan" in 1729.

WILLIAM MIDDLETON, GENT.[2]

1686–1769

WILLIAM MIDDLETON, son of Robert and Mary (Wheeler) Middleton, was born about 1686, in Charles County, being aged 57 in 1743, according to deposition. After July 13, 1710, but before April 1712, he married Elizabeth Tears, daughter of Hugh Tears by his first wife, but then the widow of John Keech. By the will of Hugh Tears, dated January 23, 1699, his daughter, Elizabeth, was bequeathed "my deceased's wife wearing apparel, rings, and one pair of Holland sheets which I have with Mr. Hawkins." His land was to be divided when she attained 16 years of age or at marriage and she was to live with her aunt Elizabeth Hawkins.

Children of William and Elizabeth (Tears) Middleton

1. Eleanor Middleton married Benjamin Tyler.
2. Robert Middleton married Ann ———. *q.v.*
3. William Middleton married Mary ——— *q.v.*
4. Hugh Middleton removed to South Carolina. *q.v.*
5. Holland Middleton removed to South Carolina. *q.v.*
6. Samuel Middleton married Elizabeth Ward. *q.v.*

From 1732 to 1741 William Middleton represented Charles County in the General Assembly. He was returned by the voters in 1748, but failed to win the election the next year.* In 1739 and perhaps other years he served as a Justice of Peace for the county.**

On November 15, 1732, William Middleton and Elizabeth his wife conveyed to Henry Holland Hawkins, of Charles County, a portion of "His Lordship's Favour" granted to Major Boarman and sold by him to Mr. Hugh Tears who devised one moyety to his wife (Tears) Eleanor and the other moyety to his daughter Elizabeth Tears, now the wife of William Middleton.

On March 9, 1735/6, William Middleton for natural love and affections deeded to "his daughter Eleanor Tyler then the wife of Benjamin Tyler" a portion of "His Lordship's Favour" which he had bought of Thomas and James Aburnathy.

On August 5, 1748, William Middleton, Sr., deeded for natural

* *Archives of Maryland*, vols. 37, 39, 40, 42, 46.

** *Archives of Maryland*, vol. 28, p. 208.

love and affections for his sons, Holland, William, and Robert, and the additional fee of £10, his manor land, "Middleton's Hope" and "Griffin's Seat."

On May 31, 1749, he leased to Hugh Mitchell, of Charles County, for 12,000 lbs. tobacco 100 acres in Zachia Manor to be held by Hugh Mitchell during the lives of William Middleton, Jr., Robert Middleton, and Hugh Middleton, the sons of the leasor.

His wife, Elizabeth, was living as late as July 16, 1748, but by August 30, 1758, she was deceased and he had married secondly Henrietta ———. On the later date he assigned to Samuel Hanson for a consideration of £28/4/3 "Henrietta's Rich Thickett" of 100 acres, but reserved the use of it to him the said William Middleton and his wife Henrietta during their lives.

The will of William Middleton, dated May 15, 1769, was probated in Charles County on November 15, 1769. To his grandsons, Isaac Middleton and Hugh Middleton, and his son, Robert Middleton, he willed his wearing apparel provided that his son, Robert "makes application for same within 10 months after my death," otherwise the son's share was to go to the testator's grandson William Morris Middleton. The residuary personal estate was bequeathed to his wife, Henrietta, whom he named executrix.

SMITH MIDDLETON [3]

1720–179–

SMITH MIDDLETON, son of James and Sarah (Smith) Middleton, was born about 1720, being aged 56 in 1776. He married Mary Hawkins, born about 1731, being aged 45 in 1776, when she and her husband were residents of St. John's Parish in Prince George's County.

In 1758 he purchased from Randolph Morris Hawkins the plantation "Goat's Lodge" in Charles County, which he conveyed to John Barnes and Thomas How Ridgate on July 3, 1771, for £242. Mary Middleton, his wife, waived dower rights. He removed to Prince George's County where he was living at the 1776 census of St. John's Parish, with 13 slaves. In that county in March, 1778, he subscribed to the Oath of Allegiance before Judge Lee.

On May 16, 1778, as a resident of Prince George's County, he conveyed to Samuel Hanson three parcels of land being portions of

"Jordan," 97 acres, which he bought of the said Samuel Hanson; 150 acres, which was his mother's portion of the tract, and 125 acres, which he had acquired from Walter Smith.

By March 1, 1788, he had removed to Charles County, when he deeded to James Middleton 150 acres of "Jordan" which had been given him by James Middleton and Sarah his wife, both parents of the grantor, then deceased. No wife waived dower.

By the will of Edward Semmes in 1789 he as the grandfather was made the guardian of the Semmes orphans. According to the census of 1790, he was living alone in Charles County with 5 slaves. He was later declared an insolvent, and on December 6, 1790, he delivered to Thomas Andrew Dyson, Sheriff of Charles County, who had been appointed trustee by the court, his personal estate for "by reason of many misfortunes he was unable wholly to satisfy his creditors."

No administration of his estate was made by the court at his death, and the only proof of an issue is a daughter Sarah who married Edward Semmes. Theodore Middleton, however, is placed as a son, and it is believed that Ann Middleton who married Francis Tolson in Prince George's County by license of February 21, 1782, is likewise a daughter.

JAMES MIDDLETON [3]
1726–1790

JAMES MIDDLETON, son of James and Sarah (Smith) Middleton, was born March 29, 1726, at "Jordan," Charles County. He is reputed to have had three wives, but the names of the earlier unions are not known. As is not uncommon ~~in Maryland~~, he had two daughters named Elizabeth; though by different wives.

Issue of James Middleton by Wives Unknown

1. Ignatius Middleton, *d.s.p.* 1816.
2. James Middleton married Nancy Corry. *q.v.*
3. Eleanor Middleton married John Baptist Thompson. *q.v.*
4. Elizabeth Middleton married Joseph Thompson. *q.v.*

His last wife and, ultimately, widow was Catherine ——, who was the mother of the two younger children.

Children of James and Catherine Middleton

1. Francis Middleton, born Feb. 11, 1784, *d.s.p.* 1839.
2. Elizabeth Middleton, born Sept. 4, 1787, married Lawrence Posey.

At the 1775 census for Charles County he was a resident of Port Tobacco East Hundred; in 1790 he was the head of a family with himself and another male over the age of 16, one male under 16, four females, and 49 slaves.

He died on August 24, 1790. His will was dated August 10, 1790, being proved in Charles County on September 14, following by Alexander McPherson, Jeremiah Dyer, and Henry Mudd.

Wife Catherine 9 Negroes, and other personalty.

Son Ignatius 10 Negroes, and 14 Negroes bought of Edward Jenkins.

Son James 10 Negroes.

Daughter Eleanor Thompson 15 Negroes.

Son Francis Middleton 8 Negroes.

Daughter Elizabeth Middleton 8 Negroes.

Sister Sarah Jenkins and her 4 daughters, Eliza, Mary, Sarah, and Charity personalty.

Wife Catherine during widowhood one-third of the following tracts —part of "Jordan," the dwelling plantation, "Middleton's and Askins Progress," but if she marries, then one-third of the land devised to son Francis.

To sons James and Ignatius the dwelling-plantation "Jordan" and also "Middleton's & Askin's Progress" and all vacant land, reserving one-third for the use of wife during widowhood, son Ignatius to have the part whereon stands the mill, but the other children were to have free grinding; son James to have his portion laid out on the land bought of "brother" Smith Middleton and the part called the old quarters.

To son Francis all that tract "for which I have deed of trust from Edward Jenkins," 340 acres, also tract bought of John Barton, Ignatius and Henrietta Montgomery called "Pyes Hard Shift" and also tract bought of State of Maryland called "Mongery's Adventure."

To son Ignatius "Batchelor's Hope" of 108 acres during the life of sister Sarah Jenkins and also reserving wife's thirds in the said lands in case she should marry.

To wife and children—Ignatius, James, Eleanor, Francis, and Elizabeth—the residue equally, but if the wife refuses to abide by this bequest then after her thirds be paid, the residue to be divided equally among said children.

The £7 subscribed by Edward Jenkins for building a chapel to come out of his estate.

Executors—sons Ignatius and James.

At the June Court of 1791 for Charles County his two minor children Francis aged 7 and Elizabeth aged 4 were placed under the guardianship of their mother Catherine Middleton, with John Gardiner and Thomas Reeves as her bondsmen. On November 24, 1793, according to the Catholic Church at Bryantown, she married Henry Hardy.

The inventory of his estate listed 63 Negro slaves, and showed that six had been delivered to James Middleton, Jr., at the time of his marriage and the like number to Eleanor Middleton at the time of her marriage. James Middleton and Eleanor Thompson approved the valuation as the kinsmen.

On May 17, 1798, Henry Hardy gave his receipt to Ignatius Middleton as having received the estate of his wife's two children. On September 24, 1804, it was reported at court that Catherine Hardy, the guardian to Francis and Elizabeth, was deceased. Henry Hardy died testate during 1805 and bequeathed to "Francis Middleton and Elizabeth Middleton the children of my third wife Catherine" the privilege of choosing two Negroes and having them appraised and the appraised value divided between the two Middleton orphans, and also 9 Negro slaves and the silver spoons marked "ICM."

On June 6, 1808, Lawrence Posey gave his receipt to Ignatius Middleton for the balance due his wife from the estate of her father James Middleton. On the same day John Baptist Thompson gave his receipt for his wife's share.

His son, Ignatius Middleton, died without issue in 1816, making a number of bequests to his kinsmen and the Catholic Church. Among his heirs were his brothers: Francis and James Middleton; his sisters Eleanor Thompson and Elizabeth Posey; his nieces and nephews Mary Ann Thompson, Elizabeth Thompson, Ann Thompson, Henrietta Thompson, Adeline Posey, Eliza Ellen Posey, James H. A. Middleton, Alexander Middleton, and David Middleton; his brother-in-law Lawrence Posey, and the following of no stated relationship—Joseph Thompson and Ann Rosaly Middleton. He also mentioned "Middleton's and Askins' Progress" which he had purchased from his uncle Marmaduke Semmes, deceased. He appointed his brother Francis Middleton and his brother-in-law Lawrence Posey the executors and trustees.

His youngest son, Francis, though married, died without issue in 1839, bequeathing one-third of his estate of his wife Elizabeth A. Middleton, and $500 to his friend Major George W. Mathews whom he appointed the guardian of his two nephews – Francis and Lawrence Posey. The residue of his estate was willed to his two nephews equally.

IGNATIUS MIDDLETON [3]

17– –17–

IGNATIUS MIDDLETON, son of James and Sarah (Smith) Middleton, was born in Charles County. After November 16, 1761, he married Anne, the childless widow of John Marshall Hawkins, of Charles County, and the daughter of Francis Goodrick, late of Charles County. On September 9, 1767, he and Ann his wife were cited by the court for their failure to pass an account upon the estate of her deceased husband.

Francis Goodrick negotiated his will on April 8, 1745, it being proved in Charles County on January 22, 1745/6, providing for his daughter Ann Goodrick and his wife Mary. His widow married secondly John Hanson who died in 1754. As Mary Hanson on October 5, 1764, she made deeds of gifts to her grandsons Francis Goodrick Middleton and Henry Goodrick Middleton. After that date she married as his third wife Charles Smoot, but she maintained her separate estate and died intestate prior to June 21, 1766. Her husband, Charles Smoot, administered upon her estate and in 1768 it was distributed among her heirs – Ignatius Middleton. William Stone, Charles Sewell, Francis Goodrick, and the heirs of Edward Goodrick.

Children of Ignatius and Ann (Goodrick) Middleton

1. Mary Middleton, born 1768.
2. Francis Goodrick Middleton.
3. Henry Goodrick Middleton.

On March 14, 1772, he conveyed to James Middleton for £225 the portion of "Jordan" which had been given him by his father and mother. He can not be placed in the 1775 census for Charles

County, nor did he take the 1778 oath in that county. The Charles County court of August, 1783, placed Mary Middleton, aged 15, under the guardianship of Charles Sewell who had married her mother's sister.

HATTON MIDDLETON[3]

1705–1733

HATTON MIDDLETON, son of Thomas and Penelope (Hatton) Middleton, was born December 9, 1705, in St. John's Piscataway Parish. Before 1731 when he and his daughter, Penelope, shared in the will of his grandmother, Mary Hatton, he had married Jane ———.

Children of Hatton and Jane Middleton

1. Penelope Hatton Middleton married ——— Jones.
2. Martha Middleton.

He died intestate in Prince George's County. The administration bond of his widow, Jane Middleton, was dated June 1, 1733, with Thomas Middleton, Sr., and Thomas Middleton, Jr., as her sureties. Sarah Middleton and Thomas Middleton approved the valuation of the personal estate as the kinsmen on August 11, 1733. At the account filed on July 8, 1734, it was shown that the widow had married John Goddard and that Martha and Penelope were the only orphans of the deceased.

John Goddard died intestate in Prince George's County during 1765, possessed of an affluent estate. The only kinsman who approved the inventory was Patrick Beall, with the following notation: "The Deceased had no other relation in this part of the world except the above Person who married his daughter." The Piscataway Parish Register records the mariage of Patrick Beall and Elinor Goddard on March 2, 1756. The sureties for the widow were William Bayne and Charles Finley, Jr.

The widow Jane Middleton-Goddard dated her will as of December 16, 1768, which was probated in Prince George's County on February 20, 1769. She named the following heirs: daughter Penelope Hatton Jones; son-in-law Patrick Beall; and grandchildren Elizabeth Brooke Beall and Jane Bayne Beall. Although she named Francis King as the executor, Patrick Beall and Philip Jones as her executors filed the final account on May 10, 1771.

THOMAS MIDDLETON [3]

1708–17–

THOMAS MIDDLETON, son of Thomas and Penelope (Hatton) Middleton, was born January 29, 1707/8, in Prince George's County. According to family tradition, he married Ann Bayne, a maiden of Piscataway Hundred. Some evidence exists for the marriage, as a grandchild carried the name of Anne Bayne Owsley. The names of his children were furnished by a late historian of the family in Georgia.

Children of Thomas Middleton

1. Mary Middleton, born 1730, died Sept. 15, 1808, aged 78 in Madison Co., Ky., married Thomas Owsley, born in Va., died testate Madison Co., Ky., Nov. 1, 1796.
2. Thomas Middleton.
3. Hatton Middleton, reputed to have been captain of Ga. Militia during Revolutionary War.
4. Walter Middleton.
5. Sarah Middleton.
6. Benjamin Middleton.

As Thomas Middleton, Jr., he was a tithable in the Upper Piscataway Hundred in 1733, according to the tax list for that year. In 1745 he approved the inventory of his father's estate, and shortly afterwards settled in Fairfax County, Virginia. In 1763 he was one of the purchasers at the estate sale of William Owsley, late of Loudoun County, Virginia, deceased. The appraisement of the latter's estate had been made on December 14, 1762, by Holland Middleton, Walter Middleton, and William Taylor.

ROBERT MIDDLETON [3]

17– –18–

ROBERT MIDDLETON, son of William and Elizabeth (Tears) Middleton, was born in Charles County. In August 1748 his father deeded him a portion of "Middleton's Hope." On August 14, 1750, he sold to Samuel Hanson 95 acres of "Maiden's Pleasure," at which time his wife Anne waived dower. He was apparently living out of

Maryland when his father wrote his will in 1769. He settled in Richmond County, Georgia, but left his three sons—Isaac, Hugh, and William Norris Middleton—in Maryland with his father.

Children of Robert Middleton

1. Hugh Middleton. *q.v.*
2. Isaac Middleton.
3. William Norris Middleton.
4. Robert Middleton in Georgia by 1770.
5. ——— Middleton married Gen. David Morgan.

After the Revolution he removed to Fayette County, Kentucky, and is said to have owned much of the land on which the city of Lexington is now built. About 1800 he went to Natchez where he died.

WILLIAM MIDDLETON [3]

17– –1756

WILLIAM MIDDLETON, son of William and Elizabeth (Tears) Middleton, was born in Charles County. His wife was Mary ———, who is believed to have been connected with the Smallwood family. In 1759 Smallwood Coghill by his will bequeathed personalty to his "beloved cousin Isaac Smallwood Middleton."

Issue of William and Mary Middleton

1. Isaac Smallwood Middleton. *q.v.*

On May 8, 1749, as William Middleton, Jr., he leased to Hugh Mitchell 110 acres of land in Zachia Manor during the lives of the said William Middleton, Jr., Robert Middleton, and Hugh Middleton, sons of William Middleton, Sr.

On August 15, 1753, William Middleton and Mary his wife, conveyed to George Maxwell for 2,000 lbs. tobacco "Griffin's Seat" of 24 acres lying in Charles County.

He died intestate. The inventory of his personal estate was made on March 12, 1756, with William Gammell as the administrator. Samuel Middleton and Robert Middleton approved the valuation as the next of kin. Apparently no accounts were filed with the court.

HUGH MIDDLETON [3]

1715–1803

HUGH MIDDLETON, son of William and Elizabeth (Tears) Middleton, was born about 1715 in Charles County. He settled in South Carolina on the Savannah River in what is now McCormick County. When he applied for land in 1768 he stated that he was married and the father of six children. According to his great-grandson, he had four wives, but the name of the first two are not known.

Children by Earlier Marriages

1. Mary Middleton.
2. Sarah Middleton married ——— Quarles.
3. Susanna Middleton.

His third wife was Lucy Williams whom he married in South Carolina. His fourth and last wife by whom there were no issue was Agatha Garrett.

Children of Hugh and Lucy (Williams) Middleton

1. Hugh Tear Middleton married Mildred Martin.
2. John Middleton, died Edgefield Co., S. C., 1846, aged about 80.
3. Elizabeth Middleton married Alexander Spear.
4. Martha Middleton married ——— Tenant.
5. Adelia Middleton married Andrew Calhoun Hamilton.

In 1786 and 1787 he was one of the county magistrates of Edgefield County. In 1790 he was the head of a family in that county with two males under 16 years, six females, and 26 slaves. He took a leading part in the civil life of his community and it is said that he was the Major Hugh Middleton of the Revolutionary War.*

He named his plantation "Locust Hill" after his ancestral estate in Maryland, and at his home on the Savannah River about three miles west of Clark's Hill Depot he died and was buried on

* On June 29, 1785, Major Hugh Middleton was issued £73/18/6 for militia duty in 1780 and 1781. Ref.: *Stub-Entries to Indents Issued in Payment for Claims against S. C. Growing out of the Revolution*, Book R-T, by A. S. Salley, p. 283. In 1781 he was in his mid-sixties, and it is possible that he was the major. The service could also be that of his son, Hugh, who lived in Laurens Co., S. C., where he was the head of a family in 1790, and who died a few months before his father in 1803.

November 30, 1803. No will is extant, but the administration accounts show that his surviving children were John Middleton, Martha Tenant, Sarah Quarles, Mary Middleton, Elizabeth Spear, and Adelia Hamilton.

HOLLAND MIDDLETON [3]

17– –1795

HOLLAND MIDDLETON, son of William and Elizabeth (Tears) Middleton, was born in Charles County. On December 28, 1737, he bought of Thomas Middleton, Sr., the plantation "Long Point" of 135 acres in Prince George's County. On June 5, 1738, he and Sarah his wife conveyed a portion of the tract to John Tolson with dwelling-house, and on October 14, 1740, he and Sarah his wife sold another portion of "Long Point" to William Luckett. By February 2, 1767, he had removed to South Carolina, for on that date as of the "Colony of South Carolina" he conveyed his interest in "Wheeler's Purchase" to Elizabeth Middleton who is identified as the widow of Samuel Middleton.

He settled ultimately in Hancock County, Georgia, and there it is believed that he married his second wife Mary ——— who survived him. He died testate in Hancock County, in 1795.

Children of Holland and Sarah Middleton

1. Sarah Middleton married ——— Dickinson.
2. Susanna Middleton married ——— Berry.
3. Elizabeth Middleton.

Children of Holland and Mary Middleton

1. Zachariah Middleton.
2. Parks Middleton.
3. John Middleton.
4. Robert Middleton.
5. Benjamin Middleton.
6. Mary Middleton.

SAMUEL MIDDLETON [3]

17– –1764

SAMUEL MIDDLETON is established as a son of William Middleton and Elizabeth Tears his wife, though no direct document can be found for absolute proof. As he and his descendants were Anglicans, he is placed in that group-pattern, and he and Holland Middleton, proved definitely as a son of William, held interest in "Wheeler's Purchase." Furthermore, on February 14, 1749, he, Holland Middleton, and William Middleton gave their bond to James Keech and James Middleton who held a lien against William Middleton, Sr., for 122,000 lbs. tobacco which was later increased to 180,000 lbs. As Holland and Williams are proved as sons of William Middleton, Sr., it looks as if all three sons were giving security for their father. No instrument has been found to disprove the above-mentioned inference. Smith Middleton approved the valuation of his estate as a kinsman, but the age of the two men were such that a father and son relationship was impossible.

He married first Sarah, daughter of William Hutchison, who died intestate in Charles County before December 3, 1735. The latter's widow Anne married secondly John Maconchie and thirdly Robert Hanson.* As Anne Hanson on March 25, 1751, she settled the estate of her husband, William Hutchison, and accounted for £206/8/- due to "Samuel Middleton who had intermarried with Sarah a daughter of William Hutchison, deceased." If any issue resulted from this first union, none has been proved.

His second wife was Elizabeth Ward who was certainly not in her teens at time of marriage, and from the birth of their children it is concluded that the union occurred about 1754. She was the daughter of Henry Ward and Margaret his wife, of Prince George's County, and was styled in her father's will of April 13, 1738, as his eldest daughter and made joint-executrix with her mother. And she was of age to qualify as an executrix at probation on June 4, 1739. Her mother's will was written on November 12, 1762, but was not probated in Charles County until December 21, 1774. She bequeathed her daughter Elizabeth Middleton one iron pot and her granddaughter Ann Middleton one heifer.

Children of Samuel and Elizabeth (Ward) Middleton

1. Ann Ward Middleton, born 1756, married Feb. 16, 1775, Benjamin, son of John and Eleanor (Howard) Douglas.
2. Horatio Ward Middleton, born 1758, married twice. *q.v.*
3. Samuel Ward Middleton, born 1760, married Catherine Taliaferro Hooe. *q.v.*

---

* For the Hanson family, see, Newman's *Charles County Gentry*.

On May 8, 1751, he purchased 300 acres of " Wheeler's Purchase," and on November 12, same year, he conveyed 118 acres to Benjamin Ward. No wife of Samuel Middleton waived dower. Both were styled " Gent." in the deed, and the plantation was situated on the Potomac River at the mouth of St. John's or Pomonkey Creek and had been patented on July 10, 1663, by John Wheeler for 500 acres.

He died intestate in 1764. His widow was issued letters of administration with her bond dated June 15, 1764, and Thomas McPherson and Benjamin Ward as her sureties. Smith Middlleton and Benjamin Ward approved the valuation of the personal estate as the kinsmen. The final account was rendered on July 6, 1765, when the balance of £1,054/15/10 was distributed among the widow and the three children, Ann Ward Middleton aged 12 August last, Horatio Ward Middleton aged about 10, and Samuel Ward Middleton aged 8 years May next.

On February 2, 1767, his widow, Elizabeth Middleton, purchased from Holland Middleton, of the Colony of South Carolina, for £100 and a silver watch all his right and interest in " Wheeler's Purchase " on Pomonky Creek whereon the said Elizabeth Middleton then resided and which her husband, Samuel Middleton, died possessed of. No wife waived dower.

The will of his widow, dated July 26, 1783, was probated in Charles County on September 12, 1784, by Francis H. Marbury, Thomas Ward, and Elizabeth Ward.

To son Horatio Middleton " the land whereon I now live reserving the house I now live in as a home for my son Samuel Ward Middleton whilst he remains single."

To son Samuel Ward Middleton " the crop now growing."

To daughter Ann Douglas during her life " the use of the Negro girl Mille, now in her possession, and at her death, her increase to be equally divided between my grandson Richard Henry Douglas and my granddaughter Matilda Douglas "; one feather bed and an arm chair.

To son Samuel Ward Middleton 10 Negroes, and other personalty.

To grandson Samuel Middleton Douglas a Negro and three years of schooling.

To granddaughter Ann Middleton Negro.

Executor—son Samuel Ward Middleton.

CAPTAIN THEODORE MIDDLETON[4]

1758–1845

THEODORE MIDDLETON is placed as a son of Smith and Mary (Hawkins) Middleton. With no settlement of the estate of Smith Middleton by the courts, it is difficult to prove his heirs, but the Christian name of Theodore was a Smith name, and although Dr. Edward Semmes who married a daughter of Smith Middleton in his will styled Theodore Middleton "friend" and appointed him the executor of his estate, a close relationship is indicated.

On May 1, 1778, Theodore Middleton was appointed 2d Lieutenant of the Middle Battalion of Prince George's County. He may be the Theodore Middleton who subscribed to the Oath of Allegiance in Charles County before Joshua Sanders in 1778. On March 30, 1781, Ensign Theodore Middleton of the extra regiment was ordered to be paid £50 by the Auditor General. On April 25, 1781, Theodore Middleton was appointed Captain-Lieutenant of a Company of Foot to serve one year. On March 7, 1782, Theodore Middleton was referred to as a late lieutenant of the extra regiment.*

On November 20, 1789, he secured license in Prince George's County to marry Julia Hoxton. In 1790 he was the head of a family in Charles County with himself, two males under 16, 1 female, and 7 slaves.

On October 5, 1789, Dr. Edward Semmes named him as his executor; in April, 1791, he was cited by the court for not passing a final account upon the estate, and in the same month the Orphans' Court granted him permission to sell a portion of the personal estate to meet some debts of the deceased.

In February, 1833, as a resident of Prince George's County, he applied for a pension by rights of his service in the Revolutionary War. He stated that he was born 1758 in Charles County, and was commissioned a lieutenant of the 2d Md. Regt. under Captain Mountjoy Bailey, Major Giles, and Colonel Alexander Smith. He participated in the Battle of Guilford Courthouse, but was released in October, 1781, as a supernumerary officer. After his return to Maryland, he was commissioned a captain under Colonel Uriah

* *Archives of Maryland*, vol. 21, p. 63; vol. 45. pp. 367, 414, 418; vol. 48, p. 94.

Forrest and did recruiting duty for nine months in Annapolis. He died in 1845.

JAMES MIDDLETON [4]

17– –18–

JAMES MIDDLETON, son of James Middleton and his wife, was born in Charles County. During 1778 he subscribed to the Oath of Allegiance in his native county before Judge Joshua Sanders. On April 23, 1789, he married Nancy Corry, daughter of Dr. John Corry and Elizabeth Neale his wife. Dr. Corry died testate 1772 in Charles County, and referred only to his daughters in his will, but his widow Elizabeth Corry died testate in 1798 and bequeathed her daughter Ann Middleton one riding chair and other personalty. Letters of administration were issued to her son-in-law James Middleton as the greatest creditor.

Children of James and Nancy (Corry) Middleton

1. Alexander Middleton, born Aug. 12, 1790, married Jan. 26, 1817, Mary Ann Thompson, and May, 1827, Elizabeth Attaway Jameson.
2. David Middleton.
3. James Henry Augustus Middleton.
4. Ann Rosalie Middleton died unmarried 1823.*
5. Lucretia Middleton.

In 1793 he and his brother Ignatius Middleton purchased from Walter Smith, of Charles County, all title to the surplus land in "Jordan" which "my grandfather John Smith, deceased, made over to me the said Walter Smith by a deed of gift except 97 acres where James Montgomery now lives also 122 acres which was formerly laid out for Smith Middleton." On September 28, 1803, he and his brother and Thomas Isaac Reeves agreed to arbitrate over the boundaries of their respective portions of "Jordan." Reeves claimed that portion which John Smith had devised in 1716 to his daughter Priscilla who married John Moore, then deceased, whereas James and Ignatius Middleton claimed title to the portion which John Smith had devised to his daughter, Elizabeth, who married Robert Middleton.

* According to the recorded will, it was written on Oct. 8, 1803, but not probated until 1823. If the date of writing is correct, then she cannot have been the daughter of James Middleton by his wife Nancy Corry.

His unmarried daughter, Ann Rosella Middleton, by her will of June 7, 1803, devised her estate to her sister Lucretia Middleton. The witnesses were Walter Baker Brooke, David Middleton, and James H. A. Middleton.

On January 17, 1825, James Middleton, James H. A. Middleton, and Lucretia Middleton conveyed to Elizabeth Montgomery for $1,100 two portions of "Jordan" and part of "Middleton and Askin's Progress."

LIEUT. ISAAC SMALLWOOD MIDDLETON [4]
17– –18–

ISAAC SMALLWOOD MIDDLETON, son of William and Mary Middleton, was born in Charles County. His wife was Eleanor ———.

At the census of 1775 he was domiciled in the Upper Port Tobacco Hundred. On February 11, 1771, he sold to Henry Hardy, Jr., of Prince George's County, 290 acres of "Gardener's Meadows Enlarged," beginning at a white oak on Mattawoman Swamp. His wife, Eleanor, waived all dower rights. On the same day, he bought of Henry Hardy, Jr., for £220 "Duke's Delight" of 100 acres in Charles County, "Gantt's Enlargement Enlarged" of 13½ acres, and "Molley's Delight" of 103 acres, all contiguous. Mary Hardy, wife, waived her dower interest.

On May 9, 1778, he was commissioned 1st Lieut. of the 26th Battalion of Militia in Charles County in the company of Captain Samuel Smallwood.* In the same year he subscribed to the Patriot's Oath in Charles County before Magistrate Joshua Sanders.

He was not the head of a family in Maryland at the 1790 census, and his name does not appear upon the deed index after 1771, nor are there any references in the Orphans' Court.

An Isaac S. Middleton, living near the Navy Yard, is listed in the first (1822) Federal City directory.

* *Archives of Maryland*, vol. 21, p. 72; Militia List, p. 62, Maryland Historical Society.

HUGH MIDDLETON [4]

17– –18–

HUGH MIDDLETON remained with his grandfather in Maryland, when his father, Robert, settled in Georgia. During the Revolutionary War he served as a private in the Charles County Militia company of Captain Thomas H. Marshall.* By 1782 he had settled in Fairfax County, Virginia, where he was a tithable with seven whites and four blacks in his household.

LIEUT. HORATIO MIDDLETON [4]

1753–1795

HORATIO MIDDLETON, son of Samuel and Elizabeth (Ward) Middleton, was born 1753 in Charles County. His mother by her will of 1783 left him the dwelling-plantation and a number of Negro slaves.

The following is from the register of St. John's Piscataway Parish: "On the 25th Day of May 1775, Horatio Middleton and Susanna Stoddert was (*sic*) married by the Rev. Thomas Thornton and the following are their Issue: Samuel, son of Horatio Middleton and Susanna Middleton, born 31 March 1776."

Children of Horatio and Susanna (Stoddert) Middleton

1. Samuel Middleton, born Mar. 31, 1776.
2. William Stoddert Middleton, born 1780.
3. Elizabeth Middleton, born 1782.

At the beginning of the Revolutionary War he served as a sergeant of the county militia. On May 9, 1778, he was commissioned an ensign of the 26th Battalion of Charles County, and later was promoted to 1st Lieutenant, serving in the company of Captain George Dent.**

On April 6, 1785, he bought of John Ward, of Charles County, for 15,000 lbs. tobacco "'Ward's Wheal" of 140 acres lying in Charles County. Mary Ward, wife, waived all dower rights. On May 6, 1794, in order to meet an obligation he sold a portion of

* Militia List, p. 55, Maryland Historical Society.

** Militia List, pp. 55, 68; *Archives of Maryland*, vol. 21, p. 72.

"Wheeler's Purchase" which his mother had bought of Holland Middleton.

He died intestate. His widow was Joanna. The administration bond was dated October 12, 1795, and the widow was granted permission by the court to dispose of a portion of the estate to meet some obligations. When the inventory of the personal estate was filed on March 7, 1796, the widow had married George Ward. The appraisement amounted to £731/19/3, but at the final account George Ward and his wife Joanna showed an overpayment of £194/14/9.

At the April term of the court in 1796, William Stoddert Middleton, an orphan of Horatio Middleton, aged 16 on August 1 next, made choice of George Ward as his guardian. At the same time his sister, Elizabeth Middleton, aged 14, was placed under the guardianship of George Ward. In August, 1800, William S. Middleton, aged 20, was still under the guardianship of George Ward.

SAMUEL WARD MIDDLETON [4]
1760–1803

SAMUEL WARD MIDDLETON, son of Samuel and Elizabeth (Ward) Middleton, was born 1760 in Durham Parish, Charles County, where his father was a communicant. After May, 1788, he married Catherine (Hooe) Winter, the widow of Captain William Winter of the Revolution, with four children—William, Anne, Elizabeth, and Richard Hooe Winter. She was the daughter of Richard and Anne (Ireland) Hooe and the granddaughter of Rice and Catherine (Taliaferro) Hooe, of Virginia. On the maternal side she was the granddaughter of Gilbert Ireland and his wife Anne Dent who was the daughter of Colonel George Dent, of Nanjemoy, Charles County.*

Children of Samuel Ward and Catherine (Hooe) Middleton

1. Catherine Anne Ireland Middleton married Richard Thompson Semmes. *q.v.*
2. Harriet Middleton married Ignatius Semmes. *q.v.*
3. Taliaferro Hooe Middleton married ——— Smith.
4. Mary Ann Dent Middleton.
5. Elizabeth Ward Middleton married ——— Davis.

---

* For the Ireland and Dent ancestry, see, *Charles County Gentry*, by Newman.

The 1800 census reports him in Durham Parish, Charles County, himself between 26 and 45 years of age, 1 male between 10 to 16, 4 females under 10, 1 female betwen 16 and 26 years, 1 female between 26 and 45, and 33 slaves.

His will, dated October 19, 1800, was probated in Charles County on December 5, 1803. He bequeathed one-third of his estate to his wife, Catherine, and the remainder to his unnamed children, providing also for an unborn child.

His widow married thirdly Richard Meek and they both distributed the estate on September 10, 1812, to the five heirs—Catherine Anne Ireland Middleton, Harriet Middleton, Elizabeth Ward Middleton, Taliaferro Hooe Middleton, and Mary Ann Dent Middleton.

During the lawsuit over the affluent estate of Robert Townsend Hooe, who died in Alexandria, Virginia, during 1796, without issue, it was stated that Catherine Meeke, the wife of Richard B. Meeke, of Maryland, was his only legal heir. She, however, had not been mentioned in his will.

Although Richard Meek dated his will February 15, 1810, and devised his wife the use of his plantation during life, he outlived her, for his will was probated on April 2, 1819. Her will, as that of Catherine T. Meek, was proved on December 7, 1818. She bequeathed her estate equally to her five daughters—Catherine Ann Ireland Semmes, Harriet Simms, Elizabeth Ward Davis, Taliaferro Hooe Smith, and Mary Ann Dent Ireland Middleton. She appointed her son, William H. Winter, of the Mississippi Territory, the executor.

NEALE FAMILY

The Neale family of Charles County with the background and position which it held in England and later in the Colonies takes its place among the leading aristocratic colonial families of America. The progenitor was Captain James Neale, Gent., son of Raphael Neale, of Drury Lane, London, and Wollaston, Northamptonshire, who at the age of three in 1618 appeared in the Visitation of Bedfordshire.* And the family's rights to the use of armorial bearings are unquestionable.

James Neale, a royalist, maintained an enviable position at the court of Charles I, and it has been stated many times that his wife, Anne Gill, was one-time lady-in-waiting to Queen Henrietta Maria. The 17th century ring which has come down to posterity is testimony of his devotion to the Crown and was worn in that day by the Stuartians in defiance of the Cromwellians. Tradition has it that it was given by the Queen to Madam Neale, one of her maids of honour.**

On July 25, 1641, Cecilius, Lord Baltimore, requested his brother Governor Leonard Calvert to survey for James Neale, Gent., a

* The material in *Semmes and Allied Families*, published in 1918, stating that the Neales were from a long line of ancient Irish kings is erroneous. For the English background, see the " Visitation of Bedfordshire," *Harleian Society Publications*, vol. 19, pp. 33, 43; also Christopher Johnson's article on the Neale family in the *Maryland Historical Magazine*, vol. 7, p. 201.

** It is a hinged ring of blue enamel set in gold with a jewel in the center. The miniature in enamel is a full face showing a white collar, dark doublet, and a blue ribbon denoting an order. The size would indicate that it was made for a small feminine finger. The ring is now in the Maryland Historical Society, having been given by Clara Goldsborough Hollyday, a descendant. Also was given a pendant which had belonged to Henrietta Maria Neale, eldest daughter of Captain James Neale.

The curator of British and mediaeval antiquities of the British Museum, writing in 1923, stated that the ring would " certainly appear to date from the 17th century, but the ring is English and the pendant is of Spanish origin. Enamelled memorial rings in memory of Charles I were made in considerable numbers after his death for adherents of the House of Stuarts. I should say that yours belongs to this class, that is, it is a Stuart ring worn in memory of the beheaded king."

THE CHARLES I MEMORIAL RING

(Illustration approximately twice actual size. Gift to the Maryland Historical Society of Miss Clara Goldsborough Hollyday.)

manor of 2,000 acres, with full manorial rights. He named his manor "Wollaston" after his paternal grandfather's lordship in Northamptonshire, and it was accordingly laid out on the west bank of the Wicomico River on the neck formed as the river meets the Potomac. The 17th century manor house stood there as late as 1900.

His first attendance at an early Assembly was in August, 1642, but by April, 1643, he had been appointed to the Privy Council. This office of state was soon followed by his appointment as one of the Commissioners of the Treasury. In 1644 he was commisioned a magistrate of the local court.

After September 18, 1644, he returned to England and was absent from his Maryland holdings for fully 15 years, but before departing he commissioned Nathaniel Pope his attorney and presumably made him the steward of his manor and manager of his other Maryland interests.

From 1644 to 1659 during the Civil Wars and the Puritan supremacy he was either in England or in Europe as an ambassador for Charles I at the Spanish and Portuguese Courts and also agent for "his Royall highness the Duke of Yorke in Severall Emergent Affaires."

Upon his return to England he married Anne Gill, a gentlewoman, the daughter and heiress of Benjamin Gill, Gent., who had come to the Province about the same time as he, or about 1641. Benjamin Gill was a business partner of John Pile, of Sarum, but somehow his family remained in Europe and none of them joined him in Maryland. He died in 1658, whereupon Robert Cole, Gent., who had come from Middlesex, declared himself as his nearest of kin in the Province.

Children of James and Anne (Gill) Neale

1. Henrietta Maria Neale married (1) Richard Bennett and (2) Philemon Lloyd.
2. James Neale married (1) Elizabeth Calvert and (2) Elizabeth Lord. *q.v.*
3. Dorothy Neale married Roger Brooke.
4. Anthony Neale married (1) Elizabeth Roswell and (2) Elizabeth Digges. *q.v.*
5. Jane Neale married William Boarman. *q.v.*

On January 9, 1650/60, Lord Baltimore addressed a communication to his Maryland Governor to the effect that Captain James Neale had been absent for some years, but was desirous of returning with his family. Accordingly, he sailed on November 16, 1660, from the Isle of Wight in an English ship with instructions from His Lordship for the Governor of Maryland to reduce the Dutch on Delaware Bay who were encroaching upon his sovereignty.

He was immediately appointed to his former seat in the Council, but some political change occurred ultimately, and he seemed to have lost his seat in the Upper Chamber. In 1666, however, he entered the Lower House as a delegate from Charles County.

In 1666 he petitioned the General Assembly to naturalize his four children by his wife Anne who had been born during his "divers yeares in Spain and Portugall," namely, Henrietta Maria, James, Dorothy, and Anthony.

With the encroachment of the Dutch on Delaware Bay and settlements made up the river prior to Penn's expedition, Lord Baltimore was anxious to cement his claims, thereupon on July 20, 1669, he made Neale the commander of that area. "I Pray cause that portion of Delaware Bay on which the Dutch are Seated and a convenient quantity of Land to it to be Erected into a County and appoint the said Captain Neale Commander of it." The Maryland settlement in that area was known as Whorekill, but an actual county with Captain Neale as Commander apparently did not materialize.

On December 24, 1681, he deeded to his son and heir, James, one-half of Wollaston Manor with the understanding that he would enjoy full manorial rights. In August, 1682, a pre-nuptial agreement was made between him and William Roswell, of St. Mary's County, Gent., whereby he made a deed of gift of the remaining portion of the manor to his second son, Anthony, in consideration of his bethrothal to Elizabeth, the daughter of William Roswell.

Captain Neale died testate in 1683. His will, dated November 27, 1683, was probated in Charles County on March 29, 1684.

To sons James and Anthony confirmation of gifts already made.

To grandson Raphael Neale 100 acres which had been purchased from Arthur Turner.

To grandchildren Roger, James, and Dorothy Brooke livestock but they were to be retained by his son, Anthony, and his son-in-law, William Boarman, until grandchildren came of age.

To granddaughter Jane, daughter of William and Jane Boarman, personalty.

To grandson James Lloyd 5,000 lbs. tobacco.

To the poor of St. Giles' Parish near London £5 to be distributed by Father Henry Warren.

His sons were to pay their mother 10,000 lbs. tobacco annually during her life.

To wife Anne, son Anthony, and daugters Henrietta Maria Lloyd and Jane Boarman residuary estate.

The original will of Captain Neale is on file at the Hall of Records. It shows his signature in a very intelligent hand besides which is an indistinct impression of a seal in red wax. Under a magnifying glass one of the charges could be a helmet above an armorial shield. The impression being so faint, no definite conclusion can be made.

Madam Neale died in 1698. Her will, dated June 28, 1697, was admitted to probate in Charles County on June 3, 1698. Personalty were bequeathed to her sons, James and Anthony, and their wives, also to her granddaughter, Mary Neale, and to her grandchildren, the children of William Boarman.

JAMES NEALE [2]

16– –1725

JAMES NEALE, son of Captain James Neale and Anne his wife, was born on the Continent of Europe, emigrated with his parents to Maryland, and was subsequently naturalized.

He married first Elizabeth, the daughter of William Calvert and his wife Elizabeth Stone,* being the granddaughter of two provincial governors—Leonard Calvert, Esq., and Captain William Stone, Esq., who held lordship on Poynton Manor. His wife Elizabeth was alive, on May 17, 1684, when she joined him in a deed of conveyance to Giles Blizzard.

Issue of James and Elizabeth (Calvert) Neale

1. Mary Neale married (1) Charles Edgerton, (2) Jeremiah Adderton, (3) Joseph van Sweringen, and (4) William Deacon.

---

* For the ancestry of Elizabeth Stone, see, Newman's *The Stones of Poynton Manor.*

James Neale married secondly Elizabeth Lord, the daughter of Captain John Lord, a magistrate of Westmoreland County, Virginia, who had come down from the Connecticut Colony. On November 28, 1687, he, styled "Gent." of Westmoreland County, conveyed to James Neale, of Wollaston, Charles County, Maryland, inasmuch as a marriage was about to be solemnized "between James Neale, and Elizabeth daughter of the said John Lord," a tract of land lying in the forest of Nomoni near the Court House containing 800 acres and also a tract lying in Upper Machodoc containing 400 acres, and also the tract lying in Stafford County near the mill of Mr. Giles Brent containing about 500 acres which had been given the grantor by the will of Joseph Edmonds. The deed of gift was signed by John Lord and Elizabeth his wife in the presence of John Matthews, Anthony Neale, and Henry Wriothesley.

Children of James and Elizabeth (Lord) Neale

2. James Neale married twice. *q.v.*
3. Henry Neale married Mary Gardiner. *q.v.*
4. Benjamin Neale married Mary Edelen. *q.v.*
5. William Neale married Anne ———. *q.v.*
6. Joseph Neale *d.s.p.*
7. Mary Neale married Thomas Taney.
8. Anne Neale married Edward Cole.
9. Margaret Neale married Richard Edelen * and Zachariah Bond.
10. Mildred Neale married Thomas Wheeler.
11. Elizabeth Neale, *d.s.p.*

On December 21, 1710, by a deed of gift he distributed 13 Negro slaves among his eight children, namely, James, Henry, Benjamin, Joseph, Elizabeth, Ann, Mary, and Margaret.

On April 26, 1716, James Neale, Sr., and Elizabeth his wife made a deed of gift to James Neale, Jr., "son and heir apparent of the said James Neale" 1,000 acres of "Wooleston Manor," where the great gate stood and the Wicomico River and bounded by St. Raphaels' Creek and Potomac River, being the portion whereon the manor house of the said James Neale, Sr., stood. On the same date he gave to his son, Henry, 500 acres of "Gill's Land" on the west side of the Wicomico River.

On March 30, 1720, James Neale and Elizabeth his wife, of

* For ancestry of Richard Edelen and his descendants, see, Newman's *Charles County Gentry*.

Charles County, deeded to their second son, Henry, for natural love and affection the tract lying in Copley Parish, Westmoreland County, near the courthouse which had been given to James Neale and his wife by "John Lord, Gent., father of the said Elizabeth Neale."

Styling himself James Neale, Sr., of Wolleston Manor, his will was dated April 1, 1725, but not probated in Charles County until October 11, 1727.

> To eldest son James, Jr., he confirmed the deed to Wolleston Manor; personalty.
>
> To second son Henry 500 acres of "Gills Land" was confirmed; personalty.
>
> To son Benjamin and heirs 500 acres of leased land; if he died without issue, then to son William; personalty.
>
> To son William 500 acres of leased land and all land at Mattawoman bought of George Hinson; if he died without issue or in minority, then to son Benjamin; personalty.
>
> To wife Elizabeth interest in 340 acres at Upper Machoteck, Va., and one-half of personal estate.
>
> To daughters Mary Deaton (formerly Vanswerring), Mary Tawney (formerly Neale), Anne now wife of Mr. Edward Cole, and Margaret personalty.
>
> To daughter Mildred £30 at age or marriage.

By a codicil his son, William, and daughter, Mildred, were to have no interest in their bequests until they gave bond to acquit themselves and heirs of all interest in certain slaves once the property of the testator's daughter Elizabeth.

His widow, Elizabeth, died testate in Charles County, and by her will dated January 17, 1733/4, and proved April 22, 1734, she bequeathed 5 shillings each to the following children—Henry Neale, Benjamin Neale, Ann Cole, Mary Tawney, and Margaret Egglin [Edelen]. To her son, William, she devised the tract on Machodock Creek, Virginia, and personalty, while the residuary estate was to be divided equally between her son William and daughter Mildred. The latter two were named as executors, with Edward Cole, of St. Mary's County, as the overseer.

His daughter Mildred, widow of Thomas Wheeler, died without issue in Harford County, Maryland, and by her will probated in 1776, she divided most of her estate among her Neale kinsmen. Among her heirs were her niece Mildred Greenwell, of St. Mary's County; niece Eleanor Green, daughter of Benjamin Green; nephew

John son of William Neale, late of Charles County; and the latter's sons Francis and Joseph Neale; and her nieces Elizabeth McAtee of Charles County, and Mary Ann Boarman. The residuary estate was bequeathed to John, Francis, Joseph, and Sarah Neale, the children of her brother. John Neale, of Charles County, and Benjamin Green, of Harford County, were named the executors.

LIEUTENANT ANTHONY NEALE [2]

16– –1723

ANTHONY NEALE, second son of James and Anne (Gill) Neale, was born on the continent of Europe, while his father was residing temporarily in the Iberian Peninsula. Being brought to Maryland at a young age, he was subsequently naturalized and granted all rights of a British subject.

About 1680 he married Elizabeth, daughter of William Roswell, of St. Mary's County, and his wife Emma, one-time widow of William Johnson. William Roswell by his will, dated September 17, 1694, and probated on May 14, 1695, devised his grandson, Roswell Neale, 500 acres of "St. Winifred" after the death of the testator's widow, Emma, and to his grandson, Anthony Neale, 265 acres of "Williams' Folly," and to his third grandson, Thomas Neale, 200 acres of "The Meadows."

Children of Anthony and Elizabeth (Roswell) Neale

1. Roswell Neale married (1) Mary Brent and (2) Elizabeth Blackistone. *q.v.*
2. Anthony Neale, no further record.
3. Thomas Neale, no further record.
4. Raphael Neale, born 1683, married Mary Brooke. *q.v.*
5. James Neale, *d.s.p.* 1719.

His wife, Elizabeth, died young leaving minor children, and he married secondly Elizabeth, daughter of William and Elizabeth (Sewell) Digges. His mother-in-law, Madam Elizabeth Digges, dating her will September 30, 1705, bequeathed legacies to her daughter, Elizabeth Neale, and appointed her son-in-law, Anthony Neale, as the executor. The instrument, however, was not proved in Charles County until June 17, 1710. He was likewise named the executor of the will of his brother-in-law, Edward Digges, who died

1714 in Prince George's County, when he devised land lying at the head of Port Tobacco Creek to his nephews, Henry and Edward Neale, and various bequests to his sister, Elizabeth Neale, and his niece, Mary Neale.

Children of Anthony and Elizabeth (Digges) Neale

6. Henry Neale, accepted Holy Orders, died 1767.
7. Edward Neale married Mary Lowe. *q.v.*
8. Mary Neale.
9. Charles Neale married Mary Smith. *q.v.*
10. Bennett Neale, accepted Holy Orders.

He particpated in the Nanticoke Indian War on the Eastern Shore and for his services he was voted 830 lbs. tobacco by the General Assembly.* On January 20, 1686/7, he was recommended by Captain Randolph Brandt as a lieutenant in the provincial militia.**

His will, dated November 20, 1722, was probated in Charles County on July 12, 1723.

Personalty to the following priests—Thomas Mansell, William Hunter, and John Bennett.

Personalty to George Newman and James Gates.

To son Raphael " Williams' Folly " and personalty.

To son Henry if he does not enter the priesthood 1/5 of personal estate, but should he take Holy Orders or die during minority, his portion to testator's four younger children—Edward, Charles, Bennett, and Mary.

To son Edward one-half of dwelling-plantation " Aquenseek " and personalty including the silver chalice and the suit of church stuff—to remain in the dwelling house for the use of the family

To son Charles residue of " Aquenseek " and personalty.

To son Bennett in event he does not enter priesthood, lease of 200 acres and 1/5 of personal estate, but if he should take Holy Orders or die during minority to testator's four younger children.

To sons Edward and Charles the store house and lot in Chandler Town bought of Philip Hemsley and Mary his wife.

Executors—sons Edward and Charles.

---

* *Archives of Maryland,* vol. 7, p. 101.

** *Archives of Maryland,* vol. 5, p. 539.

JAMES NEALE [3]

1694–1730

JAMES NEALE, son of James and Elizabeth (Lord) Neale, was born about 1694, being aged 27 in 1721. At that time he deposed that his father, James Neale, had paid Charles Calvert for land given by William Calvert to his daughter, which had not been recorded. In 1716 he received from his father 1,000 acres of Wollaston Manor, including the original manor house. His first wife was Elizabeth ———, who was living as late as 1725.

Issue of James and Elizabeth Neale

1. Elizabeth Neal.

On April 1, 1725, James Neale, Sr., deeded to his " brother-in-law Richard Edelen of Charles County for brotherly love " four Negro slaves and placed him in peaceful possession by the acceptance of " one coyned piece of silver commonly called six pence." The next day Richard Edelen, Sr., " for natural love and affection which I have for my well beloved sister-in-law, Mrs. Elizabeth Neale wife of James Neale, Sr." deeded the same four Negro slaves to his sister-in-law for life, and then to the youngest sons and youngest daughters of the said James Neale, Sr., husband to the said Elizabeth.

He maried secondly Jane, daughter of William and Mary (Pile) Boarman.

Children of James and Jane (Boarman) Neale.

2. James Neale.
3. Jane Neale.
4. Mary Ann Neale.

His will, dated January 7, 1731/2, was probated in Charles County on March 8, 1731/2, by Raphael Neale, John Lancaster, and Bennett Hoskins.

To son James " Wolleston Manor " reserving half of it for the testator's widow, Jane, during life; personalty, but in the event of his death without issue then to his daughters Jane and Mary Anne.

To daughter Elizabeth lands in St. Mary's County which had been willed the testator's former wife, the mother of Elizabeth, and personalty at the age of 16.

To wife Jane residuary estate.

HENRY NEALE[3]
1691–1743

HENRY NEALE, son of James and Elizabeth (Lord) Neale, was born at Wollaston Manor in Charles County, about 1691, deposing to be 46 in 1737. He married Mary Gardiner, the daughter of John Gardiner and Mary Boarman his wife, who as the Widow Gardiner married secondly Robert Slye. Wilfred Gardiner, brother to Madam Mary Neale, died 1743 without issue and named his mother Mary Slye, and his sisters Mary Lancaster and Anne Neale. The former after the death of her husband, Henry Neale, married secondly John Lancaster. Madam Mary Gardiner-Slye died testate in 1744 and willed Negroes to her daughters Mary Lancaster and Anne Neale.

Children of Henry and Mary (Gardiner) Neale

1. Richard Neale. *q.v.*
2. Henry Neale.
3. James Neale, *d.s.p.* 1772.
4. Gerard Neale married twice. *q.v.*
5. Sarah Neale married Richard Brooke.
6. Mary Neale married Richard Gardiner.
7. Henrietta Neale married Roger Smith and Ignatius Wheeler.
8. Teresa Neale married Raphael Lancaster.

His will was dated December 3, 1742, and proved in Charles County on March 8, 1742/3.

To son Richard "Gill Land."
To wife Mary life interest in "Gill Land."
Personal estate to wife and children—Richard, Henry, James, Garrard, Sarah, Mary, Henrietta, and Teresa.

At probation the widow refused to abide by the will and demanded her third. She married secondly John Lancaster and as his widow she died testate in Charles County during 1765. She devised her son, James Neale, "Chancellor's Point" near St. Mary's and her son, Gerard Neale, the plantation formerly possessed by William Deacon. Slaves and other personalty were willed to her sons James, Richard, and Gerard; to her daughters Teresa, Henrietta, and Mary; and to her grandchildren Ann ——, Mary Neale, William Gardiner, and Henry Gardiner.

Their bachelor son, James Neale, died testate in Charles County, and by his will dated 1766, and proved in 1772, he named his bothers Richard and Garrard Neale, his sister Teresa Lancaster, brother-in-law Richard Brooke, and James Neale, Jr., of no stated relationship. Raphael Lancaster and his wife, Teresa, administered on the estate, while Henry Gardiner and William Gardiner as kinsmen approved the value of the inventory.

BENJAMIN NEALE [3]
1703–1746

BENJAMIN NEALE, son of James and Elizabeth (Lord) Neale, was born about 1703 at Wollaston Manor. His wife was Mary, the daughter of Richard and Mary (Hagan) Edelen.*

Children of Benjamin and Mary (Edelen) Neale

1. Bennett Neale. *q.v.*
2. James Neale married Eliabeth Guibert. *q.v.*
3. Elizabeth Neale married John Corry.
4. Mary Neale.
5. Anne Neale.

His will, dated December 15, 1745, was admitted to probate in Charles County, on January 28, 1745/6.

To son Bennett half of dwelling-plantation called "Gills Tract," to have his choice of selection.
To son James the other half.
To daughter Elizabeth Corry half of plantation on Mattawoman given the testator by Richard Edelen.
To daughter Mary Neale the other half on Mattawoman.
To wife Mary one-third of personal estate.
Residue of personal estate to children—Bennett, James, Mary, and Anne.
To son Bennett £20 in addition to his share.
Executors—Brother William Neale and brother-in-law Edward Edelen.

The will of his widow was dated February 24, 1752, and proved in Charles County on March 14, 1752. The estate which consisted mostly of Negroes was bequeathed to her children—James Neale, Bennett Neale, Ann Neale, Mary Neale, and Elizabeth Corry. To her granddaughter, Mary Corry, she bequeathed a ring.

* For ancestry of Mary Edelen, see, Newman's *Charles County Gentry.*

WILLIAM NEALE [3]

17– –1766

WILLIAM NEALE, son of James and Elizabeth (Lord) Neale, was born at Wollaston Manor, Charles County. His wife was Ann ——.

Children of William and Anne Neale

1. John Neale, *d.s.p.* 1809.
2. Joseph Neale. *q.v.*
3. William Francis Neale.
4. Elizabeth Neale married Jacob Clements and Henry Macatee.
5. Mary Anne Neale.
6. Mildred Neale, died test. St. Mary's Co., 1816, married John Greenwell of Ignatius.
7. Catherine Neale married [Edward] Boarman.
8. Sarah Teresia Neale, born Apr. 1752, married John Hoskins Boarman. *q.v.*

On June 22, 1742, he and his wife, Anne, leased to James Berryman, of Westmoreland County, Virginia, his land on Mochodoc Creek in Washington Parish being 120 acres which had been patented to James Neale in 1695. The next day he sold the same tract to James Berryman for £37/10/–.

His will, dated October 29, 1765, was proved in Charles County on June 10, 1766.

> To first son John Neale the dwelling-plantation of 180 acres which extended to the plantation of his second son, Joseph Neale, and Mr. Lancaster.
>
> To third son William Francis the plantation known as " Henson " on the Mattawoman and Negroes.
>
> Personalty to the following children—John, Joseph, William Francis, Elizabeth, Mary Anne, Mildred, Catherine, and Sally.
>
> Legacy bequeathed the testator by his sister Cole was to be divided among his daughters.

The will of his unmarried son, John Neale, was dated October 16, 1808, and proved in Charles County on March 29, 1809. His heirs were: sisters Elizabeth Macatee, Catherine Boarman, Sarah Boarman, and Mildred Greenwell; and the nine children of his deceased brother, Joseph Neale, that is—Teresa Boarman, Urusla Boone, Monica Neale, Margaret Edelen, Mildred Neale, Harriet Lancaster, Joseph Neale, Aloysius Neale, and William Neale. Other heirs of no stated relationship were Jeremiah A. Neale and Milburn Boarman.

ROSWELL NEALE[3]

16– –1751

ROSWELL NEALE, son of Anthony and Elizabeth (Roswell) Neale, was born in Charles County. He married Mary Brent, the daughter of Colonel George Brent, of Woodstock, Stafford County, Virginia. In 1715 the maiden Martha Brent of Charles County died and named her sister, Mary Neale, and brother-in-law, Roswell Neale, in her will. William Chandler by his will dated 1725, but not proved until 1730, devised his nephew, William Neale, son of his sister [uterine] Mary Neale, then deceased, " Chandler's Hope " of 1,000 acres at 21 and certain personalty. To the second son of his sister, Mary Neale, that is, Henry Neale, he devised 600 acres of " Green Spring " and 200 acres of " Chandler's Hills." To his two nephews, Edward and Charles Neale, be bequeathed money that was in the hands of Richard Hawton.

Children of Roswell and Mary (Brent) Neale

1. William Neale married Anne Gardiner. *q.v.*
2. Henry Neale married Anne ———. *q.v.*
3. Edward Neale, apparently died young.
4. Charles Neale, apparently died young.

After the death of his first wife, he married Elizabeth Blackistone, daughter of John and Ann (Guibert) Blackistone. Thomas Blackistone, the bachelor brother of his wife, died testate in 1742 in St. Mary's County and named his sister, Elizabeth Neale, his brother Roswell Neale, and the latter's three children–James, Bennett, and Raphael.

Children of Roswell and Elizabeth (Blackistone) Neale

5. James Neale married Elizabeth ———. *q.v.*
6. Bennett Neale married Mary ———. *q.v.*
7. Raphael Neale.
8. Jeremiah Neale married twice. *q.v.*
9. Anne Neale married William Gibson.
10. Mary Neale married ——— Wheeler.
11. Elizabeth Neale.

The will of Roswell Neale, dated March 24, 1751, was probated in Charles County on May 1, same year.

To wife Elizabeth the dwelling-plantation on Tomachokin Creek called " St. Winifred " during life, then to son James, but if he died without issue to revert to testator's sons Raphael, Bennett, and Jeremiah.

To son James 30 acres of the plantation on which he was then living.

To sons James, Raphael, Bennett, and Jeremiah the watermill with 6 acres.

Residue of the landed estate to sons Raphael, Bennett, and Jeremiah, with Raphael having the plantation on which he was then living.

To children Anne Gibson, wife of William Gibson; Mary Wheeler; Elizabeth Neale; William Neale; Henry Neale personalty.

Reference was made to the marriage settlement made between him and his wife, and he confirmed all land previously given to his sons William and Henry.

Executors—Sons James, Raphael, Bennett, and Jeremiah Neale.

RAPHAEL NEALE [3]
1683–1743

RAPHAEL NEALE, son of Anthony and Elizabeth (Roswell) Neale, was born about 1683, deposing to be aged 59 in 1742. His wife was Mary, daughter of Colonel Baker Brooke and Anne Calvert his wife. She was unmarried at the death of her father in 1679, but received land on the north side of the Patuxent River in Calvert County. In 1716 Leonard Brooke, brother to Mary, named his brother-in-law, Raphael Neale, the executor of his estate.

Children of Raphael and Mary (Brooke) Neale

1. Elizabeth Neale married John Lancaster.
2. Mary Neale married Thomas Taney.
3. Henrietta Neale married Basil Brooke.
4. Monica Neale married Edward Digges.
5. Anne Neale married James Thompson.
6. Eleanor Neale married Bennett Hoskins.

He was styled " father " in the will of his son-in-law, Bennett Hoskins, in 1734 who directed that the agreement between him and Edward Neale for making over " St. John's " and " St. John's Addition " be fulfilled.

His will, dated July 20, 1743, was proved in Charles County on December 10, following.

To John Lancaster the land on which he resided during life, then to the testator's daughter Elizabeth Lancaster.
To daughter Mary Taney gifts already made were confirmed.
To daughter Henrietta Neale one-third of dwelling-plantation including mansion house.
Residuary estate to daughters Monica Digges and Anne Thompson.
To wife Mary life interest in one-half of realty and residue of personal estate.
Mention was made of grandchildren Ralph Taney, John Lancaster, Raphael Lancaster, Mary Boarman, and Anne Hoskins.

He also desired that what was due to his grandchildren "the Hoskinses" be fully paid including what "Mary Hoskins now Mary Boarman hath already had."

His widow died in St. Mary's County in 1763, her will having been written on September 29, 1760.

To daughter Ann Thompson Negroes and other personalty.
To grandchildren Raphael Thompson, Eleanor Thompson, Mary Eleanor Comb, John Francis Tawney, John Digges, Raphael Brooke, and Eleanor Digges, personalty.
Old slave Nell was to choose one of the testatrix' three living daughters.
Sons-in-law John Lancaster and Edward Digges personalty.
Tobacco to the clergy and the poor.
Executors—daughter Ann Thompson, sons-in-law Thomas Tawney and Bazil Brooke.

EDWARD NEALE [3]

1704–1760

EDWARD NEALE, son of Anthony and Elizabeth (Digges) Neale, was born 1704 in Charles County. He married Mary, daughter of Colonel Henry Lowe, and his wife Susanna Bennett, of St. Mary's County. She was unmarried in 1717 when Colonel Lowe negotiated his will and devised his daughter "Woods Quarter," but as Mary Neale she was an heir of her brother, Nicholas Lowe, of Prince George's County, in 1729. By the latter's will his sister, Susanna Digges, was devised "Bennett's Lowe" in Kent County, "Green Oak" in Kent County, and "Spries Hills" in Cecil County on condition that her husband, Charles Digges, make over to the testator's sister, Mary Neale, all rights and interests in the testator's dwelling-plantation in Prince George's County. In the event that Charles Digges should refuse, then the two last named tracts were to revert to his sister, Mary Neale, and to the latter he willed in fee 1,500 acres of " Barbadoes " in Charles County which had been exchanged with John Digges.*

Children of Edward and Mary (Lowe) Neale

1. Eleanor Neale married Henry Rozier.
2. Mary Neale married Nicholas Digges.
3. Martha Neale married Francis Hall; she died May 31, 1789, aged 50 years and 5 months.

Edward Neale removed to Queen Anne's County and his house " Bolingly " at Queenstown is one of the present show places of the Eastern Shore. His tombstone in the private burying grounds reads: " Here lyeth the Body of Edward Neale, Esq., who departed this life the 28th day of December 1760 Aged 60 years."

His will, dated December 22, 1760, was admitted to probate in Queen Anne's County on February 6, 1761. He devised his daughter, Martha Hall, the wife of Francis Hall, the entire landed estate, and to his daughter, Eleanor Rosier wife of Henry Rosier, and his granddaughter, Eleanor Digges, personalty. He named his sons-in-law, Henry Rosier and Francis Hall, as the executors and requested that John Lewis, of Cecil County, be granted £50 for the purchase of land in Queen Anne's County for his residence near the congregation of Catholics in the county.

CHARLES NEALE [3]

1705–178–

CHARLES NEALE, son of Anthony and Elizabeth (Digges) Neale, was born about 1705, being aged 39 in 1744, according to his de-

* Christopher Johnson in his article on the Neale family in the *Maryland Historical Magazine* (vol. 7, pp. 201-218) believed that his wife, Mary Lowe, was deceased by 1729 at the writing of her brother's will. After reading the will carefully, I saw no evidence of Mary Neale, sister of Nicholas Lowe, as being deceased. In other words, in that instrument I saw no proof that Edward Neale's widow, Mary, could not have been the daughter of Henry Lowe, and the mother of all three daughters.

position. About 1732 he married Mary Smith, daughter of Major Walter Smith, but then the young widow of Clement Brooke, Jr., mariner.

Clement Brooke upon a voyage to England with his wife, Mary, and daughter, Rachel, dated his will August 31, 1731. He devised his wife and daughter his entire estate, but in the event that his wife, Mary, should die before her return to Maryland, the entire estate was to revert to his daughter. The will was proved in Charles County on November 28, 1732.

A correct list of the children of Charles Neale has not been proved. The following were obtained from family records and published by the late Dr. Christopher Johnson in his article on the Neale family in 1912.

Children of Charles and Mary (Smith) Neale

1. Elizabeth Neale married Leonard Smith, of Frederick Co.
2. Mary Neale married Benjamin Smith, of Charles Co.
3. Henrietta Neale married Lawrence O'Neal, of Montgomery Co.

On September 9, 1741, Charles Neale, of Charles County, Gent., and Mary his wife, conveyed to Thomas Williams, of Prince George's County, Gent., 250 acres of "The Three Sisters" which "Walter Smith by his last will and testament devised to his daughter Mary the party to these Presents and now intermarried with Charles Neale."

Sometime after the above date Charles Neale removed to the Lower District of Frederick County, where on February 10, 1759, he leased from Edward Lloyd, Esq., Agent and Receiver of the Lord Proprietary, 200 acres of the Manor of Conegocheegh.

On October 6, 1769, he and his wife Mary, of Frederick County, deeded to George Fraser Hawkins, of Prince George's County, all the landed estate that had been devised to Mary, by her former husband, Clement Brooke, Jr., to be held in trust for the use and benefit of Rachel Darnall, daughter of the said Mary Neale, and not subject to the control of the husband of the said Rachel Darnall.

At the formation of Montgomery County in 1776, his plantation fell into the newly made county, and at the census for that year he was listed as "Dr. Charles Neale," aged 71, and other persons in his household were Ralph Neale aged 36, and 13 Negro slaves. On

March 3, 1778, he subscribed to the Patriot's Oath in Montgomery County before Judge Elisha Williams.*

On June 3, 1778, he conveyed to Lawrence O'Neale, husband of his beloved daughter, a lease he held on "Aix La Chapelle" and three slaves on the condition O'Neale maintained him in comfort for the rest of his life.

No record of a will nor the administration of his estate can be found in Montgomery County, but he was probably deceased by 1790, as he was not listed as the head of a family at the first census.

RICHARD NEALE [4]

17--1772

RICHARD NEALE, son of Henry and Mary (Gardiner) Neale, was born in Charles County.

Children of Richard Neale

1. Henry Neale, *d.s.p.*
2. Mary Neale, born Jan. 6, 1759, died Dec. 8, 1812, aged 53, buried at Cobb Neck; married first Dr. Benjamin Leslie Corry, son of Dr. John Corry and Elizabeth Neale his wife, and secondly Aug. 27, 1780, Thomas Jenkins.

His will was dated August 22, 1772, and probated in Charles County on October 15, 1772. He devised his son, Henry, the dwelling-plantation on the Wicomico River, but in the event that he died without issue then to the testator's daughter Mary. The latter was to enjoy the rents from the plantation on which William Boarman lived and was bequeathed Negroes and other personalty. He named his friend, John Lancaster, the executor who subsequently renounced.

The administration was granted to his brother, Gerard Neale, who died shortly afterwards and the administration fell to Gerard's widow. On March 22, 1774, "came Ann Neale administrator of Gerard Neale who was the administrator of Richard Neale" and swore that she believed the appraisement of the estate of Richard Neale at £428/3/7 was just and proper. Joseph Lancaster and Bennett Neale signed as the next of kin.

* Brumbaugh-Hodges, *Revolutionary Records of Maryland*, p. 10.

Anne Neale, the administratrix of Richard Neale and of her deceased husband Gerard Neale, married Roger Brooke, and they both settled the estate of Richard Neale. On April 23, 1777, they showed that Henry Neale, the son and heir, had died a minor and that the whole estate reverted to his sister Mary Neale.

GERARD NEALE [4]

17– 177–

GERARD NEALE, son of Henry and Mary (Gardiner) Neale, was born in Charles County. He married first Elizabeth Guibert, the widow of his kinsman, James Neale, who died in 1761. She was deceased by July, 1768, for by that time he had married secondly Anne ——, who became the mother of his only son Joseph.

He died intestate in Charles County; by November 25, 1778, his widow had married Roger Brooke. On that date they filed an account upon his estate, when £2,017/17/5 were distributed between the widow and Joseph Neale, aged 7 years. Jesse Matthews and Walter Pye were sureties for the widow.

BENNETT NEALE [4]

17– –1788

BENNETT NEALE, son of Benjamin and Mary (Edelen) Neale, was born in Charles County. In 1778 he subscribed to the Oath of Allegiance in that county before Judge John Lancaster. He probably married a daughter of Eleanor [Elizabeth] Medley, of St. Mary's and Frederick Counties.*

* Eleanor Medley by her will, dated Dec. 22, 1774, proved in Frederick Co., Jan., 1775, bequeathed her daughter, Elinor Sprigg Neale, the rents due from her townland during life and then to the children of her daughter, Elinor. She furthermore stated that Bennett Neale should not have the "liberty to sell or dispose of the money or anything I leave behind without ye executor's Leonard Smith and if Leonard Smith should die then to his son Joseph Leonard Smith." On Nov. 24, 1777, Leonard Smith, of Frederick Co., and Elizabeth (*sic*) Sprigg Neale, of St. Mary's Co., conveyed to Thomas Yeates, of Montgomery Co., "Mistaken Rival." On Mar. 5, 1779, Leonard Smith, executor of Eleanor Medley, deceased, leased to Francis Smith, son of the said Leonard, a lot in New Town at the rate of 6 p. yearly during the life of Elizabeth Sprigg Neale, wife of Bennett Neale, and at her death to the children of the said Elizabeth Sprigg Neale.

Children of Bennett Neale

1. Bennett Neale. *q.v.*
2. Edward Neale married Grace Fenwick. *q.v.*
3. Priscilla Neale.
4. James Neale married Elizabeth Boarman. *q.v.*
5. William Neale.
6. Henry Neale.
7. John Neale.

Styling himself Bennett Neale, Sr., of Cob Neck, his will was dated September 4, 1788, and proved on January 5, 1789.

To sons Bennett and Edward 5 shillings each.
To son James the dwelling-plantation "Gill's Land" of 250 acres; if he died without issue then to William, to Henry, to John, and to Priscilla.
To daughter Priscilla Neale Negroes and other personalty.
To sons James and William the lots in Carrolsburg on the Potomac.
To Mary Beekanan and Elizabeth Martindale 5 shillings each.
Residue equally to his children—James, Priscilla, William, Henry, and John.

JAMES NEALE [4]

17– –1761

JAMES NEALE, son of Benjamin and Mary (Edelen) Neale, was born in Charles County. By the will of his father in 1746, he received a portion of the "Gill Tract." His wife was Elizabeth Guibert, daughter of Thomas Guibert, of St. Mary's County.

His wife was a minor at the death of her father in 1728, who bequeathed his daughter, Elizabeth Guibert, the Negro wench called Lucy, but the increase was to be divided equally between his two daughters, namely, Elizabeth and Ann Guibert. On November 30, 1743, James Neale, who had married Elizabeth Guibert, and Ann Guibert agreed on the division of the Negroes.

Children of James and Elizabeth (Guibert) Neale

1. Mary Neale.
2. Walter Neale, born Mar. 25, 1742.
3. Jane Neale, *d.s.p.*
4. Margaret Neale, *d.s.p.*

He died intestate. The inventory of his personal estate was made on July 3, 1761, and appraised at £829/11/8½. William Neale and

Bennett Neale approved as the kinsmen, while Elizabeth Neale, the widow and administratrix, filed at court. The widow married Gerard Neale, but she was deceased by July 5, 1768, when Gerard Neale filed the final account upon the estate of James Neale. In the meantime the children, Jane and Margaret, had died under age "after the death of their father and before the death of their mother." The balance was distributed to the two heirs—Mary Neale of age and Walter Neale aged 15.

JOSEPH NEALE [4]
17— -1798

JOSEPH NEALE, second son of William Neale and his wife, was born in Charles County. The name of his wife is unknown, as she predeceased him. In 1778 he subscribed to the Oath of Allegiance before Magistrate John Lancaster and he also served as a private in the militia company of Captain Jonathan Yates of Charles County.*

Children of Joseph Neale

1. Joseph Neale, born Feb., 1783.
2. Aloysius Neale, born 1786. *q.v.*
3. William H. Neale, *d.s.p.* 1829.
4. Teresa Neale married Michael Boarman. *q.v.*
5. Monica Neale, died spinster 1811.
6. Margaret Neale married John Edelen.**
7. Mildred Neale, died spinster 1829.
8. Anne Harriett Neale married ——— Lancaster.
9. Jeremiah Neale married twice. *q.v.*
10. Ursula Neale married Joseph Boone.

His will, dated February 20, 1798, was probated on May 14, same year, in Charles County. He devised his three named sons and six named daughters one-half of the plantation where the mansion house stood, to be laid out from the head of old Duck Cove to the head of Shalot's Cove. His son, Jeremiah, was devised the other half of the plantation, that is, to the south and contiguous to the dwelling of Captain Jenkins. The personal estate was to be divided equally among all children except Jeremiah.

* Militia List, p. 49, Maryland Historical Society.

** For the Edelen family, see, Newman's *Charles County Gentry.*

At the October term of the court in 1803, Joseph Neale aged 20, Aloysius Neale aged 17, and William Neale aged 14 were placed under the guardianship of their sister Teresa Neale and their uncle John Neale.

At the distribution of the personal estate on May 30, 1809, Joseph Boone and John Edelen in right of their wives received their shares of the estate.

The unmarried daughter, Monica Neale, died testate 1811 in Charles County, naming her brother Aloysius Neale, sister Mildred Neale, and brother-in-law Michael Boarman.

The will of the bachelor son, William H. Neale, was dated October 17, 1829, and proved in court on November 3, following. He bequeathed legacies to the Catholic Church on Cobb Neck and to his sister Mildred Neale.

The spinster daughter, Mildred Neale, drew up her will on November 6, 1829, it being probated three days later. She named her nephews Columbus, Ignatius, Calvert, Francis and Joseph Lancaster; her sisters Ursula and Margaret; and the unnamed children of her brother Aloysius. She mentioned money due from the estate of Henry Macatee, and the money due from Michael Boarman was not to be demanded during the life of her sister Teresa Boarman. Cash legacies were bequeathed to the Roman Catholic Church on Cobb Neck and to Francis Neale, no relationship stated.

WILLIAM NEALE[4]

17--1763

WILLIAM NEALE, son of Roswell and Mary (Brent) Neale, was born in Charles County. He was provided for generously by his wealthy uncle, William Chandler, receiving in 1725 "Chandler's Hope" where it is alleged that the first convent organized in Maryland was located, later moving to Mt. Carmel.

Family tradition states that he married Anne, the daughter of Leonard and Anne (Boarman) Brooke. Anne was unmarried when her father, Leonard Brooke, wrote his will on November 1, 1718, and devised her and her heirs an unnamed tract of land in the fork of the creek that ran into Colonel Henry Lowe's landing.

Children of William and Anne (Brooke) Neale

1. William Chandler Neale, Jesuit, died at Manchester, Eng., 1799.
2. Leonard Neale, 2d Archbishop of Baltimore, died 1817.
3. Charles Neale, Jesuit, died at Mt. Carmel, Md., 1823.
4. Francis Ignatius Neale.
5. Raphael Neale married Sarah Howard. *q.v.*
6. Clare Neale, born 1739, married (1) [Henry] Brent and (2) George Slye.
7. Mary Neale married William Matthews. *q.v.*
8. Eleanor Neale married (1) John Holmes and (2) Raphael Boarman. *q.v.*

His will, dated February 3, 1763, was probated in Charles County on February 8, following:

To son Raphael the dwelling-plantation "Chandler's Hope" and "Chandler's Addition," lying near Port Tobacco Creek next to Mr. John Hanson's land; but if he died before age 21, then to next youngest son Francis Ignatius.

To wife one-third of dwelling-plantation during life, that portion along the main road that leads to John Hanson's called Courthouse.

To son Charles portion of "Chandler's Hope."

To son Leonard the portion of dwelling-plantation at death of his mother.

To wife, sons Raphael, Francis Ignatius, Charles, and Leonard, and daughters Clare Neale, Eleanor Neale, and Mary Matthews Negroes.

To son William Chandler Neale 20 pistoles "if he returns to this part of the world."

Legacies to the Catholic Church and clergy.

His sons, Charles and Francis Ignatius, were to be sent "home" for their education, and in the event that any of his sons accepted Holy Orders or died before 21 years, their portions were to be divided among the survivors. The debt owed him by his son-in-law, William Matthews, was cancelled. His wife, Anne Neale, and son-in-law, William Matthews, were named executors and guardians of the minor children.

The will of his widow, Anne Neale, was probated in Charles County on January 7, 1786. She bequeathed £40 to her son, William Chandler Neale, and silver plate to her daughter, Eleanor Boarman. Negroes and other personalty were willed to her son, Rev. Leonard Neale, and to her Matthews grandchildren, that is, Joseph, Ignatius, Anne, Margaret, and William Matthews. To the monastery Ares in France she left £5.

HENRY NEALE [4]

17– –1767

HENRY NEALE, son of Roswell and Mary (Brent) Neale, was born before 1725 in Charles County. He married Anne, daughter of John and Mary (Boarman) Gardiner. She was made an heir in the will of her father who died in St. Mary's County during 1717 and who was possessed of the plantation "Hillalee." As Anne Neale, she was an heir in the will of her brother, Wilfred Gardiner, in 1743, and she with her daughter, Mary Neale, was an heir in the will of her mother, Madam Gardiner-Slye, in 1745.

Children of Henry and Anne (Gardiner) Neale

1. Wilfred Neale married Elizabeth Digges. *q.v.*
2. Henry Neale married twice. *q.v.*
3. Mary Neale married ——— Roach.
4. Henrietta Neale married John Ford.

He and his wife came into possession of "Hillalee," a Gardiner plantation in St. Mary's County, which they leased to Luke Smith. In May, 1764, according to the testimony of Luke Smith, Henry Neale and Anne his wife "entered with force and ejected" him, when he had a ten-year lease. Smith sued in the Provincial Court and was upheld.

Henry Neale settled in St. Mary's County. His will was dated November 20, 1766, and probated on February 9, 1767. He appointed his son, Wilfred, the executor and willed him all his land in Charles County. He cited several gifts of Negroes and livestock to his daughters, Mary Roach and Henrietta Ford, at time of marriage, and then devised the residue of his estate to his four children —Wilfred, Mary, Henrietta, and Henry.

JAMES NEALE [4]

17– –1753

JAMES NEALE, son of Roswell and Elizabeth (Blackistone) Neale, was born in St. Mary's County. By the will of his father in 1751, he with his brothers Raphael, Bennett, and Jeremiah, were devised the water mill and six acres of "St. Winifred's Freehold."

His wife was Elizabeth ——. He died in January, 1753, leaving James Neale (*q. v.*) as his son and heir. The inventory of his personal estate was filed at court on October 25, 1753, with Robert Yates as the administrator. Raphael Neale and Bennett Neale approved as the next of kin. The widow shortly thereafter married James Dunbar. Ultimately, a lawsuit was instituted in the chancery court for a division of the water mill on " St. Winifred's Freehold " with John Dunbar and his wife, Elizabeth, appearing in behalf of the orphan, James Neale, Jr., against the three uncles represented by Stephen Bordley as their attorney.

BENNETT NEALE [4]
17- -1771

BENNETT NEALE, son of Roswell and Elizabeth (Blackistone) Neale, was born in Charles County. His wife was Mary ——.

Children of Bennett and Mary Neale

1. Benoni Neale married Eleanor Neale. License St. Mary's Co., Dec. 29, 1798.
2. Charles Neale *d. s. p.* 1798.
3. Elizabeth Neale married Kenelm Cheseldine.
4. Sarah Neale *d. s. p.* 1816.
5. Anne Neale *d. s. p.* 1816.
6. Eleanor Neale married James McWilliams. License St. Mary's Co., Dec. 30, 1802.

His will, dated February 23, 1771, was probated in St. Mary's County on May 3, following.

To eldest son, Benoni, " St. Winifred " which the testator had received from his father.
To second son Charles " Wee Bit " and the proceeds from the sale of the mill at Tomacokin to be sold by George Slye.
To daughter Elizabeth the wife of Kenelm Cheseldine Negroes.
Residuary estate to wife Mary and his five children—Sarah Neale, Anne Neale, Eleanor Neale, Benoni Neale, and Charles Neale.

The widow died testate in St. Mary's County, her will being dated December 6, 1791, and probated January 23, 1792. She bequeathed one guinea, to her daughter Susanna Greenwell.* Slaves

* Susanna was probably a daughter by a previous marriage, as she was not

were bequeathed to the following children—Sarah Neale, Anne Neale, and Eleanor Neale. To her sons, Benoni and Charles, she willed all her share of the estate willed her by her granddaughter, Mary Neale Cheseldyne.

Her unmarried son Charles died testate in 1798 and devised his entire estate real and personal to his sisters, Sarah A. Neale, Ann Neale, and Eleanor Neale, and also to his brother Benoni Neale.

The spinster daughter, Sarah A. Neale, drew up her will on March 15, and bequeathed legacies to her sister Eleanor McWilliams and certain Negroes at her death were to revert to the testatrix's niece Margaret McWilliams. Other bequests were made to her sister Anne Neale and nephew Benoni Neale. The other unmarried daughter, Anne Neale, made her will on March 20, five days after her sister and devised the dwelling-plantation "Wee Bit" to her niece Margaret McWilliams during life and then to her friends James McWilliams, John McWilliams, William Plowden, and Raphael Neale. To her sister, Eleanor McWilliams, she devised the land adjoining "Wee Bit," namely "St. Dorothy," and to her niece, Margaret Ann McWilliams, slaves. She named the Rev. Leonard Neale and the Rev. Leonard Edelin the executors. Both wills of the sisters were probated in St. Mary's County on April 30, 1816.

JEREMIAH NEALE[4]
17--1809

JEREMIAH NEALE, son of Roswell and Elizabeth (Blackistone) Neale, was born in Charles County, but upon his maturity he settled in St. Mary's County among his Blackistone kinsmen. During the Revolution he was listed as one of the able-bodied men capable of bearing arms in St. Mary's County.* The name of his first wife and the mother of his older, if not all, of his children is not known. On February 6, 1797, he secured license in St. Mary's County to marry Catherine Rapier [Rapour].

Children of Jeremiah Neale

1. William Neale.

---

named as a daughter by Bennett Neale nor were any Greenwell kinsmen mentioned in the wills of the unmarried children.

* Militia List, p. 171, Maryland Historical Society.

2. Francis Neale.
3. Benedict J. Neale.
4. Mary Neale married ——— Neale.

His will, which was drawn up on September 24, 1808, was probated in St. Mary's County on November 15, 1809.

To his wife Catherine all debts due from the estate of William Rapour, deceased; she to have the privilege of living on the dwelling-plantation and drawing one-third of the profit annually.

To sons—William, Francis, and Benedict J. Neale—the dwelling-plantation.

To daughter Mary Neale and testator's three grandchildren—William, Jane, and Elizabeth Neale one-half of the property that may be recovered in his right in the town of Alexandria.

To Rev. Francis Neale of Georgetown legacy.

To daughter Mary Neale a Negro.

BENNETT NEALE [5]
17– –1805

BENNETT NEALE, son of Bennett, was born in Charles County. The name of his wife has not been proved.

Children of Bennett Neale

1. Ann Mary Neale.
2. Susanna Neale.
3. Ann Elizabeth Neale.
4. Benjamin Neale.
5. Walter Hoxton Neale, born Jan. 15, 1801.
6. James Henry Neale, born Oct. 8, 1802.
7. John Edward Neale, born Feb. 14, 1804.

His dwelling-plantation lay in William and Mary Parish, where he subscribed to the Oath of Allegiance to the State of Maryland in 1778 before Magistrate John Lancaster. He is placed as the Bennett Neale who at the beginning of the Revolution served as a private in the Flying Camp under Captain Philip Maroney.*

His will, dated October 22, 1805, was admitted for probation in Charles County, on August 19, 1806 He devised his three daughters —Ann Mary, Susanna, and Ann Elizabeth—during their single lives

* *Archives of Maryland*, vol. 18, p. 45.

the dwelling house and 100 acres. To his four sons—Benjamin, Walter Hoxton, James Henry, and John Edward—the residue of the landed estate and also reversion in the 100 acres devised to the daughters. He named his brothers, Edward Neale and James Neale, the guardians of his children and the executors of the estate

On October 11, 1806, William Chandler Brent, of Charles County, conveyed to Ann Mary Neale, Bennett Neale, Susanna Neale, Elizabeth Neale, Walter Hoxton Neale, James Neale, and John Neale for £29/17/11 a 250-acre portion of "Gill's Land." Dorothy Brent, wife of William Chandler Brent, waived dower rights.

On February 11, 1817, Walter Hoxton Neale aged 16, James Henry Neale aged 15, and John Edward Neale aged 13, were placed under the guardianship of Horatio Edelen, with Lewis Edelen and Malachi Robey as his sureties.

EDWARD NEALE [5]

17– –1814

EDWARD NEALE, son of Bennett Neale and his wife, was born in Charles County. He married Grace Fenwick, the daughter of Edward Fenwick, of St. Mary's County. In 1799 he and his brother-in-law, Wilfred Manning, administered upon the estate of their father-in law, late of St. Mary's County. The estate of his mother-in-law, Ann Fenwick, was distributed in St. Mary's County in December, 1800, when he in right of his wife received their share of the estate.

Children of Edward and Grace (Fenwick) Neale

1. Priscilla Neale.
2. Elizabeth Neale.
3. Olivia Neale.
4. Edward Neale.
5. Leonard Neale.
6. Anthony Neale.

His will was dated January 2, 1814, and proved in Charles County on March 5, 1814.

> To his wife Grace the land lying near the monastery whereon Lowe's mill stood which had been purchased of Basil Spalding; Negroes and personalty; also his dwelling-plantation purchased from the Rev. Leonard Neale but then in dispute before Chancery Court.

To his children—Priscilla, Elizabeth, Olivia, Edward, Leonard and infant son Anthony—Negroes at age or marriage.

Executors—James Fenwick, Benjamin Lancaster, Francis Digges, and Henry Neale.

JAMES NEALE [5]

17– –1800

JAMES NEALE, son of Bennett, was born at "Gill's Land," in William and Mary Parish, Charles County. On March 5, 1789, as James Neale, Jr., he conveyed 250 acres of "Gill's Land" which he had received from his father's estate. No wife at that time waived dower. By 1767 he had married Elizabeth, the daughter of Richard Bennett and Mary Ann (Hoskins) Boarman. She was living as late as 1792, when she and her two daughters, Elizabeth and Polly, were heirs in the will of her mother Mary Ann Boarman.

Children of James and Elizabeth (Boarman) Neale

1. Catherine Neale.
2. Elizabeth Neale.
3. James Neale.
4. Robert Neale.
5. Charles Hoskins Neale married Eleanor Brooke. *q.v.*
6. George W. Neale.
7. Mary Neale married ——— Lancaster.

His seat was in the Lower Hundred of William and Mary Parish where he took the Oath of Allegiance before John Lancaster in 1778. He also served as a private in the militia company of Captain Jonathan Yates.*

His will, dated January 16, 1798, was proved on April 29, 1800. He devised his daughter, Catherine and Elizabeth Neale, the use of 100 acres of the dwelling-plantation during their single lives, reserving one-half of the mansion house for their use, then to go to the testator's son James. Negroes were willed to his children—Robert Neale, Charles H. Neale, George W. Neale, and Mary Lancaster.

* Militia List, p. 48, Maryland Historical Society.

ALOYSIUS NEALE [5]

1786–18–

ALOYSIUS NEALE, son of Joseph, was born 1786 in Charles County, but settled in Alexandria, Virginia. On August 15, 1808, he sold part of his patrimony to Michael Boarman. " Whereas Joseph Neale, of Charles County, deceased, by his will devised to Aloysius Neale one-ninth of the dwelling-plantation," therefore he conveyed his share for a valuable consideration. No wife waived dower. On January 8, 1816, " of Alexandria," he conveyed to Jeremiah A. Neale all land devised him by the will of Monica Neale, and on March 21, 1817, he disposed of the realty which he had received by the will of John Neale. In 1829 his unnamed children shared in the will of his spinster sister Mildred Neale.

JEREMIAH A. NEALE [5]

17– 1815

JEREMIAH A. NEALE, son of Joseph Neale and his wife, was born in Charles County. Sometime before October, 1798, he married a daughter of James Johnson, of Charles County. In that month James Johnson drew up his will and devised his grandson, James Neale, the dwelling-plantation after the decease of his widow, Mary Johnson. In the event that the grandson died without issue, then Jeremiah Neale, the father, was to receive £100, and the landed estate was to revert to Mary Johnson, daughter of the testator.

Issue of Jeremiah and ——— (Johnson) Neale

1. James Neale.

His first wife died before December 22, 1795, for on that date he married secondly Mary E. Fenwick of St. Mary's County.

Children of Jeremiah and Mary E. (Fenwick) Neale

2. Jane Neale.
3. Ann Olivia Neale.
4. Caroline Neale.

He settled in Alexandria where he died testate in 1815, his will having been dated July 26, 1812. He devised his wife, Mary E.

Neale, the use of all his estate in Maryland and his place in Alexandria during her single life, and his daughters, Jane, Ann Olivia, and Caroline, all his estate real and personal in the State of Maryland and in Alexandria. To his son, James Neale, he bequeathed his watch and wearing apparel, " having already been provided for."

At the probation the widow and executrix refused to abide by the provisions and demanded her third. On May 16, 1826, Mary Elizabeth Neale, presumably the widow, and Ann Olivia Neale and Mary Caroline Neale, all of Washington, D. C., sold to George W. Neale, of Charles County, for $1,397.50 realty which had descended to them from the estate of Jeremiah A. Neale, being a portion of "Gill's Land" adjoining Cobb Neck and also the "Rock Hall" tract. They appointed George W. Matthews, of Charles County, their attorney.

RAPHAEL NEALE [5]

17– –1784

RAPHAEL NEALE, son of William and Anne (Brooke) Neale, was born in Port Tobacco Parish, Charles County. He was sent to England for higher studies, and there he met Sarah Howard whom he married. He took the Oath of Allegiance in 1778 before Walter Hanson of Port Tobacco East Hundred.*

Children of Raphael and Sarah (Howard) Neale

1. Joseph Neale married Jane Stonestreet. *q.v.*
2. Charles Neale.
3. Mary Anne Neale.
4. Eleanor Neale.

His will, dated March 5, 1784, was admitted for probation in Charles County on May 1, 1784.

To wife Sarah the dwelling-plantation, but in event she died before his daughters married, then the daughters were to have two rooms in the mansion during life.

To son Joseph the dwelling-plantation after the decease of his mother, and also that portion of the plantation then in

* He is believed to be the Raphael Neale who on Nov. 18, 1779, was appointed an ensign in the company of Capt. Charles Jordan, St. Mary's County Militia. *Archives*, vol. 43, p. 18.

possession of the testator's mother, being on Port Tobacco Creek.

To brothers Leonard, Charles, and Francis the plantation where the testator's mother then lived.

To children Charles, Mary Anne, and Eleanor Neale, personalty.

Executor—Wife Sarah and nephew William Chandler Neale.

His widow died shortly afterwards, her will being probated on May 22, 1784. She placed her children under the guardianship of her sister-in-law, Clare Slye, who was to enjoy the " tuition " of her three children–Mary Anne, Eleanor, and Charles–during their minority.

WILFRED NEALE [5]
17– 1808

WILFRED NEALE, son of Henry Neale and his wife, was born presumably in St. Mary's County. On July 23, 1767, declaring himself to be the son of Henry Neale, late of St. Mary's County, he sold to William Hamilton and Patrick Hamilton for £100 " Green Spring " which had been inherited from his father. No wife waived dower.

He married Elizabeth, daughter of Edward Digges, of St. Mary's, after June 9, 1769. The latter negotiated his will on that date and made his daughter, Elizabeth Digges, one of the executors. A lawsuit developed in 1789, whereby Wilfred Neale requested that he be permitted to dispose of some of the land of his deceased father-in-law, and be made guardian of the heir-at-law, but Bernard O'Neale, of Montgomery County, who had married another daughter of Edward Digges objected.

Children of Wilfred and Elizabeth (Digges) Neale

1. Charles Neale.
2. William Gardiner Neale married Mary Williams. License St. Mary's Co., Nov. 26, 1810.
3. George Neale.
4. [Daughter married William Henry Roach].

Wilfred Neale was among those who met at the courthouse in Leonardtown on July 1, 1776, and assured Daniel Wolstenholme, Esq., Collector of His Majesty's Customs, a safe departure from the Province.*

* *Archives*, vol. 12, p. 100.

The will of Wilfred Neale was dated August 7, 1807, being probated in St. Mary's County on February 10, 1808. He cancelled all claims against his son-in-law, William Roach, except the purchase of a Negro slave. The estate was to be divided into three parts, with one share to his son Charles, another share to his son Willy Gardiner Neale, and the remaining third equally to the children of his son, George Neale, namely Elizabeth Neale and Edward Neale.

COLONEL HENRY NEALE [5]

17– –1816

HENRY NEALE, son of Henry Neale and his wife, Anne Gardiner, was born in Charles County. He established his seat in St. Mary's County. On January 2, 1776, he was elected by the Convention an ensign or 3d lieutenant of Captain John Allen Thomas's Independent Company in St. Mary's County. On August 7, 1776, by the Council of Safety he was advanced to 2d lieutenant. After the war he was commissioned a colonel by the Governor of Maryland with active service in the local militia.

Before August 4, 1785, he married Margaret Brent Plowden, daughter of Edmond and Henrietta (Slye) Plowden, of St. Mary's County. He and his wife were heirs to the estate of George Slye, of Bushwood, who died testate in 1773 and made his Sister Plowden's children the contingent heirs

Children of Henry and Margaret Brent (Plowden) Neale

1. Mary Gardiner Neale married Edward I. Heard. License St. Mary's Co., Jan. 24, 1804.
2. Margaret Brent Neale married William H. Hammersley. License St. Mary's Co., Nov. 30, 1807.

After the death of his first wife he married secondly Eleanor Hammersley.

Children of Henry and Eleanor (Hammersley) Neale

1. Anne Neale.
2. Eleanor Neale.
3. William Henry Neale.
4. Francis Neale.
5. Robert Neale.

Styling himself Colonel Henry Neale of St. Mary's County, he drew up his will on February 13, 1812, but it was not probated until January 29, 1816. He bequeathed his wife, Eleanor, during her life the use and profits from his estate. He referred to legacies already given to his married children, and named his three sons—William Henry, Francis, and Robert Neale.

JAMES NEALE [5]

17– –1809

James Neale who died testate in St. Mary's County in 1809 is believed to have been the son and heir of James Neale who died in 1753. In August, 1781, Joseph Ford, Commissary for St. Mary's County, was ordered by the legislature to pay James Neale £50.* The name of his wife has not been proved.

Children of James Neale

1. Mary Neale married John Coode. License St. Mary's Co., Feb. 17, 1795.
2. Elizabeth Neale.

His will, dated December 6, 1809, was probated in St. Mary's County on February 13, 1810. He devised his wife all land whereon he lived, being part of a plantation which he had purchased of Philip Key. At her death the plantation was to descend to his two daughters—Mary Coode and Elizabeth Neale.

CHARLES HOSKINS NEALE [6]

17– –18–

Charles Hoskins Neale, son of James and Elizabeth (Boarman) Neale, was born in Charles County. By license obtained in St. Mary's County on January 9, 1809, he married Eleanor Brooke, sister to John M. T. Brooke, of Charles County.

John M. T. Brooke by his will named his sister, Eleanor Neale, and nieces—Elizabeth and Mary Henrietta Neale. He furthermore bequeathed a legacy for the education of his nephew, James F. Neale, at the discretion of the nephew's uncle, George W. Neale. The witnesses to the will were James K. Neale, James R. Brent, and John E. Neale.

* *Archives*, vol. 45, p. 582.

JOSEPH NEALE[6]

17– –1804

JOSEPH NEALE, son of Raphael and Sarah (Howard) Neale, was born in Charles County. He married Jane, the daughter of Captain Henry Stonestreet of the Revolutionary War, by his wife Mary Noble Edelen.*

Children of Joseph and Jane (Stonestreet) Neale

1. Dr. Francis Neale married (1) Mary Clare Brent and (2) Sarah Maria Pye.
2. Mary Eleanor Neale married George Brent and James H. Neale.
3. Catherine Neale married Robert Digges.

At the census of 1775 he was domiciled in the Lower Hundred of William and Mary Parish, where he subscribed to the Oath of Allegiance before John Lancaster in 1778.

He died intestate about 1804, and his widow married shortly thereafter Henry Digges. On August 10, 1805, Robert D. Semmes and Ignatius Semmes sued Henry Digges and Jane his wife for an indebtedness contracted by Joseph Neale on February 10, 1803, for £38/14/6 and which had remained unpaid at the time of his death. It was stated that Joseph Neale died intestate possessed of 345 acres of "Chandler's Hope" and a large personal estate. Besides his widow he left three children—Mary, Francis, and Catherine Neale.

His widow as Jane Digges died testate in Charles County. Her will dated September 24, 1830, was proved on August 31, 1832. She devised her one-third interest in "Chandler's Hope" to her daughter Mary Eleanor Neale, and a number of slaves to the following: children of her daughter Catherine Digges; son Francis Neale; daughters Catherine Digges and Mary Eleanor Neale; and grandchildren Mary Ophelia Digges, Mary Cordelia Neale, and Jane Dorothy Neale.

* For the Edelen family, see Newman's *Charles County Gentry*.

INDEX

www.ingramcontent.com/pod-product-compliance
Lightning Source LLC
Chambersburg PA
CBHW071630270326
41928CB00010B/1857
9780788423086